THE
EAST INDIA COMPANY IN
EIGHTEENTH-CENTURY
POLITICS

THE
EAST INDIA COMPANY IN EIGHTEENTH-CENTURY POLITICS

BY

LUCY S. SUTHERLAND
PRINCIPAL OF LADY MARGARET HALL,
OXFORD

OXFORD
AT THE CLARENDON PRESS
1952

Oxford University Press, Amen House, London E.C. 4

GLASGOW NEW YORK TORONTO MELBOURNE WELLINGTON
BOMBAY CALCUTTA MADRAS KARACHI CAPE TOWN IBADAN

Geoffrey Cumberlege, Publisher to the University

PREFACE

PROFESSOR Namier, in considering the earlier years of the reign of George III, has drawn attention to the need for elucidation of the part played by the East India Company in the politics of this time. The need exists to a greater or less extent throughout the century. For Professor Namier was alluding, not to the significance in the history of British Imperialism of the territorial expansion in and after the Seven Years' War, nor to the issues raised in the greatest *cause célèbre* of the eighteenth century, the trial of Warren Hastings. He was drawing attention to the way in which a large financial, trading, and territorial corporation, itself undergoing great administrative and political strain, could be affected by, and itself affect, the intricate workings of politics at Westminster, and the unending struggle of the governments of the day to maintain the 'connexion' on which their survival depended.

This book is an attempt to meet the need for the years preceding the introduction of Pitt's East India legislation, a landmark in the development of the relations of State and Company and the point at which Dr. Philips's excellent study of the subject begins. Though much has been written on East Indian affairs during this period, this is an aspect which has been neglected—a fact that is not altogether surprising. The spectacular figures whose fortunes were involved in these affairs have provided a more attractive subject for investigation— Clive, the *conquistador*, arrogantly conjuring up before the eyes of an eighteenth-century House of Commons the fantastic treasure houses of Eastern princes; Warren Hastings, the great administrator, first of the 'pro-consuls' who have always failed to make themselves understood by those they served, and himself the victim of a system which ensured that he touched pitch and did not remain undefiled; and Edmund Burke, entangled in partisan and personal motives, yet also inspired by a hatred of the oppression of the weak by the strong. Interest in these personalities and in the vast public display of Hastings's impeachment has made for a treatment of the part played by East Indian affairs in English politics which is episodic rather than continuous; while a great part of the work of historians has lain outside

England, in tracing the evolution of British rule in India. Yet the political forces which formed the background of spectacular episodes at home and of developments abroad must also be examined if either are to be fully understood. Such a study is also of value for the understanding of eighteenth-century government.

The method employed in such a study is necessarily intricate and laborious. It involves working out the personnel and relationships of groups both in Parliament and in that vast network of interests, the East India Company. It also involves an attempt to keep in mind the various fields of activity within the Company, commercial, financial, administrative, and political, and to assess the comparative influence of 'management' and public opinion in both the Company and the nation. And though the great figures of the time make their appearance, much of our attention must be reserved for the lesser men of affairs with whom the day-to-day conduct of business rests. A peculiar difficulty of the study is that the sources of many of the events to be considered arise in two very different worlds—in the political, financial, and commercial world of which London and Westminster were the centre, and in the strange and complex Indian world where 'country powers' and Company were meeting. I have been acutely aware throughout how superficial and imperfect is my understanding of this Indian scene.

The arrangement of the book reflects the remarkable growth in intricacy and importance of the relations of State and Company during the second half of the century. After an introductory chapter designed to show what the seventeenth century handed on to the eighteenth in achievement and promise, there are twelve chapters, one of which deals with the first half of the century up to about 1758; five with the years 1758 to 1771, and six with 1772 to 1784.

The material for such a study both in printed and manuscript form is voluminous, and indeed almost overwhelming, though the proportion which throws real light on the springs of action is much smaller. In addition to the material, printed and manuscript, preserved in the great public collections, in particular in what was the Library of the India Office (now at the Commonwealth Relations Department), in the British Museum, and in the Public Record Office, I am indebted to a number of private owners for permission to examine and make use of the material in their possession: to the Earl of Powis for permission to use the papers of Robert Lord Clive, preserved at Powis Castle; to the Marchioness of Lansdowne for permission to use those of Lord Shelburne preserved at Bowood; to the late Lord Abergavenny for permission to use the papers of John Robinson which he kindly sent to the British Museum for my inspection; to Earl FitzWilliam and the Trustees of the Wentworth-Woodhouse Estate for permission to quote the papers of the Second Marquess of Rockingham and of Edmund Burke deposited in the Sheffield Public Library, and to Earl FitzWilliam for permission to quote the Burke papers deposited at Lamport Hall in the charge of the Northamptonshire Record Society (I am also grateful to the Librarians of these two institutions for their kindness during my search); to the late Marquess of Bute for permission to use material from the Bute MSS. of which Professor L. B. Namier kindly gave me transcripts; and to the University of Nottingham for permitting me to consult and quote the Portland MSS. deposited in their library. The Governor and Directors of the Bank of England also kindly gave me permission to work on the East India Company Stock records preserved in their Record Office.

In quoting from this contemporary material I have sought to follow the principles with regard to spelling, punctuation, and the use of capitals, applied by Professor Namier.

In the preparation of this book I have received much help from Miss K. M. E. Murray, Miss V. Lamb, and Miss M. Mackie. Mrs. J. Carmichael has kindly undertaken the task of drawing up the index.

In conclusion, I should express my deep sense of obligation to Professor Namier and Professor Pares who have found time among their many avocations to read through my text and to give me much valuable advice on its form and contents. To Professor Namier I am indebted for generous help and encouragement ever since I first ventured on historical research.

L. S. S.

CONTENTS

ABBREVIATIONS
FOR THE CHIEF MS. SOURCES USED

Add. MSS.　　　　　Additional MSS. British Museum. The main collections used have been:

> The correspondence, &c., of the first Duke of Newcastle. Add. MSS. 32686–33072.

> The political correspondence of the first Earl of Hardwicke and other members of the Yorke family. Add. MSS. 35349–35918.

> The political correspondence of the first Earl of Liverpool in the correspondence of the first three Earls. Add. MSS. 38190–38468.

> The correspondence of Warren Hastings.
> Add. MSS. 28973–29236.
> Add. MSS. 39871–39904.

> The correspondence of Sir Elijah Impey.
> Add. MSS. 16259–16271.

> The correspondence between George III and John Robinson. Add. MSS. 37833–37835.

MSS. Eur.　　　　　European MSS. Commonwealth Relations Department.

> The correspondence of Philip Francis.

> The correspondence of Francis Fowke.

O.V.　　　　　　　Orme Various (MSS. of Robert Orme). Commonwealth Relations Department.

Court Books.

Committee of Correspondence (Reports).

Committee of Correspondence (Memoranda).

Bengal Despatches.

Bombay, Public Consultations.

Bombay. European Inhabitants.

Home Miscellaneous.

Records of the East India Company, Commonwealth Relations Department.

Bodl. North MSS.　Correspondence of Frederick Lord North, second Earl of Guilford. Bodleian Library.

Stock Ledgers
Transfer Books
East India Stock records, Bank of England Record Office.

Publ. Rec. Off.　　Public Record Office. The chief materials used are: the Correspondence of the first Earl of Chatham, and the Treasury papers.

Portland MSS.	Correspondence of the third Duke of Portland, Nottingham University Library.
FitzWilliam MSS. (Sheffield).	Correspondence of the second Marquess of Rockingham and correspondence of Edmund Burke deposited by the Trustees of the Wentworth-Woodhouse Estates in the Sheffield Public Library.
FitzWilliam MSS. (Northants.)	Correspondence of Edmund Burke deposited by Earl FitzWilliam in the care of the Northamptonshire Record Society.
Powis MSS.	Correspondence of Robert Lord Clive in the possession of the Earl of Powis.
Lansdowne MSS.	Personal correspondence of the first Marquess of Lansdowne in the possession of the Marquess of Lansdowne.
Bute MSS.	Correspondence of the third Earl of Bute in the possession of the Marquess of Bute.
Robinson MSS.	Correspondence of John Robinson in the possession of the Marquess of Abergavenny.

I
THE SEVENTEENTH-CENTURY BACKGROUND

THE history of the East India Company in the eighteenth century may be said to begin with the formation in 1709 of the United Company of Merchants trading to the East Indies, as a result of the union of the 'Old' and the 'New' Companies which had been fighting for the monopoly of the East India trade. Lord Godolphin's award of the previous year had finally brought to an end the conflict between these rival companies which in the last ten years had dislocated the India trade, racked the City, and played a not inconsiderable part in intensifying national political faction. The charter of 1709[1] reflected a situation in which the Company's monopoly trading rights, its powers in its settlements, its place in the London money market, and its relations with the State, had taken a form which created the framework of the future. This framework bore the marks of a century of development and conflict.

From the year 1599–1600, when merchants normally trading with the Levant turned their attention during a slump in their own trade to the opportunities of the sea-borne commerce with the East, the trade had been organized on a joint stock basis. The Company which obtained the monopoly of this trade was indeed one of the earliest of its kind, and, though it had achieved a form something like that of a modern joint stock company well before the United Company came into existence, its progress to that goal was in its earlier years slow and uncertain.[2] Nevertheless the growth of its activities and organization was rapid both at home and overseas. The problems it met with were in part the outcome of purely temporary circumstances but in part, both in its trading activities and in its relations with the State, they were the result of factors of more permanent significance.

[1] *Charters relating to the East India Company from 1660 to 1761, reprinted from a former collection with some additions and a preface* by J. Shaw, Madras, 1887, pp. 226–9.
[2] W. R. Scott, *The Constitution and Finance of English, Scottish and Irish Joint Stock Companies to 1720*, Cambridge, 1910–12, ii. 89 seq.

In India the activities of the English Company were from the first limited by the fact that it was, in comparison with its Portuguese and Dutch rivals, late in the field and that it had far less support from the State than the Portuguese had enjoyed in the past or the Dutch were enjoying at the time. It thus failed, despite considerable efforts, to get and hold a share of the Spice Islands trade, then so greatly prized, and on the mainland had to seek trading relations where a permanent display of force was unnecessary. Hence it was in alliance with, and under the protection of, the Mogul Emperors that the English Company established its first trading settlement at Surat in 1613 and formulated the policy of peaceful trade without territorial responsibilities, to which something more than lip service was being paid almost a hundred and fifty years later when the Company was becoming mistress of India. 'A war and traffic are incompatible', said Sir Thomas Roe, James I's ambassador to the Mogul,[1] and the aim of the Company was to evade both the dangers of war and the expense of defended positions by restricting its activities to areas where the Mogul Emperor could protect them.

But this aim was impracticable for two reasons. In the first place the attractions of new and profitable trading situations proved irresistible, particularly since the competition of other European countries had to be taken into account; the nuclei of all the later Settlements were formed before 1670. These expansionist moves drew the Company away from the centre of strength of the Moguls to the fringes of their Empire or to its semi-dependent outposts. In the second place, the power of the Mogul Emperors was itself, from the middle of the century, beginning to crumble, and with it the peace which they had imposed; leaving in its place the political chaos which was to provide both the opportunities and the dangers of the eighteenth-century European Powers in India.

How greatly these developments were bound to affect the Company's policy was first seen by its servants in India—Gerald Aungier told his employers that 'the times now require you to manage your general commerce with your sword in your hands'[2] —but those guiding its fortunes at home, particularly the able

[1] W. W. Hunter, *History of British India*, 1899–1900, ii. 241.
[2] Ibid. ii. 227.

and resolute Sir Josia Child, also quickly saw it. Already in 1674 the exposed position of Bombay had led to a treaty of alliance with the rising Hindu federation of Mahrattas, and by 1684 the Company recognized the necessity of fortifying it. 'Though our business is only trade and security, not conquest which the Dutch have aimed at, we dare not trade boldly nor leave great stocks . . . where we have not the security of a fort'.[1] Finally after undertaking in Bengal the first of the wars against the country powers, the Company concluded that the days of 'fenceless factories' were over.

This admission was the thin edge of a great wedge. Not only is defence often best served by aggression, but the possession of fortified areas made necessary a great elaboration of administrative machinery. The sharpest stimulus was financial. The Company soon saw the advantage of the Dutch practice of defraying the expenses of fortification by raising revenue from those they protected. By 1689 they were telling their servants in Bombay:

The increase of our revenue is no less the subject of our care and must always be yours, as much as our trade. . . . 'Tis that must make us a nation in India. Without that, we are but as a great number of interlopers, united by His Majesty's Royal Charter, fit only to trade where no body of power thinks it their interest to prevent us.[2]

Side by side with fiscal developments went the evolution of judicial and administrative arrangements for the rule of Europeans in these settlements, and for the control, so far as this was necessary, of the Indian inhabitants, arrangements devised as need arose to meet concrete problems but coloured by the assumptions and experience of English seventeenth-century politics.[3] By the end of the century the administration of the three Presidencies had taken the general shape which it was to preserve throughout the first half of the succeeding century, and many of its most serious problems had become apparent. Prominent among these were the relations of the Company in England with its servants in the East; to them (permitted as they were to engage in private trade to supplement their very low salaries) these developments opened up new opportunities

[1] Ibid. ii. 232.
[2] Quoted by Hunter, op. cit. ii. 273.
[3] See C. Fawcett, *The First Century of British Justice in India*, Oxford, 1934.

and temptations which their distant masters found it difficult to control.

The main problems of Company rule in India had thus become apparent by the end of the century; so, too, had the complexities of the relations of State and Company in the East. From the beginning, the prestige of the Crown was employed on occasion to assist the Company in its relations with the Indian powers and sometimes in the control of its servants. The dispatch of Sir Thomas Roe, in 1615, as ambassador from James I to the Mogul but at the Company's expense was typical of their relations.[1] When after the charter of 1661 the Company's territorial rights and power of declaring and waging war against all non-Christian peoples were recognized, and the Company began increasingly to exercise the powers of a sovereign in its Presidencies, it began to claim that its powers were those of delegated sovereignty. In 1684, when an Admiralty Court was set up in Bombay, Sir Josia Child told the king that 'he had ever been of opinion that no person in India should be employed by immediate commission from His Majesty',[2] and in a private letter he wrote:

The first consideration, in my poor opinion, ought to be abstractively what powers a National East India Company ought to have for the public good to hold up against the Dutch and other foreign nations in India; and I say and will maintain it against all mankind by reason and experience, that it ought to be not less than absolute sovereign power in India.[3]

These claims were by the end of the seventeenth century tacitly recognized in matters concerning the control of the Company's settlements and their relations with the country powers. There was, however, the further complication of the relations between the Companies of the various European Powers in India. In time of peace the States to which they were subject normally left the Companies themselves to solve the conflicts arising out of their rivalries; but in the great Anglo-Dutch sea wars their commercial discussions became submerged in the national conflicts, royal navies fought with the aid of what ships the

[1] W. Foster, *Embassy of Sir Thomas Roe*, Oxford, 1926, p. xiii.
[2] Quoted J. Bruce, *Annals of the East India Company*, 1810, ii. 592.
[3] A. F. W. Papillon, *Memoirs of Thomas Papillon of London, Merchant 1623–1702*, Reading, 1887, p. 89.

Companies could raise, and clauses affecting the possessions of the Companies were negotiated in the peace treaties which followed the wars. In the eighteenth century the chief European enemy was France instead of Holland but the relations of the State and Company with respect to the national enemy remained basically unchanged.

In India the United Company inherited, then, territorial powers and responsibilities as well as trading connexions, and a complex though fluid system of relations with the country powers, the rival European Companies, and the English Crown. In England, too, the lines of future development had been laid down, both in the internal development of the Company and its relations with the State. In the relations of the Company and State three basic conditions were already apparent in the seventeenth century, and retained their significance at least up to the seventies of the next. The first was the fact that the Company depended for its very existence on the renewal of its charter, and this, as also its convenience and prosperity in a number of other ways, depended on the favour of governments. In the political and constitutional conflicts of English history it was therefore normally to be found among the supporters of the Crown and the Ministry of the day. The second, however, was the fact that, though from time to time kings or ministers might concern themselves in the Company's affairs in the interest of national prestige in war, of trading prosperity, or (towards the end of the century) of the stability of the rising London money market, the main cause of any intervention into the Company's affairs was the needs of public finance. The Company in fact needed the support of government, and a succession of governments from James I to the ministries of the mid-eighteenth century were prepared to give it in exchange for contributions to the public purse. Though the Company might grow restive under this pressure and their relations with government become strained, in the last resort they were always obliged to submit. Under James I and Charles I, like other monopolies, they paid dearly for their privileges, and even so had constantly to make contributions to check infringements on their monopoly. Under the Commonwealth they suffered severely because, through the pressure of interests hostile to their monopoly, they were for some years unable to obtain government support, but when in 1657 Cromwell finally granted them a charter it was again because of the financial needs of the State. Under Charles II and James II, the Company's leader Sir Josia Child obtained, by a regular series of gifts, the closest and most satisfactory relations between the Crown and the Company which was to be known until Walpole's day. Finally, in the desperate struggle of the 'Old' Company for survival against the rivals who began to threaten it after the Revolution of 1688, it was by the support of the administration as well as by its trading strength and weight in the City that it gradually triumphed, and in the course of the struggle both the 'Old' and the 'New' interests had contributed more heavily than ever before to the needs of public finance. It was for this reason that the United Company which emerged in 1709 was one of the major creditors of the State in the new system of funded debts that had grown up since the Revolution.

The third basic condition of the relations of the State and Company was the result of the first two. Since the Company was perforce closely associated with the Government of the day, it was always in danger, in times of political faction, of becoming itself entangled in political issues. The cause of commercial enemies jealous of its privileges, or of factions within itself hostile to its leaders, was apt to be taken up at such times by the Parliamentary opponents of the Government. So long as the Company was certain of the support of government and the Government itself was stable, the danger of this alliance was not serious, but in times of sudden change or political uncertainty seventeenth-century experience had already shown that the peril could be grave indeed. At the outbreak of the Civil War the Company was fortunate in that its relations with Charles I had been strained; though it had made terms with Cromwell, its fate during the Commonwealth and some subsequent disagreements with Richard Cromwell ensured it favourable treatment at the Restoration. But the flight of James II left it in a highly vulnerable position both because it was closely identified with the Crown and because in 1682 a revolt within the Company against the rule of Sir Josia Child had greatly strengthened its enemies in the City, and in the early years of the new reign it narrowly escaped destruction by the political supporters of its rivals. The struggles between the 'Old' and the

'New' interests during the ten years 1692–1702 were fought out more in Parliament and the council chamber than in the City, or on their markets. And all the results of this entanglement, discreditable and unfortunate both from the point of view of the nation and of the Company—results which were to be seen again between 1763 and 1784—were displayed in their crudest colours in the distractions of those years.[1] Seventeenth-century experience had shown in an unmistakable way both the dependence of the Company on the State and the dangers to which this dependence exposed it whenever political instability on the one side and dissension within the Company on the other came into combination. The circumstances of the times might change and, in the second half of the eighteenth century, new and more complex problems might arise out of the growth of the Company as a territorial power, but these basic political considerations remained unchanged throughout the period.

From the point of view of Company organization the seventeenth century had bequeathed to the United Company a sound administration, a place on the rising London money market, and a constitution which, for good or evil, bore the marks of past achievements and more recent battles. The Company had been slow in achieving the organization of a 'permanent joint stock'; it was long a congeries of different 'terminable stocks' and 'voyages' several of which might be running at the same time. But by Cromwell's charter of 1657[2] a permanent joint stock was finally recognized. The management of the Company was, by its original charter, placed in the hands of a Governor, Deputy Governor, and twenty-four 'Committees' (Directors). Nothing was said in the original charter of their stock qualifications, but from 1628, when the matter first seems to have aroused attention,[3] it was always a fairly high one, varying from £1,000 to £4,000, and after 1698 settling down at £2,000.

Nothing was laid down in the original charter about the relations of this Court with the main body of the proprietors, but the first records surviving show that what came to be called the General Court or Court of Proprietors was active, not only

---

[1] The struggle of the two Companies in and out of Parliament is studied in detail by Scott, op. cit. ii. 150 seq.   [2] This charter is lost.
[3] *Calendar of State Papers. E. Indies, 1625–9*, pp. 506, 524.

in electing the Committees or directors, but in the detailed business of the Company. From the beginning until the position was changed by Pitt's East India Act of 1784 it was accepted that the General Court could, if it so wished, over-ride any decision of the Court of Committees or their successors the Court of Directors. Nevertheless, it was essential that the Committees or directors should be able to control the proprietors and to obtain their support, and this they were in general able to do. As early as 1629 they had reduced the regular meetings of the General Court to the quarterly routine meetings which continued throughout the Company's history for 'the satisfaction of divers noblemen and gents who are in towne only in Terme time',[1] and though in 1635 the relations between the two Courts of the Company were so bad that the Committees resolved to abolish General Courts altogether as having no sanction by charter (a resolution they had not the courage to press)[2] in general they succeeded in keeping their predominance, even in times of commercial and political difficulties, without too much friction.

In this they were assisted by a succession of leaders prominent and respected in the City, and the personal influence of these men was supported for much of the century by a system of cumulative voting in the General Court. At least from 1657 on every £500 stock carried a vote with it, so that the bigger proprietors, who were often themselves Committees, were able through their cumulative votes to make a powerful *bloc* in the General Court. Indeed Sir Josia Child was credited with such strength when he was Governor that a revolt arose which led to a change in the voting arrangements,[3] for the faction which rose against him from 1682 onwards concentrated much of their fire on this issue. As a result of the political influence of his opponents the total number of votes to be enjoyed by any one proprietor was progressively cut down until, in the United

---

[1] *Calendar of State Papers. E. Indies, 1625–9*, p. 665.
[2] *A Calendar of the Court Minutes, etc., of the East India Company*, E. B. Sainsbury, Oxford, 1907, i. 13–19.
[3] Scott, op. cit. ii. 142, was of opinion that Child's holdings and the degree of control exercised by a *bloc* of large holders were exaggerated by contemporaries. More recent research by Mr. K. G. Davies (reported in a paper read at the 1951 meeting of the Economic History Association) has tended to support the contemporary view.

Company, no proprietor could exercise more than one, however great his holdings.

Provisions whereby General Courts could be called at the instance of several proprietors owed their origin to the same movement. But eighteenth-century experience was to show that alternative methods of control might be quite as effective. The Court of Directors could strengthen their position by the support of interests dependent on them. Already in the seventeenth century there are signs of at least one of these organized interests. The shipping interest composed of those connected with the ships the Company hired for its trade was already taking form.[1]

While the Court of Committees were learning how to control the General Court they were also developing their own methods of business. The standing committees, which in the eighteenth century managed so much of the Company's business, began to come into existence, and were permanent features of its organization as early as the sixteen sixties. Behind the scenes the Secretary and other officials steadily developed that routine of business which was to win the unwilling admiration of the parliamentary committees who investigated the Company a hundred years later. The powerful personal position of the Governor (in the United Company to become the Chairman) in the Court was already apparent.

The Company's financial developments were particularly significant. In book-keeping it had from the beginning been advanced (perhaps, as has been suggested, because of the Mediterranean associations of its earliest members). Well before the end of the century the concept of 'shares' as the profit on a proprietor's 'stock' capital, of 'bonds' as capital borrowed at interest for limited periods, and of book credit, was fully developed and clearly differentiated. The Company at first bore the marks of the regulated Companies with which its earliest members were familiar. A proprietor was a freeman of the Company and the sale of his stock meant disfranchising him and enfranchising another by purchase in his place. Though no objection was raised to such transfers (or transports as they were long called) and in 1615 some stock was even auctioned

---

[1] See pp. 36–38 below and my *A London Merchant 1695–1774*, Oxford, 1933, pp. 88 seq.

'whereby they (the Committees) may better know the worth of their adventures, which will give a good reputation to the voyage if it shall be well sold',[1] the early Court Books show such sales to be few. Though the numbers increased with the passing of time, it was not till 1682, when a number of Sir Josia Child's opponents sold out their holdings, that the list of transfers became at all numerous. By May 1676, however, separate transfer books had been opened[2] (books which by the charter of 1693 had to stand open for inspection) and by 1684 the Court decided that as 'the number of Transports of Credits in the Company's stock is of late much increased beyond all former precedent' a transfer fee of 5s. should be imposed.[3]

This development reflects the place which East India Stock was beginning to acquire on a growing London market. A market in stocks and shares where a day-to-day price becomes quotable does not seem to have existed before the Restoration, but after that period the advance of credit facilities, the multiplication of joint stock companies, and the consequent growth of intermediaries in London led to the development of a stock market on lines already laid down by the earlier and far more important market at Amsterdam.[4] The growth of this market tended, as time went on, materially to increase the range of persons from whom capital could be recruited and the early and in some ways remarkably mature development of speculative dealings on it brought the advantages as well as the dangers of professional activities. The importance of this mobilization of capital should not, however, be exaggerated. Except in occasional outbursts of company promoting in the late seventeenth century, it did not touch the finance of industry nor the greater part of the wide range of commercial enterprise. It was the government-funded debts and the stock of a few great joint stock companies which were primarily affected by this development. The East India Company was prominent among them. Its transfer books show the widening range of investors who as time went on were encouraged to invest in this stock by its negotiability.

---

[1] *Calendar of State Papers. E. Indies, 1513–1616*, p. 434.
[2] This is the date of the first book of this kind preserved with the Company's financial records at the Bank of England Record Office. There is no evidence that it was the first.   [3] Court Book 34, p. 7.
[4] R. D. Richards, *Early History of Banking in England*, London, 1929, pp. 205 seq.

To contemporaries, it is true, the value of this development was largely obscured by alarm at the less desirable aspects of the speculative activities it made possible. The highly developed speculative technique and even the phraseology of the Amsterdam market was early reflected in the lesser market in London; and the absence of any organization such as the later Stock Exchange to check undesirable practices among the jobbers and brokers who had sprung up, and the opportunities for combinations which were given by the comparatively small quantities of stock on the market led to a violent outcry against the 'infamous practice of stock-jobbing'.[1] The inquiries into, and litigation about, measures taken in 1693 and the succeeding years to maintain the value of India Stock during the struggle between the two Companies show that advanced speculative techniques were employed in business in East India Stock and that there was close contact between the London and Amsterdam markets in speculative transactions. The activities revealed strongly resemble (though the sums involved are far smaller) those which were to cause scandal in the Comapny in 1766–9.[2]

India Stock then already played a prominent part on the London market. India Bonds, which by 1744 were said to be the favourite short-term investment of the City, were also acquiring the form which they were to retain. The short-term loans raised by the Company for financing its trade had become by the later years of the century very considerable. In 1696 the total stood at more than £746,000 and for some years it had rarely been below £400,000.[3] For some time the Company distinguished between its loans of 'standing' and 'transient' money, but well before it was forbidden by statute to raise money for less than six months[4] its bonds had in fact run for six-month

---

[1] Acts were passed in 1696–7 to 'restraine the number and ill practice of Brokers and Stock Jobbers' (8 & 9 Will. III, c. 32) and 1734 to 'prevent the infamous practice of stock-jobbing' (7 Geo. II, c. 8). Both were ineffective and both would have checked the development of useful as well as deleterious practices had they been effective.

[2] A good deal of information on this subject is available in Court Book 36, pp. 257v seq. and Bodleian, Rawlinson MS. A303, ff. 43 seq., depositions in Chancery involving Sir Thomas Cooke and others (c. 1701). Defoe's *Stock Jobbers Detected* (1701) and *Anatomy of Exchange Alley* (1719) are also relevant. For an account of the struggles of the 'Old' and 'New' interests see Scott, op. cit., pp. 156 seq.

[3] Scott, op. cit. ii. 172.

[4] 9 & 10 Will. III, c. 44.

periods, falling due at one or other of two fixed dates.[1] The investment was generally a popular one on the market; in good times the Company could borrow 'transient' money at 4 per cent. and 'standing' money at 3 per cent., and on occasion money was offered at the Company's cash without interest on the understanding that it would be given preference when bonds were issued.[2] In 1681 those managing the affairs of the French Protestant refugees petitioned the Company to help those who had fled bringing their fortunes with them by 'accepting such monies as they should pay into the Company's Cashier at moderate interest . . . until they could find out other ways of improving their estates'. The Company agreed to accept any money so offered at 4 per cent. for three months and then at 3 per cent. until the owners wished to withdraw it, when they undertook to pay capital and interest without waiting for the bonds to mature.[3] In times of financial stress the Company felt the burden of this considerable short-term indebtedness. In 1682 for instance, when the withdrawal of Sir Josia Child's opponents coincided with 'a generall and unparalleled Run or Demand for money upon all the publick Funds in this City and particularly on this Company',[4] they had to renew the bonds falling due first at 5 per cent. and then at 6 per cent.; and in the years of the contest between the 'Old' and 'New' interests, they frequently had to borrow at these high rates.

The significance of these bonds as an influence on the market was recognized by the Treasury as early as 1698, when the first attempt was made to regulate them by Statute.[5] It was not till 1720 that a statutory limit was set to their issue—£5,000,000[6] to which a further £1,000,000 was added in 1744.[7] It can be no coincidence that in 1697 and 1698 the Company, under some pressure from the Treasury, took part in the circulation of the Exchequer Bills, which were becoming the dominant short-term security issued by the Government.[8]

[1] Court Book 33, p. 168, 14 September 1683. The dates were 30 March and 30 September, i.e. after each of the two big sales.
[2] e.g. Court Book 31, p. 25, 12 July 1678.
[3] Court Book 32, p. 179, 16 December 1681.
[4] Court Book 33, p. 97^v, 29 December 1682.
[5] 9 & 10 Will. III, c. 44.   [6] 7 Geo. I, st. 1. c. 5.
[7] 17 Geo. II, c. 17.
[8] Court Book 37, pp. 310 seq., 22 March 1697, &c.

Finally there were those forms of Company credit which, not becoming negotiable,[1] only indirectly affected the market, its considerable book credit (offset as this was to some extent by the credit it allowed to purchasers at its sales) and, what was to become a serious problem to it in the future, the bills drawn on it by its servants abroad. It was in 1680 that the remittance of private fortunes from India by draft on the Company was first encouraged.[2] Though the possible inconveniencies of such drafts were recognized, and in 1676 a limit had been set on their use in the factory at Bantam to finance purchases there,[3] conditions in the East were not yet such as to cause the grave results which followed from the excessive use of this practice in the second half of the next century. To sum up: directly through its stock and bonds and indirectly through its non-negotiable liabilities, the Company was already recognized as an important constituent of the London money market, and in this as in the other aspects of its activities the seventeenth-century developments laid down inescapable conditions for the future.

[1] So long as the Company owned some of the ships employed in the trade they also issued 'bottomry bonds' which were in effect a method of insurance on these ships. Scott, op. cit. ii. 172.
[2] Court Book 32, p. 15, 15 July 1680, and p. 64, 3 November 1680.
[3] Court Book 30, p. 121, 9 October 1676.

II
THE MONIED COMPANY

I

THE United Company of Merchants Trading to the East Indies was brought into being with difficulty, but along a way which had been well prepared. For more than ten years the inevitability of some form of union between the 'Old' and 'New' Companies had been recognized, and the complex financial settlements of Godolphin's award had their parallel in personal readjustments between their leaders, and in the compromises and safeguards which were incorporated in the constitution of the newly formed Company. How serious were the underlying strains can be seen from a comment made some eighteen months before the union:

Our good friend Sir Thomas [Cooke] reigns as much as ever [in the 'Old' Company]. The agitators with him are Mr. Moore and Mr. Craggs; the last-named being, on account of his intimacy with the Duke of Marlborough, as well as his own merits, in high favour in the City. Sir Gilbert [Heathcote] is Sovereign of the New Company, and holds great sway in the City; he is supported by Messrs. John Ward, Eyles, Dodington and Shephe[a]rd. The snake in the grass is jealousy of power. It is uncertain in which interest authority will centre; and the New Company being apprehensive of defeat at the first election [of Directors] are anxious to tie down their antagonists to as humble terms as possible.[1]

---

[1] *H.M.C.*, 13, appendix part iii, Fortescue MSS. i. 30. Letter from E. Harrison to Governor Pitt—25 July 1707. The persons referred to are on the one side Sir Thomas Cooke, M.P. (d. 1709), son-in-law to Sir Josia Child, Governor of the 'Old' Company; Arthur Moore (1666?–1730), M.P., Commissioner of Trade and Plantations 1710, South Sea Director; James Craggs (1657–1721), M.P., Postmaster-General, Army contractor, later implicated in the South Sea disaster; and on the other Sir Gilbert Heathcote (1651–1733), M.P., Lord Mayor 1710–11, a founder of the 'New' Company, Director of the Bank of England; John Ward (d. 1726), M.P., later knighted, Governor of the 'New' Company 1701–3, Lord Mayor 1718–19, Director of the Bank of England, nephew of the better known Sir Patience Ward; John Eyles (d. 1745), M.P., later Baronet, Lord Mayor 1726–7, later a well-known Sub-Governor of the South Sea Company; George Dodington (d. 1720), M.P., Cashier of the Navy, a Trustee for the subscribers for the circulation of Exchequer Bills, uncle of the notorious George Bubb Dodington, who inherited his fortune; Samuel Shepheard (d. 1719), M.P., a promoter of the 'New' and later the South Sea Company of which he became Sub-Governor.

The main problems of the newly constituted Company were: to settle its leadership; to draw up its constitution and arrange its machinery of business; to tidy up some financial anomalies surviving from the past; to decide on its policy in India, and to establish its relations with the State. In all of them it showed that it had learnt a lesson from the recent past. Compromise rather than conflict, steady attention to business, and a determination to avoid political controversy are obvious in all the actions of its early years.

The question of leadership was determined in the first elections of directors. Voting was at first very heavy and in the elections in 1709 and 1710 complete lists of twenty-four candidates were put forward by both 'Old' and 'New' interests. The first and crucial election, however, showed signs of co-operation as well as conflict, for eight candidates chosen in equal numbers from the leaders of the rival interests were included in both lists—were 'double-listed' as their successors would have said. The proprietors by no means all voted the full lists; 'scratchings' were numerous and the result was a triumph for the 'Old' interest but also a substantial representation of the 'New'.[1] In the following year the list of the 'Old' interest obtained a considerably increased majority,[2] and by 1712 the divisions appear to have died down, contests becoming limited to a few individuals or disappearing altogether.

The constitution of the Company showed similar signs of compromise—it was based on that of the 'Old' Company but borrowed freely in nomenclature and in special provisions from that of the 'New', and considerable pains were taken to limit the exercise of influence over the General Court to assuage the suspicions and fears that had been expressed before the union. The Court of Directors, as they were henceforth to be called (borrowing the title used in the 'New' Company), was to consist of twenty-four persons each holding at least £2,000 stock, who were to choose among themselves a Chairman and Deputy Chairman annually. Earlier attempts to prevent this Court from becoming a permanent oligarchy were perpetuated in the

[1] Committee of Correspondence. Memoranda, vol. i (no pagination), and Court Book 43, pp. 492–3.
[2] In this year the 'Old' interest polled 244 complete lists and the 'New' 159. The total number of voters was recorded this year. It was 948. Committee of Correspondence. Memoranda, vol. i.

provision that no director should serve for more than four consecutive years, though this provision proved easy to circumvent, since directors could stand down for a year and then return to office (this was later called 'going out by rotation'). The General Court or Court of Proprietors was to consist of all holders of £500 stock, and provisions in the 'New' Company's charter designed to ensure the independence of the Court were adopted; no one proprietor was to exercise more than one vote and Courts must be summoned by the directors at least every quarter or whenever one was demanded by nine or more proprietors. A further by-law tried (ineffectively, as the future was to show) to cut off another method by which the proprietors with big holdings could exercise an undue influence, the collusive transfer of stock to create voting qualifications—the 'splitting' of stock of which so much was to be heard later.[1]

The Company in its relations with the State was equally circumspect. The new directors were no more able to isolate themselves from politics than were their predecessors. They had the same dependence on government and the same interests to protect. In 1711 they had to enter into negotiations to ensure that the privileges given to the new South Sea Company did not infringe their charter.[2] When the South Sea Company obtained by Statute perpetual trading privileges, they sought a similar concession, though they only succeeded in getting the term of their charter prolonged by seven years to 1733.[3] At the same time they were petitioning strongly against a duty on (amongst other commodities) calicoes and muslins and tea.[4] Such political activities as these, however, arose directly from the Company's own needs and did not involve it in party politics. Only once, indeed, even in the faction-ridden last years of Queen Anne's reign, were they forced, despite all their care, to take sides on a controversial political issue. This was in 1713, when the Whigs won their great success against the Tory Government in defeating, with the aid of commercial agitation, the treaty of commerce these were seeking to make with France. Feeling ran so high in the City that the Company could not

[1] By-laws of the United Company of Merchants of England Trading to the East Indies (1709), Bodleian, Folio θ 658.1.
[2] Court Book 44, pp. 441–9.
[3] Court Book 45, pp. 33–75. The Statute was 10 Anne, c. 28.
[4] Court Book 45, p. 41.

fail to be affected. In the General Court of 4 June 1713 there were signs of excitement and strong disagreement, and a majority resolved, against the advice of the directors, to join those petitioning against the treaty, and demanded special safeguards for the trade in East Indian goods. But the directors, reluctant to aline themselves with the enemies of the administration, managed to evade the necessity of presenting their petition by obtaining the insertion of a clause in the bill which they maintained to be adequate, and the Company was unrepresented among the commercial bodies opposing the measure.[1] Except on this occasion it would be impossible to deduce from the Company's records anything of the turmoil of these years, of the change of dynasty and the downfall of the Tory party, dragging down with it the party system which had dominated the fate of the Company as well as of the nation for almost half a century.

The Company had, indeed, already set the course which it was to follow successfully for the next fifty years. It was on its way to becoming the prosperous, respectable, and sound commercial and financial corporation which was not only far and away the biggest and most complicated trading organization of the country, but was (together with the Bank of England and the South Sea Company) the centre of the financial market rising in London and of the Government's political and financial interest there.

The position was one which it could hardly have achieved had it not been for the great changes that were taking place in the political life of the nation. The events of 1713 had shown that it was still impossible for the Company, however circumspect its leadership, to remain detached from political faction when this was running high, and the experience of their predecessors illustrated the disastrous effects on the Company's fortunes of partisanship in times of political instability. It was the long period of political peace which is associated with the name of Robert Walpole that gave the Company (like so many

---

[1] Court Book 45, pp. 401–5 and G. M. Trevelyan, *England under Queen Anne*, 1934, iii. 254 seq. D. A. E. Harkness in 'The Opposition to the Eighth and Ninth articles of the Commercial Treaty of Utrecht', *Scottish Historical Review*, vol. 21, pp. 219 seq. has misunderstood the position of the Company, as R. G. Mathias, 'The Economic Policy of the Board of Trade 1696–1714' (unpublished thesis), has pointed out from the Board of Trade records.

other English institutions) its chance of peaceful development, and it was the characteristics of the political system built up by Walpole that determined the Company's place in the life of the City and the nation in the reigns of the first two Georges.

The rapid transition which took place in the political scene from the bitter dissensions of the last years of Anne's reign to the stable if inert political system of Hanoverian England is one of the most striking changes in English history. Its deep-seated causes are no doubt to be sought in the good sense and absence of rancour of the English landed and commercial classes in a society both prosperous and expansionist. It was also due to the skill and determination shown by a few men, in particular Robert Walpole and his successor Henry Pelham, in consolidating and manipulating political power under the curious conditions of their time.

The political system which Walpole built up and his successors maintained was founded on four bases: the confidence of the Crown; the solidarity of interest of a knot of important Whig families who often inaccurately described themselves as the 'Revolution' families; a co-ordinated use of public and private patronage managed with economy to achieve directly or indirectly the requisite parliamentary majorities; and the support of a strong financial interest in the City of London. The use of the power thus gained was almost entirely negative. As David Hume said in one of his essays: 'We are . . . to look upon all the vast apparatus of our Government as having ultimately no other object or purpose but the distribution of justice or, in other words, the support of the twelve judges.'[1] In fact to maintain the machinery of law and order at home; to keep up (however inefficiently) the strength of the armed forces so that they would not prove wholly inadequate to the demands made upon them by the balance of power in Europe and the pressure for expansion in the areas of colonial conflict; and to be able to lay hands on financial resources sufficient for these purposes—these may be said to sum up the public obligations of a government of the time. It was with these limited public obligations in mind (as well as a wide variety of private obligations to individuals which might frequently prove more obtrusive) that

[1] David Hume, *Essay on the Origin of Government*, *Essays, Moral, Political and Literary*, ed. T. H. Green and T. H. Gross, 1875, i. 113–14.

the machine was constructed. In this machine, which, apart from occasional checks, ran with reasonable smoothness until the death of Henry Pelham in 1754, and did not wholly break down till the fall of the Duke of Newcastle in 1762, the East India Company was a cog and quite an important one.

In the first place, even in this period, there was always a small body of members of Parliament with East Indian interests. Several of the twenty-four directors usually had seats, attracted thither, like other prominent merchants, by the prospect of government contracts and other profitable rewards for support of government.[1] Some of these were men of great influence in the City and in close touch with the Government on all matters concerning its relations with that body.[2] The Company's stock ledgers[3] also show a number of other Members of Parliament to be large holders of stock and therefore likely to react with the directors on matters concerning the Company. The East India interest in Parliament was not at this time so strong either as it had been during the struggles of the 'Old' and 'New' Companies in the preceding century, or as it was to be when the enriched Company's servants sought seats in the House and the Company's affairs once again became the object of parliamentary scrutiny. It was far less strongly represented than the West India interest or the more loosely articulated but numerous body of persons with interest, direct or indirect, in the trade with the American colonies. Nevertheless, the Government did not disdain its parliamentary alliance, and the support of the Company had one special advantage in that it widened the scope of ministerial patronage. As the *Craftsman* pointed out, the directors had in their bestowal 'several Governments of much greater value than any in his Majesty's gift'[4] and they appointed to a great number of minor positions at home and abroad. The recipients of this patronage were for the most part those serving or connected with the Company. The day had not yet come when the fame of the 'Nabobs'' riches made a writership or a commission in the East Indies the goal of the younger sons of

---

[1] See L. B. Namier, *Structure of Politics at the Accession of George III*, 1929, i. 56 seq.
[2] e.g. Alderman Sir William Baker, M.P. for Plympton 1747–68; an eminent American merchant and friend and adherent of the Duke of Newcastle. For many years Director and in 1749 and 1752 Chairman of the East India Company.
[3] Preserved, with its stock transfer books and other records of its stock, in the Bank of England Record Office.   [4] The *Craftsman*, i. 97–98.

England and Scotland, and the senior posts a haven for the
jackals of great men seeking to recoup their own and their
patrons' fortunes. Still, public men were already aware of the
openings that existed for the relatives of some of their lesser
supporters, and ministers were already exploiting their connexions with the Company to this end.

In the second place the East India Company, with its wide
commercial connexions, was clearly an important element in
the politics of the City of London, not only when it came to
Parliamentary elections but in those of the City government in
which, in view of the unique importance of the City, the
Government often thought it necessary to concern themselves.
The reasons for this arose from the necessity of combating the
activities of opposition as well as from the needs of government
itself. Though the existing party structure had dissolved with
the collapse of the Tory party, the elements of an opposition to
the triumphant group of Whigs in power soon began to become
apparent. In addition to the scattered bands of Tories left in
permanent opposition, there were from time to time groups of
'rebel Whigs' who broke off from the ruling connexion and
declared hostilities against it. So complete was the collapse of
the old party divisions that there was nothing to prevent these
two types of opposition from fusing into a common 'Country
party' opposition to administration, and this from time to time
they did. As early as 1716 a startled Jacobite agent noted the
disappearance of all real party divisions. Reporting the debate
on the Septennial Act he said:

The most remarkable thing was that the Tories talked like old
Whigs and Republicans, against monarchy and ministers, etc. and
the Whigs magnified the advantages of unlimited absolute power
and prerogative, vilified the mob, ridiculed the people and exalted
the Crown.[1]

It was this fact that made possible united oppositions such as
that in which Bolingbroke joined with Pulteney and Carteret
in their assault on Walpole. Such oppositions—weaker or
stronger according to the age of the reigning king, the relationships between prominent political personalities and the appearance of good popular issues—could normally aim at no more
than the reversion of power in a future reign or the chance to

---

[1] H.M.C., Stuart Papers, ii. 122.

force on the ministry a few of its leaders. In the clamour of unsuccessful war it could, however, even drive a government from power.

The strength of such an opposition must lie in the support of something of the nature of public opinion both within and outside the House. As Edmund Burke remarked later, 'we know that all opposition is absolutely crippled, if it can obtain no kind of support without doors'.[1] Such a public opinion was found among the independent country gentlemen and among the lesser merchants of London and a few of the bigger outports, and these very different interests found themselves in consequence from time to time joined in a curious alliance. The watchwords of this oddly assorted coalition were derived from the Whig traditions of the past; demands for a place or pensions bill, for the return to triennial (or even to annual) Parliaments, and for the abolition of the standing army; and, unreal as those issues were, they had sufficient hold on contemporary imagination to embarrass a government, particularly if brought forward just before a General Election. The real issues by which, whenever this opposition grew formidable, they wooed public opinion were, however, of a different kind; the opposition to the Excise Bill in 1733, complaints of the weight of the Land Tax or, the only really effective rallying point, discontent at failure in the waging of war. Among the factors which predisposed a considerable section of the London merchant classes to hostility to government, particularly during war, was their jealousy of the small class of rich merchants and financiers and of the 'monied Companies' on account of their privileged position in government finance. It was said of Robert Walpole that 'He is hated by the city of London because he never did anything for the trading part of it, nor aimed at any interest of theirs but a corrupt influence over the directors and governors of the great moneyed companies.'[2]

The City of London was thus a battleground in eighteenth-

[1] *Correspondence of the Right Honourable Edmund Burke*, ed. Earl FitzWilliam and R. Bourke, 1844, ii. 51–52.

[2] *Some Materials towards Memoirs of the Reign of King George II by John, Lord Hervey*, ed. R. Sedgwick, 1931, i. 138. A. J. Henderson, *London and the National Government, 1721–1742*, Duke University, 1945, examines with interesting results City politics at this time, but ignores the influence of government financial technique in stimulating anti-ministerial forces there.

century politics. The Government needed and obtained the support of the monied interest there, the rich merchants who might act as contractors or subscribe to government loans and the great corporations on which national credit depended. The Opposition sought the support of their enemies, 'neither the top nor the bottom',[1] as one of their leaders called them. The position of the three Companies and the methods of Treasury finance at the time gave a real unity to this monied interest which was the object of so much suspicion and envy from their fellow citizens. Though by law no director of one of the Companies could serve on the Court of the others, the three Corporations were on close and friendly terms. The East India Company had, it is true, watched with some suspicion the rise of the South Sea Company and had protected itself against the compulsory engrafting of some of its stock after the collapse of the Bubble,[2] but its negotiations with the unfortunate Company were quite friendly and their later relations easy. With the Bank of England its relations were closer, since the latter was its banker and had come to be the supplier of the short-term credit necessary for the smooth flow of its trade between its sales.[3] It also provided much of the silver bullion which at this time was exported to the East. The three Companies co-operated in their dealings with the Government when their common interests were involved. Together they consulted about protesting against the imposition of duties on the transfer of stock;[4] one after another they waited on new First Lords of the Treasury when they came into office, and they formed the centre of the *bloc* of state creditors who frustrated the attempt to reduce the interest on the National Debt under Walpole in 1737, and who had to be bought off by concessions when Pelham succeeded in carrying out his conversion operation in

[1] Notes of a speech on the address (November 1761) by William Beckford, M.P. (1709–70), West India planter and merchant and later Lord Mayor of London. Add. MS. 38334, ff. 29 seq.

[2] Court Book 49, pp. 113 seq.

[3] Court Book 43, p. 199, 22 October 1708. The United Company took over the arrangements with the Bank which had been entered into by those temporarily managing the early stages of the union of the two Companies. The use of the Bank simplified the routine of their business markedly and was particularly valuable in the provision of short-term credit which eliminated the need for capital calls on the shareholders.

[4] Court Book 45, pp. 19 and 23, 2 and 7 May 1712.

1749.[1] It was an indication of those close relations that the East India Company permitted directors and ex-directors of the Bank and the South Sea Company to share the privileges of its own directors at the Company's regular sales.[2]

The Company was thus of political significance to the Government in the City as part of the ministerialist monied interest there which clashed with an anti-ministerialist popular interest both in Parliamentary and City elections. Its main significance, however, in the governmental machine lay outside the realm of party politics and in that of public finance. Eighteenth-century governments depended for their fiscal requirements partly on a system of taxation which was from the modern point of view both rigid and unproductive and partly on credit raised in the form of short- and long-term loans. For obtaining this credit they depended on the growing London money market, with the Bank of England rising to a central position in it, and (in the case of long-term loans) on the power of the London market to mobilize the funds of the *rentier* class not only of the British Isles but also, at least in some degree, of various continental countries, particularly the Dutch.[3] This power gave particular strength to Great Britain in the great wars of the century. The East India Company was a factor in the arrangements for both short- and long-term credits.

The Company's influence on the short-term credit arrangements was exercised indirectly. As Sir John Clapham has shown,[4] governments were throughout this period coming increasingly to rely on the Bank of England to provide their short-term credit needs. No longer was there question, as in 1698, of the East India Company being pressed to subscribe money for the 'circulation' of Exchequer Bills, and the advances made by prominent individuals as advances on the Land Tax were being gradually eliminated.[5] The influence of the Company arose from the fact that it was itself a big issuer of short-term credit instruments in its India Bonds, the total issue of which had

---

[1] See my article 'Samson Gideon and the Reduction of Interest, 1749–50', *Econ. Hist. Rev.*, 1946, xvi.   [2] Court Book 48, p. 41, 20 June 1718.
[3] C. Wilson, *Anglo-Dutch Commerce and Finance in the Eighteenth Century*, Cambridge, 1941.
[4] J. Clapham, *The Bank of England: A History*, Cambridge, 1944, vol. i.
[5] e.g. The Duchess of Marlborough. See *Selection from the Papers of the Earls of Marchmont*, 1831, ii. 272.

greatly increased since the union of the Companies until in 1744 the maximum was raised to £6,000,000. These bonds had become by convention negotiable on the market, were in convenient denominations, and became so popular that it was argued that 'money will always be borrowed at a lower rate on those bonds than in any other way'.[1]

The rate at which the Company could raise money on bond varied with the prosperity of its trade but also with the general state of public credit. In 1711 the directors instructed their Committee of Treasury to consider means for bringing their bonds 'into better reputation'.[2] They then bore interest at 6 per cent. By 1715 it had been reduced to 5 per cent., and by 1718 to 4 per cent.[3] In 1719, during the speculative boom of the Bubble they had to pay 5 per cent. and it was not till 1724 that they were able in view of 'the present situation of the Company's affairs and the general credit of the nation' to reduce it to 4 per cent.[4] After two further fluctuations an attempt was made in 1732 to reduce it to 3 per cent. on the initiative of a body of shareholders anxious to avoid a reduction in the Company's dividend at a time of trade depression. The attempt failed but a reduction to 3½ per cent. was finally achieved[5] and this rate remained constant until 1746, a year of great credit difficulties on account of the Jacobite rebellion and the war with France, when the directors were forced to raise it to 4 per cent.[6] When peace came and Pelham began to plan the great conversion of the National Debt from which the 3 per cent. Consols emerged, it is significant that the first step he took was to get one of his most trusted financial advisers, the Jewish jobber, Samson Gideon, to organize in 1749 a successful subscription for the reduction of the interest on India Bonds to 3 per cent., the lowest level they had ever achieved.[7]

In the raising of the long-term funded loans the Company exercised a similar indirect influence (since its stock was, with that of the Bank and the South Sea Company, the only stock

---

[1] e.g. in [A. Dalrymple] State of the East India Company . . ., 1780, p. 26.
[2] Court Book 44, p. 427, 9 May 1711.
[3] Court Books 46, p. 309, and 47, p. 583.
[4] Court Books 48, p. 249, and 51, p. 61.
[5] Court Book 55, pp. 82 seq.   [6] Court Book 61, p. 469.
[7] For this and the account of the closed subscriptions which follows see my article 'Samson Gideon and the Reduction of Interest, 1749–50', loc. cit.

other than government securities always quoted on the market) but also a more direct one. The Government no longer depended for its loans on direct contributions from the great Corporations, though it still extorted them on such occasions as the renewal of their charters. Subscriptions from the monied public had come to predominate and by 1749 only some 26 per cent. of the 4 per cent. annuities were made up of loans from the three monied Companies. Nevertheless their position on the market put them still at the centre of public credit and the method employed by the Treasury in raising their loans emphasized the fact. The normal Treasury procedure when floating a loan at this period was what was known as the 'closed subscription' and had as its aim the procuring of a body of subscribers of sufficient financial strength to keep up the price of the stock when it came on the market as soon as the first instalments of payments were made. They began by asking for applications from individuals with whom the Treasury was in touch. It was understood that each applicant spoke for a considerable body of would-be subscribers as well as himself; certain of them represented the foreign capitalists, particularly the Dutch, who were beginning to constitute an important element in the body of public creditors; prominent merchants and government contractors, often themselves Members of Parliament, had the names of a number of members (particularly of government supporters) on their lists, and other special interests, such as that of the Jewish financiers, might be included. While these proposals were being formulated there was a period of active discussion behind the scenes between the Treasury and the more prominent of the applicants; then a meeting was convened to settle the terms. Contemporary references confirm the accuracy of Lord North's description in 1781 of what happened at such a meeting:

The rule of the meeting was to convene all the monied men who had made applications and offers and to convene the heads of all the great public Companies who usually assisted the Government with money, but who never made any applications previous to that meeting; by these gentlemen so collected the terms were settled and it was always usual to expect that the gentlemen who were present were to take up a pretty considerable share of the loan among them.[1]

[1] *Parl. Hist.* xxi. 1355. Two or three other Corporations, such as the insurance

The list was in fact nearly always over-subscribed and, after the terms of the loan had been passed by Parliament, the final list of subscribers was drawn up by the Treasury, usually with the advice of some City supporter. Among the subscribers there appeared, not the names of the Companies in their corporate capacity, but those of their directors, with considerable sums against them. When a list of applicants has survived, as well as the list of those on whose behalf they made successful application, the position of the Companies becomes clear. In 1759–60, for instance, when what was then the large sum of £8,000,000 was to be borrowed there stands before the names of the nineteen private applicants, 'Mr. Burrell for the Bank of England £466,000, Mr. Bristow for the South Sea Company £330,000, Mr. Godfrey for the East India Company £200,000.'[1]

The East India Company thus maintained, in the more favourable conditions of Hanoverian England, its traditional policy of alliance with the Government of the day; its direct and indirect contribution to the establishment of public credit was one of its chief claims to government favour. As the directors boasted in 1720 they could 'by several instances, and some very late ones, make it evident that they had been as zealous as any of their fellow subjects to support the publick credit'.[2]

They were wise to foster their connexion with government and fortunate in that financial considerations strengthened the case for supporting them, for the tide was running strongly against both monopolies and the joint stock organization in trade, and in favour of unrestricted commercial enterprise. The hostility shown by Adam Smith towards the Company in his famous *Wealth of Nations*[3] followed a line of criticism that had never died out since the seventeenth century, and the Bubble Act of 1720 had effectively checked the development of this form of organization. The East India Company had the further disadvantages that its imports were regarded with suspicion by powerful groups of British manufacturers and that, until the sixties, it was a considerable exporter of bullion. As late as 1754

corporations, were subscribing by this time; they do not appear to have done so earlier. ·In the Revolutionary wars the method of subscribing had somewhat changed, rival 'lists' of subscribers being submitted.

[1] Namier, *Structure of Politics*, i. 68.
[2] Court Book 49, p. 200, 22 December 1720.
[3] Adam Smith, *Wealth of Nations*, ed. E. Cannan, 1904, ii. 129 seq.

an attempt was made in the City to get up a petition against it on this count.[1] The stability of the Government they were allied with, however, preserved them from any serious danger from an Opposition who might take up the case of their opponents, while the freedom from serious internal faction which their good sense and moderation had ensured, enabled them to present a united front to any attack.

But even in these years of peace they could not hope always to take their place in the Government camp without attracting the attention of the parliamentary Opposition. When a good issue and a favourable parliamentary situation were found in conjunction, attacks were launched on the Company which served both to recall in a less violent form the assaults of the past and to prepare for those of the future. Only two such attacks attained any importance during this period and neither was really formidable. The first was in 1730 when, the term of the Company's charter nearing its end, a group of merchants in London and the outports sought to supplant it by setting up in its place a new regulated company. The second was in 1758–9, when a group of dissatisfied tea-dealers tried to force a breach in the monopoly of the Company's tea sales. Both owed what political importance they achieved to issues far outside the range of the Company's own concerns.

The first of these incidents occurred in the years when the opposition to Walpole was being built up and the *Craftsman* was the most effective organ of Opposition opinion. The Company's affairs had come into prominence because of the part played in the complex diplomacy of the day by a rival Ostend East India Company which was being fostered by the Emperor and (since it was believed to be composed of Jacobite exiles) was widely held to be part of a political threat to England as well as a commercial threat to the Company. While it was only one factor in an intricate and potentially dangerous situation, in which the threat to Gibraltar was far more serious, it attracted much attention, and it was as part of the successful solution which at least kept England temporarily out of European war,

---

[1] Committee of Correspondence. Memoranda, vol. xiv, has a copy of a petition to this effect alleged to be from several merchants and traders of the City of London. A manuscript note at the bottom states, however, that it was advertised to lie open for signature at the King's Arms Tavern, Cornhill, on 4 December 1754, but that, though one Packenham attended, no signatures were obtained.

that the Emperor agreed to suspend the Company in 1727 and abolish it in 1731.[1] During this crisis the Opposition was unfriendly to the Company, as to all interests allied with the Government, but made no serious attack on it. An occasional writer inveighed against it as a monopoly[2] (but the South Sea Company was at this time drawing most of their fire) and when fraud was discovered at its sales the *Craftsman* savagely assailed it;[3] but on the major issue of the suppression of the Ostend Company there was no real difference of opinion. An Opposition speaker said in the House in January 1727: 'As to the Ostend Company, he owned it to be a national concern, and a very just motive to a war with the Emperor; but that it had been an easy matter to nip that project in the bud',[4] and the *Craftsman* in the following March gave the same grudging support:

As to the affair of Ostend, though the abolition of that Charter is no doubt of some consequence to the East India Company and perhaps to the Nation, yet it cannot upon any account be brought into competition with a place upon which so much depends [Gibraltar].[5]

It was before this issue was finally settled, but on quite different grounds, that an assault on the Company was delivered.

In 1730 the Company was already in unofficial negotiation with the Government for the renewal of its charter. At the same time there were signs of a concerted anti-Government move in the City. The first sign was an assault on the Court of Directors of the South Sea Company, where the autocratic rule of their Sub-Governor Sir John Eyles was challenged at the election of directors. This was defeated by his supporters, 'the Court party', a contemporary said, 'coming in universally for Sir John Eyles'.[6] A few weeks later it was known that the East India Company was to be attacked. As early as 5 February there had

[1] The issue is treated by W. Michael, *Englische Geschichte im Achtzehnten Jahrhundert*, Berlin, 1934, iii. 371 seq. and G. B. Hertz, *England and the Ostend Company*, E.H.R., 1907, pp. 255 seq. The latter has attributed a number of pamphlets against the East India Company which arose from the attack on its charter in 1730 to this incident. He has therefore been led to exaggerate the hostility of the Opposition to the Company during the diplomatic crisis.
[2] *Reasons against the War by an Old Whig*, 1727.
[3] The *Craftsman*, 19 December 1726–16 January 1727, i. 39 seq.
[4] A. Boyer, *Political State of Great Britain*, 1727, xxxiii. 97.
[5] The *Craftsman*, i. 202..
[6] Boyer, *Political State of Great Britain*, op. cit., xxxix. 208.

been a slight fall in the price of the Company's stock and on the 24th the Press reported 'There is handed about here a scheme for a free and open trade to the East Indies.'[1] Two days later there was laid before the House, to the surprise of normally well-informed members, a petition signed by more than 200 respectable London merchants,[2] and supported (obviously by arrangement) by similar petitions from merchants in Liverpool and Bristol, demanding a subscription for a new regulated Company to take over the monopoly of the trade to India.

The attack followed closely on the lines of those of the late seventeenth century; so closely, indeed, that it was thought worth while to reprint some of the pamphlets of that era.[3] Sir John Barnard, the leader for many years of the popular party in the City, was at the centre of the scheme and opened the debate in the House on it.[4] Prominent members of the Opposition, Sir William Wyndham for the Tories, Pulteney and Captain (later Admiral) Vernon for the Whigs attacked the Company as a monopoly and one with a peculiarly bad reputation. The defence of the Company was somewhat confused by an ill-advised attempt to argue that it, like the South Sea Company, had been given perpetuity of trade by the Act of 1712, and the Government spokesmen, though they rallied to their ally, were anxious to repudiate excessive claims on its part lest it be encouraged to adopt an intransigent attitude in the bargaining for the renewal of its charter; but the alliance was in no degree shaken, and the petition was rejected by 231 votes to 131. There seems to have been little serious fear that the attack would prevail; the decline in the price of East India Stock was small and the Company itself did not think it necessary to submit a counter-petition to Parliament. Instead the directors continued their negotiations with the ministry and five days later informed the proprietors that all danger was over, and asked for their sanction in accepting a proposal shortly to be made by the ministry 'which may be advantageous both to the Publick and

<hr/>

[1] *Whitehall Evening Post*, 21–24 February 1730.

[2] Ibid., 24–26 February 1730. There was also behind these petitions some of the genuine hostility of the outports to London, a perennial sentiment which flared up from time to time.

[3] *A Collection of Papers relating to the East Indian Trade*, 1730.

[4] There is a detailed report of the earlier part of debate in the diary of Lord Egmont (*H.M.C., MSS. of the Earl of Egmont*, Diary, i. 65 seq.).

the Company'.[1] Next day the proposal was laid before the House in Committee and the following morning accepted by the Company. In return for a reduction of the interest on the Company's loan to the public from 5 per cent. to 4 per cent. and for a contribution of £200,000 the Company obtained a renewal of its charter till 1766, with the customary three years' grace if it were then terminated. When in 1744, during the war of the Austrian Succession, the Government was badly in need of funds, the Company came to its assistance with a loan of £1,000,000 at 3 per cent. and thereby obtained a further renewal of its charter until 1780. This source of weakness was not to disturb it again for many years. When it arose once more the situation was very different.

The second incident which led to an attack on the Company in the House of Commons during this period was of less general interest. It was indeed significant only because the political scene was beginning to shift and its importance lies more in the indications it gives of the situation in the future than in its immediate circumstances. It occurred in 1758–9, after the death of Pelham had left the ineffective Duke of Newcastle at the head of the connexion which had so long ruled the country, and when lack of success in the Seven Years War had forced them to take into office that dominating and incalculable personality, William Pitt the Great Commoner. It began in 1758 when an Alderman Blakiston, a member of the City popular party and something of a firebrand, at the head of a small group of dealers in tea, quarrelled with the Company and the majority of the tea-dealers about the policy of its tea sales and finally asked the permission of the Treasury to import some tea direct from Holland, where they claimed the price was much lower. After some discussions between the Treasury and the Company, it was agreed that the Company itself should import and sell some of this tea thereby preventing a breach of their monopoly.[2] In the following year, however, the malcontents again made an application for licence to import teas, and, when they seemed likely to be refused, put the matter into the hands of a prominent London merchant and Member of Parliament, William Beckford, who threatened to bring it before the House.[3]

---

[1] Court Book 53, p. 432, 3 March 1729/30.
[2] Court Book 68, pp. 41 seq.   [3] Ibid., pp. 305 seq.

Normally the Treasury would have given little support to applications of this kind; but the situation was not normal. William Beckford was one of the most prominent supporters of Pitt and his chief link with the City; the alliance with Pitt was new and uneasy and ministers were afraid that if the matter came up in the House, their formidable ally would join his supporter in attacking them. An agitated letter was sent from the Treasury to the Company warning the directors of the developments[1] and demanding an opportunity of discussion with them and with the tea-dealers. The Duke of Newcastle thought it necessary to keep the king informed of the progress of events.[2] When Beckford raised the matter he was supported by Sir John Barnard, the City leader, and by Sir John Phillips, a prominent member of the Tory Opposition. Alderman Baker, formerly chairman of the Company, the Chancellor of the Exchequer, and other ministers opposed him. The case was argued both on general and on specific lines but the defence put forward was a strong one, the voice of the Great Commoner was not raised in support of his henchman, and the matter finally dropped without coming to a division.[3] Nevertheless it was significant, firstly as an indication of the way in which the Company's position was to weaken when the united and stable governments of the first half of the century came to an end, and secondly as a foretaste of the attitude of a man who was to exercise some influence at a later crisis of its history. William Beckford, who was coming to possess in the City something of the prestige which Sir John Barnard had enjoyed there for many years, had already opposed several commercial bills in which the Company was concerned and had already declaimed against it as a 'monopolizing company' and as 'the favourite of government'.[4] His vociferations against monopoly were less significant than the fact of his ill-will to the Company; both gained importance from the close ties he had and was to retain with William Pitt.

[1] Ibid., p. 326.
[2] Newcastle's Memoranda for the King, 6 and 8 April 1759. Add. MS. 32889, ff. 384 and 416 seq. [3] Court Book 68, p. 329.
[4] Parl. Hist. xiv. 1218. For his attitude on the bills to restrain insurance on foreign ships plying to and from the East Indies (aimed at the trade from Emden) in 1752 and the bill of 1754 to extend the Mutiny Act to India see ibid., xiv. 1212–21 and xv. 265.

II

The Company used this period of political peace to develop its trade and perfect its internal organization. By 1732 when statistics first become available the produce of its sales of East Indian goods had reached the level of £1,940,000, a sum round which the total was to oscillate without more than temporary and slight deviations until the sharp rise in 1763–4 followed in 1768–9 by the further increase resulting from Clive's assumption of the *Diwani* of Bengal in 1765.[1] Its method of conducting this trade, the elaborate system of records which was to win the unwilling praise of its investigators, and the framework of its civil and military service became standardized and indeed stereotyped during this period. The same may be said of its internal organization. In general the conduct of its business continued on the lines already laid down for it. The directors were drawn from the same class of prominent merchants as were the Committees who preceded them, and the membership of the Court, despite the by-law intended to check consecutive service, was remarkably permanent. Directors were often re-elected year after year, only standing down every fifth year 'by rotation'; they attended the Courts and the Committees well, and carried on the Company's affairs in an orderly and dignified manner. The times did not call for the strong leadership of a Sir Josia Child, as in the past, or a Laurence Sulivan, as in the future, nor did the affairs of the Company demand the autocratic rule by which Sir John Eyles was re-establishing order in the South Sea Company after its debacle; but a few men certainly controlled its fortunes for a number of years and did so with only occasional friction and a good deal of success. Of these Josias Wordsworth had the longest titular ascendancy,[2] but the absence of controversy leaves him a dim figure; there is some evidence which might suggest that for part of the time at least the Quaker, John Eccleston, whom the *Craftsman* attacked, may have played the more active part.[3]

---

[1] *Third Report of the Committee of Secrecy*, 1773. *Reports from Committees of the House of Commons*, iv. 75.

[2] Director (except when 'out by rotation') 1712–39. In eight of these years he was Chairman and in five Deputy Chairman.

[3] The *Craftsman*, 1 December 1736, pp. 41–48 and 92 seq. and 16 January 1737, pp. 109 seq.

The most important development in the conduct of business in the Court of Directors was the standardization of the elaborate system of committees to which most of the detailed work of the Court was delegated and through which even matters of first-class importance normally passed before they came before the full Court. The Committees of Correspondence and Treasury and, from time to time, the Committee of Secrecy thus obtained great influence over the Company's policy. This fact, together with his control over the agenda, was a potent factor in maintaining the traditionally powerful personal position of the Chairman òf the Company, who served *ex officio* on them. Of equal importance was the development of the means of control over the Court of Proprietors. This meant two things; the control over the annual election of directors and the obtaining of a majority for any policy supported by the directors in the General Courts. The first step towards the control of elections was the institution of the House list, the drawing up each year by the outgoing directors of a complete list of candidates to submit to the electors. An unfriendly observer in 1764 described the method employed as follows:

Amongst the candidates there is generally one who, by dint of drudgery and application to the business of the India House, the principal quality hitherto possessed by or requisite to any of them, has rendered himself necessary in the direction. This person takes upon him to form a list of such directors for the ensuing year as are agreeable to him, copies of which list are usually delivered out beforehand to his own friends; but to others they are distributed at the door of the house when the proprietors assemble to vote. If the proprietor, receiving this list, dislikes any one or more names, he scratches such out, and, inserting others, delivers it in as his list. When all are delivered in, the different lists are scrutinised, and the majority declared. Thus there is always in the list a leader, and though there may be some scratches yet it has been seldom if ever known, that he failed of even one member of his list.[1]

This description appears to be substantially correct, though it probably exaggerates the part played by the individual leader. By the sixties at least it was customary for the House list to be drawn up at a meeting of those interested, sometimes after a

---

[1] *Reflections on the Present State of our East India Affairs*, London, 1764. A copy of this pamphlet was preserved at the Guildhall, London, but was destroyed by enemy action.

ballot to choose between a variety of candidates. The completed
list was published in the Press.[1] It had, of course, no official
standing, but that the name carried weight with the proprietors
is shown by the fact that in 1763, when the great civil wars of the
Company had begun, there was a vote in the Court of Directors
to decide which of two rival lists should enjoy the title.[2] From
the sixties onward the House list was frequently opposed by
a rival 'Proprietors' list' and sometimes by more than one. In
such cases it was usual for some of the candidates to be 'double-
listed' to neutralize the influence of their personal supporters.
Though it was rare in the first half of the century (after the
suspicions of the 'Old' and 'New' interests had died down) for
the House list to be challenged, there were occasions on which
rival lists were drawn up and at least one occasion in 1733 when
the challengers met with considerable success. In general, however, it is true that up to 1758 the proprietors showed themselves prepared to adopt the candidates put before them in this
way. The contest of 1758 was the beginning of new and less
happy times.

The chief reason for the success of the House list was
undoubtedly the confidence of the proprietors in the directors
and the absence of serious party divisions within the Company.
The General Court retained the over-riding powers it had
enjoyed from the origin of the Company, and the abolition of
cumulative voting checked the most obvious way of obtaining
control over it. There remained the possibility of control by
collusive transfer, 'splitting', which was prohibited by by-law,
but very difficult to control. In 1763 and the ten years that
followed this was to become a powerful weapon, when almost
the whole credit of the London market was on occasion massed
to support an intricate and dangerous method of controlling
the Company by the creation of votes. In the first half of the
century, however, the Company's transfer books[3] show con-

[1] A printed letter asking for support backed by the signatures of all the
candidates was also sent round to well-known supporters or prominent men they
hoped to influence. Several are preserved among the papers of the Marquess of
Rockingham in the FitzWilliam MSS. deposited in the Sheffield Public Library.

[2] Court Book 71, p. 361.

[3] The Company's Transfer Books preserved at the Bank of England Record
Office provide a most valuable source of information on this method of influencing
elections, particularly if used in conjunction with its Stock Ledgers. These papers
have been widely used in this study for the elections between 1763 and 1773; after

clusively that, while there was sometimes a noticeable increase in the number of units of £500 which changed hands immediately before and then again after an election of directors (notably in 1758), the scale was far below that sufficient to affect the issue of an election. Nevertheless the directors certainly exercised an efficient control over the General Court during this period, and in doing so they did not trust either to good fortune or their powers of argument. When dividends were maintained and trade went well and there were no dissensions among the directors danger of revolt in the General Court was not serious. Normally its proceedings were peaceable and largely formal; even at elections, unless there were competing lists, there was little excitement. Fewer than 200 proprietors would vote on such occasions, though when a contest took place the numbers voting might be as high as 700 in 1710 and over 1,000 by 1764.

It was, however, as the directors well knew, when things were going badly that there was reason to fear a revolt of the General Court, and when such a revolt occurred the results were incalculable. On the few occasions before 1758 when it rebelled, though it did not yet show the violence which was to make it a by-word in the future, it was already a formidable body. The report of the speeches at the General Court of 9 August 1732,[1] when the proprietors opposed a decrease of dividend advocated by the directors, shows that it could already achieve the high standard of debate observed in the years ahead, when its deliberations sometimes rivalled those of the House of Commons in interest, and could show the impatience of control which was to cause so much embarrassment to those trying to guide its destinies.

The way in which the directors built up their voting strength in the General Court to prevent such revolts or to defeat them when they occurred, was the normal eighteenth-century method of 'management' based on patronage. The directors

that date the reforms imposed on the Company by Parliament greatly reduced the effects of collusive transfers on the results of elections and also made them much more difficult to trace in the Company's records.

[1] Committee of Correspondence. Memoranda, vol. x. This report, evidently the work of a professional hired for the purpose (his fee is marked on it), is the only one which appears to exist. At a later period the London press sometimes made very full reports of important debates at India House.

exercised in their appointments to their military and civil services and in their promotions within these services a great deal of patronage. Some of this certainly went to their own relatives and connexions, but much of it was used with the intention of obtaining or assuring the support of persons and interests within the Company. There seems to be little or no evidence of directors selling such offices for money, but every indication that the friends and relatives of those favoured were expected to support the measures put forward by the directors in general and those favoured by their own patron in particular. Besides the Company's servants at home (relatively few in number) and the relatives and friends of those serving abroad, there were a large number of others whose interests were connected with them. There were the leaders of the monied interest in the City who had a concern in the credit and smooth running of the Company; there were the City supporters of government whom the latter might urge to come to the directors' assistance; and there were all the numerous people who had trade connexions with the Company. There were the clothiers and Blackwell Hall factors, whose woollens the Company bought for export; the packers and dyers who prepared them; the private bankers and brokers through whom it obtained its silver bullion; the diamond merchants whom it licensed to export coral and bullion and to bring back in exchange precious stones either on their own behalf or as the agents of foreign merchants. Finally, and most important of all because of their organization was the well-known East India shipping interest.[1]

This curious and influential organization was composed of those who, since the Company stopped building its own ships in the seventeenth century, were concerned in providing the specialized type of shipping required for its trade. Though, like most of the Company's institutions, it achieved more notoriety in the second half of the century (a notoriety which in 1796 led to the overthrow of its monopoly), the period of its greatest power was probably in an earlier period. The development of the Company's method of hiring its ships was largely dictated by

---

[1] The account which follows is summarized from Chapter IV of my *London Merchant, 1695–1774*. For the later history of the interest see C. N. Parkinson, *Trade in the Eastern Seas*, Cambridge, 1937, pp. 164 seq. and C. H. Philips, *The East India Company 1784–1834*, Manchester, 1940, pp. 80 seq.

expediency. When in 1659 one Captain Millett was guaranteed that, if he and his friends would build a suitable ship the Company would employ her in preference to any other,[1] and when in 1668 it was declared for the encouragement of owners that no three-decked ship would be considered superannuated until she had done sixteen years' service, and no two-decked ship until she had done fourteen,[2] the Company were taking steps to ensure a suitable fleet. It was for the same reason that they began to insist that the Commanders of such ships should be men in whom they had confidence. The result was that they became committed by degrees to the continuous use of certain ships and the continuous employment of certain Commanders, who were also permitted certain recognized privileges. From these commitments there gradually arose another; when the reign of one Indiaman came to an end, her place began to be taken as of right by another ship built by the same owners and commanded by the same master. In this way there grew up the two bases of the strength of the shipping interest, the 'permanent bottom' and the 'perpetual command'.

So long as the Company's shipping was expanding the existence of these two rights meant no more than that those already providing the shipping were given preference among those whose ships were taken up; but when the Company's needs were stationary it meant that certain men possessed a monopoly in the provision of its ships, and should the Company at any time have to contract its demands for ships it was clearly faced by a difficult problem. Moreover, though the system grew up for reasons of practical expedience, much of its development was affected by considerations of a personal nature. In the seventeenth century the 'Committees' themselves played a preponderant part in the ownership of the Company's shipping, and though when the United Company was formed a by-law forbade directors to be concerned in the ownership of ships hired by the Company, this prohibition was ignored. The continuation of the interests of such directors and the pressure of would-be owners was always tempting the Court to take up more ships than they required, and the right of the 'permanent bottom' made the results cumulative. As early as 1723 there was

[1] *Cal. Court Minutes*, v. 348–9.
[2] Ibid. viii. 58.

a glut of shipping[1] and by 1751 the excess was so great that a voluntary arrangement was entered into by the members of the monopoly gradually to reduce the numbers from sixty-five to forty-eight, with a preference for the 'suspended bottoms' should the Company's shipping needs increase again.[2] In the period beginning in 1758, when efficiency was constantly sacrificed to the claims of party, the number of 'bottoms' came permanently to exceed the number of ships required for trade, and an elaborate system of rotation was set up whereby the owners of a bottom waited their turn to build their ship, and even so, the number of ships taken up each year was more than the Company required.

In a monopolist system of this kind some kind of combination between those concerned was almost inevitable, and traces of it were early seen. As early as 1712 there is some evidence of concerted action among those tendering their ships to the Company, and in 1716 the directors complained that they had 'reason to believe that there was a confederacy among many of the owners to impose the freight they demanded on the Company'.[3] Its nucleus was the body of ships' husbands or managing owners, many of them men of wealth and importance and frequently managing a group of ships. We have no description of their organization until the eighties but it was evidently already well established. They are alluded to as a club or society; they have a Chairman and Deputy who represent them, sometimes with other delegates, before the directors, and on important occasions they summon general meetings of what they call their constituents, the general body of owners. These men formed the nucleus of the shipping interest. Other groups of persons within it, though their interests sometimes clashed, were in general prepared to follow the lead in dealing with the Company. Chief of these were the East India Commanders, with the officers depending on them, and the Thames-side ship-builders who enjoyed a monopoly in the building of East-Indiamen.

When it is considered that the husbands were a close body of important men in the City; that the owners comprised every

---

[1] Court Book 50, p. 404.
[2] Fifth Report of the Committee of Secrecy 1773. Reports from Committees of the House of Commons, iv. 261 and 294–5.   [3] Court Book 47, p. 86.

kind of influential person, including a considerable number of 'shipping' directors; that both the Commanders and the shipbuilders were a rich and influential group; and, finally, that a large body of ships' officers, tradesmen, and others were involved with them, it is easy to see that they formed a *bloc* in the Court of Proprietors who might give the directors trouble if their interests were threatened, but who in general would give them their support for reasons of self interest.

With the support of these 'Household troops', the directors, so long as they remained united, were able to maintain on the whole an easy control over the General Court. During this period it showed signs of getting badly out of control only on two occasions; in 1732–3 over the question of a reduction in the dividend, and in 1749 when opposition was made to the reduction in the interest paid to the Company by the State which was part of Pelham's conversion scheme of that and the following year. In 1732–3 the directors suffered something near defeat. In 1749 they were triumphant.

The difficulties they encountered in 1732–3 were serious.[1] They arose from a trade recession attributed by the directors to misconduct of their servants abroad (particularly in Bengal and among the Supercargoes on the China voyages); the competition of minor foreign companies, particularly the Swedish Company; and the widespread smuggling of tea. Whatever its causes, they decided that a reduction of the dividend from 8 per cent. to 6 per cent. was desirable, and brought this recommendation before the General Court. Reductions in dividend are seldom popular with shareholders and on this occasion the directors met with organized opposition. Under the leadership of one Miles Barne a party among the proprietors demanded that, instead of reducing the dividend, the Company should lower the interest on its bonds, and they even succeeded in raising a list of subscribers who were prepared to lend money at 3 per cent. as the basis of such a conversion scheme. The attempt was, after some delays, partially successful, a reduction to $3\frac{1}{2}$ per cent. being effected, but the directors still maintained that a dividend of 6 per cent. was all that the Company could afford. At this Barne and his followers challenged them in the General Court, and, on a ballot, forced them by a majority of

[1] Court Books 54 and 55 *passim.*

188 to 99 to adopt a smaller reduction and to announce a dividend of 7 per cent. Nor was this the end of the contest. Friction on the General Court continued and the directors had some difficulty in blocking a proposal for a Committee of the General Court to advise on dividends and a further resolution for restraining any director from being Chairman or Deputy for more than one year during his four-year term of office.

When the election to the Court came round in April, their opponents decided to put a rival 'Proprietors' list up against the House list, double-listing some but excluding others of the sitting directors. In a heated election where the voting was high they succeeded, not indeed in ousting their opponents, but in getting some of their candidates, including Miles Barne, elected. The check was, however, merely temporary. A year later the old interests succeeded in ousting the interlopers and by 1735 the opposition had died away. The Company continued without further electoral contests till those of 1758 marked the end of its period of peace.

The other conflict which temporarily disturbed the smooth relation between the Court of Directors and the General Court during this period arose out of the proposals made by Pelham to the Company as part of his conversion scheme of 1749–50.[1] Pelham negotiated terms with each of the three monied companies separately and when it came to the turn of the Company the directors obtained terms which they considered satisfactory. In all negotiations of this kind, however, the Government found it easier to come to an agreement with the directors than with the proprietors they represented, and on this occasion the General Court were already somewhat disturbed by the bitter recriminations which followed the loss of Madras to the French, reported in England two years before. Led by one dissentient director, Sir James Creed,[2] they now first of all turned down the Government's proposal and then launched a counter-attack on the directors, demanding a statement of the military condition of Madras at the beginning of the war and of the measures taken for its defence. They ended by questioning the terms of a recent contract for the purchase of silver bullion in which Samson Gideon, who had been acting as the ministry's

---

[1] Court Books 63 and 64 *passim*. Cf. my *Samson Gideon and the Reduction of Interest, 1749–50*, loc. cit.   [2] 1754–60, M.P. for Canterbury.

agent in the negotiations for the reduction of interest, was involved.

The directors, however, weathered this storm. An election of directors was imminent and it is clear that their forces were mustered, for an unusually heavy poll was recorded. The opposition, however, petered out, and on the wave of their success the directors forced through the acceptance of the Government's proposals, while the fact that Madras had been restored in the peace terms had taken the edge off the discontent at the Company's reverse in India. These disagreements were neither more numerous nor more serious than was to be expected in the vicissitudes of a vigorous commercial body composed of a large and growing number of shareholders.

The growth in the share capital of the Company, following the adoption of Pelham's conversion scheme, increased still further the importance of its stock on the London market. The London market itself, despite the abortive attempt to check its speculative developments by the Act of 1734, was steadily growing in experience and importance. The jobbers and brokers who met at Garraway's and Jonathan's coffee-houses were becoming a rich and important (though still suspect) class of men, handling the business of foreign as well as of English speculators and dealing on the Amsterdam as well as the London market. As early as 1761 there was an attempt, though a premature one, to set up the type of organization for the control of their business which after 1772 formed the basis of the Stock Exchange.[1] The East India Stock, together with the subscriptions to the Government's war-time loans and other government annuities, were the securities on which, after the Bubble years, most of the speculative activities centred. Though there is reason to believe that some of the speculative dealings so impressively detailed in the 1734 Act and common in Amsterdam were rare on the London market,[2] there can be no doubt that an extensive business in margins in East India Stock and in these other securities was carried on in both centres in these years. Nevertheless despite this fact, and the indignant

---

[1] T. Mortimer, *Every Man his own Broker*, 1762, p. xiii.

[2] In Edmund Burke's correspondence (FitzWilliam MSS., Northants.) there is a note, apparently dated 1767, describing the 'Species of dealing in stocks in Holland scarcely known in England which is the giving or taking Premiums for the Refusals or Putts for a future time'.

clamour of pamphleteers and commercial purists, India Stock
was in no sense a speculative one; it suffered few violent
fluctuations and indeed was the nearest eighteenth-century
equivalent of a 'gilt-edged' security.

It was as such that it enjoyed its chief importance on the
market. In England it was rare for the propertied class, whether
commercial, professional, or landed, to keep more than marginal
sums permanently in such securities, for they preferred the more
solid backing of the land; but by 1728[1] there are to be found
among the forty-seven persons holding £10,000 or more in
East India Stock three peers, a doctor, a spinster lady of
title, and a rich widow, all of them investors of long standing, as well as a number of rich City men, private bankers,
brokers, and jobbers. Charities, trusts (including in the mid-
eighteenth century the Court of Chancery itself), and other
bodies invested in the Company. And just as it attracted the
continental speculator, particularly the Dutch, so did it attract
the investor from the developed commercial centres of Europe.
The part which Dutch investment played on the London market,
significant as it was for the future, was also recognized (though not
with much gratitude) by contemporaries. So far as the East India
Stock was concerned it was in fact exaggerated. In 1730 contemporaries believed that at least a third of the Company's stock
was in the hands of foreign investors.[2] An examination of the
accounts of investors in the Company's stock ledger in 1728
suggests that a figure of 15 per cent. is nearer the mark; of
nearly 2,000 accounts open at that date, under 300 were in the
names of those resident abroad; their average holdings were
much the same as those of English proprietors, and among the
eight proprietors holding £20,000 or more there were the names
of no foreign residents, though four of them bore foreign names.[3]

---

[1] The particulars here quoted are obtained from an analysis of the Company's
Stock Ledger G. for the years 1723–8. Only the accounts open at the time the book
was closed are taken into account. Addresses are normally given, but are sometimes
omitted, and foreign residence at the date taken does not necessarily mean foreign
nationality or permanent foreign domicile, nor vice versa in the case of those with
addresses in England. The results may be considered, however, as approximately
accurate.

[2] Boyer, *Political State of Great Britain*, op. cit. xxxix. 240. Quoted by James
Mill, *History of British India*, 1817, ii. 26.

[3] Abraham Craisteyn, senior, Sir Peter Delmé, Moses Hart, and F. Pereira, all
of London.

Of the forty-seven holding £10,000 or more, nine were foreign residents. The proportion was, however, significant enough when it is considered that only forty-five years before even merchant strangers denizens by letters patent were only permitted to own stock as a result of the personal intervention of Charles II,[1] and the picture had changed greatly even in the nineteen years since the union of the Companies. Nor had the influx of Dutch capital yet reached its height.[2]

The influx both of foreign capital and of that of British investors not normally resident in London was eased during this period by certain technical developments, particularly the increased use of letters of attorney. As early as 1702 we have evidence that they were in occasional use, but in general the difficulties which beset such investors were those described to Moll Flanders, who was told if she bought stock 'if I wanted to dispose of it, I must come to Town on purpose to transfer it.'[3] It was indeed true until long after that the East India Company insisted on the presence both of the buyer and the seller at India House to effect the transfer of stock; but the development of the use of letters of attorney began to eliminate this difficulty for the absent proprietor. It was in 1711 that the Company first began laying down regulations for the use of such instruments,[4] all of which were to be passed by the Court and then filed by an officer of the Company. Foreign letters were more numerous than English ones and it was early agreed that such foreign letters should be passed by the Court *en bloc* while the full particulars of each of the English letters were to be read out. An attempt to assimilate the procedure on English letters with those from abroad was in 1718 firmly squashed[5] and it was not till 1751 that, to save the time of the Court, this method was finally adopted. By that time the number of such letters presented at each Court had risen from the two or three of the

[1] Court Book 33, p. 158.
[2] By 1761, when the holdings of £10,000 or more are reduced to less than half, though the average size of holding has gone up, foreign residents own almost 50% of them. The biggest individual holders are still Englishmen. (Stock Ledger O.) In 1773 the proportions are much the same (*A List of the Names of those Members of the United Company . . . who stood qualified to vote*, 1773 (Brit. Mus. 8002. b. 33)).
[3] D. Defoe, *The Fortunes and Misfortunes of Moll Flanders*, 1883 (reprinted from the third edition, 1772), p. 104.
[4] Court Book 44, pp. 328 and 360.   [5] Court Book 47, p. 574.

earlier years to twenty or thirty a time.[1] In the period ahead
the use of such instruments became almost universal among
proprietors of prominence, and much can be learnt of their
connexions in Company party warfare from the names of their
attorneys. Even in the more settled years of the first half of the
century the names of those acting in this capacity are of interest,
for though they include solicitors, business correspondents, and
family friends they comprise for the most part those who formed
the class of professional dealers in East India Stock.

The fortunes of war, the fluctuations of national credit, and
the calculations and miscalculations of the speculator and
investor, all had their effect on the stock but did not shake the
investors' confidence in it. In 1765 when the speculative boom
which was to change its character for some twenty years was
beginning, Lord Clive's agents warned him: 'You know
undoubtedly that India Stock is not like the other stocks, of
which you may buy any amount; of India Stock there is seldom
much at market.'[2] Even when the situation was already
beginning to change, it was believed that no more than £300,000
of it was available on the market at any one time.[3]

III

It has been possible to discuss both the Company's developments during this period and its relations with the state with
scarcely a reference to India, the source of all its wealth. This
was a characteristic of the time, but one which was soon to
change. It arose from the fact that, until the struggle began
between England and her French rivals for the domination of
an India in full tide of political disintegration, no major
problems in India forced themselves on the Company's attention. This did not mean that the situation there was static or
even stable. The policy forced on the Company by events in
the seventeenth century left them with the threefold problems,
in addition to any which might arise from their trading activities, of keeping peace with Indian sovereigns (both neighbours
and overlords), of checking European rivals, and of controlling
their own servants.

[1] Court Book 64, pp. 376 and 402.
[2] John Walsh to Clive, 30 March 1766. Powis MSS.
[3] George Clive to Clive, 17 October 1767. Ibid.

Even before the direct clash with the French these problems were becoming increasingly difficult, though the trading prosperity of the Company prevented either directors or proprietors from grasping their full implications. Of the three Presidencies which the United Company inherited in India, Bombay now went in fear of the growing power of the Mahrattas by land and sea; in Bengal the Company had a claim by a farman obtained from the Mogul in 1711 to land round Calcutta some of which they were not permitted to occupy, and lived in a condition of veiled hostility with the Nawab of Bengal, a hostility fanned by the abuses of privilege by Company servants and their hangers-on which were to precipitate Siraj-ud-daula's murderous attack in 1756. But it was in Madras that the complexities of Indian politics and the difficulties of the Company reached their height. It was here that the full effects were felt of the political disintegration of the Mogul Empire, accelerated by the disastrous inroads of the Persian tyrant Nadir Shah. The chaos of the breakdown was offset to some extent by the founding of what was for all practical purposes an independent dynasty by Asaf Jah, the first Nizam of Hyderabad, under the title of Subadar of the Deccan. As a feudal inferior he had the Nawab of the Carnatic from whom in their turn the Company held Madras. Even in the strong days of Asaf Jah, however, the control of the Subadar over the Carnatic was weak, and so too was the power of the Nawab. The instability of the Nawab's power was increased by two factors, both to be of the greatest importance in the future; the continued existence of a small but rich Hindu territory, relic of earlier Mahratta raids, under the rule of the Raja of Tanjore, which was sometimes forced to pay tribute, but which was never fully absorbed, and the rivalry of the English and the French, their newest European rivals.

The French Company was comparatively a newcomer to the East. It can be said to have come into permanent existence in 1664, when it obtained a site at Swally with permission to trade at Surat. Though in the early years of the eighteenth century it set up factories which competed in each of the three English fields of enterprise, it was in Madras, where the 'country powers' were weak, that their rivalry was to have spectacular results. At first it seemed as if the great struggles between England and

France, which were being fought out in all their varied spheres of influence, might pass India by, for in the War of the Spanish Succession an unofficial truce was made between the two companies. An attempt by the French to make a similar arrangement with the English Company in the War of the Austrian Succession (1740-8) was defeated, however, by the action of the English Government in sending a fleet to harass the French in these valuable possessions, and the French did not delay in taking up the challenge. Already, under the leadership of Dupleix, the French Company had been adopting a forward policy which must have brought them into acute conflict with the English Company. The war precipitated the clash, and the first honours went to the French, who captured Madras in 1746. Though peace officially followed and Madras was restored by treaty, the French Company never ceased its warlike measures. The English Company in self-defence followed after it. Their field was the trampled and confused one of Indian ambitions, where, since their nations were normally at peace, they could only appear in the contest as the 'mercenary troops of these polished barbarians'.[1] But whatever its form, both sides were aware that the struggle had become one to the death.

The period of peaceful trade which the Company enjoyed in the first half of the century really ended in India ten years before it came to an end in England. It ended with the fall of Madras. Though in England this event caused less consternation than might have been expected, partly because it was so rapidly followed by the restoration of the town in the peace terms, in India it marked the coming of the new period. The system of alliances between the Company and certain native powers already taking form now became essential. The relations between the Company and the Crown must inevitably become closer when royal forces, military and naval, were used in support of the Company. The Company's servants also were obliged to show more initiative and independence under these new conditions, and they did not always trouble to inform their masters fully of the nature of their activities. Finally, the men who were to mould the fortunes of the Company in the next forty years were already in India; Clive, Lawrence, and even the young Warren Hastings had begun their work, and Laur-

[1] Colonel M. Wilks, *Historical Sketches of the South of India*, 1817, i. 262.

ence Sulivan was gaining in Bombay the experience which was to help him to that supremacy in Leadenhall Street he was to enjoy for so many years.

The control of the Company's servants, already difficult in the seventeenth century, and to become almost impossible a little later, was the only one of the problems of India which was given much attention by the Company in this period of commercial expansion. The Company tried hard to establish orderly government in their Presidencies. The charter of 1726 strengthening the administration of justice in the Presidencies was one method employed;[1] the improvement of military discipline, also in 1754 facilitated by statute,[2] was another. Already in 1727 orders had been sent to Madras forbidding the taking of presents from merchants with whom the Company was trading;[3] the far greater temptations of the new Indian diplomacy were not yet recognized. Apart from these general reforms the chief Indian problems with which the Company dealt in the period of its peace were the quarrels of its servants among themselves, as in Bombay in 1721–2,[4] and the instances of corruption among its servants which occasionally came to its notice. The instances among servants whose responsibilities were confined to matters of trade were serious enough, as when gross peculation was discovered in 1730 among the super-cargoes of the China ships.[5] It was worse when those with governmental responsibilities were involved, as in 1732, when the directors dismissed the President and four of the Council of Bengal for disobedience to the orders from home to check a damaging increase of private trade at the Company's expense.[6] The loss of Madras, too, in 1746 was followed by painful recriminations in which the integrity of the Governor and Council was gravely impugned, though they ultimately cleared themselves.[7]

These scandals and difficulties took up only a small part of the time of an active Company. But they bring out a feature disquieting for the future. The Company was very unsuccessful in checking corruption even when it was discovered. Though

---

[1] C. Fawcett, *The First Century of British Justice in India*, pp. 214 seq.
[2] 27 Geo. II, c. 9.   [3] Court Book 52, p. 166.
[4] Court Book 50, pp. 158 seq.   [5] Court Book 54, p. 74.
[6] Court Book 55, pp. 84 seq.   [7] Court Book 63, pp. 179 seq.

discredited servants were not yet able to make sufficient interest in the General Court to force the directors to reinstate them, as they did in the period ahead, the Company found it hard to punish the guilty. This was partly because they so often had friends and connexions among the directors, but also because it was extremely difficult and expensive to pursue a case in the courts in England when witnesses were far away and the point at issue was usually complex. When the Company prosecuted the super-cargo Naish, he used against them all the technique of pro-crastination in which the law then excelled, and the case dragged on for seven years without hope of a conclusion until the Company reluctantly agreed to settle out of court.[1]

In India during this period, therefore, there was in the main a slow but steady development on the lines marked out by circumstances in the later seventeenth century. Even when after the Peace of Aix-la-Chapelle a fierce underground war began against their enemy the French, the Company did not at first see that their position had been changed, nor that their system was to be submitted to a strain in India which it had never been intended to bear. Still less did they realize that this and other causes were to revive within the Company, and in the relations between State and Company, the uncertainty and factions of which their predecessors had already had only too much experience.

[1] Court Book 58, pp. 267 seq.

III

THE RISE OF LAURENCE SULIVAN

THE peaceful development of the first half of the century was coming to an end both for the Company and for the nation, though largely for different reasons. For the Company the new era began in India in 1748 with the Peace of Aix-la-Chapelle, which brought not peace but war in another form, and in England ten years later with the first of those great contested elections for the control of the Court of Directors which marked the emergence of new strains and stresses destined to shatter its order. In the politics of the nation the crises of the Seven Years War made the first serious breach in the solidity of the connexions which had so long enjoyed power, and with the accession of the new king in 1760 their fate was sealed.

The changes which were taking place in the Company's position in India, and at home the threat to national credit which its internal disorders were to present, were bound to affect the relations of State and Company. It was unfortunate that this should happen not in a time of political stability but one of short-lived administrations with little internal cohesion, and also at a period when governments were facing problems in other spheres of national life far more serious than those which presented themselves to their predecessors. In the coming period the problems of the relations of State and Company were no longer those of a stable, if somewhat fainéant, government and a reasonably progressive 'monied' company. They were those of a company struggling to adapt itself to totally new responsibilities overseas, hampered at every turn by disorganization arising from too-sudden wealth and the speculation born of it; and a series of shifting administrations and spasmodic but violent oppositions too harassed to give much thought to Indian affairs, but whose component groups nearly all came to find some political advantage in forming connexions with interests and groups within the distracted Company. The situation was not the same as it had been in the nineties of the preceding century, but it was nearer to it than it was to that which had prevailed ever since the United Company had been formed.

The new period was to see a network of English control spread over the neighbouring Indian territories and an expansion of territorial power which the whole history of the Company in India made inevitable but which, thanks to the clash with the French and the spectacular exploits of Clive and his colleagues, came more suddenly than anyone could have expected. The Company had long had experience of the problems of government as well as those of the administration of commerce; but now (except in the rising China trade) it was those of government which began to prevail. In addition to this foreseeable development, the new period brought one that could not have been foreseen, a desperate struggle in England for the control of the Company's political machine (now become so much more valuable) between Robert Clive, the Company's greatest soldier, and Laurence Sulivan, its ablest ruler since Sir Josia Child. The harvests of this civil war were still being reaped when Clive had long been dead and Sulivan was an old man whose younger colleagues mocked him for his love of the power that had cost him so dear. It was a struggle involving issues vital for the Company and the State, but one in which personal hatreds and personal interests played the greatest part; for Clive during much of its course was fighting for the *jagir* of some £27,000 a year, which was an important part of his Indian spoils, and Sulivan in the later part of it was fighting to avert bankruptcy and ruin. The period was also to see the re-entry of East Indian affairs into the sphere of party politics and the intervention of the State in the affairs of a Company become at once so rich and so disordered. There was Chatham's first intervention in 1766–7, Lord North's Regulating Act and the minor acts renewing and amending it, Fox's India Bill, Pitt's India Act, and, as a sequel, the long-drawn-out agony of Warren Hastings's impeachment.

Much has been written on East Indian questions during this period, but it is not surprising that the historian has tended to turn away from the details of the negotiations, intrigues, and expedients of political management in which both the Company and the various administrations were involved, and to concentrate his interest on a few great figures and their exploits in the field, in administration, or in Parliament. Nevertheless neither the history of the development of British power in India nor the career of these great men is comprehensible without the study of their intricate and often unedifying background.

The investigator of the workings of any political machine tends to form a somewhat cynical impression of the nature and ends of politics. This impression may be sound but it is not necessarily the whole truth. The nineteenth-century historian was no doubt unwise to ignore the significance of this machine and its workings and to base his judgements on the impressive generalizations contained in the public utterances of political leaders and of contemporary political theorists; his successors would be equally unwise to ignore the fact that these generalizations meant something to those who spoke and heard them, and that the machine operated in an intellectual climate which was largely their product. The examination of the workings of the East Indian machine during this period and the points at which it touched that of the State, illustrates both the importance of these mechanical considerations in the formulation of policy and also the point at which considerations of another kind make their weight felt.

The crucial weakness of the eighteenth-century standard of political morality, as seen through the eyes of its successors, was that the private and public interests of those taking part in political life were insufficiently distinguished either by the sanctions of political organization or by the influence of an informed public opinion. To make a comfortable fortune in the public service and to establish those dependent on him in situations of profit was the major and (to contemporaries) the legitimate ambition of the ordinary politician. Such a man's obligations to his patron, his loyalty to his friends, and his duty to himself made up the main tenets of his political creed. But the results of this attitude in a political system where the individual was not controlled by party discipline, though they were often far from edifying, were not as disintegrating as might have been expected. This was chiefly because the ambitions of such men were kept within the bounds of moderation by the dominance of a wealthy aristocracy whose main source of riches remained outside the sphere of politics and by the traditions of a governing class which (though sympathetic to such views if pursued in moderation) in the last resort felt some responsibility for, and interest in, the maintenance of the king's government and in the prosperity and prestige of the country. As a result there emerged, not an orgy of corruption, but a fragile balance between public and private interests expressed in the system of 'political connexion' and 'political management'.

Despite its obvious weaknesses, this system stood up on the whole very creditably to the temptations which arose from the financial developments of the time—temptations which contemporaries lumped together under the generic title of 'stockjobbing'. For, after the South Sea scandals, very few men in high office succumbed to the temptation of using their official positions to gain, directly or indirectly, advantages from speculative activities, and those who were suspected of doing so were judged harshly. In the period of Company history which was just beginning many politicians intervened actively in its internal affairs, as the succeeding chapters will show; Lord Bute to try to sustain the influence of his falling ministry in the City; George Grenville in support of Clive who had offered him his parliamentary support; Charles Townshend to harass his colleagues in office; a whole series of opposition leaders, from the Duke of Newcastle to the Marquess of Rockingham and the Duke of Richmond, to embarrass their enemies in power; Lord Shelburne to build up his personal power in the City; Lord Sandwich to help in the construction of that network of patronage which made up his personal parliamentary interest; and Lord North to try to maintain an indirect control over the Government of India. No prominent politician, with the exception of Henry Fox, and with the possible exception of Shelburne at one stage of his career, ever laid himself open to the accusation of directing his activities in the Company to the ends of personal financial gain.

Nevertheless the temptations were real and continuous, and the lesser men, 'the men of business', nearly all succumbed to them, and were in fact not considered blameworthy in so doing unless their activities were remarkably indiscreet or ended in disaster. It was with these men that the East India Company came most directly into contact; while in its own political machine the same weaknesses which were apparent in national politics were to be found without the check of any political and social sanctions of comparable weight.

Nevertheless, within the Company, as within the State, a

certain conventional balance between public and private interests (though an even more precarious one) had grown up. The Company's servants in India, though they made up a rootless and shifting society composed of men all anxious to make what fortunes they could and return to their native country, were neither idle nor incompetent as a class. They organized and carried on the Company's intricate and extensive export and import trades; they kept the voluminous records demanded of them;[1] administered something resembling justice in their courts, and kept themselves on the whole surprisingly well informed of the intricate power politics of the 'country powers' with whom they were in contact. And it must be remembered that only a few of them made great fortunes (and these mostly during a short period of Company rule); that Cornwallis when he went out to Bengal in 1786 was able to choose good and conscientious officials there to carry out his reforms, and that by the middle of the next century, without any root-and-branch reform, the traditions of a service had been built up which John Stuart Mill judged to be superior to anything which the English State could then show.

The outlines of this conventional official morality can be seen in the acts and words of the Company's servants. A man should if he survived (as many of course did not) make a considerable fortune in the Company's service, but only if he had worked his twelve or fifteen years through the ranks and given the Company the benefit of his industry and acquired experience. While making this fortune through the recognized channels of perquisite, private trade, and money-lending, he need not reject presents from wealthy and important Indians, but he ought to do so if in return he had to sacrifice his employers' pecuniary interests, and he must not permit his private concerns to monopolize his attention to the detriment of his public duties. If these conditions were fulfilled his colleagues and he considered that he had served the Company loyally. Even Clive,

---

[1] Not, of course, always to their employers' satisfaction, cf. General Letter to Bengal, 11 February 1756 (Bengal Despatches, i. 413), 'Your General Books ending April 1754 are sent home without an alphabet, the Journal in various places has no totals, the Leger [sic] wants many references to the Journal . . . and the Leger in particular is copied in a very bad hand.' The social life of these servants has been explored with skill by T. G. P. Spear in *The Nabobs, a Study of the Social Life of the English in Eighteenth-Century India*, Oxford, 1932.

who did more than anyone else to upset this precarious balance, both by his example and by the opportunities his victories opened up, paid tribute to these conventions. He tried to explain them to a somewhat sceptical House of Commons in justification of the acceptance of gifts from Indian princes.

When presents are received as the price of services to the Nation, to the Company and to that Prince who bestowed those presents; when they are not exacted from him by compulsion; when he is in a state of independence and can do with his money what he pleases; and when they are not received to the disadvantage of the Company, he holds presents so received not dishonourable.[1]

The directors of the Company were submitted to fewer temptations than their servants abroad but they too felt the conflict of personal and public duties and the absence of a standard of conventional public morality to strengthen the latter. Their position gave them many opportunities for personal advantage; indeed, most of them were men well-to-do and respected in the City, but with comparatively small holdings in East India Stock, who would hardly have taken on the heavy burden of serving on the Direction if they gained nothing from it but their small official salaries. They stood to gain in various ways by the alliance in the City between the Company and the Government; they could put profitable business in the way of firms with which they were associated, and in the exercise of their patronage they could provide profitable openings for their relations. No one thought of blaming them for so doing, and under normal conditions their pursuit of their private concerns was in the last resort subordinated to their own interest in the prosperity of the Company and the fact that they stood responsible for it to the proprietors who elected them.

Between 1763 and 1773 it is true there were a number of occasions on which the real interests of the Company were sacrificed in a manner which caused open scandal. Occasionally they were sacrificed to the pecuniary interests of individuals caught up in the speculative boom that swept the Company, but even at the worst of times the Company suffered more from the reckless demands of party warfare than from the greed of individual directors. Nor were they the fluctuating body of ill-informed and indifferent nonentities which their opponents tried to suggest.

[1] *Reports from Committees of the House of Commons*, iii. 148.

The Court retained, even in the days of hotly contested elections, a large measure of permanence in its personnel. Though the quality of its membership varied and there was always a proportion of the directors whose intelligence was mediocre and whose interest in the details of the Company's affairs superficial, their leaders took pains to master and reply to the voluminous correspondence coming in from India, and many of them also carried on private correspondence with their principal servants abroad. When they had at their head the able and indefatigable Laurence Sulivan they made a genuine and by no means discreditable attempt to adapt themselves to problems of government outside everyone's experience and made more difficult by constant changes in the problems themselves and by the extreme slowness in communications. It was indeed often admitted that it was not so much the instructions which they sent out to India which were at fault as their incapacity to enforce them and to maintain steady authority at home and abroad. Even in their patronage, this mixture of public and private interests was apparent. Though in the second half of the century their employment of men with influence behind them was notorious, an able and hard-working servant without this influence was sure to make a career for himself if he persisted, though he might do so less quickly than the son of a director, the protégé of a cabinet minister, or the debtor of a great man sent out to enable him to meet his obligations.

On the other hand it cannot be denied that among the Company's servants the precarious balance between public and private interest sometimes broke down badly in the years ahead, or that the directors failed to handle their new problems in such a way as either to ensure stable administration in India or to preserve the financial and commercial health of the Company. In the Bengal Presidency during the years 1760–72 when the Company was gradually taking over the responsibilities of full territorial government there were periods of virtual chaos; while in Madras there was dislocation hardly less serious at times between 1769 and 1780 as a result of the unsatisfactory relations, political and financial, between the Company, its servants in their private capacity, and the Nawab of Arcot, the nominal ruler of the Carnatic.

In so far as the breakdown of the precarious balance of interests among the Company's servants in India was intensified by events in England, however, the responsibility lies rather on the decline in unity and authority in the Court of Directors than in their personal misdeeds. The sudden changes in India and the expectations based on them stimulated speculative interests in the Company; disorganized servants returned afraid of censure by the directors and the friends of those still in India organized themselves to protect them. All this, against a background of battle between Clive and Sulivan which gave such pressure groups the chance to bargain for terms, led to dissensions in the Court and loss of the power over the General Court which was essential to the conduct of the Company's affairs. Under the stress of the Company's civil war all scruples were thrown to the wind at an election or an important ballot in the General Court. Not only were dangerous concessions made to interested groups, but the method of fighting these contests became expensive and dangerous, involving the Company's leaders themselves in perilous speculations in the price of stock; while the steadier elements in the Company were increasingly hampered by the activities of speculators and adventurers who gathered round both in England and India as its disorganization grew. Such dubious characters as Lauchlin Macleane, John and James MacPherson, and Paul Benfield,[1] and all manner of hangers-on of the political and financial world saw their chance to fish in its troubled waters.

It was this disorganization which was directly responsible for the intervention of the State in the Company's affairs. These interventions did not arise solely or even primarily from concern at the disorganization of an important commercial body or from a sense of responsibility for the condition of India. On the contrary East India affairs first came back into political prominence because the party contests in the Company became caught up in the battles raging in Parliament over the terms of the Peace of Paris. In the same way the first attack of the State on the Company's powers in India was made in 1766, not to give good government to the Indian possessions, but with the intention of providing for the State a share in the revenues which were coming to the Company as a result of Clive's latest acquisition, the *diwani* of Bengal. So too, it was opposed by rival parlia-

[1] For these see below.

mentary interests far more concerned to embarrass the Government than to help the Company. The story of the unsteady progress of encroachment by the State on the preserves of the Company from 1763 to 1784 requires as its essential background an understanding of the conflicts of persons and groups in Parliament for whom the fate of the Company or India itself was a matter of much less concern than the rise and fall of ministries.

In all these ways the story of East Indian affairs during the period is that of the interaction of political machines. But there is another aspect to be considered. The story also illustrates two factors of a different kind. In the first place it illustrates the progress in the art of government and the growing interest in administration that was taking place below the surface of politics in the second half of the eighteenth century. The successors of the Government which in 1766 rushed into East India affairs to tap a new source of wealth for the Exchequer, began to find themselves increasingly concerned in the problems of Indian administration. The hard-working and intelligent 'men of business' who achieved new prominence in these ministries, men like John Robinson and Charles Jenkinson (whom Professor Namier has seen as the forerunners of the heads of the permanent Civil Service of the future), and rising young politicians like Henry Dundas, began to study the Indian question, to draw up schemes for the reform of the Company, and to digest the crude mass of material thrown up by the parliamentary investigations which were one of the results of the re-entry of the Company's affairs into party politics. It was the work of such men that alone made conceivable the compromise between the control of State and Company attempted in Lord North's Regulating Act of 1773 and which made the further compromise initiated by Pitt's Act of 1784 reasonably successful. Neither of these measures could have been put into effect without the assistance of this element of professional administrators in the Government, and neither would have been attempted without their belief that an orderly and reputable administration was a practical necessity.

The second factor at work was of a different kind; it was the growing demand for justice for the peoples of India. This arose (as knowledge of Indian affairs became more general as a result

of partisan battles) among independent men and was based on
the sense of decency of the ordinary country gentlemen, merchants, and professional men who made up educated opinion.
It was sharpened no doubt by some distaste for, and envy of, the
small group of 'Nabobs', the Company servants who returned to
flaunt the exorbitant wealth they had won from the revolutionary changes in India, but its roots lay in the rising humanitarian
feeling of the age and in discomfort at what they heard of the
misuse of the Company's new powers. This feeling was finally
harnessed to the use of the parliamentary Opposition, and found
in Edmund Burke a spokesman who expressed it in words that
have resounded down the centuries. It was largely for party
reasons and at a time chosen for party purposes that he stood
forth, and he had personal interests in the subject more creditable to his loyalty to his friends than to his sense of public
responsibility. But when once he had immersed himself in the
subject, he found himself carried beyond the immediate considerations of party and of persons by his passionate desire to
protect the weak from the oppression of the strong, and by the
sentiments he aroused, in himself as well as in his hearers, by
the idealized picture he created of an ancient, ordered, and
distinguished civilization borne down by the superior force
and ruthlessness of a new and cruder one.

The two figures who dominated the Company's fortunes
through most of this period were very different. Robert Clive
carried with him the qualities of a military leader; he had a
lightning grasp of a situation, was sudden in action, of violent
temper but able to make those dependent on him serve him well,
rapacious but contemptuous of petty gain. He was also arrogant,
suspicious, and intolerant of equals, and in England he moved
with a certain sullen awkwardness in a sphere where his highest
qualities were not called for. Laurence Sulivan on the other
hand was a man of peace and of many words, full of Irish buoy-
ancy and unburdened by scruples. He had risen through an
unusual aptitude for business and a power of keeping friends
which masked his ambition for pre-eminence. He gained his
ends, wherever possible, by subtlety rather than force, though
he was a great partisan and a remorseless and even vindictive
antagonist. The control of the Company was the object of his
ardent ambition, while it was only an exasperating necessity to

his rival, Clive. It was therefore the more disastrous that they could never come to terms.

Laurence Sulivan entered the Direction when the changes in the Company's position were only beginning to be felt. There had been little in his early history to suggest that he would rise to eminence. His early career, like that of many Irish adventurers of the time, is hard to trace. Young Irishmen who went forth to seek their fortunes left few traces behind them, unless they were cadets of one of the great Anglo-Irish families. But their loyalty to their kinsmen if they rose to success was so strong as to be notorious even by eighteenth-century standards of family patronage, and it is from the kinsmen whom he favoured when he ruled at India House that we can find something of Laurence Sulivan's antecedents. When Warren Hastings was ruling India as his nominee, Sulivan pressed upon the Governor-General's patronage, in addition to his only son Stephen, three brothers, Benjamin,[1] John,[2] and Richard Joseph Sulivan,[3] the sons of Benjamin Sulivan of Dromcragh, County Cork, attorney-at-law and Clerk of the Crown for the Counties of Cork and Waterford.[4] These young men were generally known to be his kinsmen.[5] Laurence Sulivan therefore almost certainly sprang from the turbulent sept of the O'Sulivans More of County Cork, Tories, rapparees, and soldiers of fortune in a number of foreign armies. Among them the name of Laurence had occurred on several occasions in the preceding century.

Laurence himself is first heard of in Bombay in 1740, then 27 years of age and not yet in the Company's service.[6] Though there is no trace of him in the Company's records he had evidently been there for some time.[7] One Daniel Sulivan, surgeon, asked permission to go to Bombay in 1730 and is then

[1] Spoken of by Sulivan as a barrister of some standing in Ireland. He went out to India as a barrister in 1777 and rose eventually to be a Judge of the High Court.
[2] Entered the Company's civil service in 1765 and served in Madras, Masulipatam, and Tanjore. 1801–05, Under-Secretary for War.
[3] Entered the Company's civil service in 1768 as a writer. Later Secretary in the Military Government at Madras. Created a baronet in 1804.
[4] Their mother was the daughter of the Rev. Paul Limrie of Scull, Co. Cork.
[5] e.g. Obituary of Rt. Hon. R. J. Sulivan, *Gentleman's Magazine*, April 1840.
[6] Bombay Public Consultations, Range 341, vol. xi, 17 March 1739/40.
[7] Correctly his name should occur in the Court Book, when the directors gave him permission to go out, and in the lists of European inhabitants, which had to be sent to England at frequent intervals. The lists were at this period, however, very incomplete.

heard of no more;[1] possibly Laurence went out in connexion
with him. He seems to have obtained employment in some
clerical capacity, and to have been employed for some time before 1740 by Governor Horne at the latter's private expense. He
evidently made himself useful to his employer, who left him as
one of his attorneys for the remittance of his fortune when he
returned to England. The new Governor, Stephen Law, who
later in England as now in India was to be patron to the young
Irishman, not only retained his services but obtained from the
directors his appointment to the position of Factor in the Company.[2] Before the demands for patronage became heavy it was
not uncommon for a man who had gained experience in India
outside the Company's service to be taken into its employ on
local recommendation, and at Bombay (an unpopular Presidency) such cases were particularly common.[3]

Sulivan thus entered the service by the least conspicuous of
back doors. He owed his advance solely to his competence, and
the respect in which his business capacities were held is shown
by the number of his colleagues and of visiting sea captains
who entrusted him with their remittance business. He was also
trusted by Governor Law and in 1742 was one of the three
Company's servants who signed the final agreement of a complicated negotiation for the settlement of the debts of two of the
Company's native brokers.[4] At the same time he made firm
friends among his colleagues, and, ambitious though he was, he
became involved in none of the impassioned feuds of the small
uncomfortable society in which he moved. In his later rise to
power the Bombay servants he had known in his youth were his
firm allies and the object of an impetuous solicitude on his part
which aroused the jealousy of those serving in other presidencies.

Shortly before he entered the Company's service he married.
The evidence seems to suggest that his bride was one Elizabeth
Owen, who first appears on the list of Bombay inhabitants in

[1] Court Book 53, p. 410. His request was referred to the Committee of Shipping,
whose records do not exist.
[2] Bombay Public Consultations, Range 341, vol. xi, 17 March 1739/40.
[3] In 1729 the Court of Directors had protested to Bombay against their taking
on servants without sanction from England. Referred to in Committee of Correspondence Reports, vol. ii, 7 March 1733/4.
[4] Bombay Public Consultations, Range 341, vol. xiii, p. 193, 1 March 1741/2.

1738, and who, in the list drawn up in January 1739/40, has given place to Elizabeth Sulivan, married woman.[1] She had presumably gone out to Bombay to a relative, Edward Owen, a Company's servant, who during the two years following the marriage was engaged in several business transactions with Laurence Sulivan. Two sons were born to them at Bombay, of whom one survived, named Stephen, presumably after his father's patron.

Governor Law's reign was not long. He had been sent out in 1738 to pursue a vigorous policy and make Bombay defensible against Mahratta attacks. In doing so he raised opposition in the Presidency and alarmed the directors by the excess of the expenses over their estimate. Early in 1742 they superseded him in favour of William Wake. Law returned to England under a slight cloud, and though he later began to assert himself in Company politics, in the meantime Sulivan's one patron was powerless to assist him.

In the succeeding years Sulivan saw man after man, with the influence in England which he lacked, pass him by. Not till 1748 did he obtain any of the important administrative offices of the Presidency. In this year he was given provisionally[2] the position of Collector of the Company's Rents and Revenues, an important post and one with lucrative perquisites. Next year he was also made Deputy Accomptant and Assistant to the Managers of the Bank. In the first of these positions in particular he showed that grasp of financial and administrative detail which was later to give him an unrivalled (and sometimes abused) comprehension of the intricacies of the Company's financial system. He began at once to put to rights an office which had fallen into a disorder not altogether free from scandal.[3] He must have regretted its loss when the position was taken from him and given to a new member of Council in 1750, though he was compensated by the chiefship of Mahim.[4] Only eight months later, however, he was recalled to it to deal with an elaborate system of fraud discovered among the native tenants through the suspicions of the Governor.

[1] Bombay European Inhabitants, 1719–87, vol. v.
[2] The position was confirmed to him in July of the following year.
[3] Bombay Public Consultations, Range 341, vol. xvii, 16 November–31 December 1750, pp. 52–53 and 95.
[4] 13 November 1750; ibid., p. 409.

By this time seniority had brought him close to the Council, and in December 1751,[1] on the departure of one of its members for England, he took his seat on the board as the next in standing, in default of any counter-orders from England. About the same time he performed his most important service to the Company. At the end of 1751 he and a colleague Henry Savage were employed as envoys in a negotiation with the 'country powers' to restore the Company's position at Surat, temporarily shaken in the struggles between the Mahrattas and their neighbours. After three months' negotiation they effected an honourable settlement.[2]

Sulivan did not remain in India long to enjoy his membership of Council. He had made a comfortable fortune from private trade and official perquisites (but boasted later that neither he nor anyone on his behalf had ever accepted a present of the value of £20),[3] and he now turned his thoughts to England, whither several of his colleagues had preceded him. In November 1752 he asked leave to return to England on grounds of health 'as a long continuance of nervous complaints leaves me no hope of relief in India',[4] and he sailed for England the next month, never to see India again.

His return to England was completely unspectacular. He was no more than a moderately successful servant from what had become the least sensational of the Presidencies. He was a well-to-do man, but he had not returned to live like a county magnate as did the 'Nabobs' of the next generation. On the contrary, he seems to have settled down to an Indian remittance business in the City, and to have worked, sometimes alone and sometimes in partnership, handling the remittance of business of Company servants from all the Presidencies.[5] His business must have prospered for by 1761 he was able to buy a country estate, Ponsborne Manor in Hertfordshire,[6] and not long after he seems

---

[1] Bombay Public Consultations, Range 341, vol. xviii, p. 544.
[2] There is full information about this episode in ibid. 553 seq.
[3] Court Book 69, p. 362, 18 March 1761. The boast was probably true, for no one among the bitterest of his enemies tried to refute it.
[4] Bombay Public Consultations, ibid., 24 November 1752, p. 397. It was customary to obtain this permission on grounds of health, as it made a return to the service later easier, if this should prove necessary.
[5] This is made clear by the numerous references in the Court Books. Reference was also made to it in some of the propaganda of his opponents. See *Impartial Query to Proprietors of India Stock, Public Advertiser,* 5 April 1758.
[6] He paid £13,500 for it. *Bengal Past and Present,* xlii. 159.

to have been able to give up, or at any rate greatly reduce, his business activities. In 1762 he entered Parliament.

The year in which he made his inconspicuous return to England, another more distinguished servant of the Company, Robert Clive, made a spectacular and glorious one, fresh from the triumphs of Arcot and the campaign which followed it. Clive's stay in England on this occasion was short, and eighteen months later he set out again for India with the position of second in Council at Madras and a Commission from both Crown and Company to serve in the joint Royal and Company land forces[1] (assisted by a naval force under Admiral Watson) which were intended to bring to an end the conflicts between the two Companies. On the arrival of these forces they found a truce in operation (the outbreak of the Seven Years War was to make it a short one), but they soon were called on to meet a crisis in Bengal when the Nawab Siraj-ud-daula had seized Calcutta, the Governor and other senior officials had fled, and a number of British subjects had been suffocated in the Black Hole. When they had recaptured Calcutta and forced a new treaty from the Nawab, they had revolutionized the position of the Company in India.[2]

The revolution they brought about was not the result of new concessions to the Company. The Treaty did, indeed, confirm and make operative territorial claims to areas round Calcutta which had been granted in 1711 but not before implemented. But the change came from the fact that the terms were dictated by men at the head of a victorious army and that this army still kept the field. The Company servants and the free merchants seized the opportunity to open up for their own profit the inland trade and to do so with the arrogance of conquerors. The military leaders found themselves courted by the factions in the disorganized court of the Nawab with which they were bound to keep in touch particularly since, with the renewal of war, the French were intriguing there. It was a variety of motives arising out of this situation that led Clive in 1757 to adopt the cause of a party hostile to the Nawab, to overthrow him at the Battle of

---

[1] For the details of Clive's career see Sir G. Forrest, *The Life of Lord Clive*, 1918, and Sir J. Malcolm, *The Life of Robert, Lord Clive*, 1836. A. Mervyn Davies, *Clive of Plassey*, 1939.

[2] For events in Bengal see S. C. Hill, *Bengal in 1756–1757*, 3 vols., 1905.

Plassey, and to set up Mir Jafar in his place. By so doing he completed the revolution in the Company's policy. By the time he left India for the second time in 1760 clear-sighted men (including himself)[1] were beginning to say that the Company (or even, if it failed to act, the British Government) must soon take over the entire responsibility for the administration of Bengal. Though the transfer was not complete till 1790, the two further revolutions of 1760 and 1763 carried out by his successor Vansittart and his own policy when he returned in 1765, brought the time steadily nearer. At the same time, while increasing thus suddenly the Company's powers and responsibilities, he gave a stimulus to factors which made it difficult for the Company to exercise these powers wisely. It was for the part they played in raising him to power that Mir Jafar gave Clive and his associates in the Company and the royal forces the lavish monetary awards which had parallels in the history of the French but not of the English Company;[2] it was through Mir Jafar that Clive himself later obtained the position of honour under the Mogul Emperor to which his *jagir* was attached, and the events of this revolution were faithfully followed, with increasingly disorganizing results, in those which came after it.

It was the early stages of this sudden development in India which gave Sulivan his chance in England. The feeling began to gain ground in the Company that men with Indian experience were needed on the Direction to deal with these unprecedented problems. Many agreed with Clive that the Company's responsibilities could not now be satisfactorily discharged 'but under the management of one or more of those gentlemen who brought home with them a just knowledge of India acquired by many years' experience'.[3] The number of returned servants among the directors had already been increasing and though they had not the compelling reasons for solidarity which the 'Nabobs' were to have in the future, they tended to form a compact *bloc*. Their leader was Sulivan's old patron Stephen Law and perhaps for that reason most of them came from the

---

[1] John Zacchary Holwell saw this in 1760. H. Dodwell, *Dupleix and Clive*, London, 1920, p. 197. Clive had already suggested to Pitt that the State should assume the absolute sovereignty of Bengal. Forrest, op. cit. ii. 175 seq.

[2] Clive's presents amounted to over £200,000 to which later the *jagir* added an annual sum of some £27,000.

[3] Clive to L. Sulivan, 30 December 1758. Quoted Forrest, op. cit. ii. 119–22.

Bombay Presidency at this time (their enemies called them 'the Bombay faction'[1]). It was presumably through Law's influence that Sulivan was put on the House list for the election of 1755 and elected without opposition. It was merit as well as the solidarity of the group which brought him two years later to the position of Deputy Chairman, carrying with it membership of the Committees where the most important business of the Court was done.

In the Court of Directors Sulivan found the field which suited him best. In his old age an unfriendly but acute critic, summing him up, said:

Mr. Sulivan has great experience and some talents—great cunning; will go through thick and thin with his party while he remains attached to it, but not to be trusted for a moment when his own views lead him to be faithless; clean handed I really believe as to money or unfair profits himself, but careless to how great a degree he supports the job of any of his connections. I think the *ruling passion* with him is the vanity of being supposed the head of the India Company and the power of giving protection to his friends in the Company's service.[2]

As soon as he became a member of the Court he began to contribute to its deliberations and the extent of this contribution is shown by the memoranda in his close, even hand preserved among the records of the Committee of Correspondence.[3] At first they deal chiefly with matters where his past experience was of value, the affairs of Bombay and the organization of the trade with Persia. Soon they begin to cover every sphere of the Company's activities and, as circumstances dictated, began to focus strongly on Bengal. The plans for the reorganization of that territory emerging as the directors hoped 'from confusion into some order and method',[4] owed much to his work and were largely based on his 'Observations on the Bengal Establishment with such Alterations and Amendments as appears [sic] absolutely necessary.'[5]

[1] Cf. [J. Z. Holwell] *Important Facts regarding the East India Company's Affairs in Bengal*, 1764, p. 7.
[2] R. Atkinson to H. Dundas, 22 July 1784. Quoted H. Furber. 'The East India Directors 1784', *Journal of Modern History*, 1933, v. 483.
[3] Committee of Correspondence. Memoranda, vol. xv. The papers become more plentiful in vol. xvi (1757), when he becomes, as Deputy Chairman, a member of the Committee.   [4] General Letter of 23 March 1759 (Bengal Despatches i. 868).
[5] Committee of Correspondence. Memoranda (1757), vol. xvi (no pagination).

But it was not his hard work on the Court and in Committee that raised him to the position of leader of the Company. It was the emergence of another issue from the revolution in Bengal, and one that augured less well for the future. In 1757 the directors split irremediably into two hostile parties, not on any general issue of policy, but over the claims of individuals in the restored Government of Bengal. Some issues of a more general kind were introduced into the conflict as it proceeded, and its course was confused by the rapidity with which events in Bengal out-ran their decisions, but the basis of the quarrel was nothing more than that the Chairman, John Payne, and fourteen other directors favoured an arrangement whereby one John Zacchary Holwell would supersede a number of the Bengal servants and would be put in the way to succeeding to the Governorship of Bengal; while the nine others, including seven with Indian experience, under the leadership of Sulivan as Deputy Chairman,[1] supported the claims of the Company servants who had been involved in the loss of Calcutta to retain their seniority until or unless they had been proved to be unworthy. With the two most senior of the servants concerned, William Watts and Charles Manningham, Sulivan and some of his supporters had close personal and business connexions.

The growth of the conflict was confused by causes which *mutatis mutandis* were to repeat themselves frequently in the years ahead. The loss of Calcutta was said to have been known in Paris since 21 May 1757, but the news first reached England at the beginning of June, coupled with the more reassuring information that a strong force was proceeding to recapture the settlement.[2] The directors showed no disunity in their measures for averting a panic on the London market, and at first there seemed no grave disagreement about the instructions to be sent out for the re-establishment of authority in the Presidency on the assumption that Calcutta would once again be in British hands by the time their dispatches reached India. Roger Drake the Governor was an experienced Company

---

[1] The eight supporting Sulivan were: P. Godfrey, C. Gough, H. Plant, T. Phipps, T. Rous, H. Savage, T. Tullie, and G. Dudley. Sulivan, Gough, Savage, Dudley, and Tullie had been in the Company's civil service; Godfrey and Plant had been supercargoes in the China trade. On the other side only Thomas Saunders, late Governor of Fort St. George, had seen service in India.

[2] Court Book 67, p. 394.

servant and the nephew of a prominent director. In view of
the scale of the disaster and his own flight during the attack,
however, there could be no question of reinstating him. The
objections were less strong, however, against either William
Watts[1] or Charles Manningham,[2] the two servants next in
seniority. The directors therefore decided as a temporary
measure to appoint Clive to the first place on the Bengal
Council, to reinstate the members of Council other than Drake,
and, until they had information on which to base further
instructions, not to appoint a Governor but to provide for the
three senior members of Council to preside in rotation.[3] This
provision was certainly an unwise one, even for a short time,
when the need of strong government was so great, and it was
later opposed with vigour by the minority of the directors, who
gained some credit from the fact. But while they appear to have
made a slight demur to it at this time they did not press their
objections, and the instructions sent out on 3 August 1757 were
not opposed.[4]

These first instructions never reached Bengal. They were
captured by a French privateer, and by the time this was
known, the directors had further information from India and
were beginning to change their minds.[5] They had learned that
Calcutta was again in British hands, they believed (wrongly)
that Clive had returned to Madras, and they had been hearing
accounts of the disaster and the events leading up to it from
John Zacchary Holwell, a survivor of the Black Hole. Holwell
was a man of some ability and much ambition who in 1752 had
so greatly impressed the Chairman and some of the directors
with his vigour and knowledge of India that they sent him out
to Bengal as permanent Zeminar to reform the administration
of justice there.[6] When Calcutta was besieged he was the only

[1] Second on Council. A Bengal servant of long experience.
[2] Next in seniority. He had been transferred from the Bombay service in 1743.
[3] Court Book 67, p. 436, 27 July 1757.
[4] [Holwell] op. cit., p. 9, mentions their hesitation. There is no reference to it in the Court Book or records of the Committee of Correspondence.
[5] Speech of Chairman at General Court (26 October 1757). Committee of Correspondence. Memoranda, vol. xvi.
[6] For his career see J. M. Holzman, *The Nabobs in England. A Study of the Returned Anglo-Indian 1760-85*, New York, 1926, pp. 145-6, and his own *Important Facts*, op. cit.

senior servant to rise to the occasion, and he was now busy exploiting (with characteristic enterprise) the prestige he enjoyed as hero of that episode and as the only man as yet to reach England with inside knowledge of what had happened there. He was already an unpopular man. He had shown zeal in his duties, gained favour rapidly, and had succeeded in arousing the dislike and jealousy of the Bengal servants by self-righteously reporting their short-comings to the directors. In consequence hostility to him had already been growing on the Direction among those with contacts with the Bengal servants,[1] and when it became apparent that his supporters were going to try to promote him over their heads, a sharp conflict arose.

It occurred at first without upsetting the agreement for the rotation of chairmen, though the minority were expressing increasing uneasiness about it. After a long wrangle on the Committee of Correspondence a compromise was arrived at whereby the institution of a fourfold rotation of chairmen was accepted, still as a temporary measure. Those sharing the office were to be the three Bengal servants next in seniority and the interloping Holwell. As it was assumed that Clive would be back in Madras, no provision was made for him in these arrangements. The new instructions were dispatched in November and in due time reached Bengal. Holwell was to leave by a later ship, being retained to advise the Court on the reorganization of Bengal.[2]

But the minority remained very uneasy about their compromise, the friction increased as Sulivan and Holwell began to spar about the details of the plans for Bengal,[3] and feeling began to make itself heard outside the Court among the proprietors, where Stephen Law began to take a lead. The rapid movement of events in India now played into their hands. In February 1758 they learned of the Battle of Plassey, of the overthrow of Siraj-ud-daula, of the appointment of Mir Jafar as his successor, and of the promises of monetary compensation for the Company's losses which he had made. They also learned

[1] Court Book 67, p. 310, 25 March 1757.
[2] Bengal Despatches, i. 627 seq. The records among the Memoranda of the Committee of Correspondence show how difficult it was to arrive at this compromise.
[3] Committee of Correspondence. Memoranda, vol. xvi.

that Clive was remaining in Bengal. An amendment therefore seemed necessary to their instructions. Both factions in the Direction were clear that Clive should be invited to take charge of the Company's affairs in Bengal and that he could only be asked to do so as Governor. Both wrote to him to assure him of the fact.[1] But when the majority tried to maintain the four-fold rotation in the event of his leaving the Presidency, the minority saw their chance of reopening the question and pro-posed the amendment that a successor to Clive should be appointed and that he should be William Watts. When the amendment was defeated, Sulivan and three others marched out of the Court, and only fifteen of the directors signed the General Letter to Bengal incorporating their decision.[2]

War was now openly declared between the two parties, and the constitution of the Company made the next step obvious. The minority appealed from the directors to the General Court. Such appeals had recently been so rare, that the majority hardly seem to have realized their danger. They were also lulled into false security by a breach of convention on the part of their opponents. It was customary then and later to indicate that a General Court would deal with matters outside its routine activities by calling it on 'special business'. When-ever it was not called by the Court of Directors officially, but at the request of individuals, the directors summoned it in this form. A Quarterly Court was, however, just about to meet and the discontented minority decided to raise their business at this Court without warning the directors. Two days only before they informed the proprietors through the Press that though the Court was 'not summoned on special affairs . . . most prob-ably some matters of the utmost importance will then be laid before you'.[3] The challengers had already begun to rally their

[1] Home Miscellaneous, vol. 808. Typed copies of Letters to Clive (from originals in Powis MSS.), f. 118. L. Sulivan to Clive, 20 February 1758 and ff. 139 seq. J. Payne to Clive, 27 October 1758 and ff. 105 seq. J. Payne to Clive, 11 November 1757.
[2] Ibid., f. 140. J. Payne to Clive, 27 October 1758; cf. Account (unsigned and undated) of proceedings in the Company, evidently transmitted to the ministry. Add. MS. 33031, ff. 204 seq.
[3] *Public Advertiser*, 13 March 1758. The result of this stratagem led to a suggestion for a new by-law to prevent it in the future (Court Book 68, p. 251, 17 January 1759). It was not passed, but the convention appears to have been honoured in the future.

supporters; the majority seem to have been caught unawares, and at the well-attended General Court that followed, it soon became apparent that the sympathies of the proprietors were not with them. In fact they completely lost their control of the Court, attempts made by their spokesmen to secure an adjournment were defeated, and the proprietors by a large majority ordered the directors to abolish the rotation and appoint a single successor to Clive.[1]

The intervention of the General Court in the administration of the Company's service, disastrously common though it became later, was then a rare and unwelcome occurrence. The personal issues known to lie behind it made it particularly ominous. The victors, however (more scrupulous than their successors in years to come), were anxious to avert attention from this aspect of the conflict, and having passed their general resolution, refrained from raising the name of a successor, ostentatiously pointing out that this was the responsibility of the Court of Directors. No doubt they assumed that the majority would now come to terms. But if so they were disappointed, for when the Court met the majority elected Holwell to fill the place, despite indignant opposition. A carefully prepared incident whereby a letter was then read out from Holwell declaring his unwillingness to supersede Charles Manningham (presumably intended to divide the opposition) did nothing to placate them.[2] The Chairman reported with short-sighted satisfaction:

> The gentlemen then [after the General Court] thought they had carried their point, but were greatly disappointed to find when the order of the General Court came to be carried into execution, that Mr. Watts was superseded by a great majority. . . . All the minority who attended could do was to refuse signing the letter, though the General Court had been procured by their means entirely with a view to serve Watts.[3]

There was, however, something else the minority could do, and they proceeded to do it. They could challenge the majority at the forthcoming election of directors. The next day a notice

[1] [Holwell] op. cit., p. 9; Court Book 67, p. 663, 15 March 1758.
[2] Court Book 67, p. 665, 22 March 1758.
[3] J. Payne to Clive, 27 October 1758. Home Miscellaneous, vol. 808, f. 140. Typed copy of letter in Powis MSS.

appeared in the London Press addressed to proprietors of East India Stock stating: 'It is desired that you would not be too hasty in promising your votes for directors till you see the lists, as in all probability there will be two lists.'[1] The day after a further notice was inserted asking on behalf of 'several proprietors' that those who had called the proprietors together for the recent General Court should now frame a list of directors at 'this very critical conjuncture'.[2] On 30 March the majority rushed out their House list (from the formation of which the minority had withdrawn) and the next day the rival Proprietors' list was published. The battle was engaged.

The first of the great contested elections in the Company presents several interesting features. The lists themselves illustrate the use of 'double-listing' and the degree to which this practice checked violent changes in the membership of the Court of Directors even in times of intense faction. Those double-listed usually fell into one of two classes; they were either men who for one reason or another were believed not to be finally pledged to either party, or they were well-known and respected directors whose names might be expected to shed lustre on the list in which they appeared even when they were not in sympathy with its leading members. On this occasion of the twelve men double-listed seven publicly protested at being included in the Proprietors' list without their consent and one (Sulivan) at being put in the House list,[3] but in general they were only too glad to have their election secured in this way. Had this practice not grown up there might well have been several occasions in the next fifteen years in which the whole personnel of the Court of Directors was changed at a single blow.

The means by which the election was fought is also of some interest. In one way the challengers showed themselves remarkably advanced. In their use of publicity they were well up to the standard of their successors. A well-attended meeting of proprietors was held at the Crown Tavern at which their list was

[1] *Public Advertiser*, 23 March 1758.
[2] Ibid., 28 March 1758.
[3] Ibid., 31 March. Eight of those put on the Proprietors' list (J. Browne, C. Burrow, R. Drake, J. Dorrien, F. Pigou, John Raymond, G. Rooke, G. Stevens) protested (one, G. Rooke, withdrew his protest on 1 April). On the same date Sulivan protested against his inclusion on the House list.

adopted, the majority censured for their policy, and the minority thanked for opposing them.[1] Letters to the Press and tendentious queries and notices repeatedly inserted in the chief London papers stirred up public opinion, and an intensive personal canvass was made of the proprietors. The majority were much less adroit, were slow to counter their opponents' attacks, and in general permitted themselves to be driven onto the defensive.

In other ways the election was very different from those which were to follow. In the first place it was, so far as we can judge, fought out entirely within the Company. Though it seems likely that the majority among the directors were able to call on some indirect assistance from the Government, there is no suggestion that on either side any serious effort was made to engage any outside interest in the election, and the Company's stock transfer books make it clear that there was no rush (as there was in later elections) by persons not normally holding stock to obtain voting qualifications. In the second place it is clear that among no section of the Company was there any large-scale attempt to influence the result of the election by the creation of votes, the collusive transfer of stock in units of £500 which later became common under the name of 'splitting'. Holwell, watching in bitter anxiety the fading of his hopes, would have been the first to include such practices among the causes he gives of the defeat of his supporters if they had been at all general,[2] and here too the evidence of the transfer books and ledgers is conclusive.[3]

Four hundred and forty-four proprietors voted—a good number considering the shortness of the campaign and the election methods employed. As usual at contested elections in the Company those who voted the whole list without change were in the minority, but 149 voted the whole Proprietors' list and only 42 the whole House list. The final result was that, in addition to the 12 double-listed candidates, the Proprietors' list carried 8 of its 12 candidates and the House list only 4. When the new Court met, Sulivan was elected Chairman and was found to command 14 of the 24 votes on controversial issues.

[1] Public Advertiser, 31 March 1758.
[2] [Holwell] Important Facts, op. cit., pp. 12–15.
[3] There was a slight increase in the number of transfers at this time, especially in units of £500, some of which (particularly those re-transferred shortly afterwards) were clearly collusive.

He was to hold this power unshaken for the next six years. There can be no doubt that his victory was generally popular in the Company, and among the servants in India it was equally well received. Clive wrote urging his correspondents to support Sulivan 'who will pursue vigorous measures now become absolutely necessary'.[1] To his father he wrote to the same effect though in words with disconcerting implications:

I cannot conclude this letter without desiring you will make use of all your interest and that of your friends in support of Mr. Sullivan [sic], and if there should be occasion to lay out any of my money in India Stock to effect my intentions, I desire my attorneys may do it.[2]

The defeated Chairman was right when he said 'I think these extraordinary measures must have extraordinary consequences.'[3]

With Sulivan in power the new era had begun. It did not require much foresight to see that his task would be a difficult one, but he tackled it with characteristic energy. The first business of the new Court was to reverse the recent decisions about the Government of Bengal and to reduce Holwell to his former place in seniority. The last ships of the season were held back for the new instructions, though this badly upset the convoy arrangements. It was a fitting end to a futile controversy that in the event neither these instructions nor those of their predecessors which had precipitated the revolution within the Company ever came into force. When the orders for the fourfold rotation reached Bengal the servants there so strongly disapproved of them that Clive was asked to act as Governor while they remonstrated with their employers; and all the attempts of the new Direction to keep Holwell out of the Governorship were frustrated by the premature return of the senior servants to enjoy their recently acquired fortunes. When Clive returned home in 1760 Holwell stepped into his shoes and enjoyed the position until Henry Vansittart, transferred from Madras for the purpose, could come and take up his duties.

Sulivan's attempts to inject vigour in the Company's administration at home and abroad were of more permanent significance. Every attempt was made to encourage the China

[1] R. Clive to W. Belchier, 29 December 1758. Malcolm, op. cit. ii. 116–17.
[2] Forrest, op. cit. ii. 118.
[3] J. Payne to R. Clive, 27 October 1758. Home Miscellaneous, vol. 808, f. 141.

trade, and the range of topics which are touched on in drafts in
Sulivan's own hand—from the trade in raw silk to the abuse of
dastaks in Bengal, and the debts of the Nawab of Arcot in the
Carnatic—are an impressive witness to his industry. He claimed
in 1761 that, since he had been Chairman, much had been
done to reduce perquisites by the provision of 'noble and
exclusive emoluments' for the Company's senior servants. He
had certainly taken steps to free the Governors from the needs
of private trade and had sought to prohibit the taking of presents
from the Nawab of Arcot, and had set on foot a number of
reforms in the Carnatic. His main task in India was, however,
the reorganization of Bengal. To this much thought was given
and extensive plans drawn up. But now as later (and with
justice) he relied above all on finding good men to place in the
most important positions. Just as later he pinned his faith on
Warren Hastings as Governor in Bengal, so now he hoped
much from the appointment of Henry Vansittart. Vansittart
had done well at Madras, and was highly praised by Clive and
others whose opinion was of value. Sulivan said of him 'from
his character he is high in my esteem, and from his virtues and
abilities I expect that lawless settlement of Calcutta will be
reformed to decency and order'.[1] But, though the misfortunes
of Vansittart's Governorship were by no means all his fault,
Vansittart was no Hastings, the tide of disorganization steadily
mounted, and without stronger rule in Bengal it is doubtful
whether any attempts at reform directed from England could
have checked it. Sulivan failed in his attempt to control the
situation there.

In the much easier task of bringing up to date the Company's
administration at home he was more successful. With the
co-operation of the Company's excellent secretary, Robert
James (to whose assistance he paid high tribute),[2] the establishment was overhauled, the methods of accountancy improved,
and the taking of fees and perquisites by the clerks of the
Secretary's Office brought to an end. In 1772-3 when the
Secret Committee of the House of Commons investigating
the Company's affairs had to depend on the assistance of

---

[1] L. Sulivan to Eyre Coote, 16 March 1761. Quoted Forrest, op. cit. ii. 182.
Clive had strongly supported the appointment of Vansittart.
[2] Court Book 69, p. 362, 18 March 1761.

the Company's clerks, they were loud in praise of their competence.

The reorganization of Bengal did not engage the directors' attention merely because of the unsatisfactory conditions there. There was evidence which touched them more nearly. Even before the revolution in the Direction they had become aware that an excessive number of bills were being drawn on the Companies by the Presidencies, in particular by Bengal.[1] Soon after Sulivan took over the reins of power it became apparent that the demands on the Company were mounting to a much greater total than they had intended and that the bills were being drawn payable at a shorter date than they had expected. The payment of the Company's local expenses by funds drawn from individuals on the spot and the financing of its 'investment' (or purchases of Indian goods for sale in England) by the same means was not in itself objectionable. The bills were repaid from the proceeds of the Company's sales. But any extravagance either in the taking up of such funds or in the terms offered for them (a serious temptation since those concerned were primarily the Company servants themselves) reflected itself in a drain on the Company's funds in England. Moreover the timing of the date at which such demands fell due was a matter of considerable concern to the Company. In 1758 the position became embarrassing and Sulivan's admiration for what he had called the Company's 'old and most capable servants'[2] began to wane.

The war with France, the expenses of convoys, increased shipping hire, and the losses of Indiamen to privateers were already placing the Company under strain (as always happened in time of war) and these new commitments were particularly unwelcome. Knowing that the Company had been promised £1,000,000 compensation from the Nawab, the directors were inclined to believe (not altogether without cause) that the influx of bills and the favourable terms on which they had been drawn were due more to disorderly administration and the pressure for remittance by their servants and the officers of the royal forces than to the real needs of the Company. In November 1758 they even considered refusing to accept the bills, but

---

[1] Bengal Despatches, i. 755, 8 March 1758.
[2] Account of affairs in the Company—evidently transmitted to the ministry. Add. MS. 33031, f. 204ᵛ.

decided that the damage to the Company's credit would be too great.[1] By the middle of 1759 John Walsh, a Bengal servant who had become the faithful friend and follower of Clive and who was back in England managing a good deal of his business, wrote to him that the Company was in difficulties.

Their servants having drawn such immense sums upon them, as have greatly distressed their affairs and enraged them against those who signed the bills. Indeed these draughts, the loss of St. David's, the taking the Grantham and apprehension of several others likely to meet the same fate from the Cruizers off St. Helena; together with the precarious state of the English squadrons in India, have reduced their credit to a very low ebb in so much that their Stock is not at more than £125 and their bonds at six and seven shillings discount.[2]

By making arrangements for the bills to pay interest and by paying them off by instalments—a settlement in which Sulivan was no doubt helped by the fact that a not inconsiderable part of the remittance business was passing through his hands in his private capacity—the directors succeeded in weathering the storm, but the tone of the General Letters to Bengal became increasingly acid and a General Letter of 23 March 1759 drafted by Sulivan himself subjected the servants there to bitter reproaches on this and other grounds. The directors could hardly believe, they said, after the leniency they had shown that their servants 'would bring such distresses upon us as were never before experienced by this Company'.[3] Careful attempts were made to dissociate Clive himself from the criticism levelled against his colleagues. The results of this letter, however, in the disorganized condition of Bengal, were not what was expected. Most of the servants involved had already made their plans for returning home to enjoy their fortunes. Holwell, who was not returning, knew he had nothing to expect from the present directors, and Clive took umbrage despite the efforts to placate him. The result was open defiance. Holwell drafted and they all signed an insolent rejoinder. By the time it reached England all but four of the signatories were out of the Company's power, but these four were dismissed and the quarrel added its quota to the troubles of Bengal.

---

[1] Court Book 68, p. 181, 17 November 1758.
[2] J. Walsh to R. Clive, 13 July 1759. Home Miscellaneous, vol. 808, f. 154. Typed copy of letter in Powis MSS.   [3] Bengal Despatches, i. 898.

It was in England, however, that the worst effects were seen, for it transferred the disorganization of Bengal to the head-quarters of the Company in London. A number of rich and influential Bengal servants began to return in a state of acute hostility to the directors. From this time can be dated the conflict between the 'Bengal squad' and those at the head of the Direction. Furthermore, when Clive himself returned home in the middle of 1760, though the misunderstandings between him and Sulivan were said to be cleared up, and Sulivan claimed not only that this distinguished servant had received 'every honour and compliment paid to his great abilities and extra-ordinary services' but that 'we have reason to believe he is sorry that he signed this letter',[1] the seeds of the great feud had been sown.

The effects of the changes which had taken place in the Company were not immediately reflected in the relations of the Company and State. The events of recent years had indeed forced the Government to pay increased attention to East Indian affairs and to keep in particularly close touch with the Company, but this was because of the needs of war or of a condition of near war. The long struggle with the French Company and the hostility of France and England had, indeed, revived some of the problems of the relation of the State and the Company which had arisen during the seventeenth-century struggles with the Dutch. The English and French Governments concerned themselves in the negotiations between the two Companies to settle their conflicting interests in 1752–3; the English Government squashed the suggestion for neutrality between the two Companies in India in the event of war, and in 1754, for the first time in the century, royal forces were sent out to co-operate with those of the Company in the protection of its possessions.[2]

The relations of these forces raised a number of problems, some, such as quarrels about precedence and the division of booty, of no great importance, others of permanent significance.

[1] Committee of Correspondence. Memoranda, vol. xviii, 13 March 1761. Sulivan's draft of General Letter to Bengal. This portion was crossed out and does not seem to have been sent (see Bengal Despatches, ii. 247–9).

[2] H. Dodwell, *Dupleix and Clive*, pp. 76 seq., examines these problems of the relations of the State to the Company.

There was significance for the future in the fact that both Indian
princes and discontented Company servants were tempted by
the direct participation of the State in India to appeal against
the Company to the Government. In 1762 the directors were
perturbed to find that one of their military officers had brought
a letter of the Nawab of Arcot to the king direct,[1] the first of
a series of such communications, and the personal relations
between prominent Company servants and politicians began
to cause alarm. In 1760 the directors complain that 'a minute
account of our affairs' is being given to great men at home,
which might be dangerous to the Company if it were not that
'the present ministry are their real and true friends'.[2] The
suggestions made by Clive to Pitt for the future of Bengal while
he was still in the Company's service would have been ill
received by his employers had they known of them.[3] Of even
greater importance was the fact that the successes of the combined forces brought up once again the degree of sovereignty
exercised by the Company in India. In 1757 the directors
thought it wise to obtain a clarification of their rights of war
and peace. They petitioned for confirmation of their right to
cede or restore fortresses and territories taken in war, and they
asked for the right to retain all booty captured by their troops
in combined operations. So far as the booty was concerned
it was agreed that the Company should have a right to everything taken by their troops while acting alone but that when
the royal and Company troops were acting in combination it
would be divided in shares to be determined by the Crown.
The right to cede fortresses and territories raised more difficulties. Legal opinion was by no means clear that they did not
implicitly enjoy it already[4] but the Law Officers were strongly
averse to giving general and explicit recognition of such a right.
It was, they said: 'not warranted by precedent nor agreeable
to sound policy nor to the tenor of the Charters . . . to make such

---

[1] Court Book 71, p. 81, 7 July 1762, and Committee of Correspondence Report
vol. vi, 29 July 1762. The officer was Major Richard Smith, later to be prominent
among the Nawab's creditors.
[2] Bengal Despatches, ii. 88. General Letter of 1 April 1760.
[3] Forrest, op. cit. ii. 175 seq.
[4] Pitt said: 'Upon some late transactions it had been inquired into whether the
Company's conquests and acquisitions belonged to them or the Crown and the
Judges seemed to think to the Company.' (Forrest, op. cit. ii. 177.)

general grant, not only of past but of future contingent conquests made upon any power, European or Indian, to a trading Company'.[1] It was recognized, however, that the Company's request was based on considerations of practical convenience and they recommended that it be given permission to cede or restore any fortresses or territory taken in the war with Bengal or in any future wars with Indian princes; possessions taken from European Powers should not be restored without the royal consent.[2] This was a first, tentative approach to the problem which was to excite so much controversy during the next twenty years, the right of the Company to enjoy territorial powers in India.

Though the Government's interests in India had increased in this way, and though relations arising out of war in India were added to those between the Government and the monied Company, they did not as yet, as they were soon to do, concern themselves in the internal affairs of the Company. As has been said there is no sign that they took any active part in the electoral contest of 1758. They seem, it is true, to have been a little put out by the defeat of their old allies on the Direction. Lord Anson, the First Lord of the Admiralty, was said to have been unfriendly when Sulivan, as Chairman, and Crabb Boulton, a supporter, waited on him about convoy arrangements after the election. Anson was said to have told them that 'their sole aim seemed to be the gratifying their private resentments and distressing his Majesty's service and embroiling their constituents' affairs'.[3] But it was always inconvenient for the Government as well as for the Company to be on bad terms, and this was particularly so in time of war, and Sulivan soon achieved civil if not very friendly relations with both Newcastle and Pitt. Nevertheless, it was not until the advent of Bute's administration and the beginning of Sulivan's personal association with Lord Shelburne that the new Chairman succeeded in restoring the close relations which had existed under his predecessors. And by the time he did so the combined effects of instability in ministries and of party in the Company had made

[1] Add. MS. 18464, f. 7. A volume of East India Documents collected up to 1767.
[2] *Charters Relating to the East India Company from 1600 to 1761* (Madras, 1887), ed. J. Shaw, pp. 284–6. Charter of 14 January 1758.
[3] [Holwell] *Important Facts*, op. cit., p. 15. Holwell, though well informed, was, of course, a hostile witness and may have given an exaggerated account.

this close connexion a danger as well as a strength. This was to
be shown by the events of 1763. The first active intervention,
since the seventeenth century, by Government and Opposition
in the internal affairs of the Company arose from a question
closely tied up with the disputes over the Peace of Paris—the
issue on which the parliamentary Opposition made their most
serious (though inept) attempt to bring down Lord Bute's
shaky administration.

IV

THE STRUGGLE FOR MASTERY: THE
FIRST PHASE

WHEN two such men as Clive and Sulivan were brought
face to face under the conditions found in the East
India Company in 1760, a conflict between them was
almost inevitable. By the time Clive arrived in England the
first rejoicings in the Company over his successes on the battle-
field and in the treacherous world of Eastern diplomacy had
already begun to give way to uneasiness at the results. The most
striking result was the unmistakable disorganization of the
Company's servants in the highly unstable equilibrium which
Clive achieved in Bengal, a disorganization found also to a
lesser degree in Madras, where the war with the French was
still dragging on. The enormous private gains both in gifts and
compensation which followed Clive's defeat of Siraj-ud-daula
and the revolution which made Mir Jafar Nawab in his place,
were a major cause of the destruction of the precarious standards
of official honesty in India. The removal of the old fear of the
native power also contributed to the disintegration, by encouraging a rapid increase of private trade in the hinterland
of Calcutta among the Company's servants and a host of
hangers-on, European, Armenian, and Indian, the abuses of
which have been very adequately catalogued in the parliamentary inquiries of the next twenty-five years, and in which
great profits could be gained. These two factors combined to
bring the Bengal servants to a sudden affluence which made
them, as Sulivan had already discovered, quite unmanageable.
Moreover their mass return to England with their wealth was
only to raise dangerous enemies in the Company at home
without improving the situation abroad, for they left no one
suitable to replace them.

Among these enriched and intransigent servants Clive himself must be counted, as the recipient of gifts from the Nawab
to the unprecedented sum of more than £200,000, and as the
Governor of Bengal who signed the letter in which the Bengal

servants defied the censures of the Court of Directors.[1] It could hardly be expected that opinion in the Company would be unmoved by the accounts of the great sums passing into the hands of their servants and the evidences of disorganization which accompanied them. Six months before Clive's return to England a General Court had passed a unanimous resolution that an inquiry should be made into the sums granted by the Nawab of Bengal to the Company, its servants, and other persons and into the purposes to which such grants were applied.[2] Though the directors appear to have thought it unwise to alienate their rebellious Bengal servants and ex-servants further and no more is heard of this inquiry, the issue of instructions prohibiting the receipt of presents from the Nawab of Arcot shows that the movement which led in 1764 to the total prohibition of the taking of presents was already under way.

The misdeeds of the Company's servants would have been less exasperating if they had not also been the cause of acute financial difficulties. The anger of the directors when individuals were allowed to remit home their gains to a sum which seriously embarrassed the Company has already been mentioned. The further report from Bengal that, despite the sums they had received into the local treasury in return for bills and in payment from the Nawab, they were apprehensive of an actual shortage of silver bullion, made dissatisfaction at home still more acute;[3] and finally the news that the Nawab, impoverished by war and his liberality to those who had engineered his accession, was finding difficulty in making payments to the Company brought their indignation to its culmination.

In these causes of complaint Clive was implicated. Though part of his fortune had been remitted home through the Dutch

---

[1] v. sup. p. 76. For Clive's fortune see Malcolm's calculations, op. cit. ii. 187. He estimates it in all at about £300,000.

[2] Court Book 68, p. 581, 10 January 1760.

[3] This was largely due to expense of administration and to the vast and in part fraudulent expenses of the new citadel at Calcutta. The General Letter of 1 April 1760 said (Bengal Despatches, ii. 111): 'This is really at present past our power to comprehend, and should it prove a truth, your grant and dazzling acquisitions will be the ruin of this Company, for it's a striking fact that although we have benefited upwards of a million sterling by the late Treaty, yet not a single shilling of this immense sum has gone in aid to our returns and by your representation the whole will be bury'd in your Citadel and the charges of Calcutta.'

Company, at some loss to himself,[1] much, too, had been brought home in the Company's bills, and, shortly before his arrival, news was received of a further grant he had obtained which raised unprecedented questions. The directors were informed in June 1760 that the annual sum of about £27,000, payable to the Nawab as rents for lands near Calcutta, was to be handed over to Clive as the *jagir* of a purely nominal office of honour to which he had been appointed under the Mogul. This was the famous *jagir*, which was to play so sinister a part in Company politics. To Clive's earlier presents the Company, however much they might dislike them, could make no official objection, since there was no regulation against them and he had only done on a large scale what had hitherto not been challenged when done on a smaller scale. Clive himself with his customary outspokenness described them in detail at the time of their grant. The *jagir* however, was a different matter. It was quite unexampled. It not only created a very curious legal position, in which Clive was a feudatory of the Mogul and placed by a sort of sub-infeudation between the Company and that other feudatory the Nawab of Bengal, but it involved several practical inconveniences to the Company. Among them was the fact that the Nawab had not yet paid in full the restitution money for the damage done by his predecessor to Calcutta. Had Clive not received this grant, the £27,000 a year would have been a fund from which they could recoup themselves for this default. It has been suggested by some of Clive's biographers[2] that the Company accepted the grant of the *jagir* as they had accepted the presents before, and that the attack that they made upon it in 1763 was entirely unexpected and unjustified. This was not the case. Though the story, as will be seen, reflects far from creditably upon the Company's politics, Clive was aware from an early date after his return that the Company had not formally accepted his claims and might challenge them.

[1] John Walsh to Clive, 13 July 1758. Home Miscellaneous, vol. 808, f. 152. Typed copies of documents in Powis MSS. A good deal was also sent home in the form of diamonds.

[2] Malcolm, who was using the papers of Henry Strachey, Clive's Secretary, containing a defence of the *jagir* of an interesting though *ex parte* kind, has a fuller treatment than succeeding biographers of the *jagir* controversy, though sometimes rather a garbled one (op. cit. ii. 216 seq.).

With these causes of discontent in the past, and of discord in the future, it might indeed appear that Clive and the directors led by Sulivan must come into conflict almost at once. But Sulivan was very anxious to avert this. The enmity of a victorious soldier, received with honour at court and in fashionable circles, who was at the same time rich and formidable in character, was a thing to be avoided, particularly when so many of his late colleagues were returning bent on opposition. Clive's support of Sulivan since 1758 had moreover been real and valuable. Hence Sulivan did everything he could to remove Clive's personal grievances (some of which were by no means rational) and to isolate him from the discontents of the Bengal servants with which he had identified himself. Nevertheless he watched Clive carefully. Their cordiality was never more than forced, and it was characteristic of his political methods that he early thought it wise to indicate to this dangerous newcomer that there were those in the Company who would like to challenge his possession of the *jagir*. Clive, two years after his return, told a friend that Sulivan could never forgive the Bengal letter, and 'never has reposed that confidence in me which my services to the East India Company entitled me to. The consequence has been that we have all along behaved to one another like shy cocks, at times outwardly expressing great regard and friendship for each other.'[1]

When Clive arrived in England in July 1760, at the age of thirty-five and with the prospects of a brilliant career before as well as behind him, it does not seem that he had thought of building up an 'interest' at India House. He believed, it is true, that he would be able to exercise great influence over Indian affairs, both political and military. He kept up an intimate correspondence with his successor in the Government, Vansittart,[2] and he assumed that he would have the chief say in the major military appointments of the Company. But his real ambitions, however, his hopes of 'future power and future grandeur', as he himself called them, centred in national politics. His first demand was concrete, a peerage as reward for his services. His further aims were less sharply defined but may

---

[1] Clive to H. Vansittart, 22 November 1762. Quoted Malcolm, op. cit. ii. 197.
[2] Vansittart was fortunate in the support of both Clive and Sulivan, both of whom claimed to be his patrons.

well have been inspired by the conduct and position of his chosen
political leader, William Pitt. In any case they demanded the
formation of a parliamentary influence.

During his previous visit to England Clive had already made
an unsuccessful attempt to enter the House of Commons. In
1754 he stood in a contested election for the borough of Mitchell
in Cornwall, with the support of Lord Sandwich who was
managing the interest of his nephew in this borough.[1] It was
in the confused period after Pelham's death, when absence of
leadership amongst the old governing connexions was joined
to the unrest of the court of an old king, and Clive fell a victim
to this confusion. Newcastle had indirectly stirred up a rival
local interest, and in a session when electoral disputes were
being used to make clear the party divisions of the House,
Clive's case was taken up by Henry Fox, who was in violent
revolt against the Government. As a result the ministerial
forces were called out (although the Lord Chancellor Hardwicke had shown some sympathy with Clive) and Clive was
handsomely beaten. He had already decided to return to India,
and left shortly afterwards, but Horace Walpole heard that the
expense was enormous, and Clive remembered the defeat
keenly. In 1757 he wrote to his father 'if I can get into Parliament I shall be very glad; but no more struggles against the
ministry; I choose to be with them'.[2]

While he was in India he had kept up some slight correspondence with Sandwich and Fox and also with Lord Hardwicke,
but by 1760 he seems to have thought that his correspondence
with Pitt, at this time in the height of his power, was of more
importance to him. This time he had no difficulty in obtaining
a seat. Before he reached England his father had been stirring
in Shropshire, whence the family derived, and in 1759, apparently with Lord Powis's support, he got Clive's name put
up for the borough of Shrewsbury. The first General Election of
the new reign took place a few months after Clive's return and
he was returned uncontested.[3] In these few months he had also
taken the first steps towards building up his parliamentary
connexion by bringing in his father for Montgomery, and his

[1] Forrest, op. cit. i. 230 seq.; Namier, op. cit. ii. 378.
[2] Quoted Forrest, op. cit. ii. 36, 10 August 1757.
[3] L. B. Namier, *The Structure of Politics*, ii. 320 seq.

supporter and friend, John Walsh, for the borough of Worcester. An attempt to bring in his cousin, George Clive, and his brother-in-law, Edward Maskelyne, for Penrhyn, was, however, unsuccessful.[1]

Having gained this first step, Clive now turned to the second, the obtaining of his peerage, and he was angry to find how little fame in one field of activity helped him in another. Nevertheless, after he had fretted for some time under disappointment, Lord Sandwich (who was always adroit in such matters) pointed out to the Duke of Newcastle that his allegiance was worth gaining and that he could probably be won.[2] As a consequence Clive found himself very glad to accept an Irish peerage (he had hoped for an English one) in return for entering the ranks of Newcastle's supporters. He had thus gained his first point. It seemed that now he could use his wealth to build up a parliamentary group,[3] with whose voting power he could bargain, and which would be the instrument with which he hoped to shape his glory.

At this point, however, a disaster overtook Clive, the significance of which it is impossible to overestimate either for himself or the East India Company. A chain of circumstance was being forged which was to wreck his ambitions and poison his life, destroying irremediably his independent bargaining power in Parliament, and driving him into a perpetual defensive. The same circumstances brought the East India Company back into the centre of politics where it had not been since 1698. These circumstances arose, indirectly no doubt from the events he had set in train in Bengal and their repercussions on the Company, but directly from the growing hostility between him and Laurence Sulivan.

[1] L. B. Namier, *The Structure of Politics*, ii. 380 seq.
[2] Ibid. ii. 353.
[3] It seems clear from his letter to H. Vansittart, 3 February 1762 (Powis MSS.), that Clive meant to use his wealth to increase his political power. Urging his friend that 'a large fortune honourably acquired will be the source of great honours and advantages to you' he adds, 'believe me there is no other interest in this kingdom but what arises from great possessions, and if after the Battle of Placis I had stayed in India for myself as well as the Company and acquired the fortune I might have done by this time I might have been an English Earl with a Blue Ribbon instead of an Irish Peer (with the promise of a Red one). However the receipt of the Jaggeer money for a few years will do great things.' This remark is not inconsistent with his remark on a letter written the same month, that he scorned to purchase a peerage (Forrest, op. cit. ii. 180).

The discontented servants who had returned from Bengal did not delay long before beginning to show their hostility to Sulivan in a number of ways. They were very probably already joined by other malcontents who were jealous of the remarkable ascendancy which, as Clive bears witness, he had gained over the Company.[1] Before the 1761 election of directors Sulivan thought it necessary to justify himself in a General Court against 'some heavy and injurious reflections that had been cast upon his character by many persons without doors'.[2] There is no evidence that Clive had any share in these aspersions, and the correspondence which occasionally passed between the two maintained its note of forced cordiality. In November it is true Sulivan found it necessary to assure Clive of the falsity of certain assertions which had been made impugning his 'regard for Colonel Clive'.[3] But by February 1762 Clive made no attempt to hide from his friends his hostility to the Company's leader, and by the same date Sulivan had thought it desirable to bring into action his strongest weapon against his potential enemy, and to let him know that the Company might decide to challenge his possession of his *jagir*.

We do not know precisely when Sulivan brought into play this threat which was to paralyse Clive's actions for two years, before driving him to desperate action. A clause in the Bengal General Letter of 13 March 1761 shows that nothing had been done about it up to that date. It runs:

Colonel Clive's long illness preventing our having any conversation with him before the despatch of these ships upon the subject of the Nabob's grant to him of the annual rent of those lands now in our possession, which was before paid to the Nabob, as mentioned in the 136th paragraph of your letter of the 29th December, 1759, we must therefore defer giving you our sentiments thereon to another opportunity.[4]

[1] In the letter to Vansittart quoted in n. 3, p. 86, he said, 'Sulivan still continues at the head of the Direction and in all probability will remain so as long as the War lasts. I before represented to you that the present set of Directors are without abilities, fortune or influence, and that it was Sulivan's policy to have such that he might have the greater sway. There are not wanting opponents but in the present distracted times, no man chooses to be concerned in any directions whatever.'
[2] Court Book 69, p. 362, 18 March 1761. He seems to have been accused of taking bribes from those to whom he gave office—Crommelin, Palk, and Vansittart. There seems to be no particle of evidence in support of this accusation.
[3] Quoted in Forrest, op. cit. ii. 190.   [4] Bengal Despatches, ii. 238.

A letter of Clive's of 27 February 1762 is the only other document bearing on the subject. It is therefore worth quoting the relevant parts of it in full:

My arrival in England was attended with every mark of respect that I could wish, and my interest in Leadenhall St. might have been of as much consequence as I could have desired, for the advantage of my friends; but a most severe fit of sickness overset all. For twelve months it was difficult to pronounce whether I was to live or die. In so dreadful a situation, I could not think much of India or indeed anything else but death. It is very natural to think the interest of a dying man could not be very great. Under these circumstances I had hints given me that either some attempts would be made upon my jaghire or some proposal made for giving it up to the Company after a certain time, on a supposition perhaps, that I had not long to live. Accordingly I was given to understand by Sulivan, that the Gentlemen of the Secret Committee would wait upon me on this subject, but health returning, this proposal was dropt, and I have heard nothing more of it since.[1]

The statement that for twelve months Clive could not think of 'anything else but death' cannot be taken literally, though he was in Bath for some months in exceedingly poor health. The suggestion that the attack was made on his *jagir* because he was thought to be a dying man seems a strange one, since he himself considered it as a life-rent, and his death might be hoped to remove the problem altogether. It seems far more likely that it was brought forward to serve the purpose which it in fact did serve, that of putting Clive under a permanent blackmail. As it was mentioned in the General Letter of 13 March 1761, this step was probably under discussion about that date. It is possible that the intimation was made to Clive at the time when Sulivan was smarting under the campaign of calumny just before the election of directors in April. When the Company in 1763 actually did stop the payments of Clive's *jagir*, Sulivan wrote to Vansittart that this measure 'would have taken place years ago' had it not been for him,[2] and no doubt he opened the question with Clive in 1761 as a friend warning him of the views of others. The measure, whatever judgement is passed on its morality and whatever its longer term results, was in the short run exceedingly successful.

---

[1] Clive to P. Amyatt. Quoted Malcolm, op. cit. ii. 190–2.
[2] Quoted Malcolm, op. cit. ii. 220.

For it bound Clive hand and foot. When he wrote grumbling at Sulivan's autocracy, he added:

This kind of political opinion has exasperated most of the gentlemen who are lately come from India, particularly those from Bengal. They are surprised I do not join in their resentments, and I should think it very surprising if I did, considering I have such an immense stake in India. My future power, my future grandeur, all depend upon the receipt of the jaghire money. I should be a madman to set at defiance those who at present show no inclination to hurt me.[1]

Though he was able to speak calmly about it, his anxiety about his position was great. At the same time he was taking with feverish activity every step he could think of to protect his interests. He was evidently uncertain what form an attack might take; the feudal law of the Moguls was obscure and complex enough to make his legal position by no means certain; the Company might, he thought, use 'chicanery' to 'obtain the Nabobs redemanding the grant with a view to getting it for the Company'[2] or a long case in Chancery might wear out his health and exhaust his resources. He canvassed his parliamentary allies; he wrote anxiously to friends in India, particularly to his successor Vansittart, at one moment boasting that he commanded sufficient political strength in England to checkmate any attempt on his property, at the next imploring their aid to make as certain as possible his claims in India. To Vansittart he wrote:

I have been assured by men of the greatest rank and power in the kingdom I might depend upon the Parliament for justice in this affair in which I am so deeply concerned. Much will depend upon your friendship and I must request you will take every step in your power to make my right to this Jaggeer as clear and perfect as the distracted conditions of affairs at Dilla [Delhi] will afford of a confirmation and that my Jaggeer be not forgotten when the confirmation of the Company's possessions are applied for.[2]

How much he fretted at his bondage is shown by an outburst in a letter to another friend in the same month:

Although I have such an interest in Court and in Parliament that I should not be afraid of an attack from the whole Court of Directors

---

[1] Quoted Malcolm, op. cit. ii. 195.
[2] Clive to H. Vansittart, 3 February 1762. Powis MSS.

united, yet all my friends advise me I should do nothing to exasperate them, if they are silent as to my jaggeer. Indeed it is an object of such importance that I should be inexcusable if I did not make every other consideration give way to it; and this is one of the reasons why I cannot join openly with the Bengal gentlemen in their resentments. It depends upon you, my friend, to make me a free man by getting the grant confirmed from Delhi, and getting such acknowledgements from under the hands of the present Nabob as may enable me to put all our enemies at defiance.[1]

That a man of Clive's stamp could not always be controlled by this ignominious threat might have been guessed by anyone who knew his arrogant and daring character. In spite of all he said, he was already deriving some satisfaction from harassing Sulivan.

I have so far fallen into their (the Bengal gentlemen's) way of thinking, as to preside at a general meeting of a club of East Indians once a fortnight; and this has all the effect I could wish of keeping Sulivan in awe, and of convincing him that, though I do not mean to hurt him, I can do such a thing if he attempts to hurt me.[2]

This was the famous Bengal Club, which became a centre for the returned 'Nabobs' in the coming years. The ill feeling between the two flared up unpleasantly a few months later on a question of military patronage. Indeed so rapidly did their relations deteriorate that it seems likely Clive would have found his caution insufficient to control him, had it not been for the fact that in April 1762 Sulivan decided to withdraw from the Direction for the year (his ostensible motive was the need to devote attention to his private business but it was generally thought that the real reason was the need to adjust the number of prominent directors out by rotation in 1763) and put Thomas Rous as a feeble man of straw in his place as Chairman. Though there is ample evidence that Sulivan continued to manage the Company's affairs from outside, and his interference seems to have driven even the wretched Rous to revolt, he had officially retired into private life. The open breach between Clive and Sulivan was postponed until February of 1763.

When it came, it arose out of the negotiations for the Preliminaries of the Peace of Paris. By November 1762 the two

---

[1] Quoted Malcolm, op. cit. ii. 191–2, 3 February 1762.
[2] Clive to J. Pybus, 27 February 1762. Quoted Malcolm, op. cit. ii. 195.

men were in total disagreement, but caution still held Clive back from throwing in his lot with the growing opposition within the Company. In February 1763 he suddenly decided that the time had come to put all to the chance, to sink his fortune and power in winning a majority in the Direction at India House, and to free himself at once of his enemy and of the threat to his wealth.

A variety of circumstances led to this decision. Clive's whole attitude to, and place in, politics had been changing of necessity while he was subject to this threat. Whereas he had thought of his Indian achievements and his Indian influence as a background for a great though indefinite part he hoped to play in national politics, he now found his bargaining power in national politics was necessary to preserve his personal interests in India. At the same time a revolution in national politics had taken place which was seriously to alter his position. The change in the balance of political forces that was to be expected under a new king had come about, though with a delay that is primarily attributable to the state of the Seven Years War. Now first Pitt in 1761 and then Newcastle and the remains of the Pelham connexion in 1762 disappeared from the stage, and the king's mentor, Bute, found himself struggling to build up a connexion to take its place. The Pelham connexion that was swept away was no more than a ghost of what it had been, but its destruction marked the end of a period of political stability, and seven years of fluctuating ministries and uneasy factions followed before a new 'system' which could do something to replace the old had been built up. Clive had given his support to the fallen ministers; Sulivan on the other hand had been for some time fostering a close friendship with a young man who was very influential among the new ones. This young man was Lord Shelburne, who thus began his intimate connexion with East Indian Company politics.[1] He was entering politics as a protégé of Henry Fox, one of the most astute and cynical politicians of the day, and he soon became equally friendly with Lord Bute.

[1] We do not know how it began, but as early as September 1761 Shelburne was concerning himself and interesting Bute in Sulivan's attempt to get into Parliament. When a first attempt failed Shelburne arranged another seat for him, a transaction in which Calcraft, Fox's 'jackal', took a part. Sulivan's letters and Lady Shelburne's diary show that he was on terms of intimacy with Shelburne. (Sulivan to Shelburne, 7 September 1761. Lansdowne MSS.)

An able young man, who by upbringing and tastes stood a little aside from the main aristocratic connexions of his day, his political career was to be marred by the suspicion and mistrust which he succeeded in inspiring (for no reason very obvious to posterity) among all those with whom he worked, but he showed at all stages remarkable political insight and sustained and intelligent ambition. He was always alive to the value to a rising politician of support from interests outside the House, and Sulivan, who had never obtained more than the civil forbearance of the late ministers whose friends in the Company he had ousted, made the most of the opportunity thus offered him.

The Peace Settlement after the victorious but costly Seven Years War was the first great problem of the new ministry. The preliminaries of the peace were signed at Fontainebleau on 3 November 1762, and the definitive treaty in Paris on 10 February 1763. As Professor Pares says, it was a settlement 'which secured the original objects of the war and satisfied the reasonable ambitions of all Englishmen but those who lived by war or war-mongering'.[1] Nevertheless the terms of both, and particularly the preliminaries, were subjected to violent criticism, attributable largely to the unpopularity of Lord Bute and his administration, which only failed to produce serious parliamentary repercussions because of the lack of organization of the opposition and the weakness of their case.

The criticisms centred for the most part on questions concerning the West Indies, the Newfoundland fisheries, and the compensation to be extorted from Spain for the return of Havana, captured when the negotiations were far advanced. The provisions for the settlement in the East Indies also aroused some controversy which had its effects on the general political situation, and still more on the internal politics of the East India Company. The final split between Clive and Sulivan arose in connexion with the negotiations with France over the preliminary treaty.[2]

In general the differences between the preliminary and definitive treaties were slight, but the clauses embodying the East Indian settlement differed both in the degree of detail

[1] R. Pares, *War and Trade in the West Indies* (Oxford, 1936), p. 610.
[2] I have examined the East Indian aspect of the peace negotiations at length in 'The East India Company and the Peace of Paris', *E.H.R.*, 1947.

included and in some of their specific terms. The definitive treaty, though it fell short in certain respects of the first demands of the English Company, was conceded by all parties to be 'very advantageous to the East India Company'.[1] The preliminary treaty, on the other hand, was admitted by all, even by those who were prepared to support it in general, to be far from satisfactory in its East Indian clause. Sulivan voted with the Government in support of the preliminary treaty; Clive divided with his political allies against it. As their final breach came over this same issue, it has naturally been assumed that it arose out of some fundamental disagreement about the terms of the peace. Since Clive announced his approval of the definitive treaty and his disapproval of the preliminary one, its origin has been sought in the first of the two documents and in the divergencies between it and its successor.

The underlying principle of the East India settlement was the surrender of all French claims in India originating since 1749 in exchange for the return of the *comptoirs* in their possession before that date; the French also engaged to erect no fortifications and maintain no troops in Bengal. The article in the definitive treaty differed from that in the preliminaries, both in its greater precision of definition and in two points of substance. In the first place the preliminary treaty restored to the French all *comptoirs* in their possession 'au commencement des hostilités entre les deux Compagnies en 1749'; in the definitive treaty the date was changed to 'le commencement de l'année 1749', thereby excluding important gains made by Dupleix at the expense of the country powers of the Coromandel Coast before the clash between the two Companies had occurred. In the second place the definitive treaty included, but the preliminary one omitted, the recognition of two of the allies of the English Company among the country powers, Salabat Jang as Subah of the Deccan, and Mohammed Ali as Nawab of the Carnatic.[2]

The attempts which have been made to discover differences of principle between Clive and Sulivan with references to these two documents have not been successful. It has been suggested that Clive wanted a 'Carthaginian' peace, while Sulivan held

[1] Clive, *Letter to the Proprietors of East India Stock* (London, 1764), p. 10.
[2] G. F. de Martens, *Recueil de Traités*, i. 97 and 112.

more moderate views,[1] but the proposals put up by the Company as a basis for negotiations in September 1762 were supported by both Clive and Sulivan, and in any case the definitive treaty which Clive approved was no more 'Carthaginian' than the preliminary treaty which he repudiated. Alternatively, since Clive himself in his *Letter to the Proprietors of East India Stock* (1764) criticized (though only mildly) the recognition given in the peace to the two Indian rulers, this has sometimes been seized on as the cause of conflict between the two men.[2] But this too is untenable, since their recognition occurs, not in the preliminaries, but in the definitive settlement. The truth seems to be that the breach, the culmination of long irritations, originated not from any conflict of principle but from misunderstandings arising in the course of the negotiations and from the exclusion of Clive from participation in the intricate bargaining which took place between the Government and Company about the precise terms to be put forward.

This negotiation was the first in which a general East Indian settlement was negotiated between the French and English Governments instead of between the two Companies. The fact that the Government took on this responsibility was in itself a recognition of the same forces which had led them to intervene in the conflicts between the Companies in India; but the recognition was only a partial one. When abortive negotiations for peace were undertaken the previous year, it had been agreed that the two Companies should as on former occasions deal directly with each other through commissaries;[3] in 1761–2 in settling the differences between the Dutch and English Companies which had arisen out of the war the same method was employed (though in fact there was much informal consultation with the Government),[4] and even on this occasion the Government adopted the attitude that they were conferring a favour on the Company by acting on their behalf and threatened, when they considered the Company pitched its terms too high, not to over-ride it, but to leave it to get what terms it could by direct negotiations. The part played by the Company in the negotiations was, therefore, first to get out a statement of its claims and

---

[1] A. Mervyn Davies, op. cit., pp. 337 seq.
[2] Malcolm, op. cit. ii. 192 seq.   [3] *Grenville Papers*, i. 379.
[4] Home Miscellaneous, vol. 96 *passim*.

then, through a Secret Committee appointed for the purpose, to try to get the Government to adopt them.

Both Clive and Sulivan were concerned in formulating the Company's terms; neither of them was on the Committee which discussed them with the representatives of the Government—the Secretary of State Lord Egremont or (more often) his vigorous and intelligent Under-Secretary Robert Wood.[1] But, while Clive after a time was quite out of touch with the negotiations, Sulivan's absence from them was more apparent than real since the Deputy Chairman, John Dorrien, who sat on the Committee was known to be his close follower, and to consult him constantly.[2] The Company was first approached on the subject of peace terms by the Government in June of 1762, when Lord Egremont and Robert Wood informally consulted the Chairman, Deputy Chairman, and Sulivan and were given a copy of the Company's claims drawn up the year before, supported by further documents.[3] These claims involved the total exclusion of the French from Bengal and the restoration only of those possessions in other parts of India which the French had held before 1745. The minister seems to have told them at once that the claims were excessive and that they could not

[1] Robert Wood, author of the *Ruins of Palmyra*, carried out most of the detailed negotiations with the Company and was in close touch with the representative of the French Court carrying on the London end of the discussions, the Duc de Nivernois. The latter described him as 'homme d'esprit, et de bon esprit, avec qui je suis fort lié. . . . C'est lui qui a conduit toute cette affaire des Indes vis-à-vis la compagnie anglaise.' (*Œuvres posthumes du Duc de Nivernois* (Paris, 1807), ii. 157.)

[2] Clive in a draft memorandum (apparently about the General Court of 15 March 1763) wrote: 'All the world knows the connection between Sulivan and Mr. Dorrien and that the latter took no step without the advice of Sulivan and of consequence that Mr. Sulivan knew from Dorrien everything that passed with the Committee when he was not present and consulted.' (Powis MSS., Box I.)

[3] This and much of our knowledge about the negotiations is obtained from a *North Briton Extraordinary* intended by Wilkes for publication in 1763 at the time of the contest for the Direction of that year, but withheld at the last minute. Press rivals (*The Auditor*, 25 April 1763) asserted that Wilkes had been bought off by Clive, as it contained matter discreditable to him, but this is not the case. It was apparently published in 1765, though no copy appears to survive, and was reproduced in the *London Magazine* of April 1765, pp. 175–81. John Almon (who did not know it had been published) also reproduced it, with minor discrepancies, in his *Correspondence of the Late John Wilkes*, 1805, i. 176–203. It was evidently intended as a defence of T. Rous, the Chairman of the Company, and it prints, or takes extracts from, a considerable amount of semi-official correspondence, of much of which we have no other record. Where it can be checked it is remarkably accurate.

expect the French to accept them. It was not till some six weeks later that the Company was formally approached and a Secret Committee of the Directors was set up to put forward proposals and to negotiate with the Government about them.[1] This Committee consulted Sulivan and Clive as well as at least one other person not on the Direction,[2] but did not succeed in reaching its conclusions till the beginning of September, just in time for the instructions going out to the Duke of Bedford, the English plenipotentiary in Paris. Though Sulivan had tried unsuccessfully to get a minor concession included in an attempt to placate the ministry, they were virtually the same as those unofficially offered to Egremont in June.

At this stage of the proceedings, though Clive was annoyed that he 'was not called upon to give my opinion about a peace for India for months after Mr. Sulivan had been acquainted with it by the ministry although he was no more a director than myself',[3] they were in general agreement about the claims to be put forward. Clive indeed claimed that they were largely based on his suggestions and in August wrote a memorandum to Lord Bute in support of them,[4] which the latter acknowledged civilly but non-committally.[5]

The Government found their proposals extremely unsatisfactory. In sending out instructions to the Duke of Bedford the ministers made no attempt to give the Company's claims more than a modified form, and they informed the directors that their terms were inadmissible as leaving no room for negotiation, while Wood expressed disappointment at not receiving 'a confidential communication of their real expectations'. Nevertheless, the Government would have found it embarrassing to force on the Company a settlement to which it had not agreed, and Wood (supported where it seemed useful by his superior) began to try to bring the Secret Committee to terms before the negotiations with the French were complete and before they were laid before Parliament in November.

It was in the course of these negotiations that differences of opinion began to arise among those responsible for the Com-

---

[1] Court Book 71, p. 98.
[2] *London Magazine*, April 1765; extract from *North Briton Extraordinary*, p. 177.
[3] Draft of a memorandum by Clive [1763]. Powis MSS., Box I.
[4] Quoted Forrest, op. cit. ii. 192–3.
[5] Malcolm, op. cit. ii. 207–8.

pany's side of the negotiation and to spread throughout the Company. It became apparent that Sulivan and his supporters believed that the Company could gain by adopting a more conciliatory attitude towards the Government, while others, of whom Thomas Rous became the nominal leader, were determined to stand firm. By the beginning of October the deadlock was still unbroken, and the news of the contest began to spread in political circles. The Duke of Newcastle, eagerly collecting material for opposition, noted:

I am told from very good hands, that, notwithstanding what has been given out by the Ministry that the E. I. Company are satisfied, the contrary of it is true. Mr. Sullivan [sic] and the Deputy Chairman Mr. Dorient [Dorrien] as creatures of my Lord Bute pretend to be so, but the Chairman Mr. Rouse [sic] and the Company in general are very far from being pleased.[1]

By 20 October no further progress had been made. At this stage the ministry decided to force the issue. On that day Robert Wood saw representatives of the Company and told them they must either come to terms or be left out of the negotiation altogether. Lord Egremont would give them two days in which to produce proposals of an acceptable kind.[2] Just before the time limit they obtained an interview with Egremont and tried to bargain with him. They were then given an official draft to accept or amend within one day. Next day they accepted it with only one modification of significance, which the Government agreed to, and (apparently) with an understanding that other points could be cleared up in the final treaty. The clause agreed to was incorporated in the preliminary treaty signed on 3 November. In accepting this article the Company agreed to the presence of the French in Bengal, but unarmed and for trading purposes only, and the restoration to the French of possessions held by them before the outbreak of hostilities between the two Companies in 1749, not only those held by them before 1745. They did not obtain any provision for the recognition of Salabat Jang and Mohammed Ali.

The news of the concessions which the Secret Committee had

---

[1] Notes of conversation. Add. MS. 32944, f. 30ᵛ.
[2] The evidence here comes from the extract from the *North Briton Extraordinary*, *London Magazine*, loc. cit., pp. 178–9.

made was ill received in the Company when it came out. Clive, whose papers show no trace that he was kept informed of the actions of the Secret Committee after the end of September, was particularly indignant. He wrote:

In September after Mr. Sulivan, Mr. Hume[1] and myself had given the Committee the meeting to consult of these matters, the Court of Directors gave their ultimatum to Lord Egremont which was founded principally on my advice and memorial; the period of the Pronunciation [sic] was fix'd to the year 1744 and the French were to be totally excluded Bengal, and the Committee persevered in their opinion till the middle of October in spight of all the threats of the Ministry to leave the Company to act and negotiate for themselves. At last poor Rous was sent for and after having been scolded and sworn at by Mr. Wood (Lord Egremont's Secretary) and then by his Lordship himself, the articles were consented to be altered as they now stand in the Preliminaries. I wish Sulivan has not been some way accessory to this timid and unpardonable step, being known to be under Ministerial influence.[2]

That this indignation was largely misplaced is made plain in a number of ways; by the general satisfaction expressed a few months later over the terms of the definitive treaty which contained no differences of principle; by the satisfactory outcome of the settlement from the Company's point of view; and from the advantages that soon became apparent (as Sulivan always pointed out when discussing the negotiation) from winning the good will of the Government by concessions on the preliminary terms when it came to discussing modifications of detail in the final terms. When the preliminary treaty had been signed, the change in the relations between the Government and Company became apparent and the Government was soon actively co-operating in drawing up proposed additions to, and amplifications of, the article and in pressing them on their own unwilling plenipotentiary and on the French Government.

The sympathy of the Government, moreover, proved to be of unexpected value, for it was found that in the hurry of the last-minute agreement between the Government and Company a slip in wording had been let through which would have been of considerable value to the French. The one point on which the

---

[1] Abraham Hume, M.P., a prominent proprietor.
[2] Clive to R. Palk, 15 December 1762. Powis MSS.

Government had met the Company at this stage of the negotiations was with regard to the limiting date for the return of the French possessions. In the official draft submitted by Wood to the Secret Committee this had been fixed at the 'Commencement of the present war', a phrase amended to the 'commencement of the present war between the two Companys, viz. in 1749'. The next day those who were preparing the instructions to be sent to Paris remembered that hostilities had preceded any declaration of war, and sending for Rous as Chairman got him to agree on his own responsibility to a change in words to 'before the commencement of hostilities between the two Companies in 1749'. In fact neither of the suggested phrases was satisfactory since Dupleix had obtained valuable acquisitions from the country powers just before the outbreak of hostilities between the two Companies, which neither the Company nor Government were anxious to see in French hands again. This error was almost at once discovered and Rous was much blamed for letting it pass. The co-operation of the Government was, however, at once sought in getting it corrected, and though the French were indignant at what they considered with some justice a change of substance, and though the Duke of Bedford considered the proposed change in date quite inadmissible and at one time despaired of obtaining it, it was finally incorporated in the definitive treaty.[1]

For this happy conclusion both Sulivan and Clive claimed the credit; but it was essentially the outcome of the policy advocated and pursued by Sulivan. It was nevertheless an error of judgement on his part to have let Clive get out of touch with events, since it was inevitable that he should resent his exclusion and be critical of concessions made by others. The misunderstandings about the negotiations had, moreover, two consequences which gravely affected both Clive and the Company. In the first place Clive's indignation about the East Indian negotiations made it impossible for him to give his support to the new administration; he rejected advances from Henry Fox to vote with the Government in the debate on the Preliminaries in

[1] The manuscript evidence is quoted in 'The East India Company and the Peace of Paris', *E.H.R.*, 1947. At one point the attempt seemed likely to break down, but information given to the Duke of Bedford by Isaac da Pinto (a Jewish pamphleteer and writer well known in Paris and in Holland) decided him to stand firm.

December.[1] By joining with the Opposition on this issue he clinched his continued support of them, though he had already expressed so strong a preference for the ministerial side and though circumstances arising in the Company were soon to make ministerial backing so much more important for him. In the second place, out of the ill-will generated during the negotiations a formed opposition to Sulivan and his majority began to grow up in the Company and Clive began to find the temptation to join it almost irresistible. Clive wrote to Vansittart in Bengal:

There is a terrible storm brewing against the next election [of Directors]. Sulivan, who is out of the direction this year, is strongly opposed by Rous and his party and by part, if not all, of the East Indians (particularly the Bengalees) and matters are carried to such lengths that either Sulivan or Rous must give way.[2]

At first he still hesitated to join in. 'I must acknowledge', he said, 'that in my heart I am a well-wisher of Rous, although, considering the great stakes I have in India, it is probable I shall remain neuter';[2] but as this the second and far greater contested election of the Company's new era got under way and the magnitude of the battle began to become apparent he changed his mind. Caution was not a quality likely to withhold him indefinitely. The offensive was more suited to his nature and on 17 February 1763 he announced his adherence to Rous's party; on the two following days he canvassed the City in person and on the 23rd he let it be known that he was prepared to stand for the Direction.[3] The great Civil War of the Company had broken out.

The second of the great contested elections of the Company was far better prepared and hard fought than that of 1758. It was also more wide-reaching in its repercussions. The foundations of the party which challenged Sulivan's supremacy in the Company were laid by the group of returned East Indian servants and those directors and others who, under the nominal leadership of Rous, had revolted against his authoritarian rule. When Clive drew attention to them in November they had already set in train their plan of campaign. They had also

[1] Namier, op. cit. ii. 355.
[2] Quoted Malcolm, op. cit. ii. 197.
[3] L. Sulivan to [Shelburne], 24 February 1763. Bute MSS.

invented their striking and disastrous contribution to the methods of party warfare, the setting up of a large-scale organization to create voting qualifications. For this their command of ready money put them in a highly favourable position, and the Company's stock ledgers enable us to trace the method they employed. They took as their agent the Hon. Richard Walpole,[1] a member of the London banking firm of Cliffe, Walpole, and Clarke, who from November onwards began steadily buying in East India Stock. In January and February he 'split' directly or indirectly £26,500 of stock, thereby creating fifty-three votes. In March, before the Company's books were closed, he was responsible for the creation of sixty more, thereby providing for his clients a bloc of eighty-three voters pledged to support them. When Clive joined the opposition his wealth was available for the same purpose[2] and Sulivan, though confessing himself 'a novice in the business',[3] had to follow suit as best he could. It is not surprising that an unexampled turn-over of Company stock is shown in the Transfer books, that the price of stock rose, and that the holdings of Dutch as well as English proprietors were mobilized for the purposes of the contest.

The vast and complicated machine that was thus rapidly improvised for the service of party warfare was in itself so remarkable and its results on the history of the Company so unfortunate, that it is worth examining in detail. It depended on the activities of several distinct classes of persons whose interest in it was purely professional. First of them were the great managers who undertook to finance and organize the campaign for the various party leaders, presumably in return for some remuneration or other advantage. They were generally bankers or other men of prominence in the City, and they administered large sums partly raised by themselves, partly placed at their disposal by, or borrowed by them on behalf of, their clients. When Clive entered the field he made some use of

---

[1] Son of Horatio, first Baron Walpole and brother of the Hon. Thomas Walpole, M.P., banker. Until 1758 he had been captain of an East Indiaman, but in that year changed to the 'steady and profitable profession of banker'. Home Miscellaneous, 810, f. 66.

[2] Malcolm, op. cit. ii. 211, states that he provided £100,000 for the purpose. I have not been able to check this with any degree of accuracy.

[3] L. Sulivan to Shelburne, 24 February 1763. Bute MSS.

the same firm, Cliffe, Walpole, and Clarke, which the other East Indians used, but he also employed the banking firm of Sir Francis and Robert Gosling,[1] in which his cousin George Clive became a partner the same year. Later his affairs were managed by a group consisting of his three attornies (John Walsh, Luke Scrafton, and his father), and both these banking firms. Sulivan, though in 1764 he used the banking firm of Child and Devon,[2] usually depended on an old Bombay colleague and business associate, Thomas Lane.[3] Lane was not a man of independent wealth, so that in fact Sulivan was running his own campaign through a 'jackal'.

It was not enough to enlist the services and the wealth of these monied men. The money had to be embodied at the right time in East India Stock. This was a particularly urgent problem in 1763 when the organization was in its infancy and when rich interests suddenly entered the field without preparation; but even when the voting strength of parties was already well organized it remained of significance since no banker or other agent wished to keep large sums permanently immobilized in East India Stock. Here the use of the large East India proprietor came in, both those who held the stock as an investment (like Sir Matthew Fetherstonehaugh, M.P., of Uppark, Sussex, or Sir Humphry Morrice, M.P., Controller of the Household, High Steward of Cornwall, and Warden of the Stannaries), and the great jobbers who were willing, no doubt for a consideration, to put their holdings at the service of one of the parties contending. The jobbers were not as active in 1763 as they were later to be. After they had become accustomed to playing their part, they were to show, as in 1766, that when their own personal interests were at stake, they were capable themselves of seizing the initiative.

[1] Later the firm of Gosling and Sharpe of Fleet Street.
[2] So called in the East India Company stock ledger. The partners in the famous bank were in that year Robert Child, Thomas Devon, Robert Lovelace, Robert Dent, and John Church. Hilton Price, *Handbook of London Bankers* (London, 1891), p. 36, says it traded under the name of Robert Child, Esq., and Co.
[3] Thomas Lane had entered the Bombay service in 1747. He resigned the service in 1751, was in business with Sulivan in England after the latter's return, and was also 'ship's husband' or managing owner of several East Indiamen. When Sulivan and he became involved in the crash in East India Stock in 1769, Sulivan indicated that he could not bear any part of the loss. I. Barré to Shelburne, 19 June 1769. Lansdowne MSS.

Farther down the scale were the smaller jobbers and brokers who perhaps could split some stock of their own or to whom a block of stock could be transferred for them to distribute in voting qualifications to trustworthy acquaintances. Finally there were the 'split' voters themselves, a miscellaneous body, but one that in time acquired an element of permanency. These classes between them made up the nucleus of the new, highly centralized and organized production of collusive votes. Side by side with this, there continued (but, with the increased sharpness of party conflict, on a much larger scale than before) the simple 'splitting' of moderate holdings by individuals to their friends or relations. Sulivan described to Lord Shelburne in a hasty scrawl the way in which this simpler system worked. He wrote:

There is no voting by proxy and every proprietor at a contested election swears the stock is his own. Therefore a man who has 1000£ stock and lends a second half of it for a qualification, a Note of Hand is given for the sum it amounts to and he pays it back hereafter, gaining or losing the difference of the market price; others again cast the sum it amounts to at the present price, gives his Note and takes the stock outright, selling him again 500£ stock as the price may prove.[1]

In other words the arrangement might leave either with the 'splitter' or the person to whom it is 'split' the chance of gain and the danger of loss as the result of a change in the prices of stock between the date of transfer and its return after the election.

The first striking features of the contest of 1763 were thus, the introduction of Asiatic wealth into the electoral activities of the Company; the personal struggle between Clive and Sulivan; and the evolution of a cumbrous mechanism for the creation of votes which called into action a number of forces in no way directly concerned with the welfare of the Company and which was to prove a veritable Frankenstein's monster to its creators.

A further feature was, however, of even greater significance. In 1763, for the first time since the struggles of the 'Old' and 'New' Companies, Government and Opposition openly took part in the contests at India House. For the first time the great Whigs now in opposition, the Marquess of Rockingham, the Duke of Portland, Lord Midleton, Lord John Cavendish, and

[1] L. Sulivan to [Shelburne], 24 February 1763. Bute MSS.

others, took up voting qualifications in the Company and went down to India House to cast their votes for a party in the Company. For the first time the Paymaster-General, Henry Fox, put the accumulated funds of his department through its own officials at the service of the rival party to procure them votes.

The reasons for this sudden development are not far to seek. They lay in the first place in the position of the Company as the traditional ally of the Government in the City. In 1763 Bute's Government was peculiarly unpopular there. To the general agitation against the terms of the Peace was added indignation among the 'popular' party at the favourable terms of a recent 'closed' subscription to a government loan and the discomforts always associated with the return to peace after a long period of war. A reverse in a traditional stronghold at this juncture would have been very unpleasant for the Government, and it soon became plain that, although Sulivan and his supporters commanded some wealth and though they could count on the support of much of the 'household troops' and what Sulivan called his 'natural interest',[1] the preponderance of Indian wealth on the other side would probably defeat him unless the Government intervened on his behalf in a more active manner than they had hitherto found necessary. Sulivan made this clear to Lord Shelburne as soon as it was certain that Clive had joined his enemies. He pointed out that, in addition to the general support of the Ministry 'agreeable to practice', he would on this occasion require their assistance in other ways.

> Your Lordship told me you had secured Lady Betty Germain's 25,000£ stock which makes fifty votes. Since I had the honour to see you here a friend acquainted me that through Lord Vere he could obtain her stock. If therefore your Lordship has met with difficulties I beg to know directly. Humphry Morrice has 16,700£, Sir Edward Turner 28,500£, Sir Matthew Featherstonehaugh [sic], 16,000£, Henry Lyell Esqr 14,500£, Marchioness Montandre,[2] 12,000£; these divided into qualifications make a number sufficient to overturn all opposition when added to my own natural interest, but I apprehend it's Government alone that can reach these, and the Ministry's influence

---

[1] L. Sulivan to [Shelburne], 24 February 1763. Bute MSS.
[2] Mary Ann de Spanheim, Marquise de Montandre, a widow residing in Grosvenor Square. Lady Betty Germain and Henry Lyall did not in fact 'split'; Sir Matthew Fetherstonehaugh and the Marquise de Montandre 'split' for Clive; Morrice and Turner for Sulivan (Stock Ledger P).

(as I have mentioned to Lord Bute) extended to all their dependents to procure qualifications for the whole; and if the enemies of Government are united against me because I am a friend of the present Ministry and are suffered to act without a counter-balance I foresee the issue. . . . By Mr. Fox's sending for a list of proprietors (he has one) weeks ago I pleased myself it was to do me essential service for much is in his power. . . . If your Lordship or friends have interest with the bankers they are the men that can do us infinite service. Messrs. Fox and Calcraft's bankers may do great things.[1]

The general considerations that might press the Government to take a more active part than usual were moreover reinforced by the form which the attack on Sulivan soon began to take. His opponents began particularly to attack him as the supporter of administration who had agreed to the unpopular terms of the East Indian Settlement in the Preliminaries to the Peace of Paris. The issue of the peace terms began to assume a prominent part in election propaganda (usually in a highly garbled form) and as early as 16 February his opponents raised it in the Court of Directors under the guise of exonerating Rous for responsibility for it.[2] Though Sulivan and his majority among the directors succeeded in blocking the motion by adjourning the Court, they could not permanently stifle it and at the beginning of March ten proprietors, including one of the returned Bengal servants (Edward Holden Cruttenden) and two of Clive's agents (Francis Gosling and John Waish), demanded a General Court for the same purpose and the directors reluctantly summoned it for 15 March.[3] It was obvious that in the debate which would arise at this Court the Government, as well as Sulivan, was likely to be attacked. Indeed, one of their City agents warned Lord Bute of this danger as soon as he heard that a General Court was likely to be called. He counselled that 'Your Lordship's friends should be prepared and proper speakers provided' lest 'in their frantic rage they should attack Government'.[4]

It seems certain that it was this last consideration which finally decided the Government that there was no alternative to large-scale intervention. Before this development Sulivan's

[1] L. Sulivan to [Shelburne], 24 February 1763. Bute MSS.
[2] Court Book 71, p. 301.   [3] Ibid., p. 320, 2 March 1763.
[4] Joseph Salvador to Bute, 25 February 1763. Bute MSS.

friends in the ministry had been causing him some uneasiness by their slowness to take action[1] and they had, in fact, been trying to avoid the conflict by employing an unofficial intermediary in an attempt to win Clive over to some kind of compromise,[2] while similar efforts were being made by those within the Company to detach Rous from the opposition.[3] Now that both these had failed they came out into the open in support of Sulivan. On 3 and 5 March respectively Henry Fox and Lord Shelburne took out their voting qualifications. Their action was in the nature of a gesture and to set the example to government supporters, a number of whom who had never before concerned themselves in the affairs of the Company, hastened to follow in their train. Even more important were the resources which the ministry could call on for the creation of votes. Richard, Lord Howe, M.P., one of the Lords of the Admiralty, obtained £13,500 stock from two proprietors and split it in his own name; Sir Humphry Morrice handed over his own holding of £16,500, as did also Paul Methuen, M.P., his smaller one to a government clerk, William Cholwich of the Six Clerks' Office, to split in the same way. Most important of all was the use which Henry Fox was prepared to make of the resources of the Pay Office. At least £19,000 of stock was purchased on his behalf and managed by two trusted followers of his, John Calcraft, Assistant-Commissary General, and a humbler servant, John Powell, a clerk at the Pay Office. When the splitting campaign of the party was complete nearly half of the votes created by the centralized organization set up for the purpose was provided by the Government.

The appearance of the ministry in this new and prominent role led immediately to a similar move on the part of the parliamentary opposition. Though the enemies of government in the City had been already ranged with those challenging Sulivan's power, there has hitherto been no sign that Clive's parliamentary allies were prepared to take up his cause. Now

---

[1] L. Sulivan to [Shelburne], 24 February 1763. Bute MSS.

[2] Copy of letter from Joseph Salvador to Clive enclosed with a letter from Salvador to Bute, 25 February 1765. Ibid.

[3] L. Sulivan to [Shelburne], 24 February 1763. 'Those I depend upon were frightened and kindly took upon themselves to seek Mr. Rous and picture to him his situation, sent him [sic] to break those connections, promising if he did, their endeavours with me that I would suffer him to continue in the Direction.' Ibid.

two days after Henry Fox and his henchmen had taken up their qualifications, the Duke of Portland and Lord Midleton took up theirs from one of Clive's agents; by 8 March the whole opposition group following the Duke of Newcastle had decided to make the issue a challenge to administration. The time to make new qualifications was short, since the books closed in two days, but Sir Matthew Fetherstonehaugh put his holding of £16,500 at the disposal of Robert Cliffe, and a number of leaders took out their voting qualifications. By 8 March the Duke of Newcastle, with a list of qualified proprietors before him, was writing letters to political supporters, not excluding the Bishops[1] to whom he had given preferment in the days of his power, asking them to exercise their vote in the Company in the support of Clive and his party. By 10 March when the books closed both parties, with the aid of their parliamentary supporters, had strained their resources to the utmost in the creation of votes.

The results of these efforts are of some interest. The ramifications of the system make it impossible to give a comprehensive account of the votes thus created. The small-scale 'splitters' leave in the Company's books no evidence to which of the parties they owed their loyalty, and the total effect of their efforts is not negligible. But the activities of the central machinery of each party can be traced with reasonable accuracy and it shows that over 220 votes were created by Clive and his allies and only about 160 votes by Sulivan's party. Of Sulivan's votes over 63 were provided from the holdings of big proprietors tapped by government influence, and at least 38 from funds made available by the Pay Office, so that about 100 of the 160 were the products of direct government intervention. Of the 220 or more votes created by Clive's party, no more than 33 appear to have been provided by their parliamentary allies. The remainder were procured by their own resources, chiefly from those of the East Indians and predominantly of course from those of Clive. At least 56 were provided from other sources, but, making allowances for arrangements which cannot be

---

[1] The Bishop of Ely sent a reply through the Bishop of Norwich that he was always ready to obey Newcastle's commands 'but that in this particular there is a kind of management which he cannot approve and that the contrivance for splitting votes seems not very consistent with his station and character; and therefore hopes you will excuse him.' Add. MS. 32947, ff. 191 seq.

traced, Malcolm's statement that Clive 'split' £100,000 of stock may not be too grossly exaggerated.

But, great as were the efforts of the campaigners, it is necessary not to exaggerate their effectiveness. The total created by both sides can hardly have exceeded 450. In the General Court of 15 March (an unusually large one at that date) 657 proprietors voted and it was thought that there were quite 800 present. At the election of directors itself the highest vote recorded (for a double-listed candidate) was no less than 1,240. Among the true proprietors every kind of influence, persuasion by personal canvass, and, not least, propaganda and speeches had effect, and in number they prevailed.

The course of the contest for which the forces were deployed is itself an illustration of this fact. The contest fell into two parts; the preliminary clash in the General Court summoned to exonerate Rous, and the election itself. The General Court was employed entirely for election purposes. It was the first of the great General Courts whose debates were sometimes to rival those of the House of Commons in the interest they aroused. The Government was represented among the speakers by Robert Wood, M.P., the Under-Secretary who had handled the Peace negotiations, and by Peregrine Cust, M.P., the brother of the Speaker. Clive, Sulivan, and Rous all spoke at length. Rous defended his conduct in the negotiations, announced his pride in having Clive as his ally, and denied that he had sought for the conflict in which he found himself engaged. His opponents deplored aimless recriminations about the past and pointed to the successful outcome of the peace negotiations. Clive disclaimed any desire to dominate the Company and assured the proprietors that if elected he would not seek election to the Chair. To the joy of the opposition, Rous was on a ballot exonerated by 359 to 298 votes.[1] Clive wrote jubilantly:

That tremendous day is over. I need not be particular about it; you will have it from many hands. I should imagine there were present not less than eight hundred proprietors. Numbers of neutral people went off; and no small number of our friends, thinking our majority was so great that there was no occasion for their presence. Indeed upon the

[1] Court Book 71, p. 337. There is a report of the Court in the *London Chronicler*, 22–24 March 1763, p. 287.

holding up of hands, I thought we were at least two to one. This is really a great victory, considering we had the united strength of the whole ministry against us.[1]

This success left Clive and his allies confident of success at the election next month, and this confidence they passed on to their parliamentary allies. The Duke of Newcastle, thanking Clive for an annotated list of voters, wrote, 'I am glad to see by it that we have a good majority'.[2] But though no new votes could be created and the only form of electioneering that could still be carried out was personal canvassing and propaganda, the conclusions they drew from their success were misleading. Far greater numbers turned out for the election than for the debate in the General Court and among these proprietors the influence of Sulivan proved to be still predominant. Rival 'House' and 'Proprietors' ' lists were duly drawn up, there was a brush on the Direction as to which list should enjoy the prestige of the former title, a brush in which Sulivan and his majority of directors won. Fourteen candidates were 'double-listed' without protest, including Henry Crabb Boulton who had been an active supporter of Sulivan but now was tending towards Rous, John Boyd, who remained loyal to his leader, and John Manship, the outstanding independent of the future. Included among the ten other names on the Proprietors' list were Clive, Rous, the Hon. Thomas Walpole, M.P., the banker, and two returned Company servants, Edward Holden Cruttenden from Bengal and Thomas Saunders, formerly Governor of Madras. Sulivan's list consisted for the most part of names already familiar in the Court of Directors. The election itself took place under a barrage of propaganda from the Government and Opposition press. The result was a triumph for Sulivan and the Government and a humiliating defeat for Clive and his allies in the Company and for the parliamentary opposition. 'The highest in Lord Clive's list was twenty below the lowest in Sulivan's', Newcastle's late Secretary of the Treasury wrote to him, adding with a touch of professional scorn 'Lord Clive must have been strangely misled in his calculations.'[3] The first round had gone against Clive, and the parliamentary Opposition had failed to make a breach in the ministerial stronghold in the City.

---

[1] Quoted Malcolm, op. cit. ii. 212–13.   [2] Add. MS. 32948, f. 69.
[3] J. West to Newcastle, 14 April 1763. Quoted Namier, op. cit. ii. 356.

V

THE STRUGGLE FOR MASTERY: THE SECOND PHASE

THE violent conflict which broke out within the Company in 1763 was obviously not of a kind to be solved by a single victory. The contest of that year proved, in fact, but the first round of a long battle, wearing and destructive to the contestants and fatal to whatever prospects the Company may have had of meeting the demands made upon it by its extending responsibilities in India. The history of past dissensions within the Company had also made it clear that sooner or later issues would arise which would extend the arena of contest outside it and into the field of national politics, particularly at a time when opposition to government was strong and when the governments were fluctuating and weak.

So far as the Government was concerned, on the other hand, it might have been expected that, after the triumph of Sulivan and his party, they would withdraw from their new participation in East Indian politics. The particular issue which had caused their incursion was over (the directors a few weeks after the election set the example to the City of voting an address in favour of the Peace); the parliamentary opposition groups had fallen back into disunion and uncertainty, and Bute's Government itself had given way to that of George Grenville, in which, with the disappearance of Bute himself and, the following September, of Lord Shelburne (who was shifting his allegiance to the camp of the elder Pitt), only Henry Fox, now Lord Holland, remained of those who had been active in the Company's affairs at the time of the 1763 election.[1]

At first these expectations seemed to be realized. The relations between State and Company lapsed into their accustomed form. George Grenville at the Treasury for a time had no more than normal relations with the Chairman and directors of the Company. These were chiefly concerned with the steps necessary to preserve the national credit during the first world credit

---

[1] Lord Sandwich was also still in office, but he had apparently not taken an active part in the 1763 election.

crisis which originated in Amsterdam in this year, spread to the European markets, and threatened that of London. The credit of the Company (as of many private houses) was thought to be in danger, as it was to be again in the next great credit crisis of 1772, the Treasury gave it their assistance in negotiating a short-term loan from the Bank of England,[1] and with this and good management (including it would seem the courage and generosity of Sulivan in pledging his private fortune)[2] the crisis was over so far as the Company was concerned by November.[3]

But the return to normality was only temporary. About the same time events were in progress which were to bring the Government once again into East Indian politics and to lead the Grenville Administration to much the same kind of intervention in the election of directors of 1764 and the activities leading up to it, as Bute's Administration had undertaken the year before. The mere fact that another intervention followed so soon after the last was in itself significant. The circumstances of this new intervention were, moreover, such as to make it less easy for the ministry to withdraw from the Company's affairs after the election was over, than it had been in 1763. The new intervention arose out of the parliamentary situation of Clive and the fate of his *jagir*.

When Clive took the plunge and risked all on defeating Sulivan at the 1763 election, he knew the stakes for which he was playing. Not a fortnight after their victory his opponents exacted the penalty. A general letter went out to Bengal on 27 April 1764 ordering the Governor and Council to stop all payments of Clive's *jagir*, to retain the monies in a separate fund, and to send home accounts of all sums already paid out to him.[4] Clive's response was immediate and violent, and his struggles to save his property dominate the politics of the Company for the next twelve months and continued to disturb them till 1768, affecting radically its capacity to deal with the problems facing it in Bengal. They also brought the Government back into the internal politics of the Company.

[1] J. Salvador to C. Jenkinson, 21 October 1763. N. S. Jucker, *The Jenkinson Papers 1760–1766*, 1949, p. 209.
[2] Stephen Sulivan to W. Hastings, 20 January 1779, seems to allude to this occasion. Add. MS. 29142, f. 413ᵛ.
[3] J. Salvador to C. Jenkinson, 22 November 1763. Jucker, op. cit., pp. 220–1.
[4] Bengal Despatches, ii. 665.

As soon as Clive knew of the Directors' instructions he wrote privately to Vansittart in Bengal and to other members of Council, asking for their personal support, and publicly to them in their official capacity, threatening them with legal proceedings if they obeyed their instructions.[1] There were, however, only two ways in which he could force the Company to resume payments to him: by suing the Company in Chancery (a proceeding the length and uncertainty of which was notorious and emphasized on this occasion by the wide diversity of eminent legal opinions obtained by the two parties),[2] or by seeking redress in Parliament. It was on the second of these resources that Clive had boasted that he could rely, thanks to his parliamentary connexions, and it was to his parliamentary allies that he now turned. But whatever would have been their response had they been in power (and there is no evidence that they would have been ready to espouse his cause in Parliament) they were now in opposition, and pleaded complete incapacity to help him. Lord Hardwicke, late Lord Chancellor, reported with professional detachment a call from Clive and his father giving an account of their plight. 'I had this from Lord Clive and his father who called upon me to discourse about it; but they either could not or were not willing to tell me what pretence of right was alleged for this proceeding. . . . This probably will produce a suit in Equity'.[3] Neither Lord Bessborough, brother-in-law of the Duke of Devonshire, nor the Duke of Newcastle, to whom these approaches were reported, proved more helpful,[4] while Pitt told him that it was hopeless to raise it in Parliament 'from the violence of party'.[5] Clive had said he wanted to be not against but with administration. He now found himself in opposition and just at the time when the support of the ministry would be most useful.

His problem was then what to do next. His answer has been obscured by the misdating of a letter in the published correspondence of George Grenville which would make it appear that Clive was already in touch with administration as early as

[1] Forrest, *Clive*, ii. 197–8.
[2] Their opinions were read in the General Court of 2 May 1764. Court Book 73, pp. 34 seq.
[3] Hardwicke to Newcastle, 30 April 1763. Add. MS. 32948, ff. 189–189ᵛ.
[4] Namier, op. cit. ii. 357.
[5] *Grenville Papers*, ii. 184.

April 1763.[1] In fact there is no evidence that he was drawing towards them until the beginning of November. Up to the end of September he appears to have thought it likely that negotiations for the re-entry of his friends into the administration would prove successful and was prepared to await their return. Only after this hope failed are there unmistakable signs that he began bargaining with Grenville, offering the ministry the support of his group in Parliament in exchange for their good offices in the matter of his *jagir*.[2] By the middle of November his shift in allegiance was affecting Lord Sandwich's activities in by-elections.[3] At the beginning of December Horace Walpole reported, with his usual combination of inside information and picturesque exaggeration, 'The Ministry have bought off Lord Clive with a bribe that would frighten the King of France himself; they have given him back his £25,000 a year.'[4] A few days later Clive was lamenting (also with some exaggeration) that he was 'discountenanced and hated by the party I have abandoned, as much as I was before respected and esteemed'.[5]

The return he obtained for his *volte face*—not the last that he had to make in the interest of his Indian wealth—was not indeed parliamentary intervention. His tentative suggestions that he might seek redress in Parliament met with no response

---

[1] There is a letter from Charles Jenkinson to George Grenville printed there (ii. 46–48) and quoted in Namier, op. cit. ii. 357, which is dated 20 April 1763. From internal evidence, however, it is clear that the correct date is 1764. Among the points which make this clear are: (1) it is said of Sulivan that he 'will do all he can to obstruct'; this represents the position after his defeat in 1764 but not when he was at the height of his power in 1763. (2) Clive is asking particulars of Henry Strachey's character with a view to employing him. Strachey was appointed Clive's secretary to go out to India with him in 1764. (3) Jenkinson will 'get Col. Draper talked to, I hope with success'. Draper was the Duke of Bedford's candidate for the red riband who was passed over for Clive in 1764 much to his annoyance (*Correspondence of John, Fourth Duke of Bedford*. Ed. Lord John Russell, 1842, iii. 261–2). (4) Finally, Jenkinson mentions a protest he received before from Long and Payne, West India merchants, about naval interference with commerce in the Spanish main. In a letter from Grenville to Jenkinson, 29 April 1764 (Jucker, op. cit., pp. 290–1) Grenville takes up this subject, saying he forgot to mention it in his last letter.

[2] *Grenville Papers*, ii. 160–1.   [3] Namier, op. cit. ii. 361.

[4] *The Letters of Horace Walpole*, ed. Mrs. Paget Toynbee (1904), v. 403. He added that John Walsh 'has behaved nobly—he said he could not in conscience vote with administration, and would not vote against Lord Clive who chose him; he has therefore offered to resign his seat'. If so, he overcame his scruples and was soon in full support of Grenville's Administration.

[5] *Grenville Papers*, ii. 183.

from Grenville,[1] and throughout the very considerable efforts made by the Treasury to help him, they took care not to commit themselves to taking up his cause in Parliament. The public opinion which was later to harden against East Indian wealth was already taking form; such an intervention would in any case have been shocking to eighteenth-century susceptibilities and, for a variety of reasons, it is improbable that any administration would have dared to enforce Clive's case by parliamentary action since the Courts were open to him. The only way in which Grenville could help him, therefore, was by influence in, and pressure on, the East India Company. It was in exerting this pressure that the ministry followed its predecessor into the maze of East India Company politics.

In the first instance Grenville seems to have done no more than promise to act as a mediator between Clive and the directors. At Grenville's request Clive laid down his terms. He asked for the enjoyment of the *jagir* for ten or twelve years for himself or his heirs, provided the lands from which it was derived were still in the Company's possession; in return he was prepared to abandon his freedom of action in East Indian affairs as completely as he offered to give up his independence of action in Parliament. Not only did he assure Grenville that 'my poor services, such as they are, shall be dedicated for the rest of my days to the King, and my obligations to you always acknowledged, whether in or out of power',[2] but he added 'If these conditions are fulfilled, I do promise, Sir, that I never will give any opposition to the present or any other Court of Directors, and never will interfere in any of their affairs directly or indirectly'.[3]

Grenville was by no means certain of the success of his attempt, though Clive was more hopeful. The Minister proved to be right. He persuaded Sulivan and his follower John Dorrien to bring Clive's propositions before the Court of Directors (they probably took some malicious pleasure in informing the Court that 'if this agreement takes place Lord Clive then promises upon his honour to give the present Court of Directors no trouble at any future election', though a later minute notes that this assurance formed no part of the terms

---

[1] *Grenville Papers*, ii. 184.   [2] Ibid. 183.
[3] Ibid. 161.

but was 'a matter of conversation only') but they evidently took no measures to persuade the Court to adopt them. On 14 December the terms were unanimously rejected.[1] No doubt Sulivan took Clive's offer as a sign of weakness and believed that he could stand out for better ones. He may have felt that his position was now so strong in the Company that he could stand out against an opposition even if it had Ministerial support. But if so, he was assuming that no catastrophe befell the Company. With Bengal in its disorganized state this was not a safe assumption. Within a month bad news from India and the measures necessary to deal with it had suddenly and drastically weakened his position.

When the negotiations for the Peace and the battles of the 1763 election were over, Sulivan and the Court of Directors, over which he held sway, had concerned themselves at home chiefly with the maintenance of the Company's credit, and abroad with the attempt to restore order in the administration of Bengal. In handling the difficulties which arose from the anomalous relations of the Nawab of Bengal and the Company and the wild disorganization of the Company's servants and their hangers-on, Sulivan dealt probably as well as any distant authority could. He retained his faith in Vansittart and heaped on him (as he was apt to do with his friends) rewards both of money and power, and he supported him loyally, as he was to do his greater successor Warren Hastings, when he thought he alone was in a position to form a judgement. On the other hand, he was by no means uncritical, and the General Letters sent out to Bengal under his orders are marked by common sense, careful attention to the information sent home, a sound idea of the Company's responsibilities to its Indian allies, and a vigorous demand for orderly administration in the spheres both of commerce and government. The same letters bear witness to the collapse of organization there; and the combination of an untenable division of authority between the Nawab and the Company, and a sovereign power too remote from the scene to send out orders that were still relevant when they arrived, made a mockery of the attempts to deal from England with the crises of these years.

Vansittart's deposition in 1760 of the Nawab set up by Clive (Mir Jafar) in favour of still another claimant, Mir Kasim,

[1] Court Book 72, pp. 238 and 242.

had been something of a shock, but the ease with which the revolution was achieved and the financial gains to the Company which accompanied it reconciled the directors, though they warned their servants that the Company had a reputation which must be shaken by such violent changes.[1] Throughout 1763 they were uneasy on a number of grounds, but particularly at the increasing friction between the Nawab and the Bengal Government about the private trade carried on duty free by the Company's servants and their agents, and by the dissensions on Vansittart's council which came to focus on the same issue. At the beginning of 1764 the letters from Bengal brought them news that these problems had reached a crisis, and that Vansittart's council were in open revolt against his attempt to reach an agreement on private trade with the Nawab. To this revolt the directors decided that only one response was possible. They promptly dismissed four senior servants, all men of some reputation in the Company and one of them, John Johnstone (of whom much was to be heard in the future), with powerful relatives and connexions there.[2] Other disciplinary action was also taken and in choosing a successor for Vansittart (a matter that came up at the same time) a servant recently moved from Bombay, one John Spencer, was put over the heads of claimants of much greater seniority in Bengal.[3]

Sulivan, in view of the circumstances of his own rise to power, must have realized the degree to which these actions would strengthen the opposition in the Company. Worse, however, was to come. Just as a strong letter had been drafted incorporating these decisions, further news reached England that the Nawab had taken up arms, that Mir Jafar was likely to be restored, that Vansittart himself was returning to England on grounds of health (enriched as Clive had been before him by gifts from the Nawabs he had assisted, though less skilful than Clive in collecting his gains and procuring their remittance to England), and that, in short, 'Bengal is again become a scene of bloodshed and confusion'.[4]

---

[1] Bengal Despatches, ii. 346–7, 7 October 1761.

[2] Major John Carnac, Peter Amyatt, second of Council, John Johnstone, tenth of Council, and William Hay, eleventh of Council. Others were suspended or reprimanded. Warren Hastings was declared free of blame. (Court Book 72, pp. 271 seq.)   [3] Ibid., p. 296, 1 February 1764.

[4] Bengal Despatches, ii. 782, 9 February 1764.

The reactions among the proprietors of the Company on the receipt of this news were, not unnaturally, strong. The Company's stock had already begun to sag in December when news of the Bengal troubles began to reach England from private sources. In January, when the directors were concerned with the dismissal of senior servants, uneasiness grew; at the beginning of February, when news of Mir Kasim's resort to arms became public, the uneasiness rose to alarm and even to panic.

It was these events which gave Clive his chance, and he was not the man to miss it. At first there is no sign that he aimed at more than building up a strong opposition against the directors, taking advantage of the general alarm and the anger of the friends of the disgraced Bengal servants. On 15 February nine proprietors asked for a General Court to consider 'the present dangerous and critical state of the Company's affairs in Bengal'.[1] The names of those making the demand are significant. They include Sir Francis Gosling and Luke Scrafton—men already handling much of Clive's business—a former Bengal servant, Edward Holden Cruttenden, who had been working with Clive in 1763, and two supporters of John Johnstone, Governor George Johnstone, his brother, and Lord Elibank, his uncle, representing the group (Scotsmen to a man) whom they were organizing on their kinsman's behalf.[2] The Court met on 27 February,[3] was numerously attended, fully reported in the press, and of inordinate length. Two adjournments were necessary before a vote was taken on 1 March. The attack on the directors took the form of a general criticism of policy in Bengal (somewhat hampered by the unwillingness of the Opposition to alienate Vansittart whose wealth might be expected to give him some importance in Company politics when he reached

[1] Court Book 72, p. 313.
[2] John Johnstone was one of a large family of brothers, sons of Sir James Johnstone of Westerhall, and of his wife Barbara Murray of Elibank. The most notable of the brothers were William, who married the heiress of the Pulteney fortune and changed his name, John himself, who had fought at Plassey, survived the Black Hole, and was said to have made a fortune of £300,000 by the time he left India, and George, who went early to sea, achieved some repute as a naval officer, rising to the rank of Commodore in commanding a squadron in 1780, was Governor of West Florida 1763, one of the Commissioners for negotiating with the Americans in 1778, and M.P. for many years. (See C. L. Johnstone. *History of the Johnstones 1191–1909*, pp. 175–81. For Lord Elibank see correspondence quoted by A. C. Murray, *The Five Sons of Bare Betty*, 1936.)
[3] Court Book 72, p. 327.

home). They inveighed against the supersession of senior servants by those moved in from other Presidencies, and the issue finally crystallized into a vote to refer back to the directors their decision to appoint John Spencer to the Government of Bengal. Throughout these long, excited, and thickly attended Courts the directors managed to keep their control though only by a narrow margin—they had taken the precaution to 'split' some stock a few days beforehand[1] though the votes so created made up but a fraction of the support they mobilized—and when the vote was taken they won it by the narrow majority of forty-eight.

Meantime the Opposition had been maturing a more far-reaching plan. The very next day nine proprietors asked for yet another General Court, and once again much can be deduced from the names of those calling for it.[2] At their head was the name of Clive himself, supported by three of his closest personal followers; once again the family of John Johnstone is represented and (a significant addition) there appears also the name of a prominent Jewish financier of the time, Joseph Salvador, who had been an active agent of the Treasury in the City under the Bute Administration and was now in close touch with both Grenville and Charles Jenkinson, the Secretary of the Treasury. The Court was called for 12 March and well before that date it became apparent that those calling it intended to put forward a proposal that Clive himself should go out and quell the disorders in Bengal (a proposal certain to be popular with proprietors anxious about the value of their stock) and that in return he should demand a favourable settlement of his claims to his *jagir* and a Court of Directors friendly to him and to the interests in the Company for the time being allied to him. It also became apparent that this plan had the support of the Treasury, if indeed their agent Salvador had not suggested it, and that they were prepared to mobilize all the ministerial forces they could in support of it.

The scheme with its two sides was complete in principle at least some days before 6 March, when Salvador referred to it in a letter to Jenkinson.[3] It involved action in three stages; first, the raising of the suggestion in the General Court of 12

---

[1] Stock Ledger Q.　　　　　　　　　　　　[2] Court Book 72, p. 335.
[3] Jucker, op. cit., pp. 270–1.

March that Clive should go back to Bengal with supreme military and civil power, and an indication from him that he could only accept office on certain terms. Next, a contest at the election of directors in April, at which not only should all forces be mobilized but the proprietors should be made to realize that Clive's acceptance of office depended on the result; and finally, after the election, the settling of terms on the *jagir* with, it was hoped, a friendly Court of Directors as well as a favourable General Court. The drawing up of a strong 'Proprietors' list' for the election was considered as important as a successful issue to the first General Court. Well before the latter, negotiations for the drawing up of the list had begun, and here too the ministry was closely concerned. Salvador made arrangements for Clive and others to meet Grenville,[1] asked for an assurance that, if a good list were formed, they could rely on 'a full exertion of our strength',[2] and reported to Jenkinson on 7 March that there had been a meeting of opposition supporters consisting of 'several gentlemen of weight and a numerous meeting, yet not such a one as that I think they can succeed unless Mr. Grenville gives us a head'.[3]

This support, it appears, they obtained. Jenkinson had already been bringing pressure to bear on ministerial supporters to qualify, and when 'splitting' for the crucial Court of 12 March began in earnest four days beforehand, the clerks of the Post Office and other government departments, and the employees of the Customs and Excise were pressed to take up qualifications.[4] The support which the Treasury thus organized for the Company Opposition was not dissimilar from that which it had on various occasions provided for the directors. But, as in 1763, it was much more intensive than in the past. A wide range of government supporters and clients were persuaded to qualify, and on this occasion, when the battle was longer drawn out and new 'splits' were made and new qualifications taken up before each of the significant General Courts, the Treasury made further contributions at each stage of the contest. As in 1763, the ministerial intervention was not confined to the Treasury. On 13 March, too late for the first General Court but in time for the election and the later courts, Henry Fox (now Lord

---

[1] Ibid., p. 272.
[3] Ibid., p. 272.
[2] Ibid., pp. 270–1.
[4] Ibid., pp. 271 and 281.

Holland) and his agent in such business, John Powell of the Pay Office, made the Pay Office contribution to the cause of the friends of the new ministry, as they had the year before to their opponents, the friends of the old one.[1] Their direct contribution was less than it had been a year before when John Calcraft (now with Shelburne in opposition) was working with them and far less than it was to be in 1766 when Lord Holland's own speculative interests were at stake, but between them they created eighteen votes in addition to any influence they may have exercised indirectly. At least one other minister, Lord Sandwich, then Secretary of State, gave evidence of his personal interest in the cause and was able to make some small contribution of 'split' votes.[2]

A comparison of the activities of both government and opposition interests in the East India disputes of 1763 and 1764 brings out some interesting parallels and contrasts. The part played by the ministry, though not dissimilar, is different in two respects. On the one hand the ministry in 1764 took much less part in 'splitting' than in 1763. Indeed the only big contribution it made directly to the 'splitting' campaign was the sum provided by Lord Holland from the Pay Office funds. Apart from this its agents confined their electioneering activities to rounding up supporters, and exhorting them to qualify and to vote for the Company opposition and its motions. Nor did many men of prominence in the ministry this year take up voting qualifications and register their vote as a testimony to their sympathies. Lord Sandwich and Lord Holland were the only ministers who qualified at this time.[3] On the other hand, in 1764 the Treasury played a far more active part in organizing the opposition in the Company, in planning its policy, and in choosing those to be put forward as directors than it had before. This fact may have been due only to the motley nature of the Company opposition, but there also seem to be signs of some sense of responsibility on the part of the Treasury for obtaining a fairly competent and reputable list of candidates if they were to give it their support.

If the part played by the ministry in the two elections differed

[1] Stock Ledger Q.
[2] Through Robert Jones, M.P., his man of business. See below, p. 124, n. 2.
[3] Stock Ledger Q.

only in detail, that of the opposition interests differed in kind. In 1763 it was fear of the opposition which led the ministry to extend so widely the field of its activities. In 1764 most of the Opposition took no part whatever in the dispute. The Newcastle connexion, whatever Clive might say of them to Grenville, showed no desire to pursue a vendetta against him. Indeed some of them who had most actively aided him in 1763 came to his assistance again in the same way. On 13 March, for instance, directly after the first General Court, Sir Matthew Fetherstonehaugh, who had split his large holding for him in 1763, split £15,500 for him again.[1] The only elements of the Opposition which concerned themselves in favour of the directors and therefore against the ministry were Lord Shelburne and his immediate followers, Colonel Isaac Barré and John Calcraft, who remained loyal to their connexion with Sulivan.[2] Shelburne himself took out a voting qualification on 3 March; Barré in time for the later Courts, and John Calcraft created fifteen 'split' votes on 25 February and fifteen more on 2 March, while both Barré and Calcraft were active participants in some of the General Courts.

An analysis of the 'splitting' activities of the two sides over these series of Courts shows, therefore, less direct contribution from those not normally concerned with the Company's politics than in 1763. It also shows that those in control of the Company had succeeded in finding means, temporarily at least, of offsetting the effects of East Indian wealth. Though the difficulties of assessing accurately the number of fictitious votes created are as great in 1764 as in 1763, enough is clear to show that with all the resources which Clive and his allies in the Company could call on, there was little difference between the total results produced by the efforts of the two sides. Neither can have produced much over 200 votes and though the number created by the opposition organization

[1] Among the Duke of Newcastle's papers (Add. MS. 33031, ff. 69 seq) there is a list of certain proprietors 'at the shutting [of the books] for Christmas 1763' nearly all with the names of those who might apply to them. There is no evidence in the Powis MSS. or elsewhere that anything was done about them.

[2] Sulivan wrote to Shelburne a letter of sympathy and enthusiastic support when he heard reports of his resignation. (September 1763, Lansdowne MSS.) Colonel Barré's activity in East India affairs was believed by his opponents to arise in part at least from a desire for office in India now that he was without a place. (e.g. John Walsh to Clive, 5 April 1765. Powis MSS.)

certainly seems to have exceeded that produced by Sulivan's machine the difference was not great, probably no more than 10 to 20 votes. The explanation of this seems to lie partly in the pains which had been taken to mobilize supporters among the directors, ships' husbands, and other 'household troops' and among those Company servants and their supporters who had reason for gratitude to Sulivan since he had come into power, but chiefly because he had brought into action the great resources of a few great bankers and brokers to offset the wealth which Clive could command. In particular he had succeeded, by means of which we know nothing, in harnessing to his cause Thomas Devon, the active partner in the great banking firm of Child, from whose resources £21,000 stock were provided for the creation of 42 votes.[1] The only other large-scale providers of stock for this purpose were Captain Samuel Hough, an old supporter of Sulivan (formerly Master Attendant of Marine at Bombay, and later a prominent member of the 'shipping' interest), who split directly and through an intermediary £14,000 stock; J. Berrow, broker, who provided £9,500; Sir Humphry Morrice (who had supported him in the previous year and who now split £9,000), and John Calcraft whose splitting of £15,000 has already been referred to. A considerable number of medium-scale proprietors, however, also played their part.

On the opposition side the provision of stock for splitting was more concentrated. The resources provided by Clive and controlled by himself and his agents totalled something over £40,000;[2] only three other men, Sir Matthew Fetherstone-haugh (£15,000), John Powell of the Pay Office (£8,000), and John Walsh (£7,000), split more than £5,000. It is noteworthy that there was no solid opposition to the directors from the returned Company servants, as in the previous year. It is also noteworthy that Clive's most active supporters with connexions among the Company's servants, the Johnstone group, could not then provide much stock for splitting. Their contribution was the provision of numbers of safe supporters for Clive and his

---

[1] This is the sum that can be traced from the Company's stock ledgers. John Walsh believed that he had split £30,000 for them. (John Walsh to Clive, 14 February 1765. Powis MSS.)

[2] By the end of the year Clive's holdings totalled £43,000. (G. Clive to Clive, 21 November 1764. Ibid.)

agents to equip with votes. At least thirty-four voters were provided from this source.[1]

To conclude this comparison of the campaign of 1763 and 1764; while two of the public men of prominence who had been active in the first contest, Henry Fox and Shelburne, continued their activities in the second and were to play, in their different ways, even more prominent parts in the future, three new figures entered the arena in 1764; George Grenville, Lord Sandwich, and Charles Jenkinson. Of these three George Grenville was destined to be of less future importance than the others. After the fall of his ministry in 1765 he was never again in power. Moreover in power or in opposition, he was careful to limit his interpositions into the Company's affairs to occasions on which they might serve an immediate political end. His main, if not his only, purpose in undertaking the intervention of 1764 was to achieve the preservation of Clive's *jagir* and thus ensure his parliamentary support. When the crucial General Court was drawing near in which the *jagir* was to be considered he wrote to Jenkinson 'I need not tell you how much I wish Lord Clive's success in everything that is reasonable';[2] he expressed anxiety that Clive should take no steps without the benefit of his friends' advice and Clive himself professed to have been guided more by Grenville's counsel than by that of all his other friends put together.[3] Though in the main 1764 was a success for the ministry and for Clive, the victory was not certain enough to allow Grenville to withdraw his forces from the Company. Nevertheless, when John Walsh, making arrangements for the 1765 election, suggested that Grenville might follow the example of some of his colleagues and nominate for the Company's direction some men 'immediately attached to himself' the offer was flatly refused, and Walsh commented in surprise 'he really seems to mean to maintain his power merely by his application to business'.[4] After Grenville went into opposition, Clive continued to owe him some allegiance (not always incompatible with political alliances elsewhere) but he was no more anxious to lead a group in the Company in opposi-

---

[1] G. Johnstone to Clive, 8 March 1764, and an undated list headed: 'List of gentlemen recommended by George Johnstone to Lord Clive to purchase stock on their note of hand.' Ibid.

[2] Jucker, op. cit., p. 290.   [3] *Grenville Papers*, ii. 310.

[4] John Walsh to Clive, 5 April 1765. Powis MSS.

tion than he was in power. Though he maintained his East Indian connexions and from time to time made use of them to help the policy of the Opposition, in the main he confined his participation in East Indian affairs to giving Clive the same sort of sound and shrewd advice on the use of his forces in the Company as on his activities in national politics.

George Grenville was thus no intentional innovator in the changing relations between the State and the Company. The same could not be said of Lord Sandwich. Sandwich was later to become notorious, in the days when ministers could not help concerning themselves in the internal politics of the Company, for his success in extending his technique of parliamentary management into the field of East India Company politics. Much that was then said of the power he exercised over the Company's machine and of the way he used this power for the ends of national politics was exaggerated. Still it is clear that he (like Shelburne in a rather different way) was quick to see the advantage which influence within the Company could give an ambitious politician when its affairs became of political importance. He was also quick to grasp the personal advantages of access to patronage within the Company now that this patronage was becoming increasingly valuable. There is no evidence that he had concerned himself with East Indian affairs before 1764, or 1763 at the earliest,[1] but when in these years the Company's affairs became of political significance, he was well placed to take part in them, since his friend and 'man of business' in the City, Robert Jones (once a sea-captain in the Lisbon trade and now a Lombard Street banker),[2] had long had a concern in the Company's affairs. As early as 1754 Jones had been introduced into the Direction by John Payne, then Chairman of the Company, and though he had lost his seat when Sulivan rose to power, he maintained some stock and interest in the Company. In 1763 he 'split' his modest holding in support of those favoured by the Bute Administration and in

---

[1] The assistance he gave Clive in his attempt to get a seat in Parliament in 1754 may have been the outcome of some contact with the Company's affairs at that time, through Robert Jones, but all he was doing was to try to get a seat for a well-to-do candidate anxious to enter Parliament.

[2] For a brief account of the career of Robert Jones and his connexion with Sandwich see G. F. Grand, *Narrative of the Life of a Gentleman long Resident in India*, ed. W. K. Firminger (Calcutta Historical Society, 1910).

1764 for those favoured by the Administration of Grenville, and in 1764 it was suggested that he might stand again for the Direction 'on Lord Sandwich or Mr. Grenville's request'. When he did become once again a director in 1765 he and another commercial protegé of Sandwich, John Stephenson, M.P. for the borough of Mitchell, were described as 'true and trusty friends' who 'would certainly follow Lord Sandwich on all occasions'.[1] From that time on, whenever Sandwich was in office, he sought to maintain a group of personal followers on the Direction, and, though he never concerned himself with the major issues of Company politics, as Shelburne often did, he made use of his influence there for purposes of patronage and whenever the exigencies of national politics demanded it.

Last of these newcomers was a man of less prominence but of even more importance in the history of the Company, that most accomplished and systematic 'man of business', Charles Jenkinson, who was, as Secretary of the Treasury, still at the beginning of his political and administrative career, whose concern in the Company's affairs arose merely as one of the preoccupations of his office, but who was gaining his first experience of the affairs of the Company over the future of which he was to exercise so great an influence.

The struggle between the two parties in the Company, with their political allies behind them, was a long and hard one. Like that of 1763, it ended in success for the side which enjoyed ministerial backing, but this time the victory was narrow and the issue in doubt to the end. At the General Court of 12 March Clive's supporters succeeded in carrying out the first part of their programme.[2] In criticizing the appointment of John Spencer as Governor of Bengal, speakers on Clive's side (particularly his close personal supporter Sir Francis Gosling) laid great stress on the need for a man with military as well as civil experience and of 'superior abilities' in both. Then, at what seemed a suitable moment a 'candid and sensible member' (as a newspaper reported) who had hitherto been silent, rose and 'as if by inspiration'[3] proposed that Clive be asked to return to

---

[1] John Walsh to Clive, 5 April 1765. Powis MSS.
[2] Court Book 72, p. 349.
[3] *London Magazine*, 12 March 1764, pp. 158-9.

Bengal with the combined powers of Governor and Commander-in-Chief. This well-timed proposal was received with the acclamation they had hoped for and Clive replied in a speech (evidently carefully prepared) pointing out that to a man of his standing office was indifferent, that he would do his duty if called on, but that he could only consider accepting office if the Court of Directors were as well disposed to him as the General Court.

The enthusiasm with which Clive's name was received by the proprietors in their anxiety (an enthusiasm which represented the real opinion of a number of proprietors as well as the synthetic approval of the 'split' votes) at once restored the initiative to him. Though Sulivan and his followers were not prepared to go down without a fight and though their position was still strong, this shift in public opinion forced them to trim their sails. They did so with commendable promptitude; four days later the directors assured Clive of their pleasure in learning that he might be willing to return to Bengal and of their unanimous desire to co-operate with him in every way.[1] By so doing they scored a temporary strategic success, for they embarrassed the Opposition in the second stage of their programme and forced them to appear as the party forcing on a contest. Clive gave a non-committal reply, and the matter rested till the next General Court, the normal quarterly General Court held on 21 March.

At this next Court it early became apparent (in a vote on the adjournment)[2] that the supporters of the directors were in a minority though the majority against them was by no means overwhelming. It also became apparent that the desire for co-operation rather than contest was strong there. After the Court had heard the letters exchanged between the directors and Clive, Clive was asked whether he had decided to accept office. When he answered, according to plan, that he could reach no decision until the result of the election of directors was known in April, his opponents tried to argue that this reply, given the urgency of the need, was tantamount to a refusal. In the heated discussion which followed Clive went further and announced either (as was reported in the Minutes

---

[1] Court Book 72, p. 358, cf. Forrest, op. cit. ii. 199.
[2] Court Book 72, pp. 361 seq. They were defeated by 322 to 252.

of the Court) that he would not accept office while Sulivan remained a director or (as he later maintained he had said) that he would not accept office while Sulivan was at the head of the Direction. This frank declaration of war seems to have out-run the sympathy of the Court, and after Sulivan had reiterated his willingness to give Clive every support while he was in Bengal, other speakers urged the advantages of an amicable agreement 'with great energy and very pathetically' to such effect that Clive had to promise to consider the question further and to give his reply in writing.

He had no intention, however, of losing his advantage and a week later he informed the directors, in an open letter published in the press, that, though he had felt bound by the pressure of the General Court to consider the possibility of working with Sulivan, he had been unable to change his mind, and maintained that the proprietors must choose between them. He continued, in words which reflected accurately his suspicion of his enemy though they give a somewhat misleading impression of his activities in the drawing up of the 'Proprietors' list':

At the same time I never desired or even wished, to name a Direction as some industriously spread abroad; I only object to one man's having the lead in the Company's affairs in whom I have so often and publicly declared I can never place any confidence and who, in my opinion, has acted and does continue to act upon principles diametrically opposite to the true interest of the East India Company.[1]

The publication of this letter opened up the second stage of the campaign, that of the election of directors which was to be held on 12 April. Already public interest had been stimulated by the debates in the General Courts and publications in pamphlets and press, and as a result a variety of issues had been raised, most of them by the party leaders in the course of their campaign, but some of them by independent proprietors. As the main thesis of the opposition was that Clive alone could save Bengal, and as they had to prove this without laying stress on the errors of Vansittart or the misdeeds of the Bengal servants whose friends were in alliance with them, they concentrated much of their attack on the alleged shortcomings of Sulivan's policy; his award of excessive powers and emoluments to Vansittart, the setting up of Secret Committees in the Presidencies,

[1] Ibid., p. 371. Quoted in full in Forrest, op. cit. ii. 200–1.

and the undue power of the Secret Committee of the Directors, and (still the best popular issue) the inequity of superseding Bengal servants by those from other Presidencies. There was one point they did not stress publicly, whatever understandings they had given privately. They were not prepared to advocate publicly the reinstatement of the dismissed Bengal servants, including John Johnstone. Though Governor Johnstone read out a long defence of him in the General Court of 12 March[1] he failed to get any public assurance of assistance and the group were afterwards bitterly to complain that their support had been a vital element in Clive's success but that they had been cheated out of their reward. As John Johnstone claimed later in his *Letter to the Proprietors of East India Stock*, 1766:

> Mr. Sulivan's conduct in these dismissions was one of the points which formed an opposition against him. No man who knows the facts will, I believe, affirm that if my friends had not engaged in that opposition, the management of the affairs of the India Company would now have been in the hands of the present set of Directors, or that Lord Clive would at present have been in possession of his princely jaghire.

That these important allies permitted themselves to be palmed off in this way for so long shows how influential public opinion within the Company was still recognized to be despite the creation of split votes and the bargains of interested groups and persons. To the representatives of this responsible opinion must also be attributed the appearance of certain proposals at this time without the initiative of either party but which neither of them cared to oppose openly. Two such proposals were of particular importance; a proposal to seek legislation to end the 'splitting' of stock and another for preventing the acceptance of presents by Company servants without the consent of the directors. The demand that 'splitting' should be checked was first raised at the General Court of 12 March, but deferred to that of 21 March when it was passed after some ineffective attempts at delaying tactics.[2] By this time it was too late for any legislation to affect the coming election, and when, at the beginning of the following year, a measure based on this resolution came before the House interested parties saw that it

[1] Court Book 72, p. 349.
[2] Ibid., 349 and 361.

was blocked on no less than three occasions; but it provided the prototype for the legislation later passed with the same object in view. The prohibition of the acceptance of presents was a matter which the Company could deal with without resort to Parliament. The motion was thought at first to be a veiled attack on Clive, but this was at once denied. No party cared to oppose it, and the result was the institution of a system whereby all Company servants were required to sign covenants binding themselves not to accept gifts without the consent of their employers, the first comprehensive (though long ineffective) attempt to check this damaging and widespread form of corruption.[1]

The election itself proved the most closely contested of the century. Twelve candidates were 'double-listed' and twelve places contested between the 'House' and 'Proprietors'' list. How strongly Sulivan had entrenched himself despite all the advantages which Clive might seem to enjoy—his personal prestige and the desire for his services in India, his 'splitting' campaign, the support he obtained from discontented elements in the Company, and the alliance of the ministry —was shown by the result. The highest number of votes received by a 'double-listed' candidate was 1,174, 51 less than last year; the votes for those not double-listed varied only between 637 and 604, but from the party point of view the result was a dead-heat, 6 of Sulivan's House list and 6 of the Proprietors' list being elected. Sulivan himself was returned, though he was at the bottom of the list, and this only after a dispute on the validity of the vote of the wife of the Archbishop of York.[2]

The position thus created was without precedent in the Company's history and caused a good deal of alarm. Salvador wrote agitatedly to Jenkinson asking for guidance whether or not Clive should be urged to come to terms with Sulivan after all, but the Treasury refused to intervene and Jenkinson after consulting his chief replied 'Mr. Grenville . . . bids me say that he shall have no objection to whatever is agreeable to Lord Clive and his friends'.[3] But the check to Sulivan was so severe as to amount to a defeat. This became clear in the election of the Chairman. Sulivan's name was at once proposed, and the

[1] Court Book 73, p. 34. [2] *Gentleman's Magazine*, 1764, p. 192.
[3] Jucker, op. cit., p. 285.

votes for and against him were exactly equal, as might have been expected. He took this as a signal of defeat and, with four of his closest followers (J. Boyd, G. Rooke, W. Thornton, and Richard Smith), left the Court, abandoning the field to his opponents. Thomas Rous was then nominated and elected to the Chair, and when the Court set about its business, Clive and his supporters were found to command even at the beginning a narrow majority. When it stood firm, the majority began gradually to grow. In July it was still precarious,[1] by November they could count on fourteen votes;[2] by the following February when another election of directors was drawing near Sulivan could muster no more than seven votes.[3]

The second stage of the great contest had now been brought to a successful close. There still remained the last, the laying down of the terms on which Clive would go to India, the most controversial part of which was the sanction of his *jagir*. Salvador, usually optimistic, was worried about this last stage of the campaign. He wrote to Jenkinson: 'We are now come to the most difficult part of our task. Whatever my Lord Clive may tell you I foresee much difficulty in carrying his points.'[4] His pessimism was unjustified, but the battle was still hard-fought. By 19 April Clive had prepared his terms.[5] They included a general indication of his plans for Bengal, a demand that John Spencer be sent back to Bombay, and a repetition of the terms for the recognition of his *jagir* which he had put forward through Grenville the previous December. Ten directors, including Sulivan, either voted against them or abstained from voting, but they passed the Court of Directors without difficulty. The battle was to be expected at the General Court called on 2 May to consider them. In preparation for this Court there was a last outburst of 'splitting', and prominent supporters of both parties, including Isaac Barré and John Calcraft in support of Sulivan, decided to attend it.

Clive's proposals for Bengal were expressed in very general terms and were not controversial. There was in them little trace of the issues on which his supporters had recently been

---

[1] J. Walsh to Clive, 3 July 1764. Powis MSS.
[2] J. Walsh to Clive, 22 November 1764. Ibid.
[3] G. Amyand to Clive, 14 February 1765. Ibid.
[4] Jucker, op. cit., p. 286.
[5] Court Book 73, p. 15.

attacking the last Court of Directors, or of the sweeping measures he in fact introduced when he arrived. Nor did any party make a stand for Spencer. The interest of the Court, one of the stormiest on record, focused on the *jagir*. But before this came to a vote, the Court passed without a division two other measures strangely at variance with each other in their underlying assumptions. The first was the resolution to prohibit the taking of presents without the consent of the directors, a non-party measure the propriety of which could not be disputed. The second was of a very different nature, the reinstatement of John Johnstone on the grounds of his 'services'.[1] Behind this measure (which created a precedent of the most sinister import for the Company) lay much intrigue and dissatisfaction. The Johnstone party had been growing increasingly uneasy at their failure to obtain any open support for the cause of their kinsman from the party in whose alliance they had trusted. After the election was over they had hoped that Clive would have made John Johnstone's reinstatement one of the conditions of his return to Bengal. When he failed to do so, their not unjustified suspicions of his good faith rose rapidly. At this Court they succeeded in forcing his hand. They got a proprietor (it was said that he was a follower of Sulivan[2]) to put forward a motion for reinstatement; Sulivan's followers did not oppose it since they saw the hope of winning the votes of the group; Clive and his followers could not do so for fear of losing votes which might be vital for his *jagir*, and by this neat manœuvre the Johnstone group achieved an end which no responsible member of the Company could approve, and in a manner fraught with danger for the future.

The debate on the *jagir* itself was so bitter and the feelings roused so strong that the Court broke up in confusion.[3] Before it broke up, however, some sort of vote had been taken and a ballot had been demanded by the opposition. When it was held three days later it was clear that the victory lay with Clive, for 583 voters supported the recognition of his rights in the

[1] Ibid., p. 42.

[2] The evidence for this comes chiefly from John Johnstone, *Letter to the Proprietors of East India Stock*, 1766, p. 11.

[3] Court Book 73, p. 62. At a General Court of 17 May protests were made about the arbitrary use of the adjournment by the Chairman, who replied that the Court had fallen into complete disorder.

jagir for ten years more, and only 396 opposed it.[1] About a month later Clive sailed for Bengal holding, at least for the present, his *jagir*, with a majority (though a small one) in the Court of Directors, and with every reason to hope that those left behind in charge of his affairs would be able to strengthen the party supporting him and to consolidate his victory in the coming year.

The purpose for which Grenville's Administration had entered into the internal affairs of the Company had thus been achieved. Once more it might have been expected that government would withdraw from participation in the Company's internal affairs. But the need for consolidating the victory prevented it from drawing out immediately. Ministers were called on to perform two further services for their allies in the Company. The first was to co-operate in the 1765 election of directors. The second was to give their assistance in dealing with the petition from the Company for legislation to prevent the 'splitting' of votes. As 1764 wore on it became apparent that Sulivan's hopes of retrieving the situation in the next year's election were very slight. The opinion gained ground that his opponents were the winning side and desertions began. Moreover, as Clive's correspondents pointed out, he had little share 'in the disposal of rewards this year', he was unlucky in the death of two of his staunchest friends and, worst of all, his monied backer, Thomas Devon of Child's, abandoned him.[2] Orme, the historian, told Clive 'Mr. Sulivan's party after the example of their friends the minority at this end of the town, threaten the Rouses and Boultons at the next election. But they will not succeed until the Shelbourne's, Calcraft's and Barry's [*sic*] succeed in the Administration. A long look.'[3] Nevertheless he continued to show fight and those managing Clive's affairs were determined to take no risks in securing his defeat.[4] As early as October they were in touch with the

---

[1] Court Book 73, p. 44.

[2] J. Walsh to Clive, 14 February 1765. Powis MSS.

[3] R. Orme to Clive, 19 November 1764. Orme MSS. O.V. 222, f. 111.

[4] Sulivan had printed by the beginning of the year handlists for canvassers with a list of proprietors for the purpose of electioneering. It excluded all foreigners and trustees holding stock. Walsh remarked that it thereby excluded more than half of the Company's capital. There were 1,144 names on it of persons qualified to vote; of these 1,032 held their qualifications at the time of the 1764 election and 790 of them voted. As all the big 'split' forces were at this time withdrawn, except

ministry about the House list for next year, the ministry urging them to get it out early because of the difficulty of pressing supporters into service at short notice.[1] The wishes of individual ministers were taken into consideration in drawing up the list, Lord Sandwich having two supporters, Robert Jones and John Stephenson, included; Lord Holland insisting on one candidate, Sir James Cockburn, being left out.[2] By February all Clive's £43,000 stock was 'split' and £20,000 of John Walsh's as well, and his agents could assure him that with the full support of the ministry, of the Bengal club, and of all the great proprietors except John Calcraft, victory was certain.[3]

Only one thing could have given Sulivan a hope of success in the face of this great display of force and this would have been the passing of the Bill to prohibit split voting in time to prevent the recent 'splits' from voting in the election. What had first been proposed in the Company on a non-party basis and what both parties had to pretend to support, thus became a weapon of party. Sulivan, declaring his willingness to support Clive in Bengal so as to remove the appearance of faction,[4] began vigorously to press the Bill. It was impossible for his opponents openly to oppose it and a petition and Bill to implement it were presented by the Company to the House when it resumed its sittings at the beginning of 1765. The three directors with seats in the House, Henry Crabb Boulton, John Roberts, and Sulivan, were instructed to give it their full support.[5] It was here, however, that the support of administration was particularly valuable, and it was also here that it became clear that when there was a difference of opinion it was Clive's followers with their parliamentary group and not the directors as such who enjoyed this support. At first it was assumed that the most that

Lord Holland's, these represented roughly the situation in the absence of collusive splitting of votes, which had added in the preceding election something of the order of 400 votes to the total. J. Walsh to Clive, 12 January and 14 February, 1765. Powis MSS.

[1] J. Walsh to Clive, 22 November 1764. Ibid.

[2] J. Walsh to Clive, 5 April 1765. Ibid. Sir James Cockburn did not become a director until 1767.

[3] L. Scrafton to Clive, 13 February 1765. Ibid.

[4] J. Walsh to Clive, 5 April 1765. Ibid.

[5] Court Book 73, p. 357. This was a rather small representation, but not remarkably low at this time. In 1765 and 1766 four of the twenty-four directors were in Parliament. In 1767 there were six and in 1769 there was the exceptionally high total of nine.

could be hoped for was a delay in the passing of the Bill until the election was safely over. Isaac Barré and Sulivan were active in pushing the Bill forward and it was a difficult one to oppose on principle. John Walsh, writing to Clive, seemed resigned to the disappearance of the political weapon they had wielded so successfully. In February, reporting that he had 'split' Clive's stock, he added 'It is troublesome and dangerous, but the Act of Parliament, which I suppose will pass, will stop it after this election.'[1] When he found Grenville and the ministry prepared to be co-operative, however, he became bolder. The directors as a whole, he said, would not have been averse to the passing of such a Bill, provided it did not affect the next election, but he, representing interests other than theirs, did not agree. He hoped, it is true, that 'splitting' would be a weapon to hold in reserve in the future 'for the difficulty of prevailing on people to take the stock and the danger of trusting them is so great that I shall be very loath to attempt it again for you or for myself', but he came to the conclusion that 'I was not for abridging at any time the weight of the great proprietors. I therefore pressed Mr. Grenville and also our friends to oppose the whole Bill.'[2] They did so and at the beginning of April it was thrown out on a technicality. Grenville had performed his last service for the party he had favoured in the Company. Sulivan and his party were sweepingly defeated, and the revolution in the Company seemed to be complete.

When the Grenville Administration fell from power in the middle of 1765 there was no East Indian question with which their successors, the first Rockingham Administration, needed to concern themselves. Clive's agents, it is true, took the precaution of returning discreetly into the fold of their parliamentary supporters[3] and reaped their reward in procuring their assistance in killing two further attempts to introduce Bills to prevent splitting, but no issues arose which called for a continuance of government concern in the affairs of the Company.

---

[1] J. Walsh to Clive, 14 February 1765. Powis MSS.
[2] J. Walsh to Clive, 5 April 1765. Ibid.
[3] Namier, op. cit. ii. 362, n. 1. When reporting Grenville's fall to Clive, Walsh said that he thought Clive's interest best served by remaining neutral, that Grenville was personally entitled to Clive's support, but his connexions were not (Malcolm, op. cit. ii. 243). From this position the transition into general support of the next administration was easy.

When the Chatham Administration which succeeded them came to make its far more spectacular intervention in East Indian affairs, it did so on quite a different issue and (at first at least) in a quite different way.

Nevertheless, the interventions of 1763 and 1764, though each appeared to be temporary and limited in aim, were the prelude to the progressively increasing intervention of the future. The reasons for this lay within the Company and the field of its operations. In the first place Clive's victory proved no more successful in ending party strife than Sulivan's had the year before; in the second place events in India were shaping in a way which could not fail to have repercussions on the Company and even on the nation.

When Sulivan was so resoundingly defeated in 1765 John Walsh remarked that it was his opponents' fault if he ever attained power again,[1] but he mentioned at the same time factors which might well redress the balance of forces. In the first place he noticed some restlessness among the directors at their dependence on a force outside their own body and some distaste for the predominance of their wealthy East Indian supporters. Their willingness to see the Bills of 1764, 1765, and 1766 against 'splitting' pass into law was the first indication of what became later a constant source of friction. In the second place he noted the return of other enriched servants whose power might challenge that of Clive, such as Lord Pigot,[2] and, most dangerous of all, Vansittart. It was difficult to see how the latter could be kept from drifting into opposition and into the arms of his former patron Sulivan. Walsh feared that the future might see the emergency of two parties, each fed by East Indian wealth, contending within the Company.[3] Nor were his fears

[1] J. Walsh to Clive, 5 April 1765. Powis MSS.
[2] George Pigot had been Governor of Madras from 1755 to 1763; he defended Fort St. George against the French and captured Pondicherry. He came back much enriched, it was believed, by the interest on loans to the Nawab of Arcot and the Zemindars at 2 or 3 per cent. interest per month 'which', as Scrafton remarked, 'though it has that bad effect that whoever the Governor lends money to becomes the adopted child of the Company, yet it cannot be called a violation of duty till it shall appear to have biased the Governors in their conduct to the Country powers.' (L. Scrafton to Clive, 9 December 1765. Ibid.)
He obtained an Irish peerage on his return and was held to be aping Clive. See p. 289, n. 1, below.
[3] J. Walsh to Clive, 27 April 1765. Powis MSS.

ill-founded, though the picture was to be more complicated. Sulivan was once more to achieve power, and this within four years, and Vansittart was to be his ally. The forces which were to complicate the situation he could hardly foresee, since most of them arose from actions which Clive was only now taking in Bengal.

In a letter written by Clive at sea on his way to Bengal he stated the two objects of his journey as the re-establishment of order in Bengal and the safeguarding of his *jagir* against all future attack.[1] The securing of the *jagir* and, eventually, the prolongation of its tenure, was certainly to be for some years a matter of preoccupation for Clive, his supporters, and the Company as a whole, but it should not be supposed that for this reason he took lightly the responsibilities he had undertaken in Bengal. On the contrary he was prepared to expend all his energies in triumphing over the difficulties he encountered there. Before he left England it had become clear that it would be his qualities as an administrator rather than as a soldier that would be called for, but the test of these was certain to be a severe one. In the heat of party controversies his supporters had attacked the unusual powers given to Vansittart as Governor; it did not pass without comment in the Company that he demanded powers at least as strong. On the major problems of the relations of the Company and the Nawab of Bengal and of the rights of private trade to be permitted to Company servants his views when he left England were in no way revolutionary.[2] It was not till later that he formulated his plan for an alternative to the private trade in salt, betel, and tobacco (a scheme which in fact the Company never accepted) or that he decided to carry a step farther on the assumption of that full control over the Government of Bengal which was the logical outcome of the expansion already undertaken. His demand from the Mogul of the *diwani* of Bengal (which gave the Company the control of the province's finance) still left the assumption of sovereignty in Bengal incomplete, but it was a big step towards it.

---

[1] Clive to unknown correspondent, seeking legal advice, 14 October 1764. Powis MSS. He inquired what would be the legal position if he sold his rights while in India.

[2] For these see Forrest, op. cit. ii. 202 seq.

Clive in fact went out not to implement a well-worked-out policy of reform, but as a strong man to grapple with problems when he met them. His successes serve to show, what neither the Company nor the State were willing for so long to recognize, how much could be done by a strong man armed with a good deal of discretionary power. His failures show, as much as anything, what he himself did not recognize, that the exercise of these powers persistently over a long period was necessary if they were to have permanent and salutary effects. The assumption of the *diwani* or financial control, while leaving the raising of revenues in the hands of the Nawab, certainly preserved an extremely inconvenient dichotomy; the belief that the Company would thereby become suddenly very wealthy had disastrous effects at home and abroad (all the more because Clive's own estimates of the results were over-optimistic). It is also certain that all his energy and determination did not permanently reform the administration of Bengal. Nevertheless, he restored some semblance of order to a civil and military administration which seemed on the verge of disintegration. That in doing so he should raise up enemies among the Company servants whom he sought to control (not only John Johnstone and his colleagues but the military officers whose mutiny he ruthlessly suppressed)— enemies who were to harass him for the rest of his life—was only to be expected. It was perhaps no more than poetic justice in view of the stimulus which his example had given to their scramble for wealth and the use he had made of their alleged grievances in the Company's party struggles.

Just before he left England, Charles Jenkinson, that acute young politician, made a remark which within a few years was to become familiar: 'The affairs of this Company seem to be become much too big for the management of a body of merchants. I think that Lord Clive will at present carry his point, but these disputes will probably end in a Parliamentary enquiry.'[1]

---

[1] C. Jenkinson to R. Wolters. Add. MS. 38304, f. 20.

VI

THE FIRST PARLIAMENTARY
INTERVENTION, 1766–7

CHARLES JENKINSON's prophecy came true more quickly than he or anyone else could have expected and under circumstances which had suddenly changed. By the end of 1767 there had been, not only the parliamentary inquiry he had foretold, but three Acts of Parliament modifying the powers and rights of the Company, and doing so in a manner which had no parallel since the end of the preceding century and which made it certain that still more sweeping measures were to come. The reasons for these sudden developments lay in the repercussion on the Company and the political world of England of the measures which Clive took on assuming his office in Bengal.

The letters which Clive sent home when his ship touched at Madras were the first indication received at home that great changes in the Company's status in Bengal were to be expected.[1] In his first public dispatches after his arrival he informed the directors that he had, on the Company's behalf, assumed the *diwani*.[2] The long-range significance of this action was that it constituted an important step toward the assumption of complete responsibility for the Government of Bengal. But its immediate significance in the history of the Company at home was that, from Clive downwards, everyone except the small number of men who really understood the Company's finances, believed that the result must be an immediate and striking increase in the wealth of the Company. Clive himself estimated the net gain at over £2,000,000 a year.[3]

It was idle for the directors to express their scepticism of these calculations and to point out that in any case revenues in Bengal could only be transferred to England either by a sharp increase in the goods exported thence or by relieving the Com-

---

[1] The letters are printed in Appendices 82 and 83 to the *Third Report of the Committee of Secrecy on the state of the East India Company*, 1773 (*Reports from Committees of the House of Commons*, iii. 404–5).

[2] Ibid., Appendix 86, pp. 437 seq.

[3] In a letter to the Marquess of Rockingham of 6 September 1766 (FitzWilliam MSS. (Sheffield)).

pany of the burden of bullion exports to other Asiatic markets.[1] Despite all they could say the result was an immediate boom in East India Stock and the introduction of a heavy speculative interest in it on the Amsterdam and Paris as well as the London markets, which soon radically altered its character as a security, and ran a fluctuating but mounting course until the world credit crash of 1772-3 for which the East India speculators were in large part responsible.[2] Still worse, in the course of this development the interest of groups of speculators, particularly those 'bulling' the market, began to have its effect on the unstable internal affairs of the Company, to rally the forces of party opposition, and employ for new purposes the machinery which had so unfortunately grown up in recent years for the creation of split votes. The results of these two developments provided an irresistible attraction for an impecunious government to intervene in the affairs of a Company apparently so rich and certainly so disorganized. The result was the first parliamentary intervention of the century into the affairs of the Company. Its peculiar course is attributable to weakness and uncertainty on the part of the Government and interaction of party faction both in Parliament and the Company. Its effect was to set in train the course of parliamentary measures which by 1784 had radically altered the relation of State and Company.

The peace established within the Company in 1765 was not likely to be of a permanent character even had there been no great changes to threaten it. Sulivan had, it is true, been signally defeated, but no leader of comparable skill arose among those who had supplanted him, and not only was the former Governor of Bengal, Vansittart, being driven into opposition as the circumstances of his rule came under the criticism of the new directors, but Clive's attempts to restore order on his arrival began to send back to England a new stream of indignant and discredited servants to play their part in Company politics. First among these new casualties was the egregious John Johnstone, who was found (on the occasion of the succession of Mir Kasim's heir) to have added to his earlier misdeeds the defiance of the Company's new orders against the taking of presents.

---

[1] G. Dudley to Clive, 17 May 1766. Powis MSS.
[2] C. Wilson, *Anglo-Dutch Commerce and Finance in the Eighteenth Century*, pp. 167 seq.

As has been shown, his relatives were already strongly organized
for his defence within the Company and were uneasy about his
future. Their fear that they had given their help to Clive in vain
was confirmed by his uncompromising exposure of John Johnstone's offences and they wasted no time in deserting their
ungrateful ally and seeking support elsewhere. Their stimulus
to action was the greater because the directors, strengthened by
the terms of the covenants they now exacted from their servants,
determined to proceed against Johnstone in Chancery. In 1766
they took their first steps against him[1] and there was also some
talk of proceeding against Vansittart.[2] In consequence in the
same year the supporters of John Johnstone and Vansittart
joined forces and by the end of it both were actively co-operating with Laurence Sulivan in a renewed struggle to get him
back into power.

While the opposition within the Company was thus beginning
to reform, the directors were weak and uneasy. Their dependence on Clive's voting strength and reputation was a circumstance his agents would not let them forget. One of these agents,
Luke Scrafton, was now a director; another, John Walsh, was
handling Clive's affairs outside. Both were highly critical of
their allies and neither made any attempt to disguise the fact
that their major concern was the interest of their patron
whether or not it conformed to the decisions of the majority
in the Court of Directors. They showed this in their attitude
towards the measures brought before Parliament to check the
splitting of votes, they were to show it whenever the directors
hesitated to accept any of Clive's measures in Bengal, and they
showed it most clearly of all when, after the assumption of the
diwani, they turned their full attention to a subject which
the directors believed to be settled, the future of Clive's *jagir*, the
term of which they began to claim should be lengthened.[3] This
division of interests among the directors still further weakened
their position, so that even when in 1767 they gained an access
of personal strength by admitting into their number the very
rich and enterprising (though reckless) banker, Sir George

---

[1] Court Book 75, pp. 62–63, 30 May 1766.
[2] L. Scrafton to Clive, 17 May 1766, and J. Walsh to Clive of same date. Powis
MSS.
[3] Correspondence from John Walsh and Luke Scrafton to Clive, e.g. letter from
the former of 5 May 1766. Ibid.

Colebrooke, M.P.,[1] this only served to increase the chances of friction between the majority of the Court and Clive's forces.

It was into this uncomfortable situation that there broke in the late spring of 1766 the news of Clive's action and the stock-exchange speculation which at once followed it. It was perhaps surprising that there had not been more speculation in India Stock before. During the Seven Years War, the most expensive war yet fought and one financed largely on credit, there had been great speculative activity both on the Dutch markets and in London. This speculation centred on the loans floated by the English Government and the various English government securities. With the coming of peace this source of business dried up and observers were quick to prophesy that the speculators would transfer their attention to the stock of the East India Company which had done so well out of the war.[2] But in fact there is no sign of any unusual speculative activity in the stock until the excitement caused by the receipt of Clive's dispatches from Bengal. These were received on 20 April 1766; the next day the stock, which had been steady at 164 for a number of months, suddenly rose to 172 and then to 190. It soon passed the 200 mark and in 1767 reached a maximum of 273. Though this rise and the fluctuations which accompanied it were not by modern standards very alarming, they were thought so by the investors of the period; East India Stock gained a new and unfavourable reputation as 'a very fluctuating and gaming Stock' and there can be no doubt that from 1766 onwards it became the chief subject of speculative dealings on the world markets and that by contemporary standards the volume of these speculative dealings was very large. The operations took place primarily on the Amsterdam and London markets, though Paris was also a centre of some activity, and the same speculators often operated on all three markets. Their operations took the form of purchase and sale of stock for future delivery, dealings in 'differences', and (on the Amsterdam market at least) dealings in options.

Though a good deal of information survives about the

---

[1] Of Colebrooke, Lesingham and Binns, Threadneedle Street. M.P. for Gatton. For his career see my 'Sir George Colebrooke's World Corner in Alum', *Economic History* supplement, *Economic Journal*, February 1936, pp. 237 seq.

[2] I. da Pinto, *Jeu d'Actions en Hollande*, pp. 310–11. Quoted Wilson, op. cit., p. 170.

activities of some of these speculators, it is not enough to give a full picture of the market, nor would it be relevant to the purpose of this study to try to construct one. What is relevant, however, is the evidence which survives of certain interests which at this time were 'bulling' the stock and which found it worth their while to intervene in Company politics in order to force the directors to pursue a policy likely to further their ends. From an early date such a group came into existence.[1] Some of them were Dutch speculators and investors whose affairs were managed for them in London by Pieter Clifford (of the Amsterdam firm of that name which finally came to grief in the crisis of 1772-3), by John Harman, a Dutch merchant of Cateaton Street, or by other lesser intermediaries.[2] The Dutch may well have had the greater financial interest; the lead in organizing the activities of the group, however, was taken by Englishmen. The Englishmen concerned fall into two categories. There were first a few rich men who had taken physical delivery of large blocks of stock in the hopes of selling it at a profit. Clive himself was one of these, though for reasons of Company politics his agents had to stand aside from the agitations raised by the others. Even before he had completed his plans for Bengal he had sent instructions to his attorneys to buy in all the East India Stock they could. They therefore added some £30,000 to his holding in 1766 (bringing the total up to £75,000).[3] The most

[1] Evidence of it can be seen in the names of those demanding General Courts on relevant topics in the Court Books, from the 'splitting' campaigns as laid bare in the stock ledgers, and in the correspondence of Clive's agents preserved in the Powis MSS.

[2] Stock Ledger Q.

[3] Clive in a cipher letter written from Madras to John Walsh (quoted Appendix 82, the *Third Report of the Committee of Secrecy on the East India Company*, 1773, loc. cit., p. 405) said: 'whatever money I have in the public Funds, or anywhere else and as much as can be borrowed in my name, I desire may be, without loss of a minute, invested in East India Stock'. Walsh told the 1773 Committee that he bought £30,000 on Clive's behalf between the date of the receipt of this letter and 9 May, only £12,000 of it before the arrival of the public dispatches from Clive in Bengal. Ibid., pp. 313 seq. This tallies fairly well with information in letters from him in the Powis MSS. where he attributes the comparatively small amounts borrowed to difficulties in borrowing the money to purchase it. Though Sir George Forrest (op. cit. ii. 258-9) has tried to exonerate Clive from the imputation of using his inside information to gain profit on the market, it seems impossible to do so. The suggestion that he was adding to his stock-holdings for Company political reasons gains no shadow of support from the correspondence of his agents or the directors, and none of them had any doubt of the explanation to be given to the instructions. George Dudley, Deputy Chairman of the Company, wrote (21 November 1766):

prominent of the others was Lord Holland, who, on the advice of Clive's attorneys, invested part of his Pay Office balances in £40,000 East India Stock.[1] Clive's attorneys themselves and a number of lesser men followed the example thus prominently set them.

The other category was larger and on balance more important; they were the speculators whose holdings of stock were negligible but who were dealing in differences on a very considerable scale. Among them there was, between 1766 and 1769, one particularly big and influential group. Its capital seems to have been largely provided by two men, Isaac Panchaud, a partner in the Parisian banking firm of Panchaud and Foley, and Lord Verney, a rich but rash and speculative peer who in politics was a follower of the Marquess of Rockingham and who was (until his ruin as a result of these same speculative ventures) the patron of Edmund Burke.[2] A number of men of wealth and position became associated with them, including some Members of Parliament, and their affairs were managed for them by two adventurers whose future careers were of some significance for the history of the Company, William Burke, the cousin and associate of the great Edmund; and one of the most remarkable adventurers of the time, Lauchlin Maclcane, first heard of as a doctor in the irregular troops in America[3] and

'I could wish you had not sent the orders you did to Mr. Walsh in your letter from Madras, or at least that they had not come in the Company's cipher, for reasons that must naturally occur. Too many persons are now acquainted with them, and the effect they have had upon India Stock has hurt the Court of Directors.' (Powis MSS.) The figures quoted are based on a letter from Walsh in the Powis MSS., 16 May 1766, and his evidence before the 1773 Committee, loc. cit., p. 313. The stock was not bought in Clive's name, so cannot be traced in the Stock Ledger.

[1] John Powell of the Pay Office purchased £40,000 on 27 May. Stock Ledger Q. This was done on Walsh's advice. (J. Walsh to Clive, 22 November 1766. Powis MSS.)

[2] The information on this group comes primarily from legal proceedings following their crash in 1769 and from the Lansdowne MSS. (see Appendix to Chapter VII). Some light is thrown upon it in Dixon Wecter's *Edmund Burke and his Kinsmen* (Boulder, Colorado, 1939).

[3] Add. MS. 21643, f. 86, L. Macleane to Colonel Bouquet, 25 May 1758. Further correspondence follows. I am indebted to Professor Namier for drawing my attention to these documents. Macleane's early career is obscure. For an account of him cf. Namier, *England in the Age of the American Revolution*, p. 316 n., and an unpublished thesis by L. Scott (Manchester University), 'Under Secretaries of State 1755-1775'. I am indebted to Mr. Scott and the authorities of Manchester University for permission to examine this thesis.

later in London working in collaboration with John Wilkes, and who now in this way began his long and discreditable connexion with the affairs of the Company.

The interest of both these groups was to encourage the rise in the price of East India Stock. It was clear that nothing could do more to help this on than an increase of dividend. But this the directors were determined not to give them, and at the June Quarterly Court succeeded in evading their demands.[1] When it became clear that they were going to stand firm also at the September General Court, the 'bulls' decided to turn to political measures within the Company to over-ride the directors' wishes. By August Clive's correspondents were reporting unmistakable signs of an organized campaign to obtain a majority in the General Court in favour of an increase of dividend and in defiance of the directors and their caution.[2]

The first need of the group was for allies among the political forces within the Company. For reasons concerned with the relation of the Company and the State (as will be explained later) they did not at once succeed in obtaining the support of Sulivan and what may be called the official opposition within the Company, though it was not long before the two sides drew together. But they did succeed at once in coming to terms with the Johnstone group, always prepared to pledge their support to any interest which would, in return, agree to help the defence of John Johnstone. Thus in 1766 the cry for an increased dividend and the demand for the abandonment of the prosecution of John Johnstone went hand in hand. Having procured this ally the 'bulls' then turned to the organization of publicity, and in this field they set up a new standard for the Company. Not only was the press deluged with pamphlets and articles, statements and letters, but at the beginning of September they even went so far as to begin to issue twice a week a propagandist newspaper, called the *East India Examiner*, a revolutionary step which forced the directors the following month to begin publishing a rival periodical known as the *East Indian Observer*.[3]

---

[1] Court Book 75, p. 87.   [2] Malcolm, op. cit. iii. 216–17.

[3] The *East India Examiner* was published twice weekly, beginning early in September. Eleven numbers appear to have been published. The *East India Observer* was not begun until October; seven numbers seem to have been pulished. Luke Scrafton was believed to have written most of it. *A Letter to the Proprietors of East*

Most important of all they set in train a 'splitting' campaign comparable to any which the Company had yet seen, though controlled by different people and run in a different way. Lord Holland, who had just gone abroad, left instructions that all his £40,000 holding was to be split[1] and the Johnstones were believed to have contributed £37,000 from John Johnstone's ill-gotten gains, but the campaign rested much less than on other occasions on the exertions of great English proprietors. The organization seems to have relied mainly on the mobilization of Dutch holdings on a large scale and on an activity among the bankers, brokers, and other intermediaries which had never hitherto been equalled.[2] The result was that although neither of the major parties within the Company was concerned and those most active on previous occasions took no part, the financial interests themselves took over for their own purposes the machinery which they had hitherto operated in the interest of the Company's parties. They succeeded, with no help outside the Johnstone group, in splitting some £150,000 stock and creating about 300 votes before the meeting of the General Court on 26 September 1766.

These operations gave them a formidable voting force and this on an issue which would naturally have an appeal to the less thoughtful among the proprietors. The caution of the majority, however, and the respect in which the directors' judgement on such a question was still held would probably have defeated their activities had the directors remained united. But unfortunately those who owed their first allegiance to Clive disagreed strongly with the policy of the rest of the Court. Not only were they and their master prominent among those who stood to gain from an increase in the price of East India Stock, but it was Clive's own reports which gave grounds for the optimism of those opposing the directors' caution; still further the success of their attempts to reopen the question of their master's *jagir* was dependent on prosperity and contentment within the Company. In consequence they reported to Clive

India Stock from Mr. H. Vansittart, London, 1767. Copies of both periodicals, bound together, are in the Bodleian.
   [1] L. Scrafton to Clive, 21 November 1766, and J. Walsh to Clive, 22 November 1766. Powis MSS.
   [2] Stock Ledger Q. The most prominent intermediary was William Fisher, partner in the broking firm of Fisher and Younger of Change Alley.

that the directors were slighting his achievements though 'for their own glory as well as your's they should have given the public the earliest taste of the advantages you have procured for them',[1] and they not only made no attempt to split any stock against the speculators but they did nothing to rally their supporters and most of them ostentatiously refrained from voting themselves.[2] It was therefore not surprising that when the General Court met, the newly constituted Opposition succeeded in overpowering the directors by a majority of 340 votes to 231, and that they raised the annual dividend from 6 per cent. to 10 per cent.[3] That this reverse could have been prevented had Clive's forces supported the directors is suggested by the fate of the other measure pressed by the opposition, the abandonment of John Johnstone's prosecution. On this question Walsh set promptly to work to such effect that its consideration was at first postponed and then quietly dropped.[4] Once again the Johnstone group had played their part in the victory of another interest without themselves reaping their reward.

The damage done to the Company's reputation by this irresponsible decision was serious. The market showed its shock by failing to respond by any proportionate increase in the price of stock, fearing, as the experienced Amsterdam firm of Hope and Son reported, 'the insufficiency of the stock to bear it'.[5] There were two even more serious indirect results: the first was the recognition of the political influence which groups of speculators could achieve within the Company if they chose to put some money and organization into a splitting campaign. It was too much to hope that in the fierceness of the struggle for power within the Company the contestants would not be tempted to enlist the aid of these allies, and if they did so each side would be tempted to outbid the other by an offer of increased dividends or other short-term financial advantages. Already by November 1766 Sulivan was beginning to work these speculators into his mixed group of followers. The second indirect result was equally serious; the triumph of the speculators occurred at a time when the State was already casting covetous

[1] J. Walsh to Clive, 22 November 1766. Powis MSS.
[2] G. Dudley to Clive, 21 November 1766. Ibid.
[3] Court Book 75, pp. 192-7.
[4] J. Walsh to Clive, 22 November 1766. Powis MSS.
[5] Hope and Son, Amsterdam, to George Clive, 3 October 1766. Ibid.

eyes on the resources of the Company and it could not fail to encourage the Government to press forward with its demands.

The Company was in fact threatened with the first parliamentary intervention into its affairs which it had known since the reign of William III. The threat came from Chatham's Administration which had taken up office in July 1766, just at the time when the hopes raised by Clive's dispatches were at their height. A month after the new ministers came into power they warned the Company that they intended in the autumn to institute a parliamentary investigation into its affairs. About the same time it became general knowledge that their purpose in so doing was to challenge the Company in its enjoyment of the profits of its territorial revenues.

The attack had indeed begun in a general way before the new ministry came into power and even before the news had been received of the changes in Bengal. It arose during debates in the House on the third and last unsuccessful attempt of the Company to petition for legislation to check the practice of 'splitting'. On this occasion the popular City leader and staunch personal follower of Pitt, Alderman William Beckford, took up the attack on the Company he had made in 1758 and raised again the old banner of the 'popular' party in the City against the rich monopolist Company. What had happened in the Company since this old cry had last been heard had given him some new forces to call upon as well as the well-tried old ones of City radicalism. There was the jealousy and dislike rising amongst the country gentry at the class of retired 'Nabobs', small in numbers but conspicuous in their wealth and ostentation, who were forcing themselves on English society.[1] More reputable, there was already some uneasiness at the conduct of the Company's servants in India, a feeling less strong than it was some years later when so much more had been written and said on the subject, but already being fed by that running commentary on events in India which was provided by returned servants bent on justifying their own actions or attacking those of others. Already the relatives of Vansittart had published a book in his defence which he himself enlarged and republished on his return,[2] and the hated John Zacchary Holwell had

---

[1] Holzman, op. cit., pp. 15–16.

[2] H. Vansittart, *A Narrative of the Transactions on Bengal from . . . 1760–1764*, 1766.

produced several pamphlets 'full of lyes and fables' as Clive's friends told him. Holwell was also believed to be in personal touch with Beckford and to be providing him with ammunition for his assault.[1]

Thus armed, Beckford, as it was reported:

Took an opportunity to abuse the Company as an unconstitutional monopoly, and that their conduct merited the enquiry of parliament; that they had a revenue of two millions in India, acquired God knows how, by unjust wars with the natives. That their servants came home with immense fortunes obtained by rapine and oppression, yet the Proprietors received no increase of dividend: that it was necessary to know how these revenues were consumed and whence these oppressions so loudly talked of and therefore he should next day move the House that the affairs of the East India Company should be laid before Parliament.[2]

Observers considered his speech to be largely the old cry for an open trade, but noted the shift to an attack on the revenues the Company was now gaining from territorial sources. Though he did not, as he threatened, move for an inquiry, they believed that he was in earnest and had some support, and Charles Townshend later stated that his speech was part of a planned assault.[3] When Clive's dispatches arrived a few weeks later the significance of the attack became greater, and John Walsh thought it wise to approach Pitt himself to sound him on his reactions to the news of the Company's changed fortunes. The results were disquieting; though the great man expressed goodwill towards Clive, he announced that he had for some time been uneasy about the Company and its affairs and that it was 'too vast'.[4] When in July he assumed office, the issue at once became of first-class importance. In August the Company was officially warned that its affairs would be brought before Parliament when it met.[5] Ministers spoke with different voices and

---

[1] J. Z. Holwell, *Interesting Historical Events relative to the Provinces of Bengal and the Empire of Hindostan*, pt. i, 1765, pt. ii and supplement, 1766-7. L. Scrafton mentioned him to Clive (Powis MSS. letter of 9 December 1765), and also indicated that Beckford was in touch with him. L. Scrafton to Clive, 12 April 1766.

[2] L. Scrafton to Clive, 12 April 1766. Powis MSS.

[3] L. Scrafton to Clive, 21 November 1766, says Charles Townshend had told him at the time that the attack was the result of a 'deep-laid scheme and would make its appearance next session'. Ibid.

[4] Malcolm, op. cit. iii. 189.

[5] Court Book 75, p. 152, 29 August 1766.

it was impossible to obtain any authoritative opinion as to what purpose they intended the parliamentary inquiry to serve, but it was soon general knowledge that, though Beckford's threats of a withdrawal of their charter need not be taken seriously, the ministry were going to make an assault on the Company's territorial revenues. All the members of the administration were agreed in making this assault; the differences between them were only whether it could best be made by denying the Company's right to the territories from which the revenues were derived and claiming this right for the State, or by demanding a share in the advantages which it was to enjoy.

It has been held by Chatham's admirers that when he launched this attack on the Company he was seeking to inaugurate a policy of far-sighted imperialism in what was to be British India; that he saw the need for the Government of Great Britain itself to take over the administrative responsibility of India from the incompetent hands of a trading Company. It is, however, impossible to substantiate such a claim. In the first place the Company itself had not fully taken over such a responsibility even in Bengal, and in the second place all the evidence makes it clear that his plan went no farther than the taking over of the whole or part of the revenues derived from the *diwani*. He certainly had formulated no plan for the transfer of authority—an intricate and ambitious operation for an eighteenth-century government—which a comprehensive scheme would have involved; his references to the question at the time contained the implication that the Company would retain its existing responsibilities, and in 1773 at any rate he explicitly denied that he had ever had such an intention.[1] The inspiration of the attack in fact, so far from being new, was old. It was the desire to extract money for the purposes of the State from a rich corporation dependent on the State for its privileges, and vulnerable because of the jealousy which these privileges aroused. The desire was, moreover, stimulated by the anxiety with which the problems of post-war public finance were regarded by Governments in these uneasy years, as the history of relations with the American colonies made manifest.

All the members of the administration, whatever their disagreements about the means, were agreed in supporting this raid

[1] Quoted B. Williams, *Life of Lord Chatham* (1915), ii. 233.

upon the Company, and they did so for the same reason. George Grenville did not misjudge them when he remarked that he, too, thought the National Debt should be reduced, though he did not believe this ought to be done by violation of charters.[1] When Chatham in his grandiloquent style said that he hoped by this assault to achieve 'the redemption of a nation, within reach of being saved at once by a kind of gift from heaven'[2] he meant precisely what his master George III meant when he said in his blunter way that it was 'the only safe method of extracting this country out of its lamentable situation owing to the load of debt it labours under'.[3]

The events of the next few years were, indeed, to show that these hopes were delusive, but it was not the recognition of this fact but lack of leadership and disorganization within the ministry which limited its success in extracting money from the luckless Company. As it was, it emerged from the contest bearing the additional burden of an annual payment of £400,000 a year to the Treasury, a burden which it proved quite unable to support, and without any help from the State in adapting itself to its great responsibilities. Indeed, the only beneficial results of the intervention were accidental ones, arising in the course of the contest and unwillingly introduced as temporary measures made necessary by its events. These were the belated passing of a Bill to check the 'splitting' of stock, based on the measure already three times rejected by the House (it proved unfortunately by no means adequate for its purpose), and the introduction of a temporary statutory limitation on the Company's dividend to restrain the influence which the speculators were gaining over the financial policy of the Company. Limited as were the ideas behind these measures they mark at least the beginning of some sense of responsibility on the part of the State for the sound administration of the Company.

The events of 1766-7 were to provide a striking illustration of the maxim that any parliamentary intervention by the State in the affairs of the Company, even the negotiation for the

[1] G. Grenville to Clive, 22 November 1766. Powis MSS.
[2] *Autobiography of Augustus Henry, third Duke of Grafton*, ed. W. R. Anson (1898), p. 110.
[3] *Correspondence of King George III*, ed. J. Fortescue (1927), i. 424, no. 437.

renewal of its charter, both stimulated dissension within the Company and linked the factions within the Company to the Government and Opposition interests in Parliament. The first effect was seen in the return of Sulivan to prominence in the Company at the head of a strengthened Opposition; by the end of November he was able to weld together on issues concerning the Company's future a group which included all the elements of discontent within it, and although the forces supporting the directors were strong enough to keep him out of power for two more years, he soon began once again to be a force they could not ignore. The second effect also became apparent; the conflicting interests within the Company began to obtain the support of parliamentary groups in government and opposition. Here the situation was complicated by several factors; by the links which had been forged in the earlier conflicts in 1763 and 1764 in which Company and national politics had become interlaced; by tergiversations both by the ministry and the parties within the Company in the course of the present conflict, and by the dissensions within the ministry itself.

The Chatham Administration, a government weak and heterogeneous even for its time, fell from the beginning into two rival groups which at any period of his career Chatham would would have found difficult to keep together. In the ill health and inertia into which he was falling he failed completely to co-ordinate them. On the one side he stood himself with the support of Lord Grafton, an inert mediocrity, and the able but unpopular Lord Shelburne. In the House of Commons they had some vigorous followers with a reputation among the 'popular' interests, the vociferous Beckford who was Chatham's chief link with the City where his reputation still stood high, and Colonel Isaac Barré and the prominent lawyer John Dunning, who had joined their fortunes with Shelburne. On the other side stood Charles Townshend in the last and most erratic stage of a most erratic career, and the correct but limited Conway, neither prepared to subordinate themselves to Chatham's leadership, and both connected with groups in opposition.

East Indian affairs were one of their earliest subjects of dissension. Chatham's attitude was simple in principle but vague in detail. He was all for delivering a direct attack on the Company, for challenging in Parliament their right to derive any revenue from Bengal on the ground that they had no right over territory subdued in a war in which the king's forces had taken part. This had not been his attitude when the subject was under discussion in 1757-8,[1] nor was it the attitude he later maintained that he had held in 1766. He claimed in 1773 that in 1766 he had held the view that 'there is in substantial justice a mixed right to the territorial revenues between the State and the Company as joint captors; the State equitable entitled to the larger share as largest contributor in the acquisition by fleets and men'.[2] But in 1767 he wrote explicitly that the right 'cannot (upon any colourable pretence) be in the Company'.[3] He intended, it is clear, that when the right had been established, the State should make some concessions to the Company in return for its continued administrative responsibilities, but what they would have been remains unknown, for as he grew increasingly ill and unfit for business he proclaimed the louder that he would make no plan, that the matter should 'find its way through the House', and informed his anxious colleagues that 'the ways to ulterior and final proceedings upon this trancendant object' (for so he always called it) 'will open themselves naturally and obviously enough'.[4] In this policy he was loyally followed by Grafton, though with some dismay as time went on, and by Beckford whose hatred of the Company was thought to reflect the views of his leader, though in fact he was often acting on his own initiative. Shelburne, Chatham's ablest supporter, was with him fully at first, but soon showed a preference for a less sledge-hammer type of intervention.

The attitude of Charles Townshend and Conway was different. They also wanted the State to share in the Company's spoils, but believed that the best way of getting good terms was to open up negotiations with the directors, keeping the threat of parliamentary intervention in the background. If it were to be argued that the Company had no legal right to its territorial possessions, there were authoritative legal pronouncements on both sides and the Opposition could say with justice, as George Grenville did, that the proper place for the determination of the

---

[1] See p. 78, n. 4 above.
[2] Quoted B. Williams, op. cit. ii. 233.
[3] *Autobiography of Lord Grafton*, p. 112.
[4] Chatham to Shelburne, 3 February 1767, quoted in Lord Fitzmaurice, *Life of William, Earl of Shelburne* (1876), ii. 24.

law was at Westminster Hall. If public expedience were to be adduced as a justification, the Government would raise up a formidable opposition based on the inviolability of private property and the sanctity of charters. Finally, Charles Townshend insisted the threat was no more than bluff.

'Perhaps I may have thought,' he wrote to Chatham, 'more than others of sounder judgement than mine, that the only way of making the issue adequate was to make it amicable; which, if it has been an error, it was an honest one, proceeding from a sincere, though it should be thought to be an extreme, sense of the endless difficulties accompanying every idea of substituting the Public in the place of the Company in the collecting, investing, and remitting the revenue; and from a fear that the knowledge of this impracticability might embolden a body of heated proprietors to stand the issue of such a measure. . . .'[1]

So well known was the disagreement within the ministry on this point that as early as September the *East India Examiner* was playing on it,[2] and in November Charles Jenkinson reported 'a quarrel . . . has arisen between Charles Townshend and Lord Chatham on India affairs and will be brought to its issue. . . . I am persuaded from many circumstances that the Government is drawing to a conclusion.'[3] That it was not, was due largely to the withdrawal of Chatham through illness and the growth of the influence of Shelburne. As it became recognized that Chatham was unfit for business, Shelburne gradually assumed control over those most closely associated with his leader and with considerable adroitness steered them away from reliance on parliamentary attack on the Company's right to its revenues and towards a negotiation with the Company for a share in them. Though the friction between the two groups within the ministry persisted, and was to show its confusing effects on the course of the negotiation, the danger of a head-on collision between them was averted.

When it became probable that negotiation rather than force was to be the order of the day, the links between the various parties in the Company and the Government began to assume

---

[1] *Correspondence of William Pitt, Earl of Chatham*, ed. W. S. Taylor and J. H. Pringle (1839), iii. 156.

[2] *East India Examiner*, no. 2, 10 September 1766.

[3] C. Jenkinson to Sir James Lowther [endorsed November 1766]. Add. MS. 38205, f. 106.

importance. Shelburne was the only minister who already enjoyed an established interest in the Company. Though he had been cultivating City interests of quite a different kind since his alliance with Chatham, he had not let his contacts with Sulivan lapse. No doubt it would have been more useful if Sulivan had still been in power but the connexion might be made useful for both sides. Sulivan was indeed constantly in his house during the latter part of 1766 and had personal connexions with both Barré and Dunning. In December Walsh found him present at a meeting of ministerial supporters where 'he did not say much, but at the ensuing debate in the House, the ministry seemed disposed to compliment him upon his great knowledge of India affairs...'.[1] About the same time Shelburne increased the closeness of his contact with the Company by taking as his Under-Secretary, in an evil moment for himself, that same Lauchlin Macleane whose speculative interests had already drawn him deep into the less reputable of the Company's activities and who henceforth worked in close collaboration with Sulivan in East Indian matters.

Though Shelburne was the only minister with ready-made East India connexions, others had no difficulty in acquiring them. Charles Townshend's attitude early brought him into touch with the directors and thus his side of the ministry was soon in alliance with the opposite camp in the Company. In September the *East India Examiner* was making reference to this alliance; he was speaking freely and indiscreetly to individual directors about the ministry's intentions,[2] and when in 1767 Sir George Colebrooke was brought into the Direction to strengthen it, the two men became intimate and Townshend took out his voting qualification for the Company through one of Colebrooke's agents.[3]

If the rival groups within the ministry tried to make and exploit connexions with parties in the Company, the various groups in opposition also sought support there and the Company interests were glad to have these parliamentary allies in their struggle. The issue was a good one for an opposition to take up and no doubt the indignant orations of George Grenville and Burke would have been called forth even had their respective

[1] J. Walsh to Clive, 21 December 1766. Powis MSS.
[2] L. Scrafton to Clive, 21 November 1766. Ibid.   [3] See p. 164.

parties had no contact with those handling the Company's affairs. In fact, however, both the Grenville group and the followers of the Marquess of Rockingham made such contacts and found them useful in planning their campaigns; and the parties within the Company, though the support of administration was far more important to them, did not despise the advantages of sympathy from the Opposition. In the Opposition, as in the ministry, different groups had different party alliances in the Company. Those of Grenville lay with the directors, where Lord Sandwich's 'man of business', Robert Jones, was still playing an active part, and among the supporters of Clive. The Rockingham party, though they had intervened in East India affairs in 1763 and, when in power in 1765-6, had enjoyed the parliamentary support of Clive, had no established links with the Company. Though they had some contact with men on both sides in the party war, they found themselves more closely connected on the whole with the Company opposition than with the directors. This was not because they had any friendship for Sulivan (for whom indeed Rockingham later expressed a strong aversion)[1] but because, through Lord Verney and the Burkes, they had connexions with the speculative interests which were supporting Sulivan and because, through one of their parliamentary supporters, the well-known Scottish M.P., George Dempster,[2] they came in touch with the Johnstone group who were also in his camp. In the Company elections of 1767 it is true, when Shelburne and his supporters in the ministry were encouraging Sulivan's bid for power, the Rockinghams joined the rest of the Opposition and Townshend's party in supporting the directors,[3] but on other occasions they often planned their parliamentary activities in collaboration with the Sulivan party. Their intervention is significant not because of anything which it achieved at the time, but because the line they took in these years determined

[1] e.g. Rockingham to W. Dowdeswell, 20 October 1769 and Richmond to Rockingham, 8 April 1774. FitzWilliam MSS. (Sheffield). Evidently the Duke of Portland shared this aversion. G. Byng to Portland, 25 October 1769. Portland MSS.

[2] For him see J. Fergusson, *Letters of George Dempster to Sir Adam Fergusson, 1756-1813* (1934).

[3] FitzWilliam MSS. (Sheffield). In a bundle labelled East India Papers there is preserved information from John Walsh to Rockingham on the state of the poll and a House list signed by all the candidates on it.

their East Indian policy in the future, and because such men as Burke and the Duke of Richmond gained their first interest in East India affairs while opposing the Government's intervention at this time.

To conclude the analysis of the relations between parties within the Company and in Parliament, it is necessary to give special consideration to the position of the followers of Clive. They were obliged to maintain their support of the Direction because the only alternative was the return to power of the hated Sulivan, but they put the interests of their patron before those of any party within the Company. Since their aim at the time when the attack on the Company was launched was the extension of Clive's *jagir*, their first thought was to ensure that this would not be endangered. In the early days of the new administration Luke Scrafton was in touch with Charles Townshend, but Walsh thought it wise to make a journey to Bath to interview Chatham himself. At this interview he appears to have pledged Clive's interest to support the State in its claim for a share in the Company's revenues and to have obtained from Chatham in return some general expression of support to the extension of the *jagir*.[1] On the strength of this, Clive's friends remained very quiet in the struggles and controversies that followed, but devoted all their energies to preparing the way for extorting from an unwilling Company an extension of the *jagir* for ten more years. After careful preparation, consultation with the ministry, and some splitting of stock (but none that actually stood in Clive's name)[2] they had the matter brought before a General Court of 24 March 1767. Despite all their care the result was a disappointing one, they succeeded but by a bare twenty-nine votes[3] which made their success hardly better than a defeat. The result showed both the strength which the Company Opposition was gaining and the strength of the enmities which Clive had roused among the Company servants, several of whom, including the John-

---

[1] J. Walsh to Clive, 22 November 1766, quoted Malcolm, op. cit. iii. 191-4.
[2] G. Dudley to Clive, 25 March 1767. £15,000 of Clive's funds were, however, split and Scrafton and Walsh also created twenty-three votes. (L. Scrafton to Clive, September 1767. Powis MSS.) There seems to have been a certain amount of last-minute confusion among Clive's supporters, some judging the timing of the motion unsuitable.
[3] Court Book 75, p. 458.

stones, split a good deal of stock to oppose the measure. Clive himself took the narrow majority as a personal rebuff, and on his return to England was not content until he had brought the matter once again before a General Court.[1] Thus the old issue of the *jagir* appeared once again as an issue affecting the relations of Company and State.

To sum up: parties in the Company were bidding for the support of the conflicting interests in the administration and at the same time making use, where they could, of any connexions they could achieve with the Opposition, to serve their own ends. Both administration and parliamentary Opposition were pursuing the same course with their own political ends in view. Neither side was actuated in their alliances by any motive other than immediate expediency. An informant warned the old Duke of Newcastle that this was the case. Speaking of the interests within the Company he said: 'If any reasonable plan should be proposed . . . neither ministerial nor opposition interest will avail anything with the Majority, who never did, nor ever will, regard anything but self and immediate advantages.'[2]

The course of events in the intervention of 1766 to 1767 falls into three stages, which correspond with the stages in the disintegration of the ministry. The first is that in which Chatham still had some grip on the ministry which bears his name. It ended at the beginning of March 1767. During this period the field was set, and Chatham's simple policy of force was tried and failed. After the intimation given to the Company in August that their affairs would probably come under consideration next session, nothing could be done officially until Parliament met in November. All the political world was, nevertheless, active. Walsh saw Chatham and other ministers at Bath; the directors were in touch with Charles Townshend, and in November Laurence Sulivan returned to the field at the head of the combined malcontents, with a coup intended both to ensure the favour of the ministry, and to weld his party together. His supporters at the end of October asked for a General Court, which was called for 14 November, at which

---

[1] Court Book 76, pp. 280–309.
[2] J. West to Newcastle, 16 March 1767. Add. MS. 32980, f. 310.

the Company might consider making the first advances to the ministry, and proposed such a plan for their consideration. The proposal was that, in return for an extension of the Company's charter by 37 years, the Company should hand over to the public the territorial revenues after deducting from them all expenses, civil and military, and £480,000 per annum for ten years as a yearly dividend of 15 per cent.; the profits of trade (calculated at more than £600,000 per annum) were to accumulate as capital for the keeping up of this dividend in the future and provision was to be made to ensure the Proprietors of a dividend of 15 per cent. in perpetuity.[1] The proposal was made with the full knowledge of Lord Shelburne;[2] how far it would have satisfied the ministry cannot be decided, for the directors not without some trouble brought about its defeat. Walsh called it a 'whimsical proposition'.[3]

Parliament opened late in November without any official contact between the ministry and the Company, and with everyone quite uncertain what was intended. It began with a bold step, a motion for a general inquiry into the affairs of the East India Company, but, though the Opposition was not yet at its full strength, it was clear that it would act together on this question and that the ministry would probably be divided. Men were astonished at the way the matter was introduced. As Walsh remarked, 'letting loose a general inquiry of this kind into the House of Commons without a preconcerted plan, without the least prior communication with the directors, without any line whatsoever for the House to go by, was certainly a wild method of proceeding'.[4] The very person who opened the question in the House of Commons made this clear, for it was neither Conway nor Townshend, the two leaders in the House, but Chatham's City supporter, William Beckford. After this motion no further action was taken before the Christmas recess except the passing of a further motion of Beckford's for the presentation of papers to assist the inquiry. Even this step was not taken without friction in the cabinet. While Chatham had retired again to Bath angrily reiterating

---

[1] Court Book 75, pp. 240 seq.   [2] Fitzmaurice, op. cit. ii. 17 seq.
[3] J. Walsh to Clive, 22 November 1766. G. Dudley to Clive, 21 November 1766, pointed out the alliance of the Johnstones and Sulivan in this Court. Powis MSS.
[4] J. Walsh to Clive, 21 December 1766. Powis MSS.

his demand for full parliamentary inquiry,[1] Townshend remained in London hoping to work with the directors of the Company to forestall this inquiry by obtaining permission from the General Court to enter into negotiations with and offer terms to the ministry.

The first move in the Company had been that of the Sulivan party in the General Court in November; a second was now made by the directors in December. They succeeded where their opponents had failed; despite a good deal of intransigence among the proprietors, on 31 December the directors were empowered in the widest terms to open negotiations with the ministry 'upon such points relative to the general state of the affairs of this Company as shall seem to them most requisite and conducive for the extending our commerce, securing our possessions, and perpetuating the prosperity of the Company'.[2] Charles Townshend looked on it as a personal triumph.

But the fact that the Company was likely to offer terms only served to bring out more clearly the antagonisms within the ministry. When Townshend saw in the Company's resolutions the hope of an 'amicable and happy issue',[3] Chatham suggested acidly that the adjective 'adequate' should be added, and defined adequate as 'assuming or deciding the question of right, and . . . considering consequently whatever portion of the revenue shall be left by Parliament to the Company as indulgence and matter of discretion'.[4] Such terms he had, he said, no expectation of seeing. Since terms were to be offered, however, he was obliged to admit that they must be awaited; so the parliamentary inquiry was postponed with many laments on the stupidity of 'enervating the principle of parliamentary inquiry, totally contrary to my notions'.[5] His sentiments were shared by his supporters in London, and their relations with Townshend and Conway became very strained. On 6 January and 6 February the directors presented the terms on which they were willing to negotiate. They wished in the first place for an extension of their charter either to 1800 as they at first claimed, or till 1817 as they later asked. For this they were willing to pay £500,000, and asked for permission to raise

---

[1] *Grafton Autobiography*, p. 110; Chatham to Grafton, 7 December 1766.
[2] Court Book 75, pp. 336-7.   [3] *Chatham Correspondence*, iii. 156.
[4] Ibid. 158.   [5] Ibid. 199.

the sum by loan, and somewhat more if necessary. They asked for alterations in the duties on tea and other articles, as compensation for their expenses in Manilla in the last war, and for parliamentary provision to strengthen their hands in dealing with their unsatisfactory servants in India, the first time the Company put forward this demand. Finally they asked that both their recent accessions and their exclusive trade should be sanctioned and guaranteed for the next fifty years. In return they proposed that after the Company's military and civil expenses and all contingent expenses at home were deducted and a sum allowed to the proprietors for profit (the amount of which they did not specify), all the surplus revenues to be equally divided between the Company and the State.[1] When these proposals came before the Cabinet on 14 February a breach between the two parties was only averted by referring them back for further explanation.[2] Thus the decision was postponed for a few days until the directors had drawn up these explanations.

Before their receipt, however, the ministry had been thrown into confusion by the mental and physical collapse of Chatham. Grafton and Beckford had for some time been imploring him to return to London from Bath. On 16 February, on his way thither, he succumbed to a violent attack of what was called gout. From that date, though his condition was not realized, his serious nervous illness must be dated.[3] He refused absolutely to consider details, refused to see Grafton, refused to consider the Company's proposals, refused to give any guidance for action in Parliament. It seems clear that the neurasthenic horror of business and responsibility which was so marked when he finally came to London in March had already overcome him.

The receipt of the directors' explanations brought to a head the antagonisms within the Cabinet. Already by the 16th these were common property. Newcastle reported as from Onslow that 'Governor Beckford went into the City abusing all the Directors; that nothing could be done with them, etc. And that Sir George Colebrooke said, Stock would fall 20 pr. Cent upon it.'[4]

[1] Court Book 75, pp. 427 seq.
[2] Grafton to Chatham, 15 February 1767. *Chatham Correspondence*, iii. 194 seq.
[3] This seems a valid conclusion to draw from his correspondence with Grafton and Shelburne.
[4] Newcastle to Rockingham, 16 February 1767. Add. MS. 32980, f. 110.

When Grafton saw the terms, he assumed, acting on Chatham's principles, that they were quite unacceptable and turned his attention to the next step, the continuance of the House of Commons inquiry. Here, however, he had to face a complete lack of preparation. 'Resolutions . . . ', he wrote to Chatham, 'must be well-weighed and worded so as to carry the effect that administration aims at',[1] and Shelburne echoed his implied request for guidance, reminding his leader that to leave the matter 'pretty largely to Parliament must naturally startle such of the king's servants whose minds went to a composition'.[2] But they obtained no help from Chatham and on 3 March the battle was fought out in the Cabinet. The majority decided to reject the Company's proposals and to fight the matter out in the House, the minority strongly opposed this decision, but the king threw in his voice with the majority. This seems to have been the Cabinet which Horace Walpole mentions as breaking up in disorder, after which Conway and Townshend would attend no further meetings.[3] Their resignation was fully expected in certain quarters.

The result was complete confusion. Though the matter was due in Parliament on the 6th no one knew how it was to be handled.[4] Beckford, the chief manager, had been obliged in February to write to Shelburne, 'Excuse my importunity in desiring a copy of the East India proposals; I love to talk and act with consistency and precision. I am at a loss for want of it.'[5] Still worse, the return of Chatham to London only increased the confusion, for, except for an abortive attempt to supplant Townshend by Lord North,[6] he was sunk in a strangely uncharacteristic inertia. Though he visited the king on 13 March he seems to have played no part in public affairs after 5 March, and it soon became only too apparent that he was quite unfit for business.

It was not surprising, therefore, that when Beckford took the

---

[1] 22 February 1767. *Chatham Correspondence*, iii. 217.
[2] [25 February 1767] Ibid. iii. 221.
[3] For date see *H.M.C.* ix; Stopford–Sackville MSS. Lord George Sackville to General Irwin, p. 27. Horace Walpole, *Memoirs of the Reign of George III*, ed. D. Le Marchant (1845), ii. 428, shows that Chatham was not there, although he had arrived in town. Ibid. for the attitude of Conway and Townshend.
[4] Rockingham to Newcastle, 5 March 1767. Add. MS. 32980, ff. 207–8.
[5] 14 February 1767. Lansdowne MSS. [6] *Correspondence of George III*, i. 459–60, no. 484, and Grafton, *Autobiography*, pp. 122–3.

long-deferred second step, and moved for the printing of the papers accumulated under the provisions of his earlier motion, the ministry showed itself in a pitiable light. Townshend opposed the motion as premature, and the differences in the Cabinet were openly exposed.[1] As a result, the Opposition, who had recently won a 'snap' victory in defeating the 4s. land tax, were encouraged to go farther than they had before intended. The followers of Grenville, in the Grenville–Bedford section of the Opposition, with their close East Indian connexions, suggested that it might be possible to hamper the ministry in its present state of disunion by getting a petition from the East India Company against printing the papers before the House on the grounds of the damage which might be done to its trade.[2] This plan received favour from the other section of the Opposition, the Rockinghams, and was rapidly and secretly put into effect.[3] On 9 March the always useful Robert Jones presented a petition from the directors to the House to this effect; and so well had the Opposition mustered their forces and so unprepared was the ministry that its motion to adjourn was only won by 33 votes.[4] It was an unpleasant experience for a divided ministry recently defeated on the land tax, and it was much shaken by it. Two days later, after the Chairman of the Company had been heard, the demand was withdrawn in a debate in which almost everyone, as the Opposition noticed, 'denied any design of force'.[5] The denial showed that Chatham's simple plan for forcing the Company to come to the aid of government finance on the Government's own terms had failed; and with it the first stage of the contest ended ignominiously for the ministry.

The next stage of East India negotiations had, however, already begun. In this it was Shelburne who took the initiative. That he had done so was not clearly seen by the Opposition.

[1] *Walpole Memoirs*, op. cit. ii. 428–30 and West's report to Newcastle, 6 March 1767. Add. MS. 32980, f. 215.

[2] Rockingham to Newcastle, 7 March 1767. Add. MS. 32980, ff. 220 seq. The *form* of action was certainly suggested by the Grenville group. It is not quite clear whose the idea was. It is possible that Charles Yorke originated it. The Rockinghams were certainly very active in pursuing it.

[3] Newcastle's Whips to supporters sent out on 8 March 1767. Add. MS. ibid. and ff. 230 seq.

[4] Portland to Newcastle, 9 March 1767. Ibid., f. 246.

[5] West's report to Newcastle. Endorsed 11 March 1767. Ibid., f. 262.

They saw indeed that Townshend's flank was turned, but they believed that Chatham as an 'invisible minister' was still controlling affairs. This was quite incorrect. Chatham took no part in the policy, which was indeed a reversal of that which he had been pursuing. On the other hand it followed logically from one already suggested by Shelburne.

The period of negotiation which Shelburne inaugurated seems to have lasted from March to May. It began by a stroke which, while it did not succeed, at least opened up the possibility of success in the future. It is characteristic of Shelburne's sphere of influence that it began in the East India Company. Sulivan had not accepted as final the defeat of his proposals of November 1766 for the basis of negotiation with the ministry. In January he worked out another, apparently more detailed, proposal which he discussed with Shelburne and asked him to communicate to Chatham. Shelburne did so with the remark that Sulivan had thought he could get the proprietors to agree to it, and 'he seems to think the same still, but is not so sanguine'.[1] Chatham, however, paid no attention to it,[2] and nothing was done. Now that the negotiations had broken down and all was in confusion the time seemed ripe to revive the proposition. This is what Sulivan proposed to do, and this was the scheme to which Shelburne gave his support and all his supporters in the ministry their assistance. In return it would appear they undertook to give their support to Sulivan at the next election of directors.

Had all gone well the directors had intended to have their proposals passed in the quarterly General Court of 12 March, but since they knew the ministry had rejected them the position might be thought to have changed. Emboldened by the success of their petition and the knowledge that they had support in the ministry itself, the directors decided to push farther, and resolved to have the terms passed by the General Court and then offered straight to the House of Commons where they could expect the support of the Opposition and part of the ministry and could turn the tables on Chatham and his parliamentary inquiry. This General Court, in consequence, acquired a new importance. Hitherto, although the election of directors was only a

---

[1] 1 February 1767. *Chatham Correspondence*, iii. 184.
[2] Chatham to Shelburne, 3 February 1767. Ibid., pp. 189-90.

month off, there seems to have been little activity in the Company. Sir George Colebrooke, who was entering the Direction for the first time, may have been preparing his ground, but on the whole the absence of splitting suggests that the Sulivan party had decided, as in the preceding year, that there was little to be gained by seriously contesting the election. But now on 10 March there was a sudden activity in splitting, clearly connected with the new political issue, and the issue itself soon became of importance in Company politics as a *ballon d'essai* for the election, which the Sulivan faction now saw its chance of contesting. The political element in this splitting was marked. On the one side, for instance, Shelburne's friend and follower, the lawyer, Dunning, split his stock,[1] while on the other, Charles Townshend took up his voting qualification from one Henderson, an agent of Sir George Colebrooke. The next day West fluttered the Duke of Newcastle by the information that he had received an 'unusual summons' to the General Court on the 12th.[2] On the 13th he reported the proceedings of the Court:

Sir James Hodges (after all the proposals and explanations . . . had been read) moved that the Court of Directors of the East India Company do lay the same before the House of Commons as the basis of an accommodation and was seconded by Sir George Colebrooke. This motion was much opposed by Mr. Sullivan [*sic*] and Mr. Dempster, as a letting the Government into a partnership with the Company would soon end in the absolute dependency and ruin of the latter.[3]

Sulivan then offered to draw up a less exceptionable plan and the meeting adjourned.

Two letters, one from Laurence Sulivan to Shelburne in the Bowood collection, and another from Shelburne to Chatham among the Chatham MSS. in the Public Record Office, explain the inner history of this move. In the first of them, written on 13 March, the day after the General Court, Sulivan explains that when the motion was made for the Court to approve the directors' propositions, he stood up and opposed them, particularly on the ground of their failure to keep the returns of trade and revenue apart. Challenged as to the possibility of

---

[1] Stock ledger, 1767-9. He split his £1,000 stock on 10 March. See p. 154.
[2] Endorsed 11 March 1767. Add. MS. 32980, f. 272.
[3] West's report, endorsed 13 March 1767. Ibid., f. 280.

such a distinction he offered to produce a plan if the Court would adjourn till Monday. He enclosed the outlines of a scheme for Shelburne's examination, adding 'More or less may be done if numbers are with us, which seem [*sic*] the general opinion of my friends, but I find is strongly contradicted by our opponents; upon this delicate ground I shall be happy to have your Lordship's and Lord C. . . 's sentiments and Directions.'

The proposals enclosed differed from those hitherto offered in several ways favourable to the ministry. Shelburne took up the matter.[1] Two days later, after failing to gain admission to Chatham he wrote telling him what was happening in the Company. After outlining the events leading up to the General Court of the 12th (though with an assumption of detachment from the affairs of the Company which was rather disingenuous) he reported that Sulivan had consulted him on a new plan which he hoped he could carry, since he found 'his own weight considerably greater than he had ever imagined, and that the Directors on the contrary certainly saw themselves very weak'. Shelburne adds: 'I have myself good authority to believe that he has a considerable majority for any reasonable purpose if he manages wisely.' The question to be considered, Shelburne suggests, is whether they should encourage him to pursue this plan. He writes:

I am at a loss however whether it's safe or rather proper, for his Integrity and Prudence is undoubted, to give him advice. On the one hand the situation of the House of Commons, too bad to be described, appears to make what passes in the City very material; on the other I easily conceive, that it were to be wished the genuine sense of the Proprietors could be had, but this the proceedings of the opposers of Government and the imprudence of these directors meeting them so entirely, makes impossible as far as they have weight.

It seems unlikely that he received an answer, but he answered his own suggestion and the plan went forward. Its effect was immediate. It took back the initiative in East Indian affairs from Charles Townshend. Newcastle wrote to Rockingham two days later:

I suppose you know that Charles Townshend is outrageous at what Lord Chatham is doing with the East India Company; where his

---

[1] Dated only Saturday morning, but internal evidence makes its attribution to 15 March perfectly clear. Publ. Rec. Off. (Chatham MSS.) GD 8/56.

creature Sulivan is to offer some better Proposals tomorrow at the General Court to be laid before the Parliament. And all this is done without the knowledge of the Chancellor of the Exchequer. Sullivan [*sic*] who is the person employed in all this is a creature of Lord Chatham, an enemy to Lord Clive and to all the present directors.[1]

Rockingham, both more cautious and more accurate, wrote the same day: 'I think, by what I hear, that he is set on by *part* of the Administration who wish for a *loophole* but probably it will fail.'[2]

The prophecy was correct so far as it went. Sulivan produced his plan which combined a scheme for dividing the territorial from the trading revenue, to please the Government, with a dividend of 14 per cent., to please his followers.[3] It proposed to request an extension of the charter till 1817, permission to increase the Company's capital by £800,000 at 250 per cent. (present proprietors having preference in the subscription). £1,200,000 of the sum thus raised was to go to paying off the Company's debts. A reduction in the duties on tea, muslin, and calicoes was also to be demanded. In return it was proposed to offer £800,000 to the Government for the above advantages, and all the revenue obtained by the Company from territorial sources after making a deduction of expenses and a sum large enough to guarantee the proprietors 14 per cent. dividend on their stock. That the directors took the strength behind the proposal seriously is shown by the fact that they did not attempt to reject it out of hand but moved that it should be referred to them for consideration. Sulivan's party, on the other hand, moved that it should be referred to a joint committee of directors and proprietors. But the directors still held the stronger hand and in a ballot of 19 March this amendment was defeated by 456 votes to 264, which meant the loss of the scheme.[4] Rockingham remarked that it 'happens extremely appropos [*sic*] and will be a very unpleasant hearing for the great man'.[5] The directors in due course turned down the plan, and, though Sulivan's supporters demanded a ballot on it, which coincided with that for the new directors on 9 April, its interest to the public was over.

[1] 15 March 1767. Add. MS. 32980, ff. 300ᵛ-1.
[2] Rockingham to Newcastle, 15 March 1767. Ibid., f. 296.
[3] Court Book 75, pp. 443 seq.   [4] Ibid., p. 452.
[5] Letter to Newcastle, 19 March 1767. Add. MS. 32980, f. 343.

Nevertheless it remained as an issue in the Company election and much use was made in propaganda of the assertion that Chatham and the ministry had approved it.[1] Though the challengers to the House list were late in engaging battle, they waged it hotly. 'Sulivan, Vansittart and the Johnstones are joined', Walsh reported to Clive, 'and with the assistance of the clan of temporary stock-jobbing proprietors threaten a smart opposition to our directors; I make no doubt they will have the full support of the present administration, that is of Lord Chatham and Lord Bute. . . .'[2] On the other hand, the directors also played their part with vigour. By bringing in Sir George Colebrooke on the House list they introduced a personality of undoubted energy and ambition, though of less certain judgement and solidity, into their forces, and they made full use of the Townshend party in the ministry and of the practical sympathy they could count on from the Opposition. Once again prominent members of Government and Opposition went down to India House to register their votes at an election of directors. This was what Horace Walpole meant when he asserted that the Opposition were encouraged to renewed activity in the House 'by success in a point that had scarcely been contested with them; this was the re-election of most of the late Board of Indian Directors. The Duke of Bedford was carried to the India House to vote—his son had not been dead three weeks.'[3]

The voting of the previous ballot turned out to be representative of the balance of forces in the Company and the House list was elected. Sulivan was not yet strong enough to oust his enemies. From the point of view of the ministry, however, the interlude had served the purpose of getting it out of its *impasse* and of opening up the possibility of further negotiation with the Company. No fewer than eleven proposals were sent in to the directors by various proprietors after Sulivan had offered his,[4] and the directors themselves, in the interest of their electioneer-

[1] *Gentleman's Magazine*, March 1767, p. 101.
[2] J. Walsh to Clive, 26 March 1767. Powis MSS.
[3] *Letters of Horace Walpole*, ed. Mrs. P. Toynbee, 1903-5, vii. 102. The Duke of Newcastle had been nervous as to the result, as is shown by Sir M. Fetherstonehaugh's letter of 9 April. (Add. MS. 32981, ff. 77-79.)
[4] Court Book 45, pp. 473 seq., and Committee of Correspondence. Memoranda, vol. xxiii, (no pagination).

ing campaign, had to abandon their original scheme and get out a counter-proposal to Sulivan's. Hence, before the election of 9 April they drew up a new set of proposals which owed a good deal to the Sulivan scheme they rejected. As soon as the new directors were established, it was understood that these offers would be made to the ministry. In them the directors slightly improved the terms they were prepared to offer. They offered the ministers £500,000 for the renewal of their Charter. They also asked leave to borrow the money for this and a further £500,000 to pay off their simple contract debts. The expenses of the Company were to be worked out; £400,000 was to be added to them for dividends for the proprietors, and the remaining revenues were to be divided equally between the State and the Company. They promised their constituents that as soon as the Company's debts were paid off they would raise the dividend until it reached 16 per cent., after which any surplus funds would be lent to the Government at 2 per cent. While these revised proposals owe a good deal to Sulivan's propositions, the directors continued to hold firmly to their disinclination to separate the territorial from the trading revenues of the Company, and their unwillingness to make any promise of a fixed annual sum to the State. They argued, with considerable justification, as the sequel was to show, that the future was too uncertain to make this possible. They also claimed, which was more dubious, that the danger of undue interference by the State as sharer in the Company's revenues could be eliminated.[1] Thus the two sides of the administration were able to come together again, and both succeeded in saving their faces, for on the one side the negotiation was now fully recognized, and on the other the parliamentary inquiry, so long postponed, could be opened by Beckford on 20 March,[2] because no one any longer attached much importance to it.

The significance of this inquiry is chiefly as the precursor of the much more important inquiries of the next twenty years. Though the opposition contested it hotly at all its stages, its

---

[1] Court Book 76, pp. 6 seq., and Court Book 75, pp. 480 seq.

[2] *Jour. H.C.* xxxi. 25. The original motion for a committee was one 'to enquire into the state and condition of the East India Company *together with the conduct of all or any persons concerned in the direction of the said Company*'. [The words italicized were finally omitted, on an amendment by Conway.] See also H. Flood to Charlemont, quoted *Chatham Correspondence*, iii. 144-5.

importance was obviously subordinate to that of the negotiation. Like the inquiries of later years it was exceedingly general in nature. It sought rather to show the corruption and lack of discipline of the Company's servants than to prove any one point. From the scanty information we have of its proceedings, it would appear that a wide range of evidence was covered, but its essential insignificance is shown by the fact that when the new negotiations were approaching fruition the inquiry faded away. In April when Parliament adjourned the ministry explicitly repudiated the use of force against the Company; 'a language very different', as was remarked, 'from that which Mr. Beckford . . . opened this affair with and which was held by the Ministers when they rejected the proposals of the Court of Directors as inadmissible'.[1]

The negotiations were much more serious. By 2 May they were so far advanced as to be satisfactory both to the ministers and directors and had only to be passed by the General Court and presented to the House of Commons. At this point, however, a new and acute difficulty suddenly arose. The second stage of the negotiations ended abruptly with a new outbreak of faction in the Company, followed by a recurrence of the former disunity in the ministry. The result was a third stage of negotiations marked by a renewed trust in parliamentary action, a curious revolution of alliances between ministry and Company, and an important change in the propositions which were laid before and accepted by Parliament.

The difficulty arose, as might have been expected, on the question of the dividend. In the proposals the directors put forward after they had defeated Sulivan's scheme they were forced, by the exigencies of Company politics, to make some suggestion of an increase of dividend.[2] Both parties in the Company had their own plans for reducing the Company's contract debt to make this possible. Both depended on getting government permission to raise a loan for the purpose. It was proposed in the directors' new plan that, as soon as this was done, the dividend would begin to rise gradually to a maximum of 16 per cent., and the Chairman had stated publicly that he expected the debts to be paid off by the following September.[1] This would make possible a rise in the next half-yearly dividend; it was believed it would be raised to an annual rate of at least 12 per cent. But in the course of their negotiations with the ministry the directors had been forced to abandon this among other points, and they had also had to agree to a limitation of the agreement to the short period of three years. These concessions made the expected rise in dividend impracticable. The directors had accepted these modifications with great reluctance, and showed an undisguised anxiety about their fate when brought before a General Court.

This change in terms was unpopular among the proprietors, but was particularly alarming to the speculators who had played for the rise and who were in force among Sulivan's party. They now showed they had not forgotten their success in 1766. Though the time was short before the General Court, they began considerable 'splitting' activity, led off by the Jewish financier, F. P. Fatio, who on 5 May split £16,000 of stock to the supporters of their cause,[2] in a campaign organized much as was that of the previous year, though on a less extensive scale. On the same day George Dempster and other prominent members of the Opposition asked that the directors' propositions and the Government's replies should be printed,[3] and the case of John Johnstone was once more raised by his friends. It became known that at the General Court next day they would press for a rise of dividend without reference to any negotiations that might be in progress. This impatient step was extremely unwise, for it was a deliberate defiance of the united ministry. Evidence as to its inner history is lacking, but there is some evidence that it represented rather a revolt from Sulivan's leadership than a development of it. His name does not occur among those pressing it, and only reappears in the Company records when he steps in to try to repair the damage which has been done. His coalition of supporters was by no means an easy one to lead.

Ministers saw the threatening danger in the Company and tried rather clumsily to avert it. They informed the Chair-

---

[1] *Letter to a Minister on the Subject of the East India Dividend*, London, 1767. (British Museum 102. i. 51, and India Office, Tr. 688.)

[2] Stock ledger, 1767-8. [3] Court Book 76, p. 33.

man that they would consider any increase in the dividend before the completion of the negotiations as a breach of faith on the part of the Company.[1] The wisdom of this open intervention was doubtful, for it caused strong feeling among the ordinary proprietors who might otherwise have stood aloof, and it only served to embolden the Opposition in the Company to brave directors and ministry alike. This opposition does not appear to have had the support of any member of the ministry in their revolt—they certainly had not that of their usual supporter, Shelburne—nor did the Grenville part of the Opposition assist them, though the Rockingham connexion gave them its help, brought in by the interests of Lord Verney and his friends. As Horace Walpole said, 'Dempster and W. Burke . . . ventured to avow their own share of the criminality.'[2] The strength of the Company opposition on this particular issue was, nevertheless, considerable, for much feeling had been aroused and the interests of many proprietors seemed, on a short view, to be on their side, facts which compensated for the absence of time to organize a splitting campaign comparable to that of September 1766. Moreover, once again, as in the preceding September, the directors were divided; Clive's supporters still thought, as he did himself when he returned home in July, that the directors were belittling his successes when they urged economy and caution, and in consequence were not prepared to exert themselves.[3]

All these mixed motives and the new excitment added by the intervention of the ministry made the General Court of 6 May, in which the directors had hoped to pass their propositions, a sweeping victory, on the contrary, for the Opposition. The dividend was raised to $12\frac{1}{2}$ per cent. to satisfy the speculators, the second rise within eight months, and this time the Johnstones and other returned servants also at last won their desire; prosecutions against former servants were incontinently stopped.[4] John Johnstone publicly thanked the proprietors, and all the directors could do was to register a protest in their Court against both these dangerous and irresponsible decisions.

---

[1] It is not quite clear what form this intimation took.

[2] *Walpole Memoirs*, op. cit. iii. 22.

[3] Malcolm, op. cit. iii. 216–18. They did not on this occasion desert the directors, but they gave them very grudging support.

[4] Court Book 76, pp. 39 seq.

The results of the first, the decision to increase the dividend, were not slow in coming. The ministry could not let this defiance pass, and they had a good deal of support in the House in their indignation at this act of 'impertinence' on the part of the Company. The following day the House demanded papers bearing on such subjects as the transfers of stock before the last General Court and other matters of Company political organization, and a parliamentary inquiry of quite a new sort seemed about to begin.[1] Grafton told the directors, who disclaimed all responsibility for the General Court, that the matter now rested with the House of Commons, 'whose attention to this great affair has been too often turned aside by fallacious appearances of accommodation'.[2] Nor could the Company Opposition expect any help from their accustomed friends. Shelburne may have temporized for a moment,[3] but he soon adopted a most rigid attitude. For the first time he is attacked by the pamphlets of the Company opposition. The day before the General Court his under-secretary Lauchlin Macleane had offered to resign as his duties to the ministry and his friends in the Company were at variance. 'If I oppose the wishes of Administration I abuse the trust reposed in me by your Lordship; if I take a contrary line I betray the interests of my friends, I betray my own independence.'[4] It seems to be about this time too that Shelburne noted down his own ideas of a satisfactory settlement with the Company which differed considerably from those he had approved two months ago. In particular he now thought it essential that a 10 per cent. dividend should be fixed by Act of Parliament 'as a particular set of proprietors may be led away by the hopes of present profit'.[5] Nor did the ministry await the conclusion of the parliamentary investigation. A Bill was at once introduced to prevent the Company from raising its dividend within the next year, without the consent of Parliament.[6]

[1] *Jour. H.C.* xxxi. 344.   [2] Court Book 76, p. 67.

[3] West reported to Newcastle on 11 May 1767 that Barré, Shelburne's mouthpiece in the House of Commons, had not committed himself at that date to 10 per cent. rather than $12\frac{1}{2}$ per cent. as a dividend, though he supported the Dividend Bill. Add. MS. 32981, f. 359.

[4] L. Macleane to Shelburne, 5 May 1767. His 'independence' meant his own stock-jobbing interests. Lansdowne MSS. See pp. 206 seq.

[5] Fitzmaurice, op. cit. ii. 19-20.

[6] 7 Geo. III, c. 49.

It was then that the full rashness of their precipitate action became apparent to the opposition in the Company. This Bill would lose them all they had hoped to gain. They determined to petition against it; they held General Courts of such violence and disorder that the only result was the introduction by a now thoroughly aroused ministry, of another Bill, rightly described as 'long overdue', intended to prevent the abuse of splitting.[1] The more sober leaders of the Company Opposition took some more practical measures. Sulivan once again appeared to the fore, leading them in an attempt to escape from the untenable position into which they had put themselves, by tactics of which he had made use before. He offered the Government once again better terms than they were offered by the directors. On 8 May, the very day on which the Bill for restraining the dividend was introduced, a proposition was made in the Court of Directors that the Government should be offered the more advantageous terms of the fixed sum of £400,000 a year, instead of a share in the profits (thus returning to Sulivan's earlier suggestion of separating the Company's and nation's shares), in return for the omission of all reference to the dividend. When this had no success with the directors, Sulivan and eight others demanded a General Court to discuss it. Accordingly one was called for 18 May.[2] Sulivan did not limit his activities to the Company. Three days before the General Court met, Bradshaw, Grafton's secretary to the Treasury, warned him

I am assured from good authority that the leaders of the last General Court have fallen upon a new plan for carrying their point and hope to bribe parliament into an allowance of their increasing their dividend by an immediate offer of a large specific sum instead of a moiety of the surplus. I think it my duty to apprize your Grace of this intention, lest, when the offer is made, or the view of it held out, any attempt should be made to conceal from your Grace the real motive.[3]

The warning meant, as the last line would suggest, that the danger lay not only in the attitude of the Opposition but of a section of the ministry. Under new conditions the old division within its ranks reappeared. Townshend and Conway were

---

[1] 7 Geo. III, c. 48. This Bill was introduced later than c. 49, but got on the Statute Book before it.
[2] Court Book 76, pp. 54 seq.   [3] Grafton, *Autobiography*, p. 180.

still insecure in their allegiance to the ministry; Townshend never more so. Though he had agreed to the Dividend Bill, he showed in his well-known 'champagne speech' of the same night both his instability and his contempt for Grafton and Shelburne as his colleagues. He was not, therefore, at all unwilling to play them the trick they had played him, and when the Sulivan party began to make higher offers to the ministry in return for the freedom to raise their dividend, it was not this time Shelburne who listened to them, but Townshend, who had before opposed them. Contemporaries speak of meetings between him, the leaders of the Sulivan party, and the leaders of the parliamentary Opposition at the St. Alban's Tavern, where he was generally believed to have pledged himself to opposition to the Dividend Bill in return for specific improvements in the Company's terms.[1] Whatever may have been the nature of the agreement the results were soon plain in the House of Commons and the Company. Townshend and Conway were again acting in conflict with the policy of the rest of the ministry, and in collaboration with the opposition interests, and the Sulivan party in the Company were again forcing the directors to offer the Government better terms than they had intended.

The Sulivan party carried out their side of the bargain. In the General Court of 18 May, one of the longest and stormiest in the history of the Company (it began at noon and ended just before 4.0 a.m. next day), they passed the minor proposals of the directors, but substituted for the major ones a proposition to grant to the State the sum of £400,000 a year. All references to the dividend were omitted, but a petition was voted against the Dividend Bill.[2] To these terms the directors had unwillingly to agree, and the propositions were handed in to the ministry and accepted by the House of Commons as the definitive agreement with the Company. The only change the ministry made was to insist on a still further limitation of the term of the agreement, which was now reduced to two years.

The other side of the bargain was, however, less successfully carried out. The sacrifices made by the Sulivan party were in

---

[1] *A Letter to the Proprietors of East India Stock, 1769*, op. cit.

[2] Court Book 76, pp. 67 seq., account of this General Court, pp. 85–88, the petition containing the terms offered to government.

vain, for the Dividend Bill was passed in spite of them. Townshend, Conway, and the united Opposition indeed were as good as their word, and they opposed it at every step, but the rest of the ministry stood firm and they had no success. Conditions were less favourable for such opposition than they had been when Chatham's inquiry was opposed in March, for Charles Townshend was by this time a good deal discredited and recent events in the Company had hardened opinion against it. Nevertheless men were somewhat surprised. Of the last debate on the measure Jenkinson wrote:

On Tuesday last [26 May] we had a long Debate whether the dividend of the East India Proprietors should be 10 or $12\frac{1}{2}$ per Cent. Opposition summoned all their strength. The two Ministers of the House of Commons for different motives joined them and were for $12\frac{1}{2}$ per cent. The Duke of Grafton thought it right to support Mr. Dyson, who had declared that by his Bill he meant it should be but 10; we thought ourselves bound to support him likewise, and though Townshend, Conway, Grenville and Dowdeswell, with their respective parties, were all against us, we beat them by 152 to 86. Townshend carried of [sic] with him only Touchet, and Conway only his two nephews and James (?) Harris. This is looked upon as the most extraordinary event that has ever happened in the House of Commons, and has convinced the world that the personal influence of these gentlemen who assert to be leaders is in fact nothing; and they are sufficiently humbled by it.[1]

When this had failed them the only hope of those who wanted higher dividends lay in the Lords. Here the Opposition considered themselves to be particularly strong and both sections co-operated in active measures against the Dividend Bill.[2] In the House both the Duke of Richmond and Lord Mansfield waged a vigorous campaign; and in the Company, though nothing was to be hoped from the Court of Directors, Rockingham himself proposed to 'some of the directors and proprietors'[3] the stratagem of combining with their petition against the Bill an offer from the Company to restrain their own dividend to $12\frac{1}{2}$ per cent. until the agreement with the Government

---

[1] C. Jenkinson to Sir James Lowther, 2 June 1767. Add. MS. 38205, ff. 174-174^{v}.
[2] In the FitzWilliam MSS. (Sheffield) there are notes for a speech by Rockingham against the Bill and correspondence on it. Cf. Add. MS. 32982, ff. 148 seq.
[3] Rockingham to Newcastle, 11 June 1767. Add. MS. 32982, f. 301. For Rockingham's active interest see also Newcastle to Rockingham, same date, ibid., f. 303.

expired. Once again, however, they failed, and, though thirty-seven peers dissented, the Bill was passed.

In this extraordinary way the East India agreement was finally made. It owed its origin to government need and Chatham's love of direct measures. Its course was determined by Shelburne's East Indian connexions, and its final form conditioned by the attempt of a faction in the Company to which Shelburne would offer no terms but with which Charles Townshend was willing to treat. It is not to be wondered that the agreement was bitterly attacked later, for its intentions were simply those of gain. But in the progress of the negotiations other issues had arisen, and the Government had been driven to two measures of a quite different kind which it had certainly not envisaged; the limitation of the dividend, though in the first place only for a year, and the regulation of voting qualifications in an attempt to check split voting. The age of intervention was perceptibly approaching, for the issues which the legislators had to face in 1772 and 1783-4 were already becoming clear.

VII

THE WATERSHED, 1768–71

AFTER the events of 1766–7 it proved no longer possible for the State to withdraw from the affairs of the Company. It was impossible at first because the agreement of 1767 lasted for two years only and, unless the State were to abandon its claim for the share in the Company's profits which it had won after so much trouble, a new settlement had to be reached within this time. Moreover, even before that date the Act limiting the Company's dividend would expire, and in the interest of its own share in the spoils as well as the wider interests of financial stability no ministry was likely to abandon this control until there was some reason to hope that the need for it had become less urgent. Up to the middle of 1769, therefore, the Government's relations with the Company were dominated by the problem of making a more permanent settlement with it. But when this settlement had been made, a withdrawal was still impossible because in the same year there broke on the Company two linked crises; a crisis in its affairs in India arising from administrative and political failures there, and a crisis in its affairs at home owing to the repercussion of bad news from India upon an internal situation rendered unstable by the combined effects of party faction and speculative mania. Though the events of 1769 were marked throughout by confusion and frustration, by the end of that year it would not have required much perspicacity to foresee the end of the Company's independent political existence.

The ministries which faced these problems were that of Grafton which emerged out of Chatham's ill-fated Administration, and that of North which arose in 1770 out of Grafton's. There was no sharp break between them, but throughout their changes in membership the tide was setting steadily towards alinements of interests characteristic of the future rather than the past. The parliamentary Opposition in consequence began also to assume the form which was to characterize it for the next fourteen years or so, that of various groups claiming to represent old connexions, which could be formidable when they coalesced

N

but which did so only rarely and temporarily. Some such opportunities arose during the years under consideration, in particular
in connexion with the violent but obscure popular excite-
ments raised by the Wilkite movement and the Middlesex
election in 1769, and in the agitation surrounding the war scare
over the Falkland Islands dispute in 1770. In both the ministry
showed weakness, but in neither did the Opposition interests
succeed in forcing their way into power. At no time during this
period did East Indian affairs provide such an opportunity.

Neither the Grafton Ministry nor its successor was by temper-
ament or situation likely to seek trouble with the East India
Company. Though they would cling to the financial advantages
which the State had gained, they were unlikely either to try to
despoil the Company further or to try to reform it. Since, however, they had to face the difficulties of negotiating a new agreement they had to pay it some attention, and men soon became
aware that the way they meant to do this was by extending their
indirect influence over the Court of Directors in the manner to
which the Grenville Administration had pointed the way. It can
be no coincidence that those in the best position to observe such
manoeuvres began to draw attention to them almost immediately after Lord Sandwich, already an exponent of such
measures, became a member of administration. It soon became
known that a small group of directors with close ministerial connexions was forming under the leadership of Robert Jones,
Sandwich's man of business, that they were looking for allies
among the more restless and ambitious of the directors and it
even became suspected that they were seeking to obtain control
over the Court.[1]

Their attempt to do so was made easier by the confused and
uneasy situation in which the Company's affairs were left after
the disorders of 1766-7. The opposition to the directors within
the Company remained strong and troublesome. Laurence
Sulivan, though he had not as yet succeeded in forcing his way
back to power, was ready to seize every opportunity of harassing
the directors; and the cause of discontented Company servants,
of Commanders of Company ships under accusation of smuggling, and of speculators pressing for relaxations which would

---

[1] The first suggestion that this was happening occurs in a letter of John Walsh
to Clive, 9 February 1768. Powis MSS.

bring up the price of the stock, were adopted by him and his
followers as they arose.[1] Furthermore, he had important financial
and moral support. Though Lord Shelburne was out of office
by October 1768 and even before this had withdrawn from the
business of government, and might be thought to have in consequence no longer an immediate interest in East Indian
politics, he maintained or even strengthened his support of
Sulivan at this time.[2] How far this was due to a belief that influence in the Company, like all influence in the City, was a
valuable asset to a rising politician, and how far it was merely
the result of the influence exerted over him by his 'man of business', Lauchlin Macleane, who had followed him into opposition and was himself engrossed in political and speculative
ventures within the Company, it is difficult to say. The result,
however, was that Sulivan's hand was strengthened and the
directors were always aware of the presence of their able and
unscrupulous enemy ready to stir up feeling within the Company against them or to benefit by any breach in their ranks.

The directors themselves were in no strong position to meet
this menace. To suspicion of the ministerialist *bloc* among them[3]
they added dislike of their active new colleague Sir George Colebrooke (whom they suspected rightly of an ambition to dominate
the Court)[4] and they were torn by personal dissensions. At one
point, in 1768, when they suspected Sir George and the ministerial *bloc* of an alliance to obtain the two Chairs, some of them
even went so far as to suggest bringing Sulivan back into power
to help restrain them.[5] Behind the Court, it is true, there still
stood the power of Clive, now back from his Governorship in
Bengal. His power was both a source of strength and weakness
to them, though at this stage the Direction gained more than
they lost by it. He was ill and impatient at the nagging claims of
East Indian controversies upon his time and energy; he was
already harassed by the new enemies he had made, particularly
the Johnstones who were to dog him, more bitterly even than
Sulivan, for the rest of his life; but, though he was exasperated
with the directors, he dared not abandon them lest worse should

[1] Court Books 76 and 77 *passim*.
[2] Lansdowne MSS., 1768-9 *passim*.
[3] For them see p. 181.
[4] J. Walsh to Clive, 9 February 1768. Powis MSS.
[5] H. Strachey to Clive, 5 April 1768, and J. Walsh to Clive, 8 April 1768. Ibid.

befall. In national politics he had, since his return, drifted into opposition, for he renewed his contact with his former patron George Grenville, and had he chosen to carry parliamentary contests into the Company he could have created a very awkward position on the Direction. But he and Grenville, his mentor, were careful not to do this, and indeed under Grenville's sensible and disinterested guidance, Clive was persuaded in these years to follow a much more cautious line than of old and to intervene as little as possible in the day-to-day controversies of the Company,[1] deploying his strength only on points of major importance to himself.

These were not points which much concerned the ministry, nor were they an issue of major policy within the Company; they were the exclusion of Sulivan from power and the checking of the intrigues of his newer enemies. Only in one other contentious issue in the Company was he seriously involved at this time, and that unwillingly and largely through the indiscretions of others. It proved of some significance for the future; it was the claim of his predecessor, Henry Vansittart, for the vindication of his administration when Governor of Bengal as a necessary condition of his appointment to a further term of office there. This was a matter of urgent importance to Vansittart, as he had found difficulty in remitting his fortune to England and had for some time been anxious to return to Bengal to try to realize it.[2] Though Vansittart was already at loggerheads with the directors and was working in close alliance with Sulivan and the Johnstone group, Clive made considerable efforts to keep on terms with what might be a dangerous enemy. In this attempt he failed, but one of the by-products of the attempt was of permanent importance in the history of India, for it was as a result of a temporary relaxation in party animosity that Warren Hastings, a loyal supporter of Vansittart both in public and in private, at

---

[1] e.g. G. Grenville to Clive, 29 December 1768. Advising him not to intervene in debates in the General Court on the new settlement between the State and the Company unless it became essential for him to take up the question in Parliament, and G. Grenville to Clive, 28 May 1769, on the question of restoring to the Company's service Sir Robert Fletcher, dismissed for his share in the Bengal mutiny. Powis MSS.

[2] There is much correspondence on this question among the Powis MSS. Clive became involved in it partly through a misunderstanding arising out of an interview between him and Vansittart, partly as a result of some directors quoting opinions of Vansittart which Clive maintained he had given them in private.

last obtained permission in 1768 to return to India as second in Council at Madras, thereby beginning his great period of Indian achievement.

The methods by which the ministry sought to strengthen its influence over the Court of Directors were various. The small group of directors with close ministerialist ties, never at this time exceeding three or four, might seek allies among the dissident groups of directors, as in 1768 when they formed a temporary alliance with Sir George Colebrooke. Ministers might get their nominees included in the House list; thus Sandwich got added to Robert Jones and Stephenson, his old supporters there, a new one, George Wombwell, who first came on to the Direction in 1766 and who was to serve him faithfully for many years to come.[1] Another government supporter who soon entered Sandwich's ambit, came into prominence at this time, William James, who first became a director in 1768.[2] Finally, they might strengthen their hold over the Direction by the part they could play in the Company elections themselves. In doing so they had to take account of the results of the Act of 1767 intended to check the effects of the splitting of stock. This Act had followed the lines proposed in the various unsuccessful petitions from the Company in 1764 to 1766. It disqualified from voting anyone who had not held his £500 voting qualification for at least six months. The intention was, not to prevent all collusive transfer of stock for voting purposes (this would clearly be im-

---

[1] A prominent London merchant, who was to play an important part in the Company until his death in 1780. In 1778 he was made a baronet for his services as Chairman. From 1774 to 1780 he sat as Member of Parliament for Huntingdon in Sandwich's interest. The terms on which he held the seat are made clear in a letter from John Robinson to C. Jenkinson, 19 October 1780, when Wombwell's death was imminent: 'There is some money transaction between Lord S. and Sir George which I have undertaken to discharge when Lord S. is called upon by Sir George's Executors. . . . Lord Sandwich never has sold his seats but has availed him of them to borrow money on his personal security.' Add. MS. 38214, ff. 229ᵛ–30.

[2] William James, originally in the Company's naval service in which he did notable service in destroying the pirate Angria. He returned with a fortune and became prominent at India House. In 1774 he entered Parliament, sitting for the borough of West Looe. In 1778 he was made a baronet, while Deputy Chairman of the Company. Through Sandwich's influence he was made Deputy-Master of Trinity House and director of Greenwich Hospital. He died from a stroke brought on, it was believed, by indignation at Fox's India Bill (Wraxall, op. cit. iii. 167–8). After 1769 he and Wombwell were to be Sandwich's leading Company supporters. After April 1769 Robert Jones did not again sit on the Direction, though for a time he remained active in the Company.

possible), but to destroy the elaborate financial organization which had grown up for the purpose since 1763. It would obviously be much more difficult to persuade capitalists to immobilize their resources in East India Stock for six months than it had been when the period was a few weeks or even days, and the risk of change in the value of stock, or failure or fraud on the part of the nominal holder, would be greatly increased.

At the first election after the passing of the Act, that of April 1768, it seemed as if it had been successful. It looked as if the old days of the directors' influence through the 'household troops', backed perhaps by some Treasury influence in the City, would again begin to prevail. John Walsh told Clive he thought it was bound to.[1] This year there were only 700 voters qualified, against about double that number in recent years; of these 610 voted and the House list obtained an easy victory. Hardly two months later, however, it became apparent to those in close touch with Company affairs that the success of the Act was purely temporary. The stakes for which the interests within the Company were playing were so high that they were prepared to incur almost any risk to win. Sulivan's thirst for power, Vansittart's need for office, the speculators' demand for action to bull the stock, stood on the one side; the determination of their opponents to keep them out on the other. A combination of opposition interests under Sulivan's lead showed that they, at any rate, were prepared to incur the risk and expense of organizing a splitting campaign six months in advance of the election, and as soon as this became clear the other side had to do likewise.[2] In consequence the only result of the Act was to add an even more savage intensity to the battles within the Company, and greatly to extend the period during which everything was subordinated to the electoral battle. Large forces now began to be put into the field by October of one year for the elections of April of the next and all actions during the intervening six

---

[1] J. Walsh to Clive, 15 April 1768. Powis MSS.
[2] J. Walsh to Clive, 19 August 1768. 'There are great movements in the India Stock and combinations against the directors, who are not a little alarmed for the next election. Shelburne it is said has got the command of one hundred thousand which is splitting against them and a subscription of many is set on foot for the borrowing of 150,000 more.' (This sum was exaggerated.) '. . . . The directors however are beating up for friends and in particular are solicitous for your support.' Powis MSS.

months were dominated by the needs of negotiations between, and manœuvres for position among, those in control of these forces.

In these new conditions the ministry sought to make their contributions to Company politics by the provision of stock for splitting as well as by influence. They did this for the 1769 election for instance through the provision of £25,000 from Lord Holland's Pay Office balances, which were managed as usual through his clerk, John Powell.[1] They also could sometimes direct the use of large holdings built up for the purpose by monied men anxious to obtain ministerial favours. In 1769, for instance, Sir Laurence Dundas, ex-Commissary of the Forces, bought up a large quantity of India Stock and permitted it to be split for the 1770 election under government orders.[2] Nor did ministers merely put these resources at the disposal of the directors. They could use them as a weapon of coercion. In February 1769 when the unity of the Direction had been greatly strained in the course of the bargaining for a settlement between the State and the Company, and there was real fear that there would be a breach between the ministerialist directors and the rest of the court before the April election, not only did Sandwich make a personal approach to Clive for a *rapprochement*, but a threat to withdraw Lord Holland's £25,000 was made at the same time. This threat restored at least the appearance of cordiality in the Court.[3]

It was with the aid of these methods that the ministry succeeded, though not without the usual protracted bargaining and friction within the Company, in arriving at a negotiated settlement on their future relations, a settlement which was embodied in the Statute of 1769.[4] They had first prolonged the Act limiting the Company's dividend, so that it should expire at the same time as the general settlement.[5] But already a number of pro-

---

[1] This is made clear by a letter from Sir George Colebrooke to Clive [26 February 1769] and its enclosures. Powis MSS.

[2] L. Scrafton to Clive, 25 July 1769. 'Sir Lawry [Dundas] has taken in £82,000 of stock and orders are issued for splitting it', and John Stewart to Clive, 7 November 1769, 'Sir Laurence has decided to go with the ministry ... in consequence of some rash and hasty promise he made last summer.' Powis MSS.

[3] See correspondence quoted in n. 1 above.

[4] 9 Geo. III, c. 24.

[5] 8 Geo. III, c. 11. The Company petitioned against it both in the Lords and Commons, but there was no great heat in the General Court about it and the

prietors with strong speculative interests in the stock had demanded a General Court to ensure that the directors should put forward as a *sine qua non* in any permanent settlement the right to raise the dividend to 12½ per cent.[1]

The Treasury, through Grafton's secretary of the Treasury, Thomas Bradshaw, opened negotiations with the directors in August 1768 and agreement was finally reached in January 1769. The ministry opened their negotiation by asserting their 'fullest confidence in the right of the Crown to the said territorial acquisitions and revenues', but went straight on to assert that they were nevertheless 'ready to receive a proposal from the directors for a new agreement'.[2] This was to become the accepted gambit in negotiations between the State and the Company in the years ahead. The agreement was from the beginning conceived strictly on the lines of that which was expiring. Discussion focused on the size of the annual sum which the Company was to pay the State (here the ministry succeeded in maintaining the sum of £400,000, though the directors tried hard to beat them down); the desire of the Company to be permitted to increase its bond debt by £500,000 and to obtain satisfaction for some claims arising out of the Manilla expedition in the last war (in neither of these were they successful); and the claim of the Company to increase its dividend at least to 12½ per cent., a claim which was admitted provided that it was raised by no more than 1 per cent. in any one year. It was conceded that, if the Company at any time had to reduce its dividend to 6 per cent., the State's claim to its £400,000 would lapse, and that any lesser reduction in dividend would be followed by a corresponding decline in payments to the State. Provision was also made for any surplus cash in the Company's hands, after the paying of its simple contract debts and the reduction of its bond debt to an agreed level, to be lent to the State at 2 per cent. In connexion with this last clause the Company was obliged to make annual returns to the State of its debt to the Treasury. Only on one point did the agreement go outside the purely financial field. The Government, giving expression to an old suspicion against the Company, insisted on their promising to export British

directors were thought to favour it. (G. Clive to Clive, 17 December 1767. Powis MSS.)

[1] Court Book 77, pp. 115–16.   [2] Ibid., p. 180.

manufactures each year to the average value of the exports of the last five years.[1] The agreement was to last for five years.

There were several significant points about this agreement. In the first place the sphere of State interference remained strictly limited. Though an attempt of the directors in 1768 to introduce a Statute increasing their control over their servants abroad had been blocked by the ministry on the ground that they did not want any piecemeal discussion of the Indian question in the House in advance of the settlement,[2] they made no move when the time came to eliminate any of the weaknesses of the Company's rule. Burke was justified in calling the result no more than a ransom.[3] In the second place the participation of the State in the profits of the Company led to some permanent loss of the Company's autonomy in finance in order to protect the State's interests. The dividend was now limited not as an emergency measure but as part of a long-term settlement, and the Company was never again free to raise it at will, and the Treasury was kept informed of some aspects at least of the Company's financial situation. Finally the fact that the settlement was limited to five years increased the power of the State over the Company since it gave new occasions for bargaining.

The Statute was couched in the form of a sanction to terms freely offered by the Company, and it was as such that North, as Chancellor of the Exchequer, introduced it in the House.[3] In fact, a good deal of pressure had been required to produce the Company's offer. Terms acceptable to administration were bound to be unpopular with the proprietors, and the directors were afraid that the Company opposition would gain support from those exasperated at what they would consider subservience to government. So while the directors attached to administration were prepared to back their patrons and pressed for the acceptance of terms favourable to them, the majority of the Court disagreed, Sir George Colebrooke now abandoning his ministerialist connexions and standing out at the head of these dissidents.[4] Clive, it is true, under Grenville's advice, thought it wisest not to oppose the proposals openly, but he too disliked

---

[1] It was argued that the Company no longer had an inducement to export British goods since it had gained its territorial revenues, but the complaint was a very old one.   [2] Court Book 76, p. 598, 24 February 1768.
[3] H. Cavendish, *Debates*, p. 265, 27 February 1769.
[4] R. Mackintosh to Clive, 5 January 1769. Powis MSS.

them.[1] The opposition interests in the Company, already strong, were well aware of the opportunities offered them, and in their different ways sought to take advantage of them. Some, as for instance the Johnstone group, came out instantly against the propositions and found themselves from an early date co-operating with Sir George Colebrooke and his friends,[2] despite their other quarrels with the directors. Sulivan and the interest which followed him, though they were more cautious, were also prepared to throw in their forces against the proposal when they judged their action would carry most weight.

In the confused General Courts in which the propositions finally passed by the directors were considered, the dissensions among the directors were as marked as the conflict of opinion among the proprietors. This was so obvious that Sulivan and the major part of the Company opposition held their fire till they could see what would emerge from the confusion (Sulivan himself absenting himself from the debates)[3] and the possibility of a split among the dominant interest on the Direction at the next election was freely admitted.[4] All the interests hostile to the terms rallied at the ballot which followed and the result was a defeat for the propositions and the ministerial party on the Direction by 248 to 207 votes.[5] On this the anti-ministerial directors took control and on 20 January laid before another General Court much more favourable terms, which were this time passed by 259 to 161 votes.[6] But now it was the ministry who stood out, the Treasury rejecting the revised terms as inadmissible.[7]

---

[1] His supporters were puzzled how to vote on the question (R. Mackintosh to Clive, 7 January 1769. Powis MSS.). When the matter came before the House of Commons he declared himself against the agreement.

[2] A. Campbell to Clive, 4 January 1769. Powis MSS.

[3] R. Mackintosh to Clive, 7 January 1769: 'and I understand his (Sulivan's) people and more generally Lord Sh[elbur]ne's people now that they see how the land lies as between the Court of Directors, and the old Opposition and the friends of the old system of direction are not to show themselves at all in this question.' Ibid.

[4] R. Mackintosh to Clive, 5 January 1769, reported a dispute at a dinner after one of these Courts between John Stewart, Colebrooke's jackal, and Robert Jones. When Stewart proposed to call the toast 'unanimity in April [i.e. at the election] notwithstanding different opinions as to a far earlier point', Jones asked if he meant it 'in thought, word and deed', and the toast was abandoned. Powis MSS.

[5] Court Book 77, p. 402.   [6] Ibid., p. 424.
[7] Ibid., p. 427.

Now the real struggle came. The directors were disunited, Clive passively hostile, and Sulivan seized the opportunity to come out strongly against any further concessions by the Company. Unless something were done quickly, the ministry would be forced to impose terms on the Company and face the parliamentary outcry that would follow. They avoided this danger by taking two measures; in the first place they made some further concessions to the Company, indicating that these were the last they would make. 'It is the ultimatum of the Treasury,' said the Chairman to the General Court when it met, 'there, Gentlemen, take it or go into Parliament and God knows the consequence.'[1] In the second place ministers appear to have blunted the edge of Sulivan's opposition by some hints of future support, possibly, as his enemies said, at the forthcoming election of directors.[2] As a result the agreement passed, though by no more than 290 to 250 votes.[3] It was in this way that the 'free offer' of the Company was brought into being.

It served its turn in avoiding a parliamentary crisis, however, as the lifeless parliamentary debates on it make evident.[4] Alderman Beckford, of course, seized the chance to inveigh against the Company as a monopoly and, following tradition, two petitions for laying open the trade to India were presented. There were references to the misgovernment of the Company abroad, and a brush between Clive and Governor Johnstone (representing his new enemies) on the subject. But North maintained that these were part of a wider question with which the Government had not been called upon to deal, and that all they had to consider at the moment was the protection of the financial interest of the public. From no one was there any real recognition of the kind of problems which were already becoming urgent and which both Company and State were soon to be called on to face.

Before the first sharp experience of these problems was forced upon them in the middle of 1769, there came an interlude which was also a prelude, the election of directors of April 1769, one of

---

[1] Quoted on the frontispiece of *A Letter to the Proprietors of East India Stock*, 1769, attributed in the British Museum copy to Governor Johnstone. It has been wrongly attributed to 1767.
[2] *Letter to the Proprietors of East India Stock, containing a brief relation of the negotiations with the Government from the Year 1767 to the present time*, 1769 (India Office, Tract 202), p. 25.
[3] Court Book 77, p. 462.   [4] H. Cavendish, *Debates*, pp. 251 seq.

the most fiercely contested of the century. In this election Sulivan made his great and at last successful drive to get back into
power. It had been known since June 1768 that he meant to do
so and there had been an unprecedented creation of votes before
the lists closed in October 1768.[1] The prospects of the election
had swayed both parties during the negotiations with the
Government, and the Government itself had actively intervened
in its course. As a result of the activities of the party leaders the
number of qualified voters leaped from some 700 in 1768 to well
over 1,400 in 1769. Under the new and dangerous conditions
created by the recent Act, the small-scale professional splitters
were less prominent than in the past, and much of the responsibility was carried by a few rich men or by coalitions of such men.
On the directors' side we have evidence of a fund administered
in this way in the names of Clive, Sir George Colebrooke, Henry
Crabb Boulton, and Robert Jones, to which the Government
contributed £25,000 stock through Lord Holland, and to which
others, such as Sir Matthew Fetherstonehaugh and Luke
Scrafton, subscribed.[2] Sir George Colebrooke and Clive in
addition carried on their private splitting campaigns.[3]

Their opponents, with less wealth to call on, were even more
ambitious in their plans. Sulivan and Vansittart were indefatigable in borrowing funds for splitting purposes and they built up
in particular one great fund of £100,000 stock, the details of
which we know owing to the financial disasters which afterwards befell its originators.[4] This was a coalition of twenty-three
persons who contributed to borrow the stock (mostly from
Dutch investors) on terms extremely favourable to the lenders.
They pledged themselves to return the stock after the election at
a price of 280, whether or not the stock then stood at this price.
This was a price higher than any to which India Stock had risen,
and in making the offer they were in effect gambling on a
number of issues. These issues included the successful termina-
tion of the negotiations with the Government and a relaxation
of the restrictions on the dividend, neither of which was certain
when the arrangement was made. The speculative character of

----

[1] Walsh mentioned it to Clive on 19 August 1768 (Powis MSS.) and the splitting
is evident in the stock ledger.
[2] Committee of Correspondence. Memoranda, vol. xxiv. Copy of bond.
[3] Stock ledgers, 1767-9.
[4] Correspondence of 1769 *passim*. Lansdowne MSS.

the undertaking reflected no doubt both the comparative weakness of the party's financial position and the recklessness of those who had planned it, of whom Lauchlin Macleane seems to have been the leader. Sulivan and Vansittart undertook some vague financial responsibility for the whole; the subscribers included Lord Shelburne (who afterwards claimed he knew nothing about it)[1] and Lauchlin Macleane, Lord Verney and William and Richard Burke, and Alderman Townsend, M.P., a City supporter of Shelburne's. The subscribers were no doubt actuated by a variety of motives, in which the interests of Company politics and speculative finance were probably equally balanced. They were supported by other Company opposition interests, bringing smaller but still significant forces into the field, in particular by the Johnstone group.

With these forces in the field for six months before the election, the result depended on how they were combined when the time came. There were many shifts of allegiance and much intrigue before the day when the rival lists were drawn up and the ballot taken. Though we have glimpses of these fluctuations, the evidence is not sufficient to enable us to follow their course in detail. It is clear, however, that whatever hopes of support the Government may have held out to Sulivan in January, he obtained little if any help from them in April,[2] when the battle was fought on orthodox party lines. The election was closely contested. It would seem that its fortunes were in the end swayed by the actions neither of the great parties nor of the ministry but by a last moment switch of the Johnstone group from their alliance with Sir George Colebrooke and thus with the directors, to the side of their opponents.[3] Two lists were drawn up, on which only five names were double-listed and none of these men of note in the party contests. A record

---

[1] L. Macleane to Shelburne, 29 June 1769. Lansdowne MSS.

[2] This seems clear from the *rapprochement* between Sandwich and Clive referred to by Sir G. Colebrooke in a letter which can be dated from internal evidence 26 February 1769 (Powis MSS.). In it he speaks of the Government's flirtation with Sulivan as already a thing of the past.

[3] J. Robinson to C. Jenkinson gave an exaggerated account of their 'splitting', 3 November 1769, and attributes Sulivan's success to this support. Add. MS. 38207, f. 151ᵛ. The *Gentleman's Magazine*, 6 April 1769, spoke of 'no less than £13,000 capital stock, issued out to qualify, by one set of gentlemen . . . . employed by him to whom the management of it was entrusted to make votes for the other' (p. 211).

number of votes were polled and when the results were known it was found that, in addition to the double-listed candidates, ten members of the House list and nine of the opposing Proprietors' list had been elected. Some prominent directors were defeated, both representatives of the 'Old' interest, such as Thomas Rous, and ministerial supporters, such as George Wombwell. So, too, was Governor Johnstone, despite his tergiversations; but Laurence Sulivan was back in power and Henry Vansittart was with him. The newcomers were not strong enough to control the Court—Sir George Colebrooke was elected to the Chair—but everyone recognized that the formidable Laurence Sulivan had returned from his years in the wilderness.

II

Sulivan thus began the second period of his influence over the fate of the Company. For four of the next five years he was in office and for much of the time the most powerful man in the Company. It was not a happy period for him or the Company. On the credit side of his balance sheet for this period must be placed the fact, admitted though grudgingly by most men, that he knew far more about Indian affairs than any other director, that he was resourceful and indefatigable, and above all that he at once began to push with all his vigour and determination the man who was beginning to obtain recognition as the greatest Company servant of his day, Warren Hastings. On the debit side must be placed the effects of the Company faction in which the struggles of the past six years had inextricably entangled him. 'The ghost of Clive haunts me', he said after his great opponent's death,[1] and his best friends including Warren Hastings would tacitly admit the liability under which he suffered. A still more serious misfortune was, however, now to be inflicted on him, to entangle him in all manner of difficulties and degradations, and to have unhappy effects on the history of the Company and the government of India for years to come. Not much more than a month after the election in which he returned to power financial disaster overtook him and many others in the Company.

In May 1769 the boom in East India Stock which, with minor

[1] Add. MS. 29136, f. 171, 14 April 1775.

fluctuations, had been in progress since 1766, and which had become intensified during the contested election, came to an abrupt end. It was stopped by the arrival of alarming news from India. Early in May there was an unexplained drop in the price of stock, due perhaps to the receipt of dubious rumours from India by private individuals. On 26 May there arrived alarming official news. From Madras came the news that Hyder Ali of Mysore was ravaging the Carnatic up to the gates of Fort St. George, and, even more alarming, there were accounts of the massing of French naval forces at Mauritius which it was feared might portend a bid on the part of France to revive her ambitions in India. From Bengal too there were accounts of uneasy relations with the native powers. By the time the news had reached England it is true the anxieties in Bengal had been dispersed, the war with Hyder Ali had ended in a peace on his terms and the French threat had come to nothing, but none of this could be known at the time, and the shock was heavy and unexpected. The stock promptly fell from 273 to 250 and by the middle of June was down to 239.

The market had been caught at an unlucky moment. The speculation in East India Stock had reached something of a climax during the negotiations with the Government and the heavily contested election which followed it. It was estimated that on the London market alone there were speculative transactions for settlement at the quarterly 'rescounters' in July of some 40 to 50 million pounds.[1] A number of 'bulls', including men prominent in the Company and outside, were among them, in particular the group which had been so active in pressing on for high dividends in the Company, of which Lauchlin Macleane was the directing spirit.[2] Moreover both sides in the recent contest were caught with their stock still in the hands of split votes. This was inconvenient and dangerous for everyone; for Sulivan, Vansittart, and their colleagues who had adopted so rash a method of borrowing it was little short of disastrous. The result was a panic which, while it was largely confined to India Stock and did not, as in 1772, develop into a general credit crisis, was devastating within its limits. 'There never was since the South

---

[1] I. Barré to Shelburne [18 July 1769]. Lansdowne MSS.
[2] This is made clear from suits in Chancery and the Exchequer arising out of their failure.

Sea year so great a crush in stock matters',[1] an observer said, using the current slang. A number of prominent speculators were badly hit. Lord Verney and all the Burkes with him were reduced to the verge of ruin.[2] Lord Holland was said to be faced with payment of 'differences' on £50,000 stock for the jobbing operations of his son Stephen,[3] an unwelcome addition to the gaming debts of the sons who cost him so dear. Lord Shelburne lost £30,000 in a vain attempt, made in circumstances that incurred him some obloquy, to save from disaster his henchman Lauchlin Macleane.[4] The latter admitted, after the crash, to debts of £90,000[5] and a number of other men were involved in his downfall. The organizers of Sulivan's coalition for the 'splitting' of stock, among whom were some of the speculators facing ruin, were equally hard hit. Vansittart through a combination of jobbing and 'splitting' was reduced to ruin and nothing but an immediate return to India could save him. Sulivan was calculated to have lost more than £15,000 on this subscription alone, was involved in Macleane's disasters, and was reduced to the most desperate straits.[6] Indeed, his private fortune never recovered from the disasters of this year followed some years later by the collapse of Sir George Colebrooke's fortune[7] and as late as 1780 he was glad to accept from Warren Hastings a gift of £10,000 to ease him of his embarrassments.[8] Of the twenty-three persons who had taken part in the coalition subscription planned by Macleane and backed by Vansittart and Sulivan, it was at first feared that at least ten were either men of straw or had lost so severely in other ventures that they could take no share in the

---

[1] I. Barré to Shelburne [16 July 1769]. Lansdowne MSS.
[2] For them see Dixon Wecter, *Burke and his Kinsmen*, pp. 23 seq.
[3] I. Barré to Shelburne [8 August 1769]. Lansdowne MSS.
[4] See Appendix.
[5] I. Barré to Shelburne, 19 June 1769. He was said to have property of value of £70,000, but this seems doubtful. He admitted to a deficit of some £19,000 exclusive of Shelburne's bills for £30,000. Many creditors came forward in the ensuing years and it seems doubtful whether he, or anyone else, had a complete picture of his indebtedness. Lansdowne MSS.
[6] I. Barré to Shelburne, 14 August 1769. Lansdowne MSS.
[7] See below, pp. 223 seq. Sulivan was a very heavy sufferer in Colebrooke's disaster since 'Sir George Colebrooke by a move of Macleanes is deeply in my debt'. (L. Sulivan to W. Hastings, 31 January 1779. Add. MS. 29142, f. 465ᵛ.)
[8] L. Sulivan to W. Hastings, 23 October 1780. Add. MS. 29146, f. 176. Hastings had made the offer the preceding June. Letters to L. Sulivan and to his attorneys, June 1779. Add. MS. 29128, f. 205.

burden falling on the rest. In fact when (after some discussion whether or not they should carry on in the hope that the stock would rise again) they wisely decided to wind up the venture, only six proved unable to meet their liabilities; the others got out at a loss of over £3,000 a head.[1]

The results of this financial crisis on the affairs of the Company were disastrous. Its leaders were distracted by their own difficulties and by the panic and clamour of ruined followers seeking means of saving themselves and the remnants of their fortunes. This was the more unfortunate since firm action was required, firstly to deal with the situation in India, and secondly to handle relations with the ministry who, on the news of danger of attack from France, at once began to take a new and agitated interest in the affairs of the Company. If the relations of the Company with the country powers was to give France an opportunity for successful aggression, the State was clearly concerned in the way in which the Company handled these relations. And when the Government was asked for naval assistance to save India from attack and some alarmists even clamoured for military aid as well, it had its opportunity to assert its interest.

Even before this new crisis arose, it had seemed to contemporaries that the influence which the ministry had recently built up in the Company was not going to die away now that, with the passing of the agreement, its ostensible cause was over. The active part that ministers played in the election of directors had seemed to suggest that they intended to continue their policy of maintaining an interest there in case it should be needed. The recognition of this fact had stirred no less an Opposition leader than the Marquess of Rockingham to one of his occasional bursts of activity.[2] His inspiration was not in this case, as in most others, Edmund Burke; Rockingham seems indeed to have concerted his early measures without consultation with Burke, planning them instead with Charles Cornwall, M.P., later Speaker of the House of Commons,[3] a competent young 'man of business' who

<hr>

[1] I. Barré to Shelburne, 14 August 1769. Lansdowne MSS.
[2] This is brought out by correspondence in the FitzWilliam MSS. (Sheffield), e.g. E. Burke to Rockingham, 31 May 1769, and a letter in the Powis MSS., H. Strachey to Clive, 13 June 1769, reporting a conversation with Rockingham on it on 11 June.
[3] Charles Wolfran Cornwall, 1735-89, Speaker of the House of Commons 1780-9, brother-in-law to Charles Jenkinson.

was rising to some fame about this time as a negotiator. Their idea was to effect a junction between Clive, Sir George Colebrooke, and Laurence Sulivan and their respective parties so as to build up a coalition against the ministry in the Company. When the financial disaster came they saw the additional advantage that a cessation of conflict in the Company would restore confidence and steady the price of stock. As Rockingham wrote to Burke on 31 May 1769 in the early days of the disaster in which Burke himself was so deeply implicated:

A conciliation between Sir George Colebrooke, Lord Clive and Sullivan [sic] would in my mind produce permanent security and the political consideration of keeping the East India direction from being tools of the Administration and in the present moment would give great force and credit to the affairs of the Company—if such an Union could be effected immediately.[1]

This idea was steadily pursued throughout the summer of 1769 by a small body of men within and outside the Company. Its organizer, Cornwall, gave much thought and address to it.[2] When he had the scheme complete it involved the sharing of offices and advantages between the parties and the drawing up (with the help of a named arbitrator, Charles Raymond the ships'-husband) of an agreed House list for the next election.[3] Its desirability was strongly felt by both sides—by Clive's followers (if not very willingly by Clive), by Sir George Colebrooke, and by Sulivan, who realized that his financial losses and those of his ally Vansittart made it quite impossible for him to attempt to fight another election on his own[4] and who needed more than anyone the immediate advantages of political power. The actions of administration in the crisis which had arisen underlined, moreover, the political arguments for such a union. Nevertheless, though the scheme often seemed on the verge of success, it finally broke down over jealousies about the share each side was to have in office and over the suspicion which each side entertained of the other.

[1] Rockingham to E. Burke, 31 May 1769. FitzWilliam MSS. (Sheffield).
[2] There are references to his activities in the Lansdowne, Powis, and FitzWilliam MSS. during this year. He was particularly adroit in avoiding the demands of Lauchlin Macleane for a lucrative position.
[3] A copy of the terms of the agreement (undated) is preserved among the Powis MSS.
[4] I. Barré to Shelburne, 14 August 1769, quoting Sulivan. Lansdowne MSS.

At first the crisis seemed to be helping those working for it to achieve their aim. The need of rapid action to re-establish the situation in India was generally felt and the idea of sending out a Commissioner or Commissioners (later generally called supervisors) with overriding powers to bring the Presidencies back to order and restore peace there was early suggested and adopted. The measure was one successfully employed on occasion by the Dutch Company and not without precedents in English and French experience. Clive gave the prestige of his support to the idea and also suggested the need of specific reforms for which parliamentary sanction would be necessary, in particular improved conditions for the Company in recruiting its armed forces.[1] The proposal for the sending out of supervisors was quickly seized on by those planning the coalition within the Company, who saw in it a way of clinching the alliance. Within a few days it was known that a proposal was taking form to send out not one but three supervisors and that the men proposed were Luke Scrafton, as representative of the one side, and Henry Vansittart, as representative of the other.[2] For a third candidate someone less strongly associated with either party was sought. The advantages to Vansittart and Sulivan of this appointment for the former were, however, so obvious that Clive's supporters felt they might safely insist on tipping the balance to their side and the third candidate put forward was one Colonel Forde who was understood to owe allegiance to them. The plan seems already to have been far advanced at the beginning of June; on the 9th the ministry were informed of it and were asked for a naval frigate to carry the supervisors to India.[3] On the 14th the directors agreed on the names of those to go.[4]

It was over the question of the third supervisor that disagreement sprang up. It showed itself first among Sulivan's supporters. Sulivan and Vansittart had seized the chance of salvation without consulting Shelburne and their other influential backers. Shelburne and his friends were not only piqued at the slight, but angry that no attempt was made in the arrangements to give Lauchlin Macleane the same chance of saving himself

[1] G. Grenville to Clive, 11 June 1769. Powis MSS.
[2] I. Barré to Shelburne, [12 June] 1769. Lansdowne MSS.
[3] Court Book 78. The correspondence between the ministry and the Company was reported at the General Court of 15 August, pp. 167 seq.
[4] Ibid., p. 72.

and his creditors which Vansittart was getting. They promptly brought pressure to bear both on Sulivan (who himself had only less financial interest in Macleane's rehabilitation than in Vansittart's) and on Cornwall, as sponsor of the union, to obtain for Macleane the third place among the supervisors or to reorganize the Commission in such a way as to make it easy for him to go out in their train.[1] Opposition also arose from other directions. The Johnstones were not only excluded from the coalition but were nervous of the investigations which the supervisors would set on foot in India; they therefore opposed their appointment altogether.[2] Finally the ministry began to show suspicion of, and hostility to, the measure. When ministers were first informed of the Company's intention they had expressed general approbation of it, though they had considered themselves justified in view of their concern in the Indian situation in asking for further particulars.[3] The demands for assistance from them in the naval field became heavier as the Company reviewed the situation, and the ministry itself was anxious to co-operate both by sea and if necessary by land. First of all General Robert Monckton, M.P., volunteered, with the king's permission, to command the Company's land forces;[4] this offer was not accepted; but the next suggestion, that the Crown should appoint a sea officer of experience to command the naval forces sent out, met with a warmer response, and Sir John Lindsay (not an impressive selection but presumably chosen as a kinsman of Lord Mansfield's) was nominated.[5] The services of these officers were certainly put forward in the first instance for reasons of military expediency; but the offers soon became entangled with issues of East Indian politics. The supporters of the ministry in the Company could not be expected to stand idle while a coalition was formed against them, and the ministry itself did not want the Company under the control of Opposition interests at such a time. The appointment of the three supervisors was the first

---

[1] See letter quoted in n. 2, p. 195, and also I. Barré to Shelburne, 19 June 1769. Lansdowne MSS.
[2] H. Strachey to Clive, 22 June 1769. Powis MSS.
[3] Court Book 78, pp. 167 seq.
[4] Ibid., 78, p. 65. Robert Monckton, 1726–82, had seen much service. Governor of New York 1761. Since 1765 he had been Governor of Berwick-on-Tweed.
[5] Ibid., p. 148. He was then thirty-two with the rank of Captain.

fruit of such an anti-ministerial coalition. Hence the ministry
began to oppose it in various underground ways, sometimes indicating a preference for the sending of Vansittart alone,[1] sometimes suggesting that Monckton or Lindsay should be the third
of the triumvirate, thus leaving a representative of the Crown as
arbiter between the representatives of the other two interests,[2]
sometimes quarrelling with the legality of their commission.[3]
These activities added to the dissension within the Company.
Lauchlin Macleane and the Shelburne interest, for instance,
made a sudden and short-lived alliance with the ministerial
party while Monckton's appointment was under discussion, because Macleane had served under him in the past, was still in
touch with him, and believed he could go out to India in his
train.[4] When this failed, and the ministry was pressing Sir John
Lindsay on the Company, the Johnstones, who had some connexions with their fellow-Scot and hoped to profit from it,
eagerly pressed his claims.[5] The sensible suggestion of Sulivan
that Warren Hastings should be made the third supervisor
went disregarded in the turmoil.[6]

The most serious trouble between the ministry and the Company arose, however, on the powers which the former claimed
for Lindsay in India as its representative, in exchange for the
help it was providing. Ministers were seriously alarmed at the
position in India. Though they did not openly press the claim
that he should be associated with the supervisors in all their
powers, they tried to obtain for him not only plenipotentiary
powers in the Persian Gulf but also—a much more sweeping
claim—full powers of treating on peace and war with the Indian
princes with whom the Company were in contact. Since the
Carnatic was believed to be the centre of trouble, the aim of this
provision was obviously to establish direct relations between the

---

[1] L. Scrafton to Clive. Letters of [28, 29 June and 1 July] 1769. In the last he
reports a rumour that a letter is to be written stating that such an appointment
would be in conformity with the King's sentiments. (Vansittart had a sister at
Court in the Princess of Wales's household.) The dates of these letters can be fixed
from internal evidence. Powis MSS.
[2] I. Barré to Shelburne [12 June] and [16 July] 1769, Lansdowne MSS., and
E. Burke to Rockingham, 13 August 1769. FitzWilliam MSS. (Sheffield).
[3] Court Book 78, pp. 156 seq.
[4] I. Barré to Shelburne, 19 June 1769. Lansdowne MSS.
[5] L. Scrafton to Clive, 25 July 1769. Powis MSS.
[6] L. Scrafton to Clive [13 June] 1769. Ibid.

Crown and the Nawab of Arcot on certain subjects to the exclusion of the Company. Indeed, it was soon frankly admitted
that this was so. Lord Weymouth, the Secretary of State, advanced the new and revolutionary doctrine that, since the
Nawab was recognized in the Peace of Paris and 'it would be
highly improper that the king should trust the execution of
engagements which he has contracted with other Crowned
Heads to the Company's servants', the king ought to have direct
intercourse with him.[1]

Behind this new and unexpected demand lay a story full of significance for the future. The claims which Weymouth advanced
were based not merely on the evidence of misrule in the Carnatic
which had reached the ministry through the Company, or
on panic at the news from India, but on the representations
of an emissary of the Nawab himself. The Nawab's representative was one John MacPherson, a plausible and ingenious
Scottish adventurer of whom more was to be heard.[2] In undertaking this mission he established his position as the pioneer of
the shady ranks of European agents sent over to England in the
coming years to further the interests of the princes of India by
appealing to the State against the Company. Though all we
know of his mission is what appears in a highly coloured report
he submitted to his employer when claiming fantastic expenses
from him,[3] there is no reason to doubt that during 1768 and
1769 he had access to Grafton and his secretary of the Treasury
Bradshaw, that he offered them presents from his master which
they refused, and that he gave them a tendentious but not
altogether inaccurate account of the relations between the
Nawab and the Company's servants in the Carnatic. No
official notice was taken of his mission,[4] but the events of 1769
showed it had not gone unregarded.

---

[1] Home Miscellaneous, vol. 101, ff. 1–11. Weymouth's secret instructions to Sir
John Lindsay, 13 September 1769; see also Court Book 78, pp. 170 seq.
[2] For his later career see below. He was a cousin of James MacPherson, author
of *Ossian* and Government pamphleteer. He went out, nominally, as purser of an
East Indiaman, to seek his fortune, and managed to attract the attention of the
Nawab. In 1770 he returned to India as a writer in the Company's service.
[3] For this document see p. 317, n. 3, below.
[4] Admiral Harland later reported that MacPherson had given some trouble to
Sir John Lindsay and himself, claiming their support in his claims on the ground
that their missions were due to him. Harland to Rochford, 1 September 1772,
Home Miscellaneous, vol. 110, ff. 495 seq.

These sudden claims on the part of the Government, however, aroused alarm not only throughout the Company but among the parliamentary Opposition, and it soon became clear that ministers had occupied a position which they dared not retain.[1] In the Company almost all interests rallied to the defence of its independence, and when ministers unwisely insisted on the calling of a General Court to hear their demands, it became apparent that they would suffer an open defeat unless they were prepared to modify their terms. But for such a clash they were not prepared. In the face of the feeling they had aroused they thought it wise to climb down, and negotiations for a compromise were soon in train. By the end of the month one was reached. It was agreed that Lindsay should be given by the Crown and the Company the rights of a plenipotentiary in the Persian Gulf, but should elsewhere have no other powers than those of assisting the Company's authorities in measures concerning war and peace with the Indian powers, special attention being paid to the relevant articles of the Peace of Paris to which the Government had appealed.[2]

The compromise on this specific point was, moreover, part of a more comprehensive *rapprochement* with the Company, and of a new attempt to pacify the contending forces there. The ministry promised support for parliamentary measures to strengthen the Company's control over its servants and to aid its recruiting; all opposition to the three supervisors was dropped; the three originally proposed, Vansittart, Scrafton, and Forde, were accepted; and the party coalition within the Company which Rockingham had aimed at was extended to embrace the ministerial supporters in the Company. Laurence Sulivan told Lord Shelburne at this time that he had been asked, in order to cement the alliance, to visit not only his old enemy Clive but the Duke of Grafton and Lord Weymouth, who would not object to the arrangement, and to 'converse occasionally' with Robert Jones.[3] When the supervisors sailed in the *Aurora* frigate early in October all groups within the Company were temporarily at peace.

---

[1] *Burke Correspondence*, i. 185.
[2] Court Book 78, pp. 144 seq. For the feeling roused see Sir George Colebrooke to [C. Yorke], 26 August [1769]. Add. MS. 35638, ff. 311-12.
[3] L. Sulivan to Shelburne, 27 September 1769. Lansdowne MSS.

But nothing done in 1769 worked out as was intended. The supervisors sailed, bearing with them both the private and desperate hopes of Sulivan and all connected with Vansittart, and the public instructions which, it was believed, would reorganize the Company's administration, particularly in the Carnatic. Even in the struggles of the last painful months Sulivan and others had been working hard on the problems of Bengal and of the Carnatic, and among other issues the problem of the Nawab's debts to the Company and its servants and his relations with the neighbouring powers and with the Company were faced openly for the first time. All this labour was, however, in vain, for after long waiting it became clear that the *Aurora* had met with misfortune and it was finally admitted that she must have foundered with all hands.

Sir John Lindsay, 'the sea officer of experience', on the other hand, arrived in safety with his small naval force to carry out on behalf of the Crown the delicate compromise of his instructions. It was even more delicate than appeared on the surface, for he carried with him, in addition to his public instructions from the Company and the Crown, private ones from Weymouth which fully justified the suspicions of the Company. He was privately instructed to inquire into the grievances of the Nawab of Arcot against the Company's servants, making direct contact with the Nawab for the purpose if necessary. His mission was, he was told, of the utmost national importance. The Company's servants at home and abroad were too selfish to consider Indian affairs from a national point of view; but a quarrel with the Company was most undesirable and he must carry out his investigation without alienating its servants. 'Whatever just arguments might be drawn from the present participation of the Public with the Company to justify a more inquisitive inspection of the management of their affairs, at present they are to be avoided as much as possible.'[1] His arrival with these powers was no less unfortunate than the failure of the Commissioners to arrive with theirs. The situation was less critical than had been believed when he was appointed, but it was even more complicated, and the young Commodore found himself trying to carry out his instructions, not in time of war when the Company

[1] Weymouth to Sir John Lindsay, 13 September 1769. Home Miscellaneous, vol. 101, f. 128.

was dependent on royal naval aid, but in conditions of uneasy peace. The result was a signal failure; he proved incapable of resisting the wiles of Eastern diplomacy and during his short term of office only succeeded in encouraging the Nawab to play off the Crown against the Company, in fostering the ambitions which led to his attack on his feudatory the Raja of Tanjore from which so much trouble arose, and in exasperating the Company's servants, good and bad alike. Not only Warren Hastings, who was doing admirable work in the Carnatic under Governor Du Pré, but the ministry who had sent Lindsay, were obliged to admit that the results of his mission were unfortunate. It is true that on his return in 1771 relations with France made North's Government consider desirable the appointment of a successor, Admiral Harland, but he went out with instructions to refrain from independent action and to impress upon the Nawab the fact that the interests of the State and the Company were the same.[1] The first attempt of the State to interfere in the Company's territorial affairs by agents on the spot was unsuccessful, damaging, and even ignominious.

At home the results were equally inconclusive. Though ministers were no doubt sincere in promising to support the Company in any parliamentary measure necessary to improve its military and civil authority in its overseas possessions, in fact they were never prepared to face the opposition of vested interests which was roused by such proposals when they were put forward, and nothing in consequence came of these efforts. In the Company itself the party truce proved more apparent than real: the ministerial supporters continued to suspect a plot against them by the opposition interests, while, on the other side, Sulivan's desperate situation made him nervous of treachery at every turn. His re-election to the Direction was of the utmost importance to him and he had good cause for alarm in the known weakness of his state. 'To me', he wrote to Shelburne at the end of September, 'all are ill-disposed, Clive and George Grenville, Colebrooke and Lord Rockingham, Cust and Administration.'[2] Still worse, even Shelburne was beginning to fail him. Lauchlin Macleane had got nothing out of the negotiations in the

---

[1] Secret instructions to Admiral Harland, f. 79, Rochford to Harland, 26 April 1771. Home Miscellaneous, vol. 109, ff. 5 seq.
[2] L. Sulivan to Shelburne, 27 September 1769. Lansdowne MSS.

Company and Shelburne (well aware that in the painful process of disentangling his follower's liabilities his own reputation was suffering) began ostentatiously to dissociate himself from the East India affairs which had worked out so unfortunately for him. Some time later he said, attributing to himself as he was wont loftier motives than the circumstances might seem to justify: 'I interfered a good deal at one time in the affairs of the Company, but upon its taking a very corrupt turn I scrupulously shut my door against them.'[1]

In this unfriended position Sulivan took the precaution, only two days after the coalition was thought to be settled, of trying to reinsure himself with the ministry lest Clive and Colebrooke should try to throw him over.[2] Nor was it long before the occasion arose to make use of this insurance. As early as October, for reasons which the evidence leaves obscure, the coalition seems to have begun to break down, and a flurry was caused in the Company and even some comment in parliamentary Opposition circles, by the news that Sulivan had promised his support to the ministerial side and that the supporters of Clive and Colebrooke were hastily preparing for a contest at the next election of directors. Burke told the Marquess of Rockingham, who had heard rumours of it in the country: 'I forgot to mention anything to your Lordship on the revolution in the India House. . . . Sullivan (sic) has gone over to the Court. When I was told this, I said to my informer, as I do to your Lordship, that I could not blame him.'[3] By the end of November Shelburne considered that he was now 'acting in a very opposite line to ours.'[4]

At first it looked as if he would be successful, and his opponents were loud in their indignation;[5] but his luck did not hold. Sir George Colebrooke had foretold that he would probably get

---

[1] Fitzmaurice, *Life of Shelburne*, op. cit. i. 318.
[2] L. Sulivan to Shelburne, 29 September 1769. Lansdowne MSS.
[3] *Burke Correspondence*, i. 210–11, 6 November 1769. On 20 October Rockingham wrote to Dowdeswell: 'When I was at Lord Albemarle's in the beginning of last week, an account came there of a strong suspicion that Sullivan (sic) . . . was gone off to Administration . . . and by what I have since heard from London I imagine there was good foundation to believe that Sullivan was playing pranks.' FitzWilliam MSS. (Sheffield). George Byng told the Duke of Portland, 25 October 1769: 'Sulivan is certainly gone over to the Duke of Grafton. He took a solemn and weeping leave of Lord Shelburne.' Portland MSS.
[4] Shelburne to I. Barré, 30 November 1769. Lansdowne MSS.
[5] The reactions in the Company are reflected in the Powis MSS. Letters from 6 November 1769 seq.

his way if the ministry remained in power,[1] but at the end of
1769 Grafton was seeking an escape from the office he had never
greatly desired and his ministry came to an end in January
1770. When North succeeded him there was a reshuffling of
persons and of dominant interests in administration. Among
those whose views became much more important were North
and Sandwich, and both of them had become averse from encouraging the continuation of the party battles in the Company.
As early as November 1769 it had been significant that, though
officially the ministry was understood to be backing Sulivan
against the parties owing allegiance to Clive and Colebrooke,
Lord Sandwich had already told Colebrooke that he stood
'neuter'.[2] By the time the April election of directors was due
North's Government was well established in power and Sulivan,
whose friends complained of 'dreadful treachery',[3] was defeated,
and again found himself in the wilderness.

But North's new administration, while not prepared to back
him against his old rivals, was equally disinclined to back his
rivals against him. They soon set to work to achieve the coalition
which the Opposition leaders had sought to bring about the
year before, though in a form which admitted the reduction in
Sulivan's bargaining power since his recent catastrophes. The
tale was told by Colebrooke in October 1770:

Lord North took the occasion very early to express his good wishes
towards the East India Company and the Court of Directors. Some
time after this he sollicited as a Favour done to himself, the taking in
of Mr. S.(ulivan) as a single director. At the time he had not seen
Mr. S—. However when Mr. S—. saw Lord North he gave him a list
of eight names, which he said was a list of his friends, out of which he
proposed the Direction to choose two or three and claimed one of the
Chairs. When it was given to me, I told the first Lord of the Treasury
that I was sure the directors would not agree to it—that I was ready
to carry any measure to the Court of Directors—that I could not
answer for them what they would do, but I was sure I could answer
for them what they would not do. It was thought proper to bring it

[1] Letter from Colebrooke undated [November 1769]. Powis MSS.
[2] As soon as Colebrooke and Clive learned of the alliance they began to take
vigorous steps to counter the threat, including the setting up of a fund, with Clive's
name at the head, to insure holders or distributors of 'split' votes against loss
through fall in the price of stock (G. Colebrooke to Clive, various letters in November 1769; also J. Stewart to Clive, 7 November 1769. Powis MSS.).
[3] 24 April 1770. W. Waller to W. Hastings. Add. MS. 29132, f. 372.

on before the Court of Directors the week previous to the last day of splitting of stock which was last Wednesday [10 October]. Accordingly I received Lord North's letter on the morning to request of the Court of Directors, which was stated to them. They were told it was a matter not of our seeking, but coming recommended from above. We had reduced it to a precise point; notwithstanding which it would be better to put some question in writing upon which we were to ballot. The question agreed on was this:

> That L. S——. Esq. be a candidate on the House List of Directors on the assurances which have been given, that he will sign and support the said list and accept of being a Director without any other terms or conditions.
>
> The number of the ballot, 13 to 4.[1]

This time the coalition was achieved. At the election of directors in April Clive's friends kept some stock split in case of a last-minute contest,[2] but the precaution proved unnecessary. There was no opposition and Sulivan, humbled but in no way daunted, resumed his seat on the Direction. Though, when it became evident that Vansittart had been lost at sea, his private affairs became almost desperate,[3] he did not let them interfere with his public activities. His talents began to impress themselves again on his colleagues; he and Sir George Colebrooke soon struck up an alliance and by the end of 1771 observers began to remark 'if he remains united as at present with Sir George, he will . . . very shortly lead the India House.'[4]

Three things only emerged from the confused episodes of these years, sandwiched between the first parliamentary intervention of 1767 and the events leading directly to the second one of 1773. The first was the blurring of the edges of the feud between Clive and Sulivan which had torn the Company for seven years and done both it and the contestants great harm. Though the ani-

---

[1] G. Colebrooke to Clive, endorsed October 1778. Powis MSS.
[2] G. Clive to Clive, 13 October 1770. Ibid.
[3] *H.M.C., Palk MSS.*, nos. 169, 170, 171, 189, show how serious his position was in 1772, before the crisis of that year broke. After mortgaging everything he still owed over £17,815 against which he had no security other than debts of £9,070 owed him by Lauchlin Macleane, Lord Shelburne, Lord Verney, and a Mrs. Forest. His hopes of getting this money rested on Macleane's chances of getting out to India and retrieving his fortunes. By 1774 (loc. cit., no. 242) Macleane had begun to make some payment, but when he died he was still in Sulivan's debt.
[4] R. Leycester to W. Hastings, 1 December 1771. Add. MS. 29132, f. 465ᵛ.

mosity flared up again and its effects were still felt within the
Company for years to come, it became henceforth an incident
in, rather than the mainspring of, party dissensions there. The
second was the mounting significance of the influence of the
Government over the Company. It was the parliamentary
Opposition leaders who for their own political ends had tried
first to heal its feuds; it was North's Administration which, for
the same reason, succeeded at least in neutralizing them. At the
same time fear of French aggression in India had led to a degree
of State intervention in the Company's affairs there which was
unparalleled in time of peace, and had caused ministers to
speak plainly, at least in private, of the possibility of even more
sweeping action. Of most immediate and practical significance,
however, was the third result. In 1771 it became apparent that
some other steps must be taken to implement the reforms which
the missing supervisors would now never be able to undertake.
The appointment of successors with the same powers was discussed but, partly out of fear of the contests between persons
which would ensue, progress in making such appointments was
slow. Meantime, though the situation in the Carnatic remained
uneasy, the Indian storm-cloud had shifted to Bengal, where the
failure of Clive's successors to make his dual system work had
been becoming increasingly evident and where the disastrous
famine of 1769-70 now threatened the main source of the
Company's wealth. The appointment of a new Governor of
Bengal with increased powers was therefore considered essential,
and Warren Hastings was the man chosen. His appointment
preceded the return of Sulivan to the Direction and he seems to
have owed his nomination to a widespread appreciation of his
high qualities as an administrator rather than to party manœuvres. The reconciliation of parties, however, gave a good
augury for the support he might expect from home in the duties
which lay before him; in Sulivan he had a supporter with forward ideas on Bengal, and at the beginning of 1772 he entered
into a field in which he was to play so outstanding a part in the
development of British India and in the future history of the
relations of State and Company.

APPENDIX

Lord Shelburne's Financial Concern in the East Indian Crisis of 1769

Lord Shelburne's integrity was always suspect to his contemporaries, though it is hard to explain why. No major indictment was brought against him. Among the underground mutterings against him was the charge that he was a jobbing minister. This accusation was put forward but not substantiated with respect to dealings in government stock during the peace negotiations of 1783.[1] Suspicion was also cast upon him in 1769 during the East Indian crisis of that year through the difficulties into which he was thrown by his late Under-Secretary (Shelburne had been in office until October of the previous year) and close personal follower, Lauchlin Macleane. These difficulties involved him in a loss of more than £30,000.

Shelburne's own account of the incident was simple. He wrote in a note to his heirs: 'It may serve as a warning to my own family to be told that I have lost near £40,000 by being bond for other men . . . and all the return I had was treachery and a great deal of unjust public abuse.'[2] And when applying to Warren Hastings in 1774 for aid in recovering some of his losses from Macleane (by that time in India) he said:

> I dare presume so far upon yours as well as Mr. Impey's good opinion, that however my understanding may suffer in your judgement from your knowledge of this transaction, you will not think the worse of my heart in lending my hand as I hoped to save a drowning friend, where I could possibly have no other interest.[3]

These statements are difficult to take at their face value. It is difficult to persuade the world that a man gives another bonds to the value of £30,000 from sheer good nature, and the relations between Shelburne and Macleane were such that it was ridiculous to suggest that Shelburne 'could possibly have no other interest' but friendship in the transaction. When a statesman employs in his close personal service a man of Macleane's character and antecedents and then gives him bonds to a very large sum for debts incurred in stock dealings, and when, in addition, that statesman has recently been in office and handling matters which directly affect the price of the stock in question, it is too much to expect that he will escape 'public abuse'.

Evidence produced in several law cases arising out of the transaction, and the papers which Shelburne himself preserved and which

---

[1] *Edinburgh Review*, xxv. 212, June 1815.   [2] Fitzmaurice, op. cit. ii. 332.
[3] Add. MS. 29134, ff. 366–366ᵛ.

are now at Bowood, together with a certain amount of material from other sources, succeed only partially in clearing up the problem. They suggest, however, that neither the suspicions of the public nor the protestations of Shelburne were altogether accurate. They make it clear that Macleane was handling Shelburne's financial business and was known to be able to pledge his credit, but they also make it clear that when Shelburne gave him bonds for £30,000 to support his credit when East India Stock fell in 1769, Macleane considered that this was the help of a friendly patron rather than the support he might expect from a principal for whom he was acting. It is also clear that Shelburne and his friends considered Macleane a rich man, that he was in fact dealing on a large scale on his own account, and that they had implicit faith in his resources and uncanny skill as a speculator, and were slow to believe that he could really be ruined. Moreover, while there is good evidence that he was engaged in speculative activities on behalf of others, there is no direct evidence that he ever was so engaged on behalf of Shelburne.

It would seem that Shelburne himself had speculative concerns at one time, but also that he took steps to wind them up when he came into office. On 5 September 1766, not six weeks after he became Secretary of State, John Calcraft wrote to him about the settlement of some accounts including the half share of 'our loss on the joint concern of India Stock'.[1] Shelburne also made Macleane promise, when he took him into office as Under-Secretary, that he would not speculate on the English market while he was in office. He may also have suggested that he would prefer his subordinate not to speculate on the Amsterdam market, for Macleane wrote to him on 30 October 1766 that since he had been in Shelburne's service no one

> so deeply concerned as I was at the time of my engagement could conduct himself with more caution than I have. I promised your Lordship to have no concerns in Funds of any species in England; accordingly I gave orders to sell whatever stock I had here although at a loss, and I am not concerned in any stock in England that has been bought since the 24th September, neither directly or indirectly. My engagements in Holland with Lord Verney are paid for by a loan subsisting till next August. My other engagement on my own account in the same place subsists till February.[2]

He added that he would sell in Holland only and would abstain from all such activities while in office.

[1] On 24 February and 9 June 1767 Shelburne paid sums of £9,140 and £7,000 to Calcraft, but there is no means of determining how much, if any, of this was in payment of the debt referred to. Lansdowne MSS.

[2] L. Macleane to Shelburne, 30 October 1766. Ibid.

It is rather doubtful whether Macleane kept his promise with regard to dealings in England; he certainly did not maintain his avowed intention with regard to dealings in Holland. In a case later brought against him by an Amsterdam merchant, Gerrit Blaauw, the latter deposed that between the years 1767 and 1769 he transacted a great deal of speculative business for Macleane in East Indian Stock.[1] Macleane's affairs were fantastically elaborate, and we have no coherent account of them, but it is certain that he did a good deal of business for principals who did not wish their names to appear. Accident has given us the names of Major-General Robert Monckton and Sir John Hort, Bart.[2] It seems more than likely that Macleane is the man referred to by the *Repository or Treasury of Politics and Literature* for 1770 (i. 236), when it complains of a syndicate of Members of Parliament, who, on the failure of their speculative venture, left one of their number as a scapegoat to pay his creditors 2s. 6d. in the pound. That we have no proof that he ever speculated on behalf of Shelburne cannot be taken as evidence that he never did so.

Macleane was managing Shelburne's financial affairs during these years, and had a free hand in so doing. Between 1767 and 1769 he received sums totalling some £10,000 from Shelburne,[3] he negotiated loans for Shelburne, and he was able to pledge his participation in a very ambitious scheme for the splitting of East India Stock for the Company elections of 1769 without any written authorization.

The loss, discredit, and alarm into which Macleane plunged his patron in 1769 as a result of his own financial disaster was brought about in three ways.

1. One of them seems to have been only a transitory alarm. Macleane, raising money on his patron's behalf, had obtained £3,000 on note of hand from a Jewish broker, Ximenes, to whom he had given Shelburne's name as the principal in the transaction. The bill was due for payment in the first instance on 28 February 1769, and was twice renewed up to 25 June. When Macleane's difficulties became known, Ximenes became nervous and applied to Shelburne direct, and, as Shelburne's friends reported, was making free use of Shelburne's name until Laurence Sulivan stopped him. For some reason to which we have not got the clue, Shelburne was extremely nervous about his name coming out in this affair, but Macleane reassured him and apparently paid off this creditor. Macleane added that on other occasions when raising money for Shelburne he either lent him

---

[1] Publ. Rec. Off., Exchequer Bills, London and Middlesex, Easter, 13 Geo. III, no. 1836.
[2] The latter is mentioned in the Gerrit Blaauw case; the former in another case in which Macleane was involved, ibid., Easter, 10 Geo. III, no. 140.
[3] Pass-books. Lansdowne MSS.

the money himself or obtained it from Laurence Sulivan, and that no one but Ximenes could possibly know of the affair.[1]

2. A more serious matter was the loss incurred from the scheme for stock splitting and there was some anxiety lest its details should become public. This plan, whereby twenty-three persons jointly guaranteed to repay £100,000 stock borrowed for splitting at 280 per cent. in July 1769 has been mentioned in the text.[2] Of the subscribers we only know the names of Sulivan, Vansittart, Lord Verney, Macleane, Lord Shelburne (through Macleane), William Motteux, a director, Alderman Townsend, William and Richard Burke (Lord Verney was understood to be behind them as Lord Shelburne was behind Macleane), and Thomas Lane (merely an agent of Sulivan's).[3] Macleane must have played an important part in arranging the subscription, for the document in which it was embodied was drawn up by him (with a looseness that distressed the lawyer, Dunning, when he later inquired into it on Lord Shelburne's behalf).[4] Shelburne himself at first denied all knowledge of it, and always protested that he had not fully understood it, but Macleane reminded him that they had discussed it on several occasions, and that on one in particular he had said that it was the way in which he would prefer to help Sulivan's campaign.[5] At the time the arrangement was made no one, of course, envisaged a disastrous fall in stock prices.

When the crash came considerable loss was feared; it was rumoured that many of the subscribers would be unable to bear their share (actually seventeen of the twenty-three were able to do so), and at one time it was feared that those who held the £500 stock qualifications might become bankrupt and these sums be seized by their creditors.[6] All Shelburne's supporters rushed to his assistance; Isaac Barré, Alderman Townsend, and Dunning. Townsend, himself implicated, was the most useful to him, and, after a number of meetings and discussions, the subscribers wound up the venture at a serious loss. Shelburne's loss was £3,140. His financial difficulties were so serious, however, that he could not pay the sum to Sulivan, or part of a bill for £4,000 which he already owed him, until 1777.[7]

3. Much the most serious of his anxieties and losses were caused, however, by six bills which he had given to Lauchlin Macleane on

---

[1] Letters from Barré and Macleane to Shelburne, 18, 19, and 29 June 1769. Lansdowne MSS.   [2] See p. 188 above.
[3] I. Barré to Shelburne, 19 June 1769. Lansdowne MSS.
[4] J. Dunning to Shelburne, 7 July 1769. Ibid.
[5] L. Macleane to Shelburne, 29 June 1769. Ibid.
[6] Alderman Townsend to Shelburne, 22 August 1769. Ibid.
[7] Account receipted by L. Sulivan, 9 October 1777. Ibid.

12 May and 24 May to help him meet his liabilities in East India Stock when the price began to fall, but before the bad news from India precipitated a panic. Lauchlan Macleane had, as he himself said, great sums embarked in India Stock,[1] or rather in speculations on 'differences' in East India Stock. Some time before 11 May Shelburne must have offered to help Macleane if he were in need of money for these transactions. On 11 May Macleane wrote to him that a temporary fall in stock prices forced him to take advantage of this offer, and that he was in need of £30,000, which Lord Verney and Panchaud, a speculative banker from Paris, would supply on Shelburne's security.[2] After consultation with Laurence Sulivan, Shelburne decided to support Macleane, informing his wife that there was very little chance that he would suffer for it.[3] The correspondence makes it quite clear that Macleane did not ask for the sum to meet liabilities incurred in Shelburne's service, but when Shelburne took advice and then gave him the bills he no doubt had in mind the fact that, with Macleane's financial affairs so closely connected with his own, and with the relations which were known to exist between them, he could not escape suspicion if Macleane crashed in a spectacular way on Change Alley.

When Macleane got the bills he paid them over to Panchaud and Lord Verney, as he had said he would, but not altogether to pay his large stock-jobbing commitments for others,[4] for he already owed Lord Verney £8,000 and Panchaud £10,000 (as he admitted later under pressure) chiefly for jobbing debts, most of them he insisted incurred on behalf of others, though in Panchaud's case they were partly for a share in a West Indian estate which he was buying.[5]

Shelburne was no doubt wise to support Macleane if his downfall could be averted. Their calculations were upset by the crisis on the market that followed, however, and Shelburne, so far from saving Macleane, was involved in his ruin. After the end of May there was a *sauve qui peut*; by the middle of July Panchaud, Lord Verney, and the firm of brokers with which both Verney and Macleane did most of their business in England (Brymer and Delafontaine) had crashed.[6] Shelburne, already anxious for Macleane's solvency and his own, was now in despair at the danger of a public scandal if his bonds should

---

[1] L. Macleane to Shelburne, 11 May 1769. Lansdowne MSS.

[2] Ibid.

[3] Lady Shelburne's Diary. Ibid.

[4] For instance, in July 1769 he owed his brokers in England, Brymer and Delafontaine, £23,555. (Publ. Rec. Off., Exchequer Bills, London and Middlesex, Easter, 10 Geo. III, no. 140.)

[5] I. Barré to Shelburne [July 1769, dated Thursday night only]. Lansdowne MSS.

[6] I. Barré to Shelburne, [16 July] 1769. Ibid.

be in the hands of a bankrupt broker such as, for instance, Brymer and Delafontaine. Barré and Dunning, after cross-examining the unhappy Macleane (who preserved as they reported, 'the manliness of an Indian') scoured London for Panchaud and Lord Verney to find out what these two ruined gamblers had done with the bonds, and if possible to retrieve them.[1]

Lord Verney retired to the country, pleading sickness, but their worst fears there were not realized, for he had kept possession of the bonds and had not, as was at first feared, passed them on to his ruined broker (to whom he had lent £22,000 in a vain attempt to save him the day before he failed).[2] Panchaud, caught by them just before he fled to Paris, said that he had kept the bonds until his Paris partners had shown alarm and then sent them to Paris to reassure them. He was prepared to swear (mendaciously) that he had received them not on account of stock 'differences' but for cash.[3] These bonds were handed over by his partners to a creditor in Paris, Thomas Tierney, shortly before they went bankrupt.[4] There was, however, some doubt about the validity of their assignment in English law, and Tierney's London correspondent in August entered into negotiations with Shelburne on the subject. Since it was in the interest of Shelburne that the bonds should be in Tierney's hands rather than in those of Panchaud's creditors, and since (as Shelburne's agents pointed out) it was in Tierney's interest to keep quiet about them, lest the rest of the creditors claimed them and he had to wait his share with the rest, the assignment was made without difficulty and conditions of repayment (which were not kept to) made at the same time.[5]

Thus Shelburne managed to avoid the public scandal which he feared. Nevertheless, the matter could not be kept a secret. Charles Lloyd, George Grenville's private secretary, wrote to him on 1 June: 'Lauchlin Macleane I hear is absolutely ruined. Lord Shelburne is very deep.'[6] Shelburne's friend and adviser, Isaac Barré, wrote to him frankly on the subject:

Long before I left you, you seemed to expect that your enemies would neither be inactive nor silent about this affair of the Securities. It is far from being a secret and of course great liberties [are] taken with your name and that of some of your friends. D[unning] and I are clear of opinion (Macleane thinking so too) that it

[1] I. Barré and Macleane to Shelburne, various letters of July 1769. Ibid.
[2] L. Macleane to Shelburne. Undated [June 1769]. Ibid.
[3] I. Barré to Shelburne [? 17 July 1769]. Ibid.
[4] Publ. Rec. Off., Exchequer Bills, London and Middlesex, Trinity, 12 Geo. III, o. 1904.
[5] Alderman Townsend to Shelburne, 22 August 1769. Lansdowne MSS.
[6] Quoted C. W. Dilke, Papers of a Critic, 1875, ii. 338.

should not be attempted to keep it private. It would only increase suspicion to be too prompt in telling it, but surely it would be wise to meet it when it offers, with temper and with truth.[1]

It is not necessary here to describe the painful straits to which all the parties were reduced in their attempts to retrieve themselves, nor the expensive and somewhat discreditable litigation in which they became involved and to which we owe a good deal of our information. Shelburne's eventual losses fell far below the £40,000 at which he estimated them. By 1776, Macleane had reduced his debt to £12,445. 18s. 9d., some of it before he left England and some of it by remittances from India. Returning to England that year in the pay both of Warren Hastings and the Nawab of Arcot, he tried to liquidate his debt altogether by giving Shelburne a draft of £14,000 on John MacPherson at the Nawab's court, to be paid from that mine which Indian adventurers hoped was inexhaustible, the Nawab's treasury. The Nawab's debts, real and fictitious, were by this time, however, a public question of great urgency, and when Macleane was lost at sea the following year, Shelburne was left with little hope of receiving anything from this source, and seems never to have done so.

To sum up, Shelburne's losses arose from the fact that he had as his confidential agent a man who failed heavily in a Change Alley crisis, and whom he had tried to save because his failure would involve him in discredit and some loss. Macleane had been raising credit for him and was carrying out for him the financing of corrupt votes for East Indian elections. There is no evidence that he had ever speculated in the stock for his patron. In 1769, indeed, it seems quite clear that he had not, but as he certainly did so on a large scale for other public men, and Shelburne was aware of the fact and showed no disapprobation except to stipulate against transactions *on the English market*, when he was in power, it is rather hard to believe that he never performed the service for his patron, which he did freely for others. Lauchlin Macleane obtained great sums from many prominent persons in the course of his career, but he obtained them from men who had reason to fear his fall or to welcome his success. If Lord Shelburne were an exception to this rule, he was very unlucky.

[1] I. Barré to Shelburne, 14 August 1769. Lansdowne MSS.

VIII

1772

IN 1772 Sir George Colebrooke was elected Chairman of the
Company and Laurence Sulivan (not without strong
opposition)[1] Deputy Chairman. Their union, though one of
convenience only, was useful in preserving the peace of the
Company, and of the two men Sulivan soon asserted himself
as the abler and more experienced. Though the Company's
politics had lost the sharp two-party edge which had charac-
terized them at the height of the struggle between Clive and
Sulivan, much faction lay hidden beneath the surface.

Clive continued his defensive role and Sulivan, his faction
virtually destroyed by financial disaster, was barely keeping
himself afloat by his skill and reputation. Of the other interests,
that of the great stock-jobbers had come to an abrupt end with
the collapse of the boom in the Company's stock, only Sir
George Colebrooke of all their number remaining prominent
in Company affairs, and he himself, as was soon to become
apparent, heading for disaster. On the other hand the more
traditional shipping interest retained its vigour and was called
into some activity by the attempts to reform abuses in the
Company's shipping organization in 1772 and 1773. Moreover,
significant of the trend of the times was the rapid rise of groups
representing the interests of returned Company servants or even
of men still prominent in the Company's service. Of these the
remarkable and ferocious Johnstone group was still the most
important, but the return of General Richard Smith,[2] representing the interests of the creditors of the Nawab of Arcot, was a
foretaste of things to come; Sir Thomas Rumbold was known
to have acquired his large stock-holdings in order to further his
future career in the Company,[3] and Richard Barwell, still in

---

[1] L. Sulivan to W. Hastings, 28 April 1773: 'I must go back to April 1772 when
Colebrook (sic) and I had the game in our hands, but by an indecision habitual
almost natural to him, we lost that ground which we never could recover, and in
place of bringing in firm friends, I carried the Deputy Chair by my own vote.'
Add. MS. 29133, f. 533. Actually the voting was equal and Sulivan was elected by
the casting of lots (Court Book 81, p. 4).

[2] H.M.C., Palk MSS., pp. 120–1; cf. Court Book 81, p. 40.

[3] Thomas Rumbold entered the service as a writer at Madras in 1752, served

India, wrote to a friend: 'That the servants abroad should interfere in the election of directors and solicit votes of their friends for the nomination of men under whose orders they are to act becomes every day more and more necessary.'[1] For the time being, however, no major issue called these various interests into activity.

The absence of such issues within the Company was partly the result and partly the cause of a similar inaction among both government and opposition groups. The Duke of Grafton's ministry had merged into that of Lord North with no marked changes in policy or persons, and the new ministry, gradually taking the shape it was to retain for twelve years, began to assume a certain air of permanency which had been foreign to its predecessors of the last nine years. As old opposition leaders such as George Grenville and the Duke of Bedford died, their followers tended to gravitate to the Government, which also began to attract young men of promise either like Charles James Fox beginning their political careers, or like Charles Cornwall[2] anxious for chances of preferment. The result was a return to something superficially resembling the stable government of Walpole's or Pelham's day, but with a similarity more apparent than real. North had none of the great territorial connexions of the Pelhams[3] and, though intelligent and adroit, little of the iron nerve and driving force of Walpole. Even the vigorous and unflagging supervision of George III over all the ministry's affairs could not make it anything but an inert and badly co-ordinated body, ill devised even by eighteenth-century standards for taking decisions or for tackling problems in time to prevent their becoming serious difficulties.

But, if the ministry was deficient in political leadership, it

in the military forces and, reverting to the civil list, served in Bengal and rose to be a member of the Council. He returned to England in 1769, entered Parliament in 1770 and the Company's Direction in 1772. Was intriguing to be sent back as Governor of Madras, an ambition he satisfied in 1777. For his use of his fortune to further his ambitions see *Bengal Past and Present*, x. 245, *The Letters of Mr. Richard Barwell*.

[1] R. Barwell to R. Leycester, 5 November 1773. *Bengal Past and Present*, xi. 265, *The Letters of Mr. Richard Barwell*.

[2] See pp. 193 seq. above and pp. 242–3 below.

[3] When Lord North became Prime Minister, Lord Dacre, congratulating his father on his son's success, said that he had risen by his own merits, 'For, though nobly born he is as little indebted to connections or the powerful support of great persons as if he had been a Novus Homo.' (Bodl. North MS. D.14, f. 175.)

could command considerable administrative talent and its very
weaknesses gave its 'men of business' unusual opportunities.
Among the ministers it is true only Lord Sandwich stands out
for his administrative capacities, but a number of 'men of
business', particularly John Robinson, Secretary to the Treasury,
and Charles Jenkinson, the former Secretary to the Treasury[1]
and soon to be appointed Vice-Treasurer of Ireland and in
1778 Secretary at War, played prominent parts and were on
occasion even in direct correspondence with the king. The
result was an administration of the kind common under such
conditions, one in which major decisions are seldom taken at
the right time, but in which, in default of them, there is much
careful conciliation of interests and a series of partial solutions,
often ingenious and valuable, to urgent problems as and when
they arise. Among the major problems with which the ministry
was faced, those raised by East Indian affairs must be included.

It was customary for the Company's directors and servants
to believe at this time that the Government were pursuing a
Machiavellian policy directed to the destruction of the Company's independence and the assumption of its patronage. They
believed it to be doing this through the underground activity
of Lord Sandwich and his friends among the directors at home
and through the more open interventions of government
representatives in India.[2] In fact this was by no means the case.
The Government were well aware that Indian affairs were
unsatisfactory and from some points of view alarming and,
when once action was taken, it was true that there were among
them some who would support strong measures, but their actions
make it plain that they were extremely unwilling to embroil
themselves in East Indian conflicts and that they did so only
when forced by circumstances. It was more characteristic that
they sought to achieve peace within the Company by the
readmission of Sulivan to power; and thereafter, until the
events of 1772 forced a change of policy upon them, the relations of Government and Company were remarkably free
from political implications. Lord North's relations with the
Court of Directors were no closer than those of any First Lord

---

[1] 1763-5.
[2] Sir John Lindsay, 1770-1, and his successor Sir Robert Harland, 1772-4,
Commodores and Naval Commanders-in-Chief in India.

of the Treasury of the time,[1] while Lord Sandwich appears to have used his personal influence with the Court of Directors solely for purposes of minor patronage and for departmental ends—when, for instance, in 1771 timber conservation began to be recognized as a matter of grave importance to the Admiralty, he managed his negotiations with the Company for the limitation of the size and number of East Indiamen very adroitly.[2]

If the Government had no desire to be active in East India affairs, neither had the opposition groups at this time any reason to bring them to the fore. Opposition was now settling down into two major groups, the followers of Rockingham inspired by Edmund Burke, the descendants of the former Newcastle connexion, and the followers of Chatham, among whom Shelburne was becoming the leading figure. Apart from those created during the short-lived and disastrous stock-jobbing ventures of some of their minor members[3] (as, for instance, Lord Verney and the Burkes) the Rockinghams had few personal connexions with the Company and had never concerned themselves with its affairs except when they became a major political issue. At this time their interests lay elsewhere. The Chathamites, through Shelburne and his personal followers, had far closer connexions with the Company and a more continuous interest in its affairs, but Shelburne's own connexions with the Company had been severed, the policy with which they had been associated in 1767 was one inconvenient for an opposition party to advance, and they too were preoccupied elsewhere.

In this undisturbed political atmosphere it might have seemed at the beginning of 1771 that the Company was being given its last chance to put its own house in order, and that Sulivan, the only man in the Company with the necessary

---

[1] The most important questions he dealt with were (1) the question of Tea Duties, where an arrangement very unfavourable to the Company was made, (2) questions of naval reinforcements during the war scare of 1770, and (3) legislation the Company was trying to introduce to improve its organization; see pp. 230 seq. below.

[2] Court Books 79 and 80 *passim. Fifth Report of the Committee of Secrecy. Reports from Committees of the House of Commons*, iv. 255–96. On this question see R. G. Albion, *Forests and Sea Power; the timber problem of the Royal Navy, 1652–1862*, Cambridge (Mass.), 1926.

[3] See above, pp. 192 seq. and p. 209. Sir George Colebrooke, whose elder brother had been an adherent of the Duke of Newcastle's, had some contact with them, but he was seldom in touch with them on East India affairs.

ability and will to do it, might seize this chance. In fact the possibilities were largely illusory. Apart from everything else, party and personal factors, old enmities and desperate present needs, hamstrung the efforts of the Company's leaders. Only strong and consistent support from a government bent on assisting the Company to reform itself could have overcome these handicaps and, as events were to show, no such coherent policy could be expected from the North Administration. The attempts of the Company to save itself were thus for the most part doomed to failure.

Nevertheless real efforts were made to introduce a comprehensive and on the whole well-thought-out policy of reform, and for these efforts Sulivan can claim most of the merit. It rested on three bases. The first was the review and correction of abuses in India by a Supervising Commission sent out with wide powers to operate in the Indian Presidencies—a continuation of the plan adopted in 1769 but frustrated by the loss of the Commissioners on their voyage to India. The second was the introduction of special steps to improve the administration of Bengal; and the third was the passing of legislation through Parliament to increase the Company's control over its servants, to improve certain other aspects of its organization, and to reform the constitution of Bengal. That only one of the three aspects of this policy met with any success is symptomatic of the difficulties with which the Company leaders had to contend. The first, the appointment of a new Supervising Commission to be sent to India, failed through faction within the Company, led by the Johnstone group and other ex-servants with reasons to fear an investigation into abuses, and fed by profound personal disagreements as to who should be appointed to go out. The controversy dragged on so long that by the time a list of names was accepted by the General Court, government intervention into Company affairs had already begun, and the list was so unacceptable that Sulivan himself was glad when the Government intervened to prevent their dispatch.[1] The third, the introduction of legislation in Parliament to increase the Company's powers and reform the constitution of Bengal, failed, partly it is true because the opponents of reform in the Company found supporters among the Opposition in the House of Com-

[1] L. Sulivan to W. Hastings, 28 April 1773. Add. MS. 29133, f. 533.

mons (Governor Johnstone once again came into action to
protect the cause of his brothers in the Company), but more
because the Government through lack of internal cohesion
failed to give the Company the support which it had been led to
expect. Both the Recruiting Bills of 1770 and 1771[1] and the
Judicature Bill of 1772[2] had to be abandoned for this reason.

Only one aspect of the reform policy met with any success,
the measures for administrative reform carried out in Bengal,
and this success was due to the activities of a man who was to
play a great part in the future not only of the Company but of
India, Warren Hastings, the newly elected Governor of Bengal.
The appointment of Warren Hastings to the Government of
Bengal, a measure which ante-dated Sulivan's return to power,
but which fitted in well with his wishes, may be said to end the
period in which the personality of the Company's great military
servant, Clive, profoundly affected its affairs and to begin the
period in which the personality of its great civilian administrator had an equally marked though not altogether parallel
influence. Hastings's appointment from the beginning carried
with it the assumption that he must be a reforming Governor
and that some at least of the work which had been expected of
the supervisors must fall on his shoulders. It was, however, only
after the return to power of Sulivan that the directors decided
that the Company should 'stand forth as *diwan*', i.e. should
undertake the actual financial administration of the country
from which they drew their revenue and should end the period
of dual responsibility inaugurated under Clive. It was the need
to remodel the complete administration of Bengal that gave
the great administrative talents of Hastings their chance, and
(many as were the imperfections of the system instituted) it was
Hastings in the next few years who laid the basis for the future
prosperity of Bengal under British rule.[3]

The plans of the Company's leaders for reform were, however, only a small part of their preoccupations in 1771 and the
beginning of 1772. They constituted a gallant attempt to take

[1] *Jour. H.C.* Company's Bill to enable them to raise a military force (9 April to
10 May 1770), and Bill for raising a military force (10 December 1770 to 23 April
1771). *Parl. Hist.* xvii. 169 seq.
[2] See below, pp. 230 seq.
[3] M. E. Monckton Jones, *Warren Hastings in Bengal, 1772–4*, Oxford, 1918, pp.
166 seq.

the initiative; but the greater part of their activities had necessarily to be defensive. Three factors were combining to under-
mine their authority and to threaten their independence. The
first was the continued fear of French attempts to retrieve their
position in India. The Government were in constant anxiety not
only about the adequacy of the Company's provisions against
attack by sea, but lest the wars with the country powers in which
their servants became involved would give the French an opportunity to intervene. It was believed that only the fall of Choiseul
prevented a French attack on Bengal in 1770;[1] the reports of
the land and sea officers who were sent to India in an ineffective
and indeed often damaging attempt to strengthen its defences
were persistently disquieting. The reality of these fears was
made abundantly clear by the events of the great international
wars of the last quarter of the century. Further government
intervention to strengthen the British position in India was
inevitable. But though this need lay at the back of men's
minds[2] it was not sufficiently urgent in 1771 and 1772 to be in
itself a cause for government intervention.

Of more immediate significance to the Company was the
second factor, the information which was reaching the British
public, often in a highly sensational form, about abuses and
Company misrule in India, particularly in Bengal. So many
people had an interest in East India Stock and so many had
their own correspondents in India, that events in India could
never be kept quiet. Thus news of the horrors of the 1769–70
famine in Bengal and the sensational accounts of the inroads
of Hyder Ali in the Carnatic received immediate publicity in
England and had alarming effects on the price of the Company's
stock, in which despite the crash of 1769 there was still much
speculative dealing both in London and Amsterdam. Moreover
Clive and some of the other returned 'Nabobs' were spectacular
figures and ugly stories about them were gaining increasing
currency.[3] Early in 1771 Sir George Colebrooke, hearing that
Clive was thinking of publishing a defence of his last admini-

---

[1] A. Wedderburn to Clive, 29 October 1771. Powis MSS.
[2] Clive gave this problem an important place in the plan he drew up for
presentation to the ministry in November 1772. See *Historical View of Plans for the
Government of British India*, 1793.
[3] For the hostility to the 'Nabobs' at this time see J. M. Holzman, *The Nabobs
in England*; op. cit., pp. 15–16.

stration, thought it necessary to warn him against drawing attention to himself and the Company's affairs.[1]

But India was so far away and its institutions so unfamiliar to those who made up English public opinion, that some special scandal was necessary to bring the widespread uneasiness to a head. Such a scandal was now provided. In 1769 there had been deported from Bengal to England a peculiarly disreputable free merchant named William Bolts[2] who had been a partner of John Johnstone there and who had succeeded for years in defying the efforts of the Bengal Government to suppress him. He now returned, bent on making trouble, bringing with him certain Armenian merchants, his agents, to institute proceedings against Governor Verelst in the English Courts.[3] His case was, of course, taken up by the Johnstone party in the Company and they soon saw the advantage of extending their attack from Governor Verelst to include his predecessor Clive. In this attack all Clive's newly won enemies joined, and though the directors, including his old enemy Sulivan, were at first reluctant to become concerned in it, they were gradually drawn in.

At first the attack was confined to the Company. One John Petrie (one of the officers cashiered by Clive in 1766) laid a charge against him and others before the directors of setting up illegal monopolies and of committing other offences.[4] The charges could not be ignored, pressed as they were by the Company opposition, but the directors showed no enthusiasm in pursuing them. They first sent Clive a copy of the charges against him and asked for his observations on them.[5] When he refused to reply, they began to obtain legal opinion on them, but all in the most leisurely way.[6] Though the Company's servants complained later in the year when they were attacked in Parliament that the directors allowed them to become scape-

[1] G. Colebrooke to Clive, 8 January 1771. Powis MSS.

[2] For this episode see N. L. Hallward, *William Bolts, a Dutch Adventurer under John Company*, Cambridge, 1920.

[3] *Select Committee, 1772, Second Report. Reports from Committees of the House of Commons*, iii. 265 seq.

[4] R. Palk to W. M. Goodlad, 2 February 1772. *H.M.C., Palk MSS.*, p. 170.

[5] Forrest, *Clive*, op. cit. ii. 384.

[6] A summary of the legal proceedings, evidently drawn up for Charles Jenkinson, exists among the Liverpool MSS. (Add. MS. 38398, ff. 36 seq. endorsed 'Hints respecting the Prosecution against the Salt-Traders, Receivers of the Mahtute Tax etc.').

goats, and though there were then recriminations between Clive and the directors in the House, the luke-warmness of the directors in this early stage of the conflict not only aroused the indignation of Clive's assailants, but caused them to shift their activities first into the Press and then into the House of Commons.

The attention of the reading public had already been aroused by the two editions in 1768 and 1770 of Alexander Dow's *History of Hindustan*.[1] The author, who had been implicated in the 1766 mutiny, was hostile to Clive, but his comments had been veiled and discreet. The egregious William Bolts showed no such restraint and his publication *Considerations on Indian Affairs*,[2] which appeared in the early months of 1772, took the form of a sustained and copiously documented attack on Clive, his associates, and his successor in the Government, Verelst. Inspired by this example, Dow, who had been swept into the Johnstone orbit, now published a third volume of his *History*, bringing events in India up to date and adopting a much more outspoken and contentious method of presentation than he had used before. These works, which were followed by several minor publications, were very effective. Horace Walpole, no longer active in politics but still one of the best barometers for gauging political opinion, remarked of them:

The oppressions of India and even of the English settled there under the rapine and cruelties of the servants of the Company had now reached England and created general clamour here. Some books had been published, particularly by one Bolts and Mr. Dow, the first a man of bad character, the latter of a very fair one, which carried the accusations home to Lord Clive; and the former represented him as a monster in assassination, usurpation and extortion, with heavy accusations of his monopolizing in open defiance of the orders of the Company . . . To such monopolies were imputed the

---

[1] Alexander Dow, d. 1779. Formerly secretary to Governor of Bencoolen. Captain in the Company's service 1764. Implicated in the mutiny, but 1769 Lieutenant-Colonel. In addition to his *History*, the basis of which was a translation of Firishta's history, he wrote two tragedies. He was later reappointed to India and died there. John MacPherson claimed to have contributed a good deal to the second edition of the *History*.

[2] *Considerations on Indian Affairs, particularly respecting the Present State of Bengal and its Dependencies*. Two editions were published in 1772, the second considerably enlarged to counter a retort by Harry Verelst, late Governor of Bengal, *View of the Rise, Progress and Present State of the English Government in Bengal, including a Reply to the Misrepresentations of Mr. Bolts and other writers*, 1772.

late famine in Bengal and the loss of three millions of the inhabitants. A tithe of these crimes was sufficient to inspire horror.[1]

These views were echoed by the periodicals that formed educated opinion, and the accusations came, as a 'Nabob' himself said, 'at an unlucky time, mankind in general being willing to suspect that so many great fortunes cannot be fairly acquired'.[2]

The result was undoubtedly the formation of a *bloc* of opinion within and without the House which was inspired by genuine and disinterested dismay at a situation many of the facts of which might remain obscure, but which could not be represented in any but a highly discreditable light. Though no spokesman arose, as Burke did later, to stimulate their humanitarianism and to stress their responsibility for deeds done in the British name, the existence of this body of opinion helped the leaders in the Company to push forward with their schemes for reform, was directly responsible for the setting up by the House of Commons of the Select Committee under Burgoyne to investigate abuses in India, and limited the range of Opposition activity when government intervention was finally undertaken.

The immediate influence of this opinion should not, however, be over-estimated. It did not lead to support in the Commons for the Company's attempts to reform itself. Lord Shelburne remarked as late as April that 'the East India affairs . . . do not catch the active public';[3] and the driving force behind the work of the Select Committee when it got to work was much less disinterested indignation than personal vendettas. Events were to show that pressure of quite a different kind was needed before the Government intervened to reorganize the Company's affairs.

It was a third factor which precipitated a crisis in the Company's affairs, raised what Burke called 'the phrenzy of the people',[4] and forced the Government to intervene decisively in Company affairs. What stimulated the Government to a degree of constructive activity which few had expected of it, what clinched and gave direction to the indignation of the ordinary citizen whose conscience was already uneasy, and what raised

---

[1] *The Last Journals of Horace Walpole*, ed. A. F. Steuart, 1910, i. 72.
[2] R. Palk to W. M. Goodlad, 2 February 1772. *H.M.C., Palk MSS.*, p. 171.
[3] *Chatham Correspondence*, iv. 209–10.   [4] *Burke Correspondence*, i. 362.

a howl of fury among the large body of shareholders of and speculators in East India Stock, was the Company's sudden threat, in September 1772, to pass its next half-yearly dividend. This threat was the more alarming since it came in the midst of the acute financial crisis which had seized London the previous June, which was rapidly spreading to the continental bourses, and which was becoming the biggest international credit crisis which Europe had yet seen.

For this crisis itself the leaders of the East India Company in their corporate capacity bore no direct responsibility, though the same could not be said of all of them in their private capacities. The Company held two main sales in London, in March and September, of the goods they imported from India. While waiting for the receipts of the March sales they were accustomed to borrow on short term from the Bank of England sums varying from £200,000 to £400,000. These they repaid before the September sale, borrowing again similar sums in October to be repaid before the first sales of the following year.[1] In the spring of 1772 they had procured their normal loan from the Bank, which stood at £300,000 on 1 May. Then early in June the crisis broke on the market with the failure and flight of the Scottish banker Alexander Fordyce. Twenty important houses fell within three weeks; others were only saved by the interposition of the Bank, or, like the Chairman of the East India Company Sir George Colebrooke himself, only succeeded in limping on for a short time before stopping payment.[2] Though the actual crisis in London was short-lived, it was followed by parallel disasters on the continent; stagnation of credit and trade depression continued until well into 1773.[3]

The crisis immediately affected the Company in two ways. Firstly there were heavy calls on them for payments which normally would have been delayed. A correspondent describing the situation to Warren Hastings wrote:

A very alarming bankruptcy in London and Edinburgh has shook the publick credit, and the merchants of London have met to

---

[1] *Committee of Secrecy, Second Report. Reports from Committees of the House of Commons*, iv. 19.

[2] See my article *Sir George Colebrooke's World Corner in Alum, 1771-3*, loc. cit.

[3] There are many contemporary references to it, e.g. Shelburne to Chatham, 25 April 1773 (Publ. Rec. Off. GD. 8/4). Part of this letter is printed in *Chatham Correspondence*, iv. 261-2.

sustain the credit of the Bank and that of private bankers. The East India Company keep their books open for the inspection of their Proprietors lest there should be a run on them and paid £100,000 to different tradesmen which was not due.[1]

Secondly the sums due in receipt of their May sales were very slow to come in. In June the Company postponed the date for their 'prompt payments'[2] for three weeks and further postponements were made, some to 6 November; in August some £320,000 was still outstanding.[3] The result was that instead of being able to pay off their loan from the Bank, they had in July to negotiate a new short-term loan. In September the debt was renewed till the end of October, to be repaid out of the proceeds of the September sales.[4] Repayment proved, however, to be impossible. The Company found the prevailing shortage of money so great that they had to postpone the most important part of their sale, that of Bengal goods, until November, and the sale was still going on at the end of the month.[5]

The same difficulties had led the Company on 7 August to ask the Treasury to permit a postponement in their payment of customs due to the value of £203,619 and again on 24 September and 24 November they had to ask for a respite.[6] On 22 September the directors were obliged to inform the Court of Proprietors that the declaration of a dividend must be postponed, as they were in negotiation with the Government for a loan.[7] On 28 October the Government, whose tribute of £400,000 per annum from the Company was tied up with the continuance of its dividends, informed them that the terms they proposed were not acceptable.[8] On 29 October the Bank refused to renew their loan.[9] Parliament had already been summoned to meet before Christmas to discuss East Indian

[1] G. Stratton (of Vizagapatam) to W. Hastings, 28 January 1773, quoting news from England of the preceding 7 July. Add. MS. 29133, ff. 355–355ᵛ.

[2] *London Chronicle*, 24 June 1772, p. 608.

[3] *Committee of Secrecy, Eighth Report. Reports from Committees of the House of Commons*, iv. 392.

[4] Copy of Letter from Secretary, Bank of England, to the Chairman and Committee of Treasury of the East India Company, 10 September 1772. Add. MS. 38397, f. 228.

[5] *Committee of Secrecy, Second Report*, loc. cit., p. 32. Memorial of Directors to the Treasury, 24 November 1772.   [6] Ibid., pp. 31–32.

[7] Court Book 81, p. 175.   [8] Ibid., p. 220.

[9] Copy of a letter from the Secretary of the Bank to the Chairman of the East India Company. Add. MS. 38397, f. 240.

affairs. The days of the Company's independence were numbered.

This startling collapse was not due simply to temporary financial embarrassments caused by the credit crisis. If it had been it would probably have been staved off by temporary measures. The gravity of the Company's position was due to a far more serious financial unsoundness, as they themselves soon frankly admitted. The annual payment of £400,000 to the Government and the increased dividends which the Company had paid since the taking over of the *diwani* in Bengal were based upon estimates of the surplus of the territorial revenue of Bengal over the costs, military and civil, of administering the country. Though the estimates seem always to have been unduly optimistic the surplus was at first considerable. But an increase in the expenses of administration, particularly on the military side under the threat of French aggression, soon began to narrow the gap, while a trade depression in Bengal, suddenly intensified by the disastrous famine of 1769–70, inevitably cut down the territorial revenues. Between 1767–8 and 1770–1 there had been a decline in territorial collections of some £400,000 per annum and an increase in the sums spent on fortifications of some £162,000 per annum, while other administrative costs were also rising.[1]

The seriousness of the situation was masked from the Company by the determined efforts of its servants to satisfy its requirements and keep up the Company's income in England by purchasing the largest possible 'investment' of goods in Bengal for shipment to England. The value of the investment leaped from £437,000 in 1765–6 to £904,000 in 1770–1 and even in the famine year of 1769–70 did not fall below £633,000. Part of this increase represents increased prices but the representations of the Company's servants themselves show how hardly Bengal was being pressed. Moreover the Bengal Government could only find the means of financing these vast purchases first by a huge increase in the bond debt in Bengal (it rose from £297,000 in 1769 to £922,000 in 1770 and was over £1,000,000 by 1772) and, when this failed, by raising money by the issue of bills of exchange drawn on the Company in London.

---

[1] These figures are taken from the *Third Report of the Committee of Secrecy. Reports from Committees of the House of Commons*, iv. 60–61.

226   1772

This last source of supply was one easy to tap, since the problem
of remitting a fortune home from India was becoming an
almost insoluble one and the Company's servants themselves
were only too glad to seize such an opportunity. But from the
Company's point of view this method of raising funds to pay for
the investment cancelled much of its value, since the bills had
to be met in London out of the products of its sales. If the latter
should fail for any reason its position might become very
dangerous.

The danger of the excessive drawing of bills from India had
long been recognized by the directors and they had already in
recent years had occasion to tighten up their precautions against
it. In 1768 and 1769 they had laid down maxima for the bills
to be drawn from each Presidency and the terms on which they
might be drawn.[1] These precautions proved unsuccessful partly
no doubt through the indiscipline and self-interest of their
servants, but partly on account of the acute nature of the
financial difficulties in Bengal and the impossibility of obtaining
instructions from home in time to deal with them. The result
was that between April and August 1771 the directors discovered
that their servants in Bengal, who had been authorized to draw
about £212,000 in 1770 (including some £26,000 for Clive's
jagir), had in fact drawn more than £1,000,000[2] and that in
all the Company was liable to meet during the coming three
years no less than £1,578,000 for Bills of Exchange drawn from
the Presidencies.[3] Nothing gave them reason to expect an
increase in the value of their sales which could offset such a
burden and, without reserves to meet it, the directors and in
particular their Committees of Treasury and of Correspondence,
of both of which Sulivan was by now a member, were faced
with a grave problem.

Their first reaction was a wish to refuse all bills in excess of
the permitted sums, but Sulivan and the Chairman of that
year, John Purling, easily persuaded them of the damaging
effects on their credit of such a decision.[4] The bills were therefore accepted, but how to meet them when they fell due

[1] *Eighth Report of the Committee of Secrecy*, Appendices i and ii, loc. cit., pp. 401–2.
[2] Ibid., pp. 356–7.
[3] *Third Report of the Committee of Secrecy*, loc. cit., p. 58. The bills were also drawn
on terms less favourable than those laid down by the Company.
[4] *Eighth Report of the Committee of Secrecy*, 1772, loc. cit., p. 380.

remained obscure. Even had there been no credit crisis ahead the bills had come at a particularly bad time. In the first place there had been some signs of a recession in the Company's sales, which had been very profitable for several years past. The stocks of tea on its hands, one of its most important products, were growing steadily partly on account of the friction with the American Colonies. In these circumstances an arrangement recently made with the Government for the payment of duty on teas was working badly for the Company and the most satisfactory outcome to be hoped for was a composition which would involve a heavy payment.[1] In the second place the directors had been unable to resist the temptation to raise their dividend as soon as they obtained partial liberty to do so.[2] By March 1771 they had raised it to the permitted maximum of $12\frac{1}{2}$ per cent. before they realized the scale of the liabilities which were being imposed on them.[3]

The first decision which the directors had to take after the full situation became clear to them in August 1771 was whether or not they should continue their existing dividend for the next six months. Though knowledge of the details of the situation was kept to the small group of directors on the Committees of Treasury and Correspondence, their predicament could not be kept secret. What was known or suspected by the Court of Directors as a whole soon became common property, and in any case all those with correspondents in India had independent sources of information. In private conversation all those from Clive downwards who had knowledge of Indian affairs, expressed gloomy views,[4] and the Company's affairs were freely discussed in the Press. Principles of sound finance certainly counselled a reduction in dividend; future events were to show that a reduction to 6 per cent. which would have automatically freed the Company from its payment of £400,000 to the Government would have been justified. Such a step would,

[1] There is a competent account of this question in the *Gentleman's Magazine*, 1772, p. 547.

[2] By 9 Geo. III, c. 24.

[3] In April they already knew that their servants were disobeying them. It was not till August that they knew how far they were deviating from their instructions. *Eighth Report of the Committee of Secrecy*, loc. cit., p. 374.

[4] Clive to W. Hastings, 1 August 1771. 'Every man sees clearly that as matters are now conducted abroad the Company will not long be able to pay the £400,000 to Government.' Add. MS. 29132, f. 434ᵛ.

however, have led to sensational results, certainly a catastrophic fall in the value of the Company's stock, even perhaps the government intervention the Company so much feared, and it was understandable that the directors hesitated to take it. These reasons may have been reinforced in some cases by personal interests of a less creditable kind. Sir George Colebrooke (out of the Direction in rotation that year but still in the closest touch with its affairs and about to return to office as their Chairman) and Sir James Cockburn, a prominent director, were known to be 'bulling' the stock on the Amsterdam market at this time and others may well have been concerned with them.[1]

Whatever their motives, the directors decided to continue the existing dividend, and to play down the gravity of the financial position. The proprietors were only too glad to believe that they were right and, though one independent director, John Manship, challenged their decision and the very misleading accounts on which it was based, and though the Johnstone party made some small show of opposition in the General Court, the motion was passed by an overwhelming majority.[2] In March 1772, when the directors repeated their error with even less excuse, no objection was raised at all. It was scarcely three months later that the storm broke. When the facts could be compared with the six months' estimate on which the decision of March 1772 was based it was seen that the receipts from sales had been over-estimated (for which the crisis might be held responsible) but the demands on the Company for payments on bills of exchange drawn on them from India were under-estimated and for this there was no such excuse. No account was taken of the still heavier claims which would be made on the Company a few months later. In short, it can be affirmed with certainty, as the directors themselves admitted by implication when the crash came, that the Company's financial disaster of the autumn, though it might be precipitated by the credit crisis in the City, was by no means caused by it. For their failure to handle this emergency with courage and foresight all the Company's leaders must be blamed; it more than outweighed any efforts they had made to put the Company on its feet again.

[1] *Eighth Report of the Committee of Secrecy*, loc. cit., pp. 394 seq.
[2] Ibid., pp. 381 seq.

This was the background out of which the Regulating Act of 1773 emerged. The military problems were those which first engaged attention. It was as early as October 1771 that the Government reluctantly began to come to the conclusion that something would have to be done and to say that 'the very intricate and dangerous situation of our possessions in India will probably make it necessary to bring them under the consideration of Parliament during next session'.[1] The first signs of this growing feeling are some tentative approaches by North and Rochford, the Secretary of State primarily concerned, to Clive for advice, approaches actively encouraged by Alexander Wedderburn, the Solicitor-General, who had become associated with Clive when they were both followers of George Grenville, who still sat for Clive's borough of Bishop's Castle, and who was anxious to bring his patron into the orbit of the government interest.[2] Varying opinions within the ministry soon began to be reported about the extent and nature of the reorganization likely to be necessary. That section of administration still known as the 'Bedfords'—Lord Gower, Rigby, Weymouth, and their followers—was believed to favour fairly sweeping measures and to have the support of the Duke of Grafton (who still wielded some influence in the Government) and possibly of Lord Mansfield, the Chief Justice.[3]

It soon became apparent, however, that North and the majority of the administration held much more moderate views. The negotiations with Clive languished[4] and when the

[1] Forrest, *Clive*, op. cit. ii. 380.

[2] Ibid. 379–82. On p. 381 a letter from North to Clive dated only 9 November is misplaced. From internal evidence it clearly should be dated 1773. For Wedderburn's relations with Clive see Namier, *Structure of Politics*, ii. 305, and J. M. Holzman, *The Nabobs in England*, p. 58.

[3] John McPherson wrote to Warren Hastings from Madras on 12 October 1772, but giving news not later than the preceding February. (Add. MS. 29133, ff. 261 seq.) He reported lack of unanimity in the Cabinet on East Indian matters, with North unwilling to interfere, but the 'Bedfords' and the Duke of Grafton pressing him to intervene. McPherson had been in touch with the Duke of Grafton on behalf of the Nawab of Arcot when the former was still in power (see p. 198 above). Mansfield and Thurlow appear to have declared themselves slightly later.

[4] There is evidence that North was in touch with Clive throughout November —on the 17th he urged Clive to see him as soon as the latter returned to town (Powis MSS., quoted Forrest, *Clive*, op. cit. ii. 382). On 4 December 1771 he was trying to fix dates for Clive to call on him in town (North to Clive, 4 December 1771. Powis MSS.) and Clive was to call on him on 31 January 1772 (North to Clive,

King's Speech at the opening of the new parliamentary session
on 21 January 1772 referred to the

concerns of this country . . . so various and extensive as to require
the most vigilant and active attention; and some of them as well from
remoteness of place as from other circumstances . . . so peculiarly
liable to abuses and exposed to danger that the interposition of the
legislature . . . may become necessary,[1]

the speech of the seconder of the Address made it clear that all
the Government was recommending was the legislation designed
to strengthen the control of the East India Company over its
servants which Sulivan was working within the Company to
procure. Dissatisfaction with the military situation of India had
not proved strong enough to persuade the Government to take
the initiative in reorganizing the East India Company.

Equally, it had not proved sufficient to persuade the Government to support with any strength the reformers within the
Company. The attempt to co-operate with the Company in its
own reform broke down. If the Company's legislation had been
ready for immediate consideration in the House all might have
gone well. The terms of the Judicature Bill, which the Company
finally brought forward, were, so far as they went, sound and
sensible. They involved a new Charter of Justice for Bengal, the
barring of the Governor and Council from trade, and provisions for strengthening the Company's control over their
servants;[2] and much of what was proposed was incorporated in
subsequent legislation. But unfortunately it was a slow business
to get the Bill drafted, to get assurance of support for it among
the various interests in the Company (both the Johnstone party
and Clive viewed it with suspicion),[3] and to discuss it with
North and the law officers to see that it met their needs.[4] A draft
was in existence at least as early as 6 February,[5] but it was not
till 28 February that the Committee of Correspondence was
able to bring it before the Court of Directors.[6] On 4 March a

30 January 1772. Powis MSS.). After that there appears to be no contact between
them until after Parliament went into recess.

[1] *Parl. Hist.* xvii. 233.
[2] *London Chronicle*, 16 April 1772, pp. 374–5, prints an abstract of the Bill.
[3] Forrest, *Clive*, op. cit. ii. 385–6.
[4] It was clear from the debates in the House that North and Wedderburn, the
Solicitor-General, had in general approved it. (*Parl. Hist.* xvii. 328–81, 464–75.)
[5] Forrest, *Clive*, op. cit. ii. 385.   [6] Court Book 80, p. 484.

General Court of the Company adopted it;[1] but it was not until 30 March that Sulivan introduced it in the House, more than two months after the opening of the session.

A good deal, however, had happened in the intervening months. The second factor leading to intervention in the Company's affairs had come into play. Public attention had been focused on the abuses of the Company's rule by the propaganda of Bolts, Dow, and others. From one point of view this public concern was of assistance to the Company. It checked possible opposition to the Judicature Bill within the Company itself. Indeed, a correspondent wrote to Hastings that the Bill had been 'brought on by Bolts his book and . . . a petition from an Armenian in Bengal.'[2] The other effects were entirely unfavourable to the Company. Opinion within the House was much stirred both among the Opposition and that section of the administration who were already tending to favour stronger action on Indian affairs, and the atmosphere was propitious for the Johnstones to transfer their vendetta against Clive and other Company servants to a wider arena than the Company provided. The introduction of the Bill was the signal for a storm. Governor Johnstone and some of the Opposition group following Shelburne demanded a parliamentary inquiry into the abuses of the Company servants before any legislation was undertaken; Clive defended himself and attacked both his enemies and the Company; Johnstone launched a violent counter-attack upon him; and all of them combined in declaring the Bill inadequate.[3] More serious for the Bill's prospects was the fact that North's backing became tepid and there was a striking absence of the government support which had been expected. It was a private member on the Government's side, General Burgoyne (who was understood to be acting with the encouragement of the Duke of Grafton), who a few days later demanded, among general applause, that a Select Committee be set up to investigate 'the most atrocious abuses that ever stained the name of civil government'.[4] Supported by the Government and very widely throughout the

---

[1] Ibid., p. 489.

[2] H. Brooke to W. Hastings, 14 September 1772. Add. MS. 29133, f. 225v.

[3] Parl. Hist. xvii. 328–81.

[4] Ibid. 454. For Burgoyne's connexion with the Duke of Grafton see John McPherson to W. Hastings, 8 June 1773. Add. MS. 29133, f. 576.

House, the motion passed on a wave of enthusiasm, and its passing killed the Judicature Bill. It is true that North and a few supporters continued to give the Bill half-hearted encouragement, but it was very ill attended and when Wedderburn, the Solicitor-General, withdrew his support[1] it became clear that the hostile forces in the Government had triumphed. The open clash between them and the Company came on a point which was evidently unexpected. On the second reading of the Bill, an objection was raised to the appointment of judges in Bengal by any authority other than the Crown. This was a point on which Sulivan and the Company's other representatives could not be expected to compromise, since to do so would permit an important encroachment by the Crown into the Company's preserves. Consequently, though North tried ineffectually to save some part of the Bill, no one was surprised when, with the session nearing its end, it was allowed to lapse.[2]

With attention shifted to the activities of Burgoyne's Select Committee, few seem to have realized the seriousness of this fact. It marked the failure of the combined efforts of Government and Company to reform the Company from within. The Select Committee was conceived by its members as an instrument of investigation of the scandals of the past, not as one for considering the reforms necessary for the future. Still further, its composition, representative of both government and opposition interests, made it unlikely to play a constructive part even if personal animosities had not early led it into activities which were more sensational than practical. Shelburne lamented at the end of the session that they were 'an hundred miles off an honest enquiry', little could be done 'under such a ministry, such a parliament, such a direction, with an unawakened public'.[3] What was even more important, they were just as far off an honest attempt to grapple with the conditions which made such inquiries necessary. The wave of indignation against the Company had also failed to force East Indian affairs to a crisis, and had indeed interrupted the less spectacular efforts to institute reforms in them.

---

[1] *Parl. Hist.* xvii. 464–75. Burgoyne, Welbore Ellis, Thurlow, Whitworth, and Wedderburn on the Government side all spoke against the Bill.

[2] Ibid. 474–5.

[3] Shelburne to Chatham, 13 April 1772. *Chatham Correspondence*, iv. 212.

It was while Parliament was in recess and the ministers scattered throughout the country that the financial crisis blew up in the City and the storm broke on the East India Company. On 7 August the Treasury were first made officially aware of the difficulties the Company was in.[1] Though they asked to see various figures they seem at first to have taken the situation fairly lightly, but they soon began to realize that this was a mistake. By the latter part of September they had become aware that the immediate difficulties of the Company were of such a nature as to threaten a complete stoppage of payments unless something could be done to help them.[2] Such a prospect, with its implications of heavy direct loss to the Exchequer, widespread commercial dislocation, and confusion in India, would at any time have been alarming. At a time of financial crisis in the City it was doubly so. The hope of those managing the Company's affairs was that, when the postponement of Customs dues proved an insufficient relief and the Bank would only give limited credit for a very short time, some fairly unspectacular way would be found by the Treasury to help the Company out of its difficulties, without raising other issues and without recourse to Parliament. Colebrooke and Sulivan put forward a variety of expedients,[3] and both North, on holiday at Wroxton, and the members of the Treasury Board in London seemed inclined to be accommodating.[4] What help they got from the Bank was also based on the assumption that the Government would come to their assistance.

Two things combined to destroy these optimistic assumptions: the growing realization by the Treasury of the extent of the Company's obligations, both immediate and (as Bills of Exchange became due) long-term, and the sudden break in India Stock prices when the Company's straits could no longer be kept secret, a collapse which raised a frenzy of indignation among shareholders, speculators, and the public at large.

The members of the Committee of Treasury of the Court of

---

[1] *Reports from Committees of the House of Commons*, iv. 31. *Second Report of the Committee of Secrecy*, Appendix A.

[2] Accounts in Add. MS. 38397, *passim*, drawn up by the Company's officials for submission to the Treasury.

[3] E. Burke to W. Dowdeswell, 27 October 1772. *Burke Correspondence*, i. 343–4. Cf. L. Sulivan to W. Hastings, 28 April 1773. Add. MS. 29133, f. 534.

[4] E. Burke to W. Dowdeswell, 27 October 1772. *Burke Correspondence*, i. 344–5.

Directors were the only members of the Court who had known the details of the Company's accounts.[1] On this occasion they kept their counsel remarkably well. When the crash came some of them, particularly the Chairman, Sir George Colebrooke, were accused of selling out their own holdings in good time while keeping the true state of things from the public,[2] and there may have been some truth in the accusations, but no such accusation was directed against most of them and their close friends and associates were in many cases heavy sufferers.[3] By the 22 September, however, the Committee could no longer keep the directors in ignorance, as on the 24th the dividend for the next six months had to be passed by the General Court. In fact the news must have become general property a few days earlier, for after some days of sagging prices there was a sharp fall in the price of India Stock on 18 September from 200 to 187 and then to 185, its lowest level until Parliament opened and the Government decided to impose terms on the Company.[4] On 23 September an indignant but not yet thoroughly alarmed

---

[1] The Committees of the Treasury and of Secrecy were the only ones whose minutes were not open for the examination of directors (they could, however, be shown them with the permission of the Chairman or his Deputy). *Reports from Committees of the House of Commons, Eighth Report from the Committee of Secrecy*, iv. 384.

[2] For Colebrooke's relations with Fordyce in dealings in East India Stock see *Sir George Colebrooke's World Corner in Alum, 1772–3*, loc. cit.

[3] Francis Sykes, himself a heavy loser, complained that the Committee 'got clear of their Stock and communicated their situation to the directors at large, not that it was a matter of any great consequence, only a temporary difficulty' (F. Sykes to W. Hastings, 8 November 1773. Add. MS. 29134, f. 117ᵛ). Laurence Sulivan said that 'Stock purchases were all remembered: the sufferers were violent in the extreme, and it must be acknowledged (though I believe the parties innocent of any sinister views) that appearances were very unfavourable' (L. Sulivan to W. Hastings, 28 April 1773. Add. MS. 29133, f. 534). Burke spoke of Colebrooke as 'under imputations all of which he cannot remove' (*Burke Correspondence*, i. 351), and Palk, who was left a creditor of Sir George's after his failure, speaks of his sale of stock in April: 'he, who was in the secret, knowing when to sell for his own advantage what did not belong to him' (*H.M.C., Palk MSS.*, p. 244). Both Palk and Sykes considered that, having close friends among the directors, and having done them much service, they should have been warned in time to get out. Sykes complained: 'Purling and Savage told me the difficulty was of no great consequence till almost the last and [I] concluded they would hardly deceive me, so kept my stock, which with my own and what I borrowed amounted to near £30,000 capital. The situation of the Company was so little known and so partially retailed out, that most of the Stockholders suffered one third of their principal, besides interest' (F. Sykes to W. Hastings, 8 November 1773. Add. MS. 29134, f. 118).

[4] Figures taken from tables in the *London Magazine*, September 1772, p. 402; sufferers quoted more striking figures.

Court of Proprietors were told that the consideration of a dividend must be temporarily postponed since the directors were in negotiation with the Government for assistance,[1] a situation which they reluctantly accepted.

On 2 October North returned to town[2] and on the 5th had come to the conclusion that the matter must be laid before Parliament,[3] which would have to be summoned to meet before Christmas (it had been hoped that it might remain in recess till the New Year). After a three weeks' hold-up in the negotiations with the Company the Treasury gave an unfavourable reply to all its proposals for credit and demanded further papers so that 'a more proper method of assisting the Company might be considered of before the meeting of Parliament'.[4] North's administration through no initiative of their own found themselves forced to evolve an Indian policy.

Until the situation was thus rudely altered by the financial disaster, there had been an uneasy lull in the attempts to grapple with the East Indian question. Neither Company nor Government had made any progress during the recess. The Company's leaders after the failure of the Judicature Bill had fallen back on the second part of their plan, the early dispatch of supervisors to India to investigate and reform abuses. But by failing to persuade suitable persons to stand for the position[5] and by arousing personal animosities they had weakened their position in the Company even before the knowledge of the financial situation completed their discomfiture. After the crash they lost their control even over the Court of Directors and still more over the Court of Proprietors. In consequence, the list of supervisors finally passed[6] was made up in defiance of their wishes and was so manifestly unsuitable in its composition

[1] Court Book 81, p. 181.

[2] Bodl. North MS. D.24, f. 172, George North to Guilford, 5 October 1772.

[3] Ibid., D.24, f. 177, North to Guilford, printed in 'Lord North's Correspondence 1766–83', E. Hughes. (*E.H.R.*, April 1947, p. 223.)

[4] Court Book 81, p. 221.

[5] The failure was not for want of trying. Laurence Sulivan said: 'Here it was our misfortune to secure no conspicuous character (Monckton's excepted), Mr. Cornwall, Sir Jeffry Amherst, Edmund Burke, Colonel Barré, Sir Richard Sutton had refused, and last in the list myself. Among those that Sir George selected and had accepted, was Mr. Andrew Stuart, a gentleman now well known as the principal actor in the famous Douglas cause . . . being a Scotchman, it gave our enemies scope for an attack' (L. Sulivan to W. Hastings, 28 April 1773. Add. MS. 29133, f. 533). [6] Court Book 81, pp. 289 seq.

that, even had the Government not in the meantime intervened in the Company's affairs on other grounds, it could hardly have failed to take action to prevent their going to India. As it was, an Act of Parliament was hurriedly passed in December 1772[1] to prohibit temporarily the dispatch of supervisors to India and the scheme came to an end.

The Government on its side appears to have been entirely quiescent during the summer. Only one step which it took affected the East Indian issue and this no more than indirectly. During these months ministers finally saw their way to add Clive and his substantial interest to their parliamentary supporters. On the death of Lord Powis he was appointed Lord Lieutenant of Shropshire.[2] From the ministry's point of view this alliance had nothing to do with Indian affairs and it appears to have embodied no specific pledge of government support to Clive against the accusations of Burgoyne's Committee. It is probably significant that though the king, when Clive kissed hands on the 9 October, 'talked upon Indian affairs for near half an hour', North, when they met early in November, 'seemed industriously to avoid entering upon the subject of Indian affairs'.[3] But on Clive's side the usefulness of a friendly government in such circumstances cannot have been forgotten, particularly with the events of 1763 still in his mind, and observers, fully alive to this consideration, pointed out that Burgoyne's Committee had 'driven Lord Clive to the Court'.[4]

Now that Parliament had been summoned to meet on the 26 November, however, a line had to be adopted by the Government without delay. It could not expect much help from outside. Public feeling was running high, but was much confused; the Company was in disorder, the directors discredited, and the Chairman, Sir George Colebrooke (his private affairs in distraction), was described by Burke as being:

in a flutter of expedients, the instrument of the designs of other people, wholly without authority in the Company, baffled in all his attempts, under imputations, all of which he cannot remove and without any natural resources (further than some kind of resolution) to carry him through a labyrinth of difficulties.[5]

[1] 13 Geo. III, c. 9.   [2] Forrest, *Clive*, op. cit. ii. 395–6.
[3] Ibid., p. 346.   [4] *Burke Correspondence*, i. 353.
[5] Ibid. 351.

Within the Government itself there was little agreement; those who always advocated stronger measures than North was prepared to adopt were talking loudly and were now joined by Wedderburn, with Clive's interests in view. It was rumoured that some of them were in favour of sweeping extensions of Government responsibility reminiscent of the more extreme views of 1767.[1] But now, as then, there was little if any attempt to translate these views into concrete plans, or even to adopt any of the various proposals, including one from Clive,[2] that began to pour in on the Government from those experienced in East Indian affairs. On the other side, there were no signs that North and the advisers on whom he leaned had abated their objections to a sweeping assumption of responsibility by the Government in India. The sober administrators whose advice North took did not believe that the machinery of government was strong enough to take over the responsibility of governing Bengal.[3] Still less did they think it could be done in the teeth of violent opposition from the East India Company. It was, however, now accepted as axiomatic that if the East India Company were to be helped out of its financial difficulties, it must be in return for radical improvements in the Company's organization and rule. The king himself warmly supported this view[4] and it is significant that its strength lay not only in the desire to obviate financial loss or military danger to the nation, but in a wider sense of obligation for law and order in India.

The plan of action which North and his advisers devised to implement the cautious policy he favoured was carefully thought out. It began with a speech from the throne which was firm though moderate (North softened it down at the last minute with the king's rather dubious consent). The speech

[1] Ibid. 345. *Chatham Correspondence*, iv. 234.

[2] Presented to the Government on 24 November 1772. Summarized in *Historical View of Plans for the Government of British India . . .*, 1793. Clive sketched it out and Strachey elaborated it. (Forrest, *Clive*, op. cit. ii. 396-7.)

[3] On 17 January 1773 Shelburne informed Chatham (*Chatham Correspondence*, iv. 238-9) on good authority that North's supporters had opposed the taking of the territorial revenues of Bengal into the hands of the State and that an attempt to do so was now improbable. Some time later, probably in 1779, John Robinson gave a reasoned statement of the administrative and political case against the assumption of Government control much of which, while written with special reference to the position during the American War, applied also in general. See pp. 338 seq. below.

[4] *Correspondence of George III*, ii. 408, no. 1158.

stated that Parliament had been called together to consider the 'maintenance of the credit and prosperity of the East India Company' and asked Parliament, after informing themselves of the 'true state of their affairs', to 'make such provision for the common benefit and security of all the various interests concerned as you shall find best adapted to the exigencies of the case'.[1] He probably was not sorry that the mover and seconder of the address (Richard FitzPatrick[2] and Dr. Burrell[3]) should express themselves with some violence. He then himself moved the appointment of a small Committee of Secrecy with the limited and practical duty of examining the Company's books and reporting on the facts of its situation. This Committee was to be very different from Burgoyne's Select Committee (which, it had been understood, would continue its activities in the new Session and which had to be permitted to do so) in that its membership was restricted to supporters of administration, its purpose was to lead up to legislation, it was asked to report rapidly, and it was given as its unofficial *rapporteur* the highly competent and purposeful Charles Jenkinson.[4] Little attempt was made to disguise the fact that the Government were using it as an instrument of policy; the king pressed for rapid results[5] and on one occasion, just before it submitted its fifth report to the House of Commons, it was summoned to meet at 'Lord North's in Downing St.'.[6]

After taking these steps it would seem that North hoped he could stand back and await propositions from the East India Company for their own reform, which could then be used as a

[1] *Jour. H.C.*, 26 November 1772.
[2] Richard FitzPatrick, M.P. for Okehampton, friend of Charles James Fox, later a prominent Whig politician.
[3] William Burrell, LL.D., M.P. for Haslemere, antiquary and writer of law-reports.
[4] There can be little doubt that this was Jenkinson's role on the Committee. He gained considerable credit for its reports; Chatham wrote to Shelburne of the first report, it 'does credit to the Committee . . . I understood . . . that it was principally Jenkinson's' (*Chatham Correspondence*, iv. 241); the material for the reports can be found in large quantities in his correspondence and Rigby writes to him as if to the Secretary of the Committee (Add. MS. 38398, f. 38). Jenkinson's position throughout this affair is a striking illustration of Professor Namier's thesis that the 'king's friends' were in large part the rising professional administrators, who as yet could find no place in the Civil Service.
[5] *Correspondence of George III*, ii. 417, no. 1170.
[6] R. Rigby to C. Jenkinson, 21 March 1773. Add. MS. 38398, f. 38.

basis for discussion and the foundation of the future system. The king, his customary energy breaking through the restraints of punctuation, wrote to him in terms which make clear the line which the Government was adopting.

I cannot omit reminding you that though I trust when the Company finds the Committee has laid the true state before the House, that it cannot avoid coming into such an agreement as may be thought secure for its creditors and equitable for the Public and the Proprietors; but that if this should not happen that you will be prepared with a plan for conducting those affairs, if you form it yourself it will be just, and there are men of ability in Parliament will certainly support it well in the House; but if you are open to their ideas nothing will be done for everyone will have schemes incompatible with those of the others you may consult.[1]

It was the partial failure of North's hopes in the coming session and the reason for, and results thereof, that make up the story of the passing of the Regulating Bill.

[1] *Correspondence of George III*, ii. 408, no. 1158.

IX

THE PASSING OF THE REGULATING ACT

IT was with doubtful hopes and limited objectives that a session was launched which was certain to be controversial. The circumstances which had forced the Government into action also forced the parliamentary opposition groups to consider what line they would adopt. At first sight the prospect did not seem encouraging for an Opposition which was already weak and divided, since, as Burke gloomily pointed out, indignant public opinion was strongly in favour of the Government. 'By an unhappy and rare conjunction of circumstances', he wrote, 'the designs of the court coincide exactly with the phrenzy of the people.'[1] Nevertheless both the opposition groups had carried over from the debates of 1766–7 certain presuppositions and points of view which they were almost bound to adhere to in this new crisis of the Company's affairs.

The Rockinghams had stood in 1766–7 for the chartered rights of companies, and more specifically the right of the East India Company, to enjoy the revenues of the territories it had conquered. Though Burke pointed out that they need not slavishly adhere to their line of 1767, Dowdeswell as their leader in the House of Commons took the earliest opportunity of raising the question of territorial right in its most abstract form,[2] and Burke himself was soon eagerly at work stimulating their supporters to action.[3]

Burke and Dowdeswell, however, found a good deal of difficulty in rallying their supporters. Rockingham and the other leaders were reluctant to come to town for a session called solely on East Indian affairs—even the Duke of Richmond, soon to immerse himself in them, refused at first to intervene.[4] Some refused to oppose what seemed to them the necessary intervention of the Government,[5] and even the big East India shareholder,

---

[1] *Burke Correspondence*, i. 362.
[2] *Parl. Hist.* xvii. 806.
[3] *Burke Correspondence*, i. 385–91.
[4] Ibid. 386; and Rockingham to W. Dowdeswell, 30 October 1772, and Richmond to Rockingham, 2 November 1772. FitzWilliam MSS. (Sheffield).
[5] Sir George Savile, for instance, refused to take part in the matter.

Sir Matthew Fetherstonehaugh, was anxious to temporize.[1] Rockingham indeed propounded from afar (under the influence of Robert Gregory, an East Indian director who was in touch with him) a scheme whereby the Company could evade the Government's clutches by reducing its dividend to 6 per cent., thus freeing itself of its liabilities to the State.[2] But those on the spot assured him that a collapse in the price of stock would damage rather than improve the Company's case,[3] and despite the misgivings of some of their supporters the Rockingham group soon found it impossible not to support the Company in its resistance. As Dowdeswell reported to his leader, when proprietors anxious to stand firm 'come to us, open their case to us and hope for our support . . . not to hear them tends to throw the Company at the feet of Government'. On the other hand 'to hear them in the distracted state in which we are, so many of our friends panic-stricken in whatever concerns the East India Company . . . I say to hear and support them in this state is holding out false hopes to the Company and incurring the danger of great division among ourselves'.[4] Such considerations rallied their forces and, particularly after the Duke of Richmond came into action early in the new year, brought them to a reasonably united opposition to the Government's policy, an opposition which they based on the grounds that the Government by its actions was endangering the liberties of the subject and increasing the powers of the Crown.

A survey of recent East Indian history which Rockingham gave in a letter as early as October 1772 indicates their line of thought so clearly as to be worth quoting at length:

All thinking men must already acknowledge that the influence of the Crown and the means of corruption are become very dangerous to the Constitution and yet the enormous addition of power which Government are aiming at by subjecting the East India Company to their control does not strike and alarm so much as it ought.

It is very unfortunate that in the course of late years many men who have had no such intention, have nevertheless helped to forward

[1] *Burke Correspondence*, i. 396.
[2] Rockingham to W. Dowdeswell, 30 November 1772. FitzWilliam MSS. (Sheffield).
[3] *Burke Correspondence*, i. 385 seq.
[4] W. Dowdeswell to Rockingham, 20 December 1772. FitzWilliam MSS. (Sheffield).

this plan of Government. Beckford's wildness in arraigning the East India Company's right to their acquisitions was [word illegible] to the Sanctum Sanctorum and that idea was much cherished.

Many men of tender feelings on the dismal accounts of rapine and oppression in the Company's servants in Bengal, join the cry that some stop must be put to it; the interior Cabinet laugh in their sleeve at the pretence with which this helps to furnish them in their object of more control over India affairs.

These two circumstances alone might have been sufficient to have struck terror into the East India Company, but when one considers also that Government sent out Sir John Lindsay with a commission that tended to weaken and destroy the weight of the India Company with the Indian powers and that at home scarce a session can pass without some terror held out over the India Company . . . I must say that I fear the result will be that there will be neither virtue nor strength enough in the East India Company to resist Government's plan nor will the public at large see all the danger till too late.[1]

Chatham, Shelburne, and their followers did not find it any easier to determine their line of policy. Their problem was different. Until they knew precisely what the Government intended to do, it was not clear how, if at all, they could oppose it in view of their own actions in 1767. Nevertheless, as an opposition group, they were bound to feel uneasy about an aspect of the situation which they observed with equanimity when in power, the possibility of increased Crown patronage as a result of any assumption of administrative control in India.[2] They also took some pains to deny that they had ever wished to take over the control of the Company[3] and some of those on the fringes of their group, particularly Charles Cornwall, seem to have been working for a compromise,[4] but in the end they

[1] Rockingham to E. Burke, 28 October 1772. FitzWilliam MSS. (Sheffield).
[2] *Chatham Correspondence*, iv. 254–7, 264–5. Barré echoed their fear in the House of Commons. He would have 'no cousins, no younger brothers, no servile dependents to quarter upon the Company' (*Parl. Hist.* xvii, col. 826).
[3] W. Dowdeswell to Rockingham, 20 December 1772. FitzWilliam MSS. (Sheffield). This is confirmed by Chatham's own words, see p. 152 above.
Rockingham had already remarked (28 October 1772, Rockingham to E. Burke): 'Perhaps by this time something may be known in regard to what Lord Chatham's ideas may be on East Indian matters. I am not sure that his Lordship has any *or ever had any* fixed plan or idea on that subject.' FitzWilliam MSS. (Sheffield).
[4] W. Dowdeswell to Rockingham, 20 December 1772. FitzWilliam MSS. (Sheffield).

found it most convenient to concentrate their interest on the revelations of Burgoyne's Committee rather than on the Government's measures for reform, and ultimately found themselves giving the Government their general support.[1]

As a result of these difficulties, therefore, and despite some stirring debates, North found little to fear from the organized opposition groups. He found the activities both of his own more extreme supporters and of the non-party Burgoyne Committee considerably more embarrassing. So far as this Committee was concerned, an attempt was made to keep distinct its functions and those of the new Committee of Secrecy, and to limit its activities to investigations of the disorders of the past, while the Committee of Secrecy considered nothing that was irrelevant to the reforms of the future. In fact the fields of the two Committees inevitably overlapped and, though North was adroit in dissociating himself and his government from the most controversial and personal issues raised by the Select Committee, he could not prevent it from throwing a good deal of confusion into the orderly development of the Government's plans.

But the Government's most serious problems and the Opposition's most marked success in embarrassing them came from outside the House. It did not come from the general body of public opinion which habitually assailed the Government. Right at the end, it is true, the Company succeeded in calling forth a certain amount of public support for the cause of the sanctity of chartered rights, but the contrast between the public reaction to North's Act and to Fox's Bill ten years later is a remarkable commentary on the discredited position in which the Company found itself in 1773. The Government's difficulty came from within the Company itself, where some measure of co-operation was essential for the success of the ministers' schemes. This difficulty was greatly increased, if not caused, by the assistance given to the hostile forces in the Company by supporters of the parliamentary Opposition, in particular by a sudden and headlong excursion into East Indian affairs by no less prominent a person than the Duke of Richmond.

The opposition from the Company was not found in the Court of Directors. The administration found no great difficulty in bringing into conformity with its wishes either the Court in

[1] *Chatham Correspondence*, iv. 279 seq.

power during the crisis or the new Direction elected the following April. The position of the directors in power in 1772–3 was unkindly sketched by a former Company servant:

The truth is they know not what to do. Afraid to propose any measures that might seem to go beyond the bounds of the Company's charter, sensible that nothing effectual can be done while that restraint remains, willing to keep pace with the Minister's views and desirous to gain and preserve the good will of the Proprietary; all these motives operating together with their own private wishes and views for maintaining their share of power and consequence, and not without some degree of apprehension that they may be called to account for past misconduct and errors, makes their task a very difficult one.[1]

Moreover, the question of the April election was already preoccupying them. The deployment of forces had taken place, as was now necessary, in October 1772, and it is not surprising, in view of the situation at that time, that activity can be seen on the part of various interests to prepare for a hotly contested election.

The administration had taken its share in these preparations. More than £23,000 of the stock held by Lord Holland and administered by John Powell of the Pay Office had been duly 'split'. Neither Sir George Colebrooke (who had undertaken extensive precautionary operations even in the 1772 election) nor Sulivan nor Clive themselves put forces in the field, but various East Indians, whose fortunes were closely bound up with them, did. Francis Sykes, who had worked with Clive on previous occasions, 'split' £16,500;[2] Thomas Rumbold, who was at this time very closely connected with Sir George Colebrooke,[3] split £10,000, and the Barwell family, who supported Sulivan and Colebrooke and whose holdings were managed for them by

---

[1] J. Caillaud to W. Hastings, 15 March 1773. Add. MS. 29133, ff. 444ᵛ–445. Stock Ledgers 1769–1774.

[2] Sykes may have controlled considerably more votes, as he told Warren Hastings that he held nearly £30,000 including 'what I had borrowed' when prices crashed in September 1772. F. Sykes to W. Hastings, 8 November 1773. Add. MS. 29134, f. 118.

[3] F. Sykes to W. Hastings, 10 February 1773. 'R[umbol]d lent Sir George most of his fortune. On his stopping payment he has been not a little frightened, yet Sir George has been able to satisfy every claimant and a large fortune yet remains.' Add. MS. 29133, f. 381ᵛ. In fact, Colebrooke's crash was only postponed, not averted.

their redoubtable sister Mary,[1] split £12,500. In addition to these large forces controlled by individuals there were also the usual variety of smaller interests and individuals whose votes could be subjected to influence.

A force deployed so long in advance was open to casualties and to every kind of adjustment to meet changes in alliance, and the Government on this occasion met with what might have been a serious misfortune. Towards the end of November the distributors of Lord Holland's stock began to recall it and finally sold most of it off, thus cancelling the greater number of the votes that had been created. By April no more than £7,000 of the stock obtained from him seems still to have been available in the form of voting qualifications. Though there appears to have been no political motive behind this manœuvre, probably the result of the extreme financial pressure to which Lord Holland was subjected at this time in repaying his sons' debts,[2] it must have been highly inconvenient for the Government. It threw them back on the 'management' for which Sandwich was becoming noted and on the favour of the holders of large voting forces. But, helped by the disorganization of the Company's leaders and the fears of the 'Nabobs', these ultimately proved adequate for the purpose. The collapse of Colebrooke and fear of the attacks of Burgoyne's Select Committee brought Rumbold over to the camp of Clive and Sykes, already strong supporters of the government interest; only Sulivan of the Company's leaders in 1772 dared to stand for re-election.[3] Two rival lists of candidates were made up, a House list with Sulivan at its head, and a rival Proprietors' list backed by the Government and by strong East Indian interests headed by Crabb Boulton, Clive's

---

[1] Barwell Correspondence, printed in *Bengal Past and Present*, xi. 49 seq.

[2] Lord Ilchester, *Henry Fox*, ii. 351.   [3] General Caillaud told Warren Hastings (31 March 1773): 'Sir George Colebrooke and Purling have both declined standing, being both publicly accused as also Sir James Cockburn of having withheld the true state of the Company's affairs from the proprietors. Purling made his declaration of not being a candidate for the direction in the House of Commons until his conduct had been enquired into. This drew from Lord North a compliment approving and applauding his resolution, which Sulivan took up as an indirect censure on his conduct, having declared his intention of standing. For being clear in his conscience of all sense of guilt, he could despise all reports to the contrary. And that as he feared not to meet the fullest enquiry into his conduct, he thought it his duty not to decline the offer of his services, and more particularly in the present situation of the Company's affairs. His speech was short, spirited and manly, and was much approved of.' Add. MS. 29133, ff. 494ᵛ–495.

old supporter.[1] The Proprietors' list won an easy victory.[2] Crabb Boulton was chosen Chairman and Edward Wheler Deputy. Sulivan gave his account of the débacle in a letter to Hastings:

Sir George Colebrooke, pressed by misfortunes retreated, Purling in dread of the Secret Committee signified his intention of keeping out of the Direction and I was left alone to stem the torrent, which was considered by many to be a difficult task. For the Minister judging that without extraordinary attempts the Company would be in their own hands could I be persuaded to retire, every art was practised to cajole, to intimidate me; but nothing could move me for I had nothing to fear. A proposal was then made to take Robert Jones, John Pringle, Dewar and Richard Smith on the House List. I stated a truth that it was impossible for me to carry the first three. This was considered a refusal. Sandwich erected the standard, mandates were issued from every office and ministerial influence proved too hard for me, and yet . . . if Mr. Raymond had not deserted me, I had still gained the victory.[3]

Thus in this, the last election of directors under the old system, Laurence Sulivan was again (though by no means finally) ousted from power and the Government obtained a Direction which, while not altogether under their control, was unlikely to refuse co-operation in their immediate plans.

On the other hand the situation in the Court of Proprietors was very different. Angry and confused, they had already got beyond the control of the directors before the end of 1772. When this happened they were apt to fall an easy prey to demagogic leadership. The peculiar feature of the position in 1773 was that this leadership was provided quite openly and on undeniably political grounds by leaders of the parliamentary Opposition. In the earliest phase of the struggle the Johnstone group within the Company took the lead in the Court of Proprietors, and Governor Johnstone used his prestige as a promi-

[1] Add. MS. 29133, ff. 494ᵛ–495. R. Palk to W. Hastings, 8 April 1773. 'The Election [of Directors] ended yesterday but the report is not yet made, the great contest is between Boulton and Sulivan, the first assisted by Administration, which I apprehend will be too much for our friend, especially as all Indians are on the same side.' Ibid., f. 506. The Barwell interest and Palk himself, however, remained faithful.

[2] *London Chronicle*, 8 April 1773, p. 338.

[3] Add. MS. 29133, f. 534ᵛ. L. Sulivan to W. Hastings, 28 April 1773. Charles Raymond, a prominent ships'-husband, seems to have been acting as leader of the shipping interest at this time.

nent M.P. and a well-known party orator to sway the disorganized Court to his will. Now in the new year a powerful ally and rival came down to the Court from the West end of the town, by no means altogether to Johnstone's satisfaction, and stole most of his thunder, while making still more effective the opposition to directors and government. This new leader was the Duke of Richmond, who, after withstanding all Burke's blandishments, suddenly took up the East Indian cause with single-minded impetuosity when he came to town at the beginning of the year, and, with the prestige of his rank, the well-known vigour of his oratory, and the complete irresponsibility of one whose sole interest was to annoy the Government, swept the proprietors into his train.[1]

Peers had before this qualified as stock-holders and gone down ostentatiously to register their votes in the Company's elections; Lord Sandwich had thought it worth while to build up a steady interest there and Lord Shelburne had entertained even higher hopes, but for a prominent peer to stand forth as the personal leader of the discontented proprietors in the Court was entirely new, and, in the disturbed conditions of the Company, very effective. The Duke of Richmond was, moreover, particularly well suited for the work he undertook. Burke pointed out the violence of his enthusiasms. 'Your Grace', he said, 'dissipates your mind into too great a variety of minute pursuits, all of which, from the natural vehemence of your temper, you follow with almost equal passion',[2] and it was reported that Chatham said of him that 'he is in opposition the most grievous man to a ministry that ever I knew'.[3] He got only half-hearted support from his aristocratic colleagues who, though they formally approved his unorthodox activities, were somewhat alarmed at the extremes to which they led him ('The Duke of Richmond', said Rockingham, 'is now head of a *large* body of Proprietors—among

---

[1] General Caillaud wrote to Warren Hastings on 15 March 1773 that the directors were much hampered in their negotiations with the Government 'by a party among the Proprietors headed by the Duke of Richmond, with Johnstone and Dempster [for him see p. 155, n. 2, above] who disqualified as a Director ten days ago that he might be more at liberty in Parliament. The real views of this party under the plausible pretence of being the sacred guardian of the Company's chartered rights is to get matter for forming a strong opposition in Parliament against administration.' (Add. MS. 29133, ff. 445-445ᵛ).

[2] *Burke Correspondence*, i. 376.

[3] Lord Holland, *Memoirs of the Whig Party during my Time*, London, 1852, i. 118.

them men of much *natural warmth* and also men of cooler passions and yet perhaps both equally firm to the object. His Grace must act as a *moderator*');[1] but for more than a year he carried on in the Company the battle which the Opposition were unable to fight in the House. Thereby he added greatly to the embarrassments of government, while the political world followed with interest and amusement the course of this unorthodox battle.

The final results of North's intervention into the affairs of the Company are comprised in three Acts: 13 George III, c. 44, which gave the Company concessions with regard to the export of tea (which indirectly affected relations with the American colonies); 13 George III, c. 63, the Regulating Act itself, which inaugurated a number of reforms in the organization of the Company and gave the Government for the first time a share in the responsibility for the administration of India and considerable powers of control over the Company; and 13 George III, c. 64, which gave the Company, under fairly stringent financial conditions, the loan the need for which was the immediate cause of the whole reform. The forms and contents of these Acts owed much to the circumstances in which they were passed.

At first North's hopes appeared likely to be realized. The Committee of Secrecy, after reporting on the need to restrain the sending out of Supervisors, went rapidly to work, and Jenkinson, aided by the Company's clerks (whose professional skill and excellent records he warmly praised), succeeded in getting out a clear and comprehensive statement of the Company's finances contained in two reports, one published on 17 December, before Parliament adjourned for the Christmas recess, and the other on 9 February, after it had reassembled.[2] A day was fixed for a debate on them, and on further papers demanded from the Company, early in March. Meantime negotiations were going forward with the directors for proposals from the Company to be put before the House at this debate. These negotiations went at first fairly smoothly, the directors being collectively anxious to prevent a head-on collision with the

---

[1] Rockingham to E. Burke, n.d. (apparently early December 1773). Burke, Dempster, and sometimes Lord John Cavendish seem to have helped Richmond considerably. FitzWilliam MSS. (Sheffield).

[2] *Second* and *third Reports of the Committee of Secrecy*, loc cit. iv, pp. 15 seq. He used the figures previously wrung from the Company by the Treasury (Publ. Rec. Off., Treasury Papers T29/42, pp. 245 seq., and T1/488 *passim*).

Government and some of them having as individuals good reason to show their willingness to co-operate. As early as 14 January they had agreed to ask for a loan of £1,500,000 at 4 per cent. and for concessions with regard to the export of tea. Colebrooke and Sulivan consulted North on the Government's views on these demands[1] and brought back a message of cautious encouragement, but also a firm warning that no demands could be considered unless accompanied by proposals for reform.

As it is very improbable [North wrote] that Parliament will think fit to direct that an application be made for the relief of the Company without making at the same time some effectual provision for preventing the repetition of the same errors and abuses as have brought the Company into their present difficulties, and as it seems equally natural to expect that some further propositions should be made to Parliament by the Company respecting the possession of the territorial acquisitions and revenues in India, the agreement concerning which will expire in February 1774, Lord North recommends it to the consideration of the directors whether it can answer any good purpose to proceed in settling a plan of the kind proposed by them to be offered to Parliament unless they do also prepare such other propositions to be laid at the same time before Parliament as they shall judge best calculated for securing in future the better Government of the Company's affairs as well at home as in India.[2]

Thus pressed, the directors went farther, and on 3 and 6 February produced further propositions which at least by implication dealt with both points raised by Lord North. To check abuses in India they proposed the reintroduction of the Judicature Bill which had been allowed to lapse in the preceding session. They also suggested that the Treasury should have power to limit the total value of bills of exchange to be taken up by the Company; that Company servants should be forbidden to have commercial dealings with traders of foreign nationality, and that returns should be made to the Government of all civil and military expenses in India and of all sales at the Company's warehouse in London. To give the State a share in its revenues without prejudice to the Company's claim of right to its territorial conquests, they suggested that all profits over and above those necessary to ensure an 8 per cent. dividend to

---

[1] Court Book 81, p. 394. [2] Ibid., p. 415.

the Company should be divided equally between the Company and the State. Still further, they proposed that Indian revenues should be handled by special servants who might be subject to the control of the State as well as the Company.[1] North, when consulted, gave general approbation to the proposals.

Difficulties arose, however, when the directors brought them before the General Court. The proprietors had already shown their mistrust of the directors by appointing a Committee of twenty-five of their members to watch over the proprietors' interests. Strong opposition to the proposals now began to manifest itself in a series of Courts. As early as December the Duke of Richmond had suggested that the best way for the Company to embarrass the Government was to refrain from putting forward any propositions at all.[2] At a Court held on 12 February this opinion prevailed and the majority, refusing to consider what the directors put before them, instructed the Chairman and Deputy to wait on North and to ask him what terms he was prepared to consider.[3]

The step was not, from the Company's point of view, a useful one; North might sometimes be a weak negotiator, but his answer to this was simple. He promptly replied that unless the Company put forward proposals he would leave it to Parliament to do so.[4] In view of the attitude of the House at the time the threat was scarcely veiled, and was immediately recognized. With time drawing short, therefore, the directors set hastily to work to rebuild the edifice of their offer, by a three-cornered negotiation with interests among the proprietors on one side and with North on the other. In the course of it North appears to have given the Chairman some reason to believe that the Government would accept the terms which they put forward. On the strength of an assurance by the directors to this effect (which North later repudiated)[5] the General Court was persuaded to pass a petition incorporating these terms, and it was laid before the House on 2 March, two days before the date fixed for the debate. The proposals were not indeed as comprehensive as those which the directors had hoped to bring forward.

---

[1] Court Book 81, pp. 445 seq.
[2] Richmond to E. Burke, 2 December 1772. *Burke Correspondence*, i. 397.
[3] Court Book 81, pp. 463 seq.
[4] Ibid., p. 471.
[5] *Parl. Hist.* xvii, cols. 801 seq.

They asked for a loan of £1,500,000 at 4 per cent. interest repayable within four years and for measures to assist the export of tea; in return they proposed that the Company's dividend be limited to 6 per cent. until this loan was reduced to £750,000 and thereafter to 8 per cent. and that, when the loan should be repaid in full, the profits in excess of those necessary to support the 8 per cent. dividend should (as in their earlier proposal) be divided equally between the Company and the State. On the further question of 'regulations . . . proper and effectual for the more advantageous management of their affairs and for the due administration of justice in India', they now made no suggestions, but promised forthwith to take them into consideration,[1] The debate in the House was postponed until 9 March so that the petition might be studied.

When the House met, it went into Committee to consider East Indian affairs, and in this debate and in those of 23 March and 5 April the Government advanced and carried a series of Resolutions which were laid before the House on 27 April after the Easter recess. They were based on, but varied on several important points from, the Company's proposals. Their substance was:

1. That a considerable sum of money was necessary to relieve the Company from its financial distress and that it was best for the Public to advance it.
2. That a sum of £1,400,000 (against the Company's demand for £1,500,000) would be sufficient.
3. That the loan should be granted on condition that 'at the same time due care be taken to secure by proper Regulations the future good government of the Company's affairs'.
4. That the Company should be restrained from increasing the dividend beyond 6 per cent. till their debt be repaid and beyond 7 per cent. until their bond debt was reduced to £1,500,000 (terms considerably more onerous than those for which the Company believed they had government approval).
5. That, without entering into discussion about the territorial rights enjoyed by the Company, it would be for the

---

[1] *Jour. H.C.* xxxiv. 164–5, 2 March 1773.

mutual benefit of Public and Company for the territorial possessions and revenues 'under proper Restrictions and Regulations' to remain in the possession of the Company during a term not exceeding six years, and that the public would forgo all share in the Company's revenues until the bond debt had been reduced to £1,500,000, but thereafter would take three-quarters of all profits above those necessary for a dividend of 8 per cent., the remaining quarter going to the Company for use in debt redemption and the building up of reserves.

6. Finally that the concessions the Company asked for with regard to the export of tea should be granted.[1]

A strong committee on which North himself served and of which John Robinson, the Secretary of the Treasury, was to do most of the spade-work,[2] was appointed to draw up a bill to implement these resolutions, the measure later known as the Loan Bill.

So far the Government, despite some hitches, had carried out its intention. It had forced propositions out of the Company and had then modified them to some extent in the House, and was now prepared to incorporate them in legislation. But it could hardly be said to have carried the Company with it, and the proprietors' indignation at the imposition of terms they considered onerous was strengthened by the feeling that they had been tricked into offering more than they wished in the belief that the proposals met the Government's requirements. A strong petition protesting against the resolutions was passed in the General Court and laid on the table on 3 May.[3]

The differences between the Company and State were, moreover, only beginning. The resolutions to serve as the basis of the Loan Bill had taken almost two months to get through the House, and further delays were imposed by the need to await the Committee of Supply. The Bill did not have its first reading until 29 May. In the meantime the Bill for assisting the Company in its export of tea was introduced and had an uneventful

[1] Jour. H.C. xxxiv. 286, 27 April 1773.

[2] Robinson seems to have assembled the material for these complex measures and to have done much of the negotiations with interested groups which accompanied them. Charles Jenkinson appears, from later references, also to have taken a considerable part in the drafting of the legislation. See p. 262, n. 1.

[3] Jour. H.C. xxxiv. 295, 3 May 1773.

passage. It was otherwise with the reforms in the Company's organization insisted on by North as a corollary to the loans and promised in, but in fact excluded from, the Company's petition of 2 March. These had to be brought forward without delay if legislation incorporating them was to be passed that session, and here it early became apparent that the Government would have to take much more of the initiative if anything satisfactory were to be evolved. It was also clear that anything done would be highly controversial.

The Company, it is true, at once set to work to evolve proposals for reforms both in India and in England. As early as 25 February, the General Court requested the directors to prepare regulations for the reform of the Company.[1] In an attempt to get agreement the directors associated a few prominent proprietors in the deliberations of their own Committee of Correspondence and on 12 March the proprietors asked the joint body to meet daily on the subject.[2] But difficulties in reaching agreement soon cropped up. By the end of April a variety of proposals for reforms in India had been advanced, but what conclusions had been formed were described by a critic as 'very general, loose and futile'.[3] In the meantime, in an attempt to get full agreement within the Company, a committee of thirteen proprietors was appointed to draw up proposals for the reform of the Company's organization in England,[4] but it was even slower in getting to work and did not report until 20 May.

It was apparent that the Government could not await the very dubious outcome of the Company's deliberations. North, it is true, had urged the directors on 4 March to bring their proposals before the House as quickly as they could.[5] On the other hand, as early as 15 March some at least of the Government's own proposals were in draft form[6] and, during the weeks when the resolutions leading up to the Loan Act were being debated, those which were to form the basis of the Regulating Act were being knocked into shape. Those working on them were assisted

[1] Court Book 81, pp. 488 seq., and Committee of Correspondence Reports, 10, pp. 257 seq.   [2] Court Book 81, p. 528.
[3] J. Caillaud to W. Hastings, 31 March 1773. Add. MS. 29133, f. 495.
[4] Court Book 81, p. 554.   [5] Ibid., p. 511.
[6] General Caillaud told Warren Hastings (15 March 1773) that he had accidentally seen it. He reported that Hastings was already chosen for Governor-General and would have a Council of four. Add. MS. 29133, f. 443.

no doubt by the Reports of the Committee of Secrecy, by their unofficial knowledge of the various propositions under consideration within the Company, and by the advice of many individuals, including even Laurence Sulivan.[1] Consequently North was ready to submit them to the House on 3 May. They incorporated the following propositions:[2]

1. That the directors should in future be elected for four years instead of one, a quarter of the Court retiring each year.
2. That the qualification for voting in the General Court should be the ownership of £1,000 stock which must have been at least twelve months in the voter's possession, in lieu of the existing qualification which was the ownership of £500 stock which must have been in the voter's possession for at least six months.
3. That the judicial system in Bengal should be reformed, the Mayor's Court of Calcutta being confined to minor commercial causes, and in all other business should be replaced by a Supreme Court appointed by the Crown with considerably extended powers.
4. That the Government of Bengal should have predominance over those of the other Presidencies in matters likely to affect the general position of the Company's Indian possessions.

It had already been decided that the Government should consist of a Governor-General and council of four persons, and that the Governor-General should be the one Company servant with a reputation which made him at that time widely acceptable within the Company and to a wider public without, Warren Hastings, Governor of Bengal.[3]

The General Court was still further inflamed by these propositions coming on the heels of the last, and instructed the Chairman and Deputy to wait on North and to point out that

[1] L. Sulivan to W. Hastings, 13 October 1773. Add. MS. 29134, f. 69.
[2] Parl. Hist. xvii, col. 851.
[3] Various people claimed the credit of pressing him on North (e.g. Francis Sykes. F. Sykes to W. Hastings, 8 November 1773. Add. MS. 29134, ff. 123 seq.) but his appointment was early certain. Lord Pigot was understood to be a rival candidate of some importance since his family had considerable Parliamentary interest. (R. Palk to W. Hastings, 8 February 1773. Ibid., and Add. MS. 29133, f. 378.)

they were now almost ready with their own propositions and would like to discuss in the light of them the Bill he was drafting.[1] He refused and, turning to their recent petition, asked them outright whether he was to understand that they would rather reject the loan than accept it on the terms suggested.[2] That the question was one that admitted of more than one answer was shown by developments in the General Court. On 10 May a proposal by a proprietor purporting to show how the Company might extricate itself from its financial difficulties without government assistance was ordered to be printed for the consideration of the Court.[3]

At this point still further fuel was heaped on the fire as a result of an interlude in the House of Commons for which Burgoyne's Select Committee was responsible. While the Committee of Secrecy was getting out in orderly sequence its competent and cautious, though devastating, reports and the Government was laying the basis of its legislation, the Select Committee had been carrying on its more discursive investigations into the immediate past. Its revelations created more sensation than any of the Government's actions, because of their grave personal implications. It was becoming impossible for the Government to ignore them, but any action was likely to involve awkward embarrassment. This was because of the position of Clive, against whom the most serious of the charges was directed. North was very unwilling to drive him again into the arms of the Opposition (where the Rockingham party made no attempt to disguise their willingness to receive him)[4] after the efforts which had been made to win him to the Government side. Moreover, he had a zealous supporter in the ministry in Wedderburn, the Solicitor-General. On the other hand, the

---

[1] Court Book 82, p. 74.   [2] Ibid., p. 89.
[3] Ibid., p. 94.

[4] Shelburne had remarked as early as 27 February: 'the only contest seems to be between the ministry and Lord Rockingham's friends who shall be most active in protecting the guilty directors and servants'. (*Chatham Correspondence*, iv. 252.) Among the Powis MSS. is a letter from Lady Clive to her husband on 30 May 1773 saying: 'The lie of the day is that your Lordship last Thursday agreed to join the Rockingham Party and that the terms are that they are to oppose the present East India Bill and your Lordship is to support their measures against the present Administration. I heard this from two other parties.' There is correspondence between A. Wedderburn and Burke in the FitzWilliam MSS. at Sheffield which shows they were in touch at this time.

section of the ministry which was known to hold strong views on Indian questions shared the feeling widespread in the House that vigorous action should be taken against Clive and the others against whom charges were made.

The need of action was pressed on North. Charles Cornwall, for instance, now more than half-way over to the Government's ranks, told Charles Jenkinson on 4 May that he had seen North:

> I told him my sentiments very freely, that the Government would be irreparably disgraced if nothing was done this Session and that in its present situation I thought the only option was to lay hold of Burgoyne and make him the instrument of bringing forward such a scheme as was in his judgement the most proper.[1]

Whether or not the Government took this advice we have no evidence, but it is certain that Burgoyne opened a debate on the reports of his Committee six days later, on 10 May, and that North was pleased that he should do so. Ostensibly the Government completely dissociated itself from Burgoyne's action. There was no Cabinet discussion of the question[2] and it was made clear that ministers voted and spoke purely in their personal capacity. The debate was stormy and, in the absence of a ministerial lead, highly confused, and it was continued on the 19th and concluded on the 21st in a climax of excitement. Burgoyne began by proposing three very general resolutions which the House (largely, it would appear, through confusion)[3] adopted:

1. That all territorial acquisitions made by subjects belonged to the Crown.
2. That it was illegal for private persons to appropriate the revenues of such possessions.
3. That there had been appropriation of such revenues.

The first was a direct challenge to the Company on an issue where the Government had been walking much more warily. The second and third were intended to point straight at Clive and his colleagues.

The greatest excitement and confusion reigned in the House of Commons during the debates on these resolutions and on the

---

[1] C. W. Cornwall to Jenkinson [4 May 1773]. Add. MS. 38207, f. 359ᵛ.

[2] *Chatham Correspondence*, iv. 261–2.

[3] H. Walpole, *Last Journals*, i. 201.

Select Committee's reports. Both Government and Opposition were divided. On the Government side Wedderburn, the Solicitor-General, led Clive's defence and his formidable colleague, Thurlow, the Attorney-General, was prominent in the attack. North and the other Lords of the Treasury voted solidly, if inconspicuously, against Clive, but Charles Jenkinson was on his side. In the Opposition the Rockinghams, angling for Clive's support, were on the whole favourable to him, while the Chathamites, led by Barré, were foremost in the attack.[1] The feelings of the House swayed from violent hostility to sympathy with Clive in the brave fight he put up, reinforced by distaste for the discreditable personal animosities which inspired much of the attack. 'The hounds go out again next Friday', wrote that detached but appreciative observer, Edward Gibbon: 'They are in high spirits; but the more sagacious ones have no idea they shall kill.'[2] Horace Walpole, with his love of the sensational, was entranced by the arrogance of Clive's defence: 'With the frankness of Julius Caesar he promised himself an escape like Verres'.[3] Francis Sykes, whose fortunes, like Clive's, hung in the balance, wrote of the last night of the debate:

The debate began at three in the afternoon and continued till five in the morning in warm contest . . . I never suffered more in my own mind when I was prisoner with S^r (sic) Serajah ul Dowlah than I did that very night, and you may easily judge at Lord Clive's situation when he did not know that he had a sixpence to call his own in the morning.[4]

The result, Clive's exoneration by vote of the House, was due in large part to the balance of sentiments in the minds of the ordinary private members, in which perhaps a creditable dislike of exacting penalties by irregular and clamorous processes played the greatest part[5]—a tribute to the respect in which the law was held in the eighteenth century. It was also

---

[1] *Parl. Hist.* xvii, cols. 856 seq.; H. Walpole, *Last Journals*, i. 197 seq.

[2] *Private Letters of Edward Gibbon* (1753–94), ed. R. E. Prothero, London, 1897, i. 185.

[3] H. Walpole, *Last Journals*, i. 198.

[4] F. Sykes to W. Hastings, 8 November 1773. Add. MS. 29134, f. 120^v.

[5] H. Walpole, *Last Journals*, i. 230 seq. Chatham shared this feeling (*Chatham Correspondence*, iv. 264) and Lord Mansfield found his legal training stood in the way of his desire for strong action. He is said to have found 'great dangers from having recourse to parliamentary judicature in such times'. (Ibid. 263.)

due to considerations of policy among those who might have been expected to act as leaders of the House. 'It was notorious', wrote Horace Walpole, 'that [Clive] owed his indemnity neither to innocence nor eloquence.'[1] Walpole goes on to make the characteristic assertion that Clive had corrupted a 'secret junto' at Court; that the king had been glad to seize the chance to humble North and the other ministers who voted against Clive, and that North had felt his position so strongly that he was moved to write a letter of protest to the king.[2] In fact this was all untrue; the king and North were working closely together and both were at the same time relieved at the result but rather ashamed of it. The king's letter to North on the occasion indicates very clearly the mixed feelings they both experienced.

The vote carried this morning is a very strong proof of the propriety of your leaving to private gentlemen the punishing the servants of the East India Company, and by that wise conduct you as an individual have been in a minority that with every man of honour must do you credit at the same time that the Minister had nothing to do with it; but I own I am amazed that private interest could make so many forget what they owe to their country. . . . I cannot conclude without adding your conduct has given the greatest satisfaction.[3]

Though the ministry by this somewhat ignominious means escaped one difficulty, they had to face another which had been seriously aggravated. The passing of Burgoyne's resolutions made a breach with the East India Company inevitable. The General Court held on 12 May, two days after the resolutions were passed, was wildly disorderly. It resolved to petition the House to introduce a Bill incorporating the Company's own proposals for reform in lieu of those the Government had just got through. The Chairman and Deputy were instructed to wait on North and inform him that if the conditions of the loan were such as seemed to be implied, they would refuse to accept it, though they hoped that they would not be driven to this extremity.[4] A ballot demanded by fifteen friends of the Govern-

---

[1] H. Walpole, *Last Journals*, i. 198.   [2] Ibid. 234.

[3] *Correspondence of George III*, ii. 491, 22 May 1773. Walpole had made similar allegations about the king's treatment of North on the occasion of the East India Recruiting Bill, 1771 (Walpole, *Memoirs of the Reign of George III*, op. cit. iv. 319).

[4] Court Book 82, pp. 114 seq.

ment including Robert Jones succeeded in holding up a decision for two days, but the ballot resulted in a victory for the rebels by 319 to 149. North was therefore officially informed of their views.[1]

This development was extremely unwelcome to the Government. In their anxiety to avoid the accusation that they were making an attack on chartered rights, they had based their scheme of intervention on the Company's demands for a loan. If the Company refused the loan new ground would have to be adopted, and it might well prove unpopular. The Company had already set up a Committee to work up support for their opposition, which was approaching the City of London (successfully) and the other great Companies (with less success)[2] and Burke was drawing up a scheme for the organization of opposition 'out of doors' which if it had been carried out would have rivalled the agitation of 1784.[3] Moreover, it was clear that the Company could not meet its liabilities without outside assistance, and an irresponsible attempt to do so would have precipitated a further credit crisis. The king urged the strongest action. He hoped that 'the absurdity of the Proprietors' would persuade all supporters of government that there was no alternative to a bold assertion of the State's right to intervene in the Company's affairs as the territorial sovereign of their possessions in India, but

if you on consulting the ablest of your counsellors in the House of Commons, chuse to avoid coming yet to that, continue the Bill of regulations, and as the Company do not chuse to be assisted with money, pass an Act to prevent their having any dividend for the next three years. They must then come on their knees for what they now seem to spurn.[4]

The solution adopted by North was more mildly expressed, but followed on these lines. Indeed, he could not draw back. The Regulating Bill was now complete and the House awaiting it. He made it clear that it would not be held up, and in a debate

---

[1] Ibid., pp. 121 seq.

[2] Ibid., p. 194. The City of London agreed to send in a supporting petition. No other body did so. Governor Johnstone indicated in the House that there were some Directors of the Bank of England in sympathy with the Company (*Parl. Hist.* xvii, col. 887), though the Bank was called by Burke 'the grand instrument of the Court on this occasion'. (*Burke Correspondence*, i. 429.)

[3] Ibid. 427 seq. Dated only 1773, but from internal evidence applying to this period.

[4] *Correspondence of George III*, ii. 484.

in Committee on 26 May, he proposed two resolutions intended, he informed the House, to keep the Company 'to an observance of common justice and those rules and principles of payment which, I believe, were always observed by the Company when their affairs were in common order'. These were:

1. That all surplus revenues of the Company should be applied to meeting its debts.
2. That in the present circumstances it would be expedient for Parliament to secure this.[1]

These resolutions were duly passed, though Governor Johnstone put the Company's case in strong terms. They considered, he maintained, that an immediate dividend of 8 per cent. was reasonable and that when their debts were paid off they ought to have an equal share with the Government in the territorial revenues of the Indian possessions. He argued that there was no need for a loan unless the Government itself should force the issue, as all the Company's creditors other than the Treasury were prepared to give the Company time for payment. Turning to the main measures known to be incorporated in the Regulating Bill, they were, he maintained, unjust to the Company and destructive of the liberties of the people.[2]

Three days later the Regulating Bill was introduced. It followed in its main lines the resolutions of 3 May both in its reforms of the Company's organization in England and in its arrangements for the government of India. It nominated the first Governor-General and Council and made provision for government participation in the nomination of any successors during the coming five years. A careful attempt had been made to achieve some balance between the interests of Company and State in their choice. Warren Hastings, the Governor-General, and Richard Barwell represented the Company's interests; General Clavering (destined for the position of Commander-in-Chief and Hastings's successor should he resign), Colonel Monson, and Philip Francis, a team collected with some difficulty, represented the Government. The bill was a composite measure, embodying proposals advanced from a wide variety of

---

[1] *Jour. H.C.* xxxiv. 348, 29 May 1773. These resolutions were reported from the Committee of the whole House which passed them on 26 May.
[2] *Parl. Hist.* xvii, cols. 885–6.

sources. Those supporting it justly stressed its transitory character. It was intended to bridge the gap between 1773 and the
running out of the Company's charter in 1780, and made no
pretence of setting up a permanent system of government
participation in the responsibility of Indian administration. Its
friends claimed little for it but that it would create a situation in
which further reform would be easy. The king said of it:

[I] trust that it will prove a remedy to some of the many evils
that if not corrected must soon totally prevent any possibility of
preserving that great branch of commerce; besides it lays a foundation for a constant inspection from Parliament into the affairs of the
Company which must require a succession of Regulations every
year; for new abuses will naturally be now daily coming to light,
which in the end Parliament alone can in any degree check.[1]

The variety of sources from which its various provisions were
drawn and the careful balance of interests which it incorporated
is made clear by the difficulty of attributing the credit for it to
any one man. One of Clive's biographers has claimed the doubtful honour for him on the strength of his proposals of November
1772,[2] but neither he nor any informed contemporary appears
to have claimed that he was acting as Government adviser, and,
indeed, Francis Sykes, who was in fairly close touch with Clive,
said that he never could discover what man with Indian experience advised the Government.[3] Nor is such a claim supported
by internal evidence. There are proposals in Clive's scheme
which find their place in the Bill, but they are not peculiar to
Clive and many of his suggestions were completely ignored.
Sulivan might equally well have advanced a claim for the
plans he early 'conveyed to the fountain-head',[4] and Sir John
Dalrymple's proposals preserved in George III's papers have
also much in common both with the other schemes advanced
and with the Bill.[5]

The decision to appoint a Governor-General and Council in
lieu of visiting supervisors was early adopted and had been

---

[1] *Correspondence of George III*, ii. 500–1.
[2] A. Mervyn Davies, *Clive of Plassey*, p. 481. He considered that North used them
as a basis, but emasculated them. See p. 237 above.
[3] F. Sykes to W. Hastings, 8 November 1773. Add. MS. 29134, f. 121ᵛ. Clive
disapproved of several aspects of the Settlement. H. Strachey to P. Francis, 30
August 1773. MS. Eur. 21, Doc. 4.   [4] See p. 254 above.
[5] *Correspondence of George III*, ii. 418 seq.

under discussion for some time. Clive had assumed that these officers would be appointed by the Company. Sulivan and Dalrymple suggested the analogy of the Dutch Governor-General of Batavia, who was appointed by the Company subject to the veto of the Government. The characteristically elaborate compromise of the Act whereby the first holders of the offices were appointed in Parliament; the successor to the Governor-General (should he retire) was nominated; all replacements on the Council during five years were to be made by the directors subject to the veto of the Crown; and the appointments thereafter by the directors without outside control, was dictated no doubt by the exigencies of the moment. The setting up of a Supreme Court in Bengal was a provision based on the abortive Judicature Bill of 1772 (Warren Hastings' subsequent alternative proposals being ignored) and on the Government case advanced when that Bill was under discussion, for the appointment of the Judges of the Court to be vested in the Crown. Most of the provisions for the checking of corruption by the Company's servants in India also had their place in the Judicature Bill, though there were a few recent additions which owed their inclusion to specific events. At least one such proposal we know was eliminated as part of a deal with the Government's 'Nabob' supporters.[1] The provisions for the submission by the Company of all incoming dispatches either to the Treasury or the Secretary of State was an expansion of an offer already advanced by the Company with regard to questions of revenue.

The proposals for the reform of the Company in England were of equally diverse origin. Sulivan had advocated the extension of the period during which stock must be held for a voting qualification. Clive had suggested the increase of the voting qualification from £500 to £1,000. There is no reason to think that either of them originated the proposals. It was a last-minute suggestion advanced in debate by Rose Fuller, a

---

[1] Plan for Settling the Affairs of the East India Co. [1781] by C. Jenkinson; *v. infra*, pp. 337 seq., for these plans. 'I remember that I had prepared a Clause to this effect to be put into the 13th of George III but it was withdrawn at the request of several of the servants of the Company who had raised fortunes in India, and who were exceedingly alarmed at it and promised their support to the other provisions of the Bill if this was omitted'. Add. MS. 38398, f. 80. This refers to the prohibition of trade relations between Company servants and foreign merchants in India.

government supporter, which led to the reintroduction of the cumulative vote for large holders, a reversion to ancient practice which reinforced the oligarchic nature of the reform of the Court of Proprietors.[1]

This was the Bill which, introduced on 31 May, passed its third reading in the House of Commons on 10 June and after hot debates in the Lords, when the Duke of Richmond led the Opposition, became law on 21 June. Though for the time it was a complicated piece of legislation, it was by no means comprehensive, much (for instance provisions for reform of the collection of revenue) being left for incorporation in the instructions to the Governor-General and Council. It was customary at the time to speak of it as a Bill introduced in a highly imperfect form and to suggest that it was amended out of all recognition during the debates,[2] but this criticism does not seem to be justified. There were a number of amendments, but none of them were crucial and its passage through the House was not difficult.

Outside the House, however, the situation remained difficult. The opposition to the Bill itself, it is true, never became formidable. The Company failed to enlist active support outside its ranks and though the £500 shareholders petitioned vigorously against their disfranchisement[3] this was only to be expected. More serious was the evidence of the difficulty the Government was going to meet with in its co-operation with the Company in running the system it was inaugurating. This difficulty was first encountered over the appointment of General Clavering as Commander-in-Chief of the Company's forces. Not only did the General Court flatly refuse to appoint him,[4] but the opposition elements there and in the House combined to embarrass the Government by putting up another government supporter, General Robert Monckton, M.P., in his place. Even when Monckton was bought off by a grant of Crown lands in the

---

[1] *Parl. Hist.* xviii, col. 891. Though it is here stated that the proposal was rejected it was in fact incorporated in the Act.

[2] e.g. F. Sykes to W. Hastings, 8 November 1773. 'The bill when it made its first appearance in the House was so crude, so undigested and, in short, so very inconsistent that it has been cut and hacked all to pieces.' Add. MS. 29134, f. 121v. Cf. Shelburne in *Chatham Correspondence*, iv. 270–3.

[3] *Jour. H.C.* xxxiv. 362, 8 June 1773; Court Book 82, p. 210.

[4] Ibid., p. 204, 9 June 1773.

West Indies[1] the deadlock was unbroken and remained so until the early months of the following year.

Meantime the Government's financial arrangements for the Company were giving rise to even greater friction despite North's attempt to cow the Company by the threat of a complete stoppage of their revenue. The credit necessary for the loan to the Company was passed on 29 May, and the same committee which drew up the Regulating Bill set to work to draw up a bill authorizing a loan to the Company on the terms already accepted by the House. It had its first reading on 10 June, just before the Regulating Bill had its third. Five days later the Company petitioned to be allowed to withdraw their earlier petition for a loan on the grounds that the terms offered were unreasonable, and that the Regulating Bill was an infringement of their rights.[2] Time was drawing short if the legislation was to be completed before Parliament rose. It was impossible to give way to the Company, but also undesirable to have a head-on collision with it.

The Government decided to stand firm on the major issue, but to negotiate with the Company on minor points. When the Company's petition came before the House Charles Cornwall demanded that, in the interest of those shareholders of the Company who were unable to vote in the General Courts— the minors, widows, and foreign holders—the Company should be forced to save itself and the loan be made compulsory.[3] On these grounds the petition was turned down and the sitting adjourned for two days while the Bill was amended to this effect. The time was also used to patch up some kind of compromise with the more reasonable sections of the Company's Opposition. In consequence, when the Bill came up for consideration on 17 June, it was amended in several particulars. It was made clear in the preamble that the acceptance of the loan was compulsory on the Company; on the other hand all reference to the Government's share in the Company's revenues after the

---

[1] Court Book 82, p. 210. *Correspondence of George III*, ii. 494 seq. He had accepted the Company's offer to go out as one of the Supervisors in 1772. For him see p. 196, n. 4.   [2] Court Book 82, p. 210.

[3] Shelburne believed that it was Cornwall's speech in the Commons that persuaded the Government to stand firm (*Chatham Correspondence*, iv. 279–83) but in view of his relations with them at this time it is unlikely that there was no prior consultation on the matter.

reduction of their bond debt was omitted. So too was the reference to the Company's enjoyment of the revenues of their territorial possessions for a six-year period, with its implication that this enjoyment was not of right and was likely to be limited in duration.

Thus amended, the Bill had an easy passage, though some amendments of detail were made during debate. These included one important addition, the prohibition of the acceptance by the Company of Bills of Exchange from India for more than £300,000 without Treasury sanction, a measure which Robinson later believed to have been the salvation of the Company.[1] It had its third reading in the Commons on 19 June; and passed the Lords and became law on 29 June. Two days later, after the distribution of awards to the clerks of East India House for their assistance to the Committees,[2] the House was adjourned and this important session came to an end.

The session had come to an end but the initiation of the new system was not yet complete. It was the nature of the new arrangements that the passing of the legislation was no more than the prelude to new and closer relations between Company and government. It was soon to be clear that these contained their own difficulties. The passing of the legislation, moreover, did not immediately resolve all the existing difficulties and an interim period of an awkward kind had to be gone through. The internal reforms in the Company did not come into force immediately. The existing Court of Directors remained in power until April 1774, and, though cowed throughout 1773, it began occasionally to assert its independence as time went on; far more important, the enraged Court of Proprietors, with its body of £500 shareholders standing behind Richmond and Johnstone, remained in being until the beginning of October. It was generally recognized that the Government could expect to make little or no progress in the working out of the arrangements for India until the new Court was constituted.[3] This meant that both the instructions for the Governor-General and Council and the appointment of Clavering as Commander-in-

[1] Add. MS. 38398, f. 113.
[2] *Jour. H.C.* xxxiv. 385, 28 June 1773.
[3] J. Caillaud to W. Hastings, 21 January 1774. Add. MS. 29134, ff. 290–290ᵛ.

Chief and thus in effect the introduction of the new system were completely held up.

Moreover, even when the new voting qualifications came into force, the Government could not assume that it would automatically obtain a friendly majority in the Company which it had so strongly alienated. It was realized that hard work of the kind which was to become so familiar to the Government's 'men of business' had to be undertaken to achieve the desired results. A steady stream of stock purchases to make up £1,000 qualifications is noticeable in the Company's stock ledgers. The demand was indeed so large as to lead to a rise in the price of India Stock.[1] The Government was playing an active part in this movement. Burke reported that Welbore Ellis, Charles Jenkinson, and others were qualifying.[2] George Clive, more precise, reported to his patron that they had bought some £10,000 of stock, and that a mandate had gone out to government supporters to qualify.[3] Clive himself was pursuing similar tactics,[4] and though a glance at the list of qualified voters[5] makes it clear that the number of votes directly controlled by either ministers or 'Nabobs' was small, the new body was one in which the forces of 'influence' could far more readily make themselves felt than in the unwieldy assembly that preceded it. The Opposition, under pressure from the Duke of Richmond, also made some efforts to get voters to qualify, but on their side the results achieved were slight.[6]

The success of the Government seemed thus ultimately assured at least on the immediate issue, but even after the disappearance of the £500 voters it was not instantaneous. Though Richmond and Johnstone lost many of their supporters after October, they still remained powerful in the General Court. When, on 7 December 1773, the directors put forward instructions for the Governor-General and Council which had the backing of the Government, the proprietors elected a Committee

---

[1] Powis MSS. George Clive to Lord Clive, 27 July 1773.

[2] *Burke Correspondence*, i. 434.   [3] Powis MSS. See n. 1 above.

[4] Clive to W. Hastings, 25 October 1773, 'I am at present very strong in friends among the new-qualified proprietors.' Add. MS. 29131, f. 102.

[5] Printed in pamphlet form. *A List of the Names of those members of the united Company of Merchants of England trading to the East Indies who stood qualified as Voters on the Company's Books, 1 October 1773* (Brit. Mus. 8022, b. 33).

[6] Richmond to Rockingham, 10 September 1773, and Rockingham to Burke, 20 September 1773. FitzWilliam MSS. (Sheffield).

under Richmond which put up rival instructions drafted by Richmond himself[1] and for more than a month the two sides sparred and negotiated with each other, neither being sure enough of its position to risk the issue on a vote. Finally, the risk was taken and in a ballot between the two sets of instructions the Duke of Richmond suffered his first defeat,[2] the directors' instructions being accepted by 406 votes to 308. How important this success was to the Government, and how purely political the vote at the East India House had become, is shown by the eager interest of George III in the voting and his delight at this success. The result, he said, 'gives me satisfaction . . . much increased from the supposition that the Directors gave but little assistance: I desire you will now have this victory pushed as hard as it will go by carrying every question to the ballot.'[3]

The advice was taken and, though Richmond fought a gallant rearguard action, his successes were over. On 8 February Clavering was appointed Commander-in-Chief by ballot[4] and further attempts to query the legality of his appointment and to reject the Commission to Warren Hastings and the Council were defeated.[5] Richmond was met, said Horace Walpole, by 'the Treasury's influence, conducted by Robinson the Secretary and now openly by Lord Sandwich's activity and presence'[6] and

there ended the Duke of Richmond's Indian Campaign in which his spirit, address, insinuation and application had greatly distinguished him and acquired a large number of adherents, by whom he had so long balanced the power of Government at a moment when Opposition had in a manner given up the contest in Parliament.[7]

And there began, one might add, the first period of indirect control by the Government over the East India Company. During this period the 'management' of the Company became one of the regular activities of the Treasury; the king was kept as regularly informed of East Indian elections and of important votes at East India House as he was of the proceedings of Parliament, and there arose to prominence those official experts

---

[1] Court Book 82, pp. 544 seq., and Richmond to J. Adair, 1 December 1773. FitzWilliam MSS. (Sheffield). See p. 282.

[2] Court Book 82, p. 715.   [3] *Correspondence of George III*, iii. 52.

[4] Court Book 82, p. 775. The minutes of this ballot are lacking, but reference is made to it in those of General Court of 11 February.

[5] Ibid., pp. 815 and 838 seq.

[6] H. Walpole, *Last Journals*, i. 315.   [7] Ibid. 287.

in Indian affairs of whom Robinson and Jenkinson were the pioneers, and Henry Dundas the most famous.

Here too began the participation of government in the administration of India. This participation began from financial and military necessity and moved on uncertainly to considerations of sound government and just administration. It was none the worse for basing itself on no particular doctrine of the relations of government and Company, and it was probably much the better for facing the fact that the machinery of government as then constituted was entirely inadequate for the assumption of full responsibility for the administration of India. North's settlement was nevertheless a clumsy and inexpert attempt to solve the difficult problem of dual responsibility, and one that could hardly have succeeded in producing a sound administration even had it been undertaken in circumstances far more favourable than those in which it was introduced. As it was, it was not surprising that it failed altogether in India, and in England was barely kept on its feet by the exercise of personal influence and by constant and prodigious efforts of diplomacy. When the date for the renewal of the Company's charter drew near in 1779, after nearly six years of intensive experience of the working of the system, Robinson cried out in despair that something more satisfactory must be worked out, for 'I shall wish joy to the man who can imperceptibly guide *that Company* and give him great credit for his temper, patience and abilities, because I despair of its being done'.[1]

Nevertheless, a step had been taken that could not be reversed and some of the worst abuses of the Company's rule both in India and at home had disappeared for ever. The pressure for action of one section of the ministry; the desire of the king for strong action; the parliamentary adroitness of North and that section of the ministry which stood for compromise and modified reform; the disinterested anger of public opinion and the far from disinterested fury of disappointed shareholders and speculators had produced a demand for parliamentary action which a few individuals then toiled to put into a form capable of administrative application. Together they had inaugurated a revolution in policy the significance of which none of them were yet in a position to appreciate.

[1] J. Robinson to C. Jenkinson, 9 April 1779. Add. MS. 38211, f. 21.

X

LORD NORTH'S REGULATING ACT IN
OPERATION: STAGE I

THE purpose behind the temporary East Indian settlement
which North and his advisers improvised to meet the
crisis of 1772 was twofold; first to leave the Company in
control both of trade and day-to-day administration, while
checking its worst excesses at home and abroad by reforming
some of its institutions and sharing some of its powers; and
secondly, under cover of these arrangements, to prepare the
ground for a more permanent and sweeping reorganization
when the Company's charter came up for renewal in 1780.[1]
To some the second of these two aims was, no doubt, little more
than an easy excuse for procrastination, but to others, in particular the king and the 'men of business' who were to handle
East Indian affairs for the Government, it was a responsibility
to be taken seriously. The first of the aims underlay every East
Indian settlement of the century, even in some degree the
radical proposals which brought down the Government of
Charles James Fox. It was justified by the total inadequacy of
the Government's administrative machinery for the assumption
of full control in India and (so long as the Company retained
its monopoly trading rights) by the difficulty of taking over
administrative control without assuming at the same time wide
responsibilities for the conduct of commerce. The caution was
never better justified than in 1773, when the experiment of
government intervention in this distant and unfamiliar field
was entirely novel.

North had managed to push through Parliament the legislation necessary for his intricate compromise without an irre-
concilable breach with the Company with which his advisers
would have to work in the future. Despite the hostility of a
Court of Proprietors temporarily in the hands of his political

[1] They had allowed an awkward timing problem to arise. The Charter whereby
the Company enjoyed its monopoly trading rights expired in 1780, with three
years' notice if it were not renewed. The arrangements of the Regulating Act, with
their compromise on the Company's rights to the territorial revenues and possessions, expired in 1779.

enemies and the suspicion and dislike of government interference which existed even among the moderate elements of the
Company, the auspices at home were fairly favourable; while
in India the rapid revival of the prosperity of Bengal for which
Hastings' Government since 1772 can claim much of the credit[1]
gave the new system a better start than anyone had expected.
Nevertheless, North's Administration were ultimately frustrated
in both their aims. The ablest of their men of business expended
themselves on the problem, and ministers themselves gave it,
from time to time, considerable though grudging attention, but
they never succeeded in making their relations with the Company work smoothly for any length of time either at home or
abroad. So too, when the Company's charter expired, though
those handling these relations had fully grasped the principles
which led to a reasonably successful settlement under the
younger Pitt, the Government was labouring too heavily under
the distresses of unsuccessful war and the mounting attacks of
parliamentary opposition to undertake the task of constructing
a permanent Indian settlement.

It is the purpose of this and the following chapter to examine
the causes of this failure. The historian is assisted in the task by
a truly formidable mass of material both in print and in manuscript. But he is hindered in its use by the source from which
much of it flows, the great controversy which has raged round
the virtues and demerits of Warren Hastings as Governor-
General of Bengal and of Philip Francis and his other opponents
there.[2] Quite apart from the distortions arising from the aura
of partisanship which, from that day to this, has surrounded the
career of the great civilian administrator (as it has that of his
military predecessor Clive) this highly personal approach has
tended to throw out of focus the problem of the relations of
government and Company and to over-emphasize the significance of East Indian problems to the English Government of
this period. It must be remembered that this hard-pressed

---

[1] E. Monckton-Jones, *Hastings in Bengal*, op. cit.

[2] The old-fashioned biography of G. R. Gleig, *Memoirs of the Life of the Right
Hon. Warren Hastings*, 1841, is still valuable for its mass of printed material. Of the
more recent works, A. Mervyn Davies, *Warren Hastings, a Maker of British India*,
1935, and S. Weitzman, *Warren Hastings and Philip Francis* (Manchester, 1929), are
the most important. There are also some very useful studies of special aspects of
Hastings' career.

administration had far more serious problems to face, and that, for all the sound and fury of the combatants, the quarrel of Hastings and the majority of his Council in Bengal remained throughout its fluctuating course a source of irritation and inconvenience to government rather than a political danger to it. It must be remembered too that the chief Opposition group in Parliament, whose spokesmen Fox and Burke were later so vocal, remained indifferent to the struggle until it was almost over and Hastings had made his peace with the Government; that, indeed, after the defeat in 1774 of the Duke of Richmond's campaign at India House the parliamentary Opposition tended to draw out of East Indian affairs of all kinds and for some years made no more than casual excursions into them; and that when in 1777 they first began to follow the line which ultimately led them to a systematic attack on the Government's East Indian policy, and on Hastings as its agent, they were not in fact led to do so by humanitarian zeal fanned by Francis against Hastings as the spoliator of Bengal and destroyer of the peace of India. They took up Indian affairs on the contrary in support of the personal case of Lord Pigot, who had been illegally deposed from the Governorship of Madras, with whose parliamentary interest they were in alliance, whose brother Admiral Pigot organized a pressure group on his behalf, but in whose affairs Hastings was only indirectly involved.

Relations of government and Company under the Regulating Act were treated until the last year of North's Ministry as an administrative problem of ways and means (even though a peculiarly thorny one) rather than one of high policy, a matter where the views of John Robinson on questions of 'management' and Charles Jenkinson on questions of long-term policy were more important than those of the Cabinet, and in which some solution to keep the question out of Parliament was always the first consideration. It is characteristic of the period and the ignorance of Government when it took up its new responsibilities for India that both the problems and their solution were held to centre in England rather than India, but that in fact it was events in India which were to shape its course.

The history of the working of the system inaugurated by the Regulating Act can conveniently be considered in three periods; the introduction of the system, 1774–5; its dislocation as a result of breakdowns in India, 1775–7; and the last years in which a falling government, torn between short-term needs and long-term policy, distracted by war in India as well as in the West, and harassed by the attacks of a violent Opposition who were once again making India a controversial political issue, tried to patch up something that might be dignified by the name of an Indian settlement.

Under the Regulating Act there were three ways in which the Government hoped to exercise sufficient control over the Company at least to prevent the repetition of recent scandals. The first and least important was their right to receive copies of the Company's accounts and of all the correspondence on political topics arriving from India. It was not till 1781 that they obtained the right to scrutinize and if necessary to reject the Company's out-letters, which turned the right to be informed into something more powerful.[1] It was later assumed that even the rights North's Government enjoyed were neglected, but this was inaccurate. In the Secretary of State's office it is true, little, if anything, was done,[2] but John Robinson at the Treasury scrutinized carefully all correspondence, both financial and political, passed on by the Company, often with the assistance of Charles Jenkinson who retained a strong personal interest in the working of the system he had helped to introduce. Many of the papers were also seen by North and other ministers and by the king himself. Moreover, important letters sent out by the Company were habitually submitted to Robinson and often extensively amended by him.[3] Nevertheless, both Robinson and Jenkinson were hard-driven men.[4] with many other claims on

---

[1] 21 Geo. III, c. 65.

[2] When Lord George Germain was made third or 'American' Secretary of State in 1775, Welbore Ellis wrote to Philip Francis (17 November 1775. MS. Eur. E. 13, f. 270) that he, as handling 'all which concerns the commercial interests of this country', would now become prominent in East Indian affairs, but in fact the business (largely formal) done in East Indian matters in a Secretary of State's office was done in that of the Southern Department.

[3] This can be seen from the East Indian papers among the Treasury papers. (Publ. Rec. Off., T49/1–9.) E.g. T49/8.22, a draft of the General Letter of 15 December 1775, with many amendments in Robinson's hand, and notes by him for further discussion with the Chairman of the Company.

[4] The amount of work which Robinson got through in the latter years of the ministry is remarkable. He speaks of working eighteen hours a day in times of crisis, and it is easy to believe it. Jenkinson, also a very industrious man, became heavily over-burdened when in 1778 he took over the position of Secretary at

their time, and no effective and continuous control over the details of Indian administration was possible until Pitt's Act set up in the Board of Control an organization to give its undivided attention to the problems of India.

The second and far more important means of control was the nomination by Parliament for a term of years of a Governor-General and Council to administer Bengal and to enjoy some measure of ascendancy over the other Presidencies. The principle embodied in this arrangement was sound and important and it remained the basis of all future reforms. On the other hand, the deficiencies in the application of the principle were numerous and have received much attention. Not only was there no attempt to strengthen the Company's administration by giving discretion to those on the spot to deal with the complex and urgent problems of Indian government without awaiting the instructions which took sometimes two years to reach them; not only was nothing done to give the Governor-General powers on his Council which bore some relation to the executive responsibilities which he had to carry—at a time when abuse of power seemed more dangerous than weak government this was perhaps inevitable—but the new system introduced new weaknesses in administration. It is obvious that the composition of the Bengal Council, consisting as it did of two old Company servants and three new Crown nominees, was likely to lead to friction. The relations of the executive and the new Court of Judicature had been imperfectly thought out, though in quieter times a *modus vivendi* between them might have been worked out. Little thought had been given to defining the superintending powers of the Governor-General and Council over the other Presidencies, and even less either by Company or by government to strengthening this power in the instructions sent out in the succeeding years. Finally, though much attention was given to checking the worst of the scandals of Bengal (and despite the recriminations of Francis it is clear that the Company, Hastings, and Parliament between them had brought the period of its greatest scandals to an end) the ministry had shut their eyes to a situation almost as serious in

War. Correspondents expected this would mean that he dropped his detailed concern in East Indian matters, but in fact the difficulties which the Government ran into there forced him to spend more and more time on them.

Madras. This Presidency, through the corruption of its officials and their relations with the Nawab of Arcot, was becoming the plague spot of India.

North's men of business by the end of their administration recognized all these weaknesses. At the beginning they were unrecognized because the complexities of Indian administration had been under-estimated. Some local knowledge, and a tolerable standard of personal integrity among those administering India, were thought to be sufficient (at any rate temporarily) to restore the Company's financial stability and to re-establish order and security in its Indian possessions. It was for this reason no doubt that the settlement was allowed to hinge on the third means of controlling the Company, the establishment by systematic 'management' of a government-controlled majority in the Court of Directors and, when necessary, in the Company's General Court.

This 'management' was no more than an elaboration and systematization of activities which had been growing in importance ever since government interest in the internal affairs of the Company began in 1763. Its new importance was, however, reflected in changes in organization. No attempt was made to interfere with the control of those voting forces within the Company on whose support the Ministry could rely (that of Clive, which was declining even before his death in 1774,[1] and that of Lord Sandwich which on the contrary was steadily increasing) but the Treasury in the person of its Secretary John Robinson, with his experience in Parliamentary 'management' behind him, now began to take a leading part. He can be seen taking over (subject to the general control of Lord North) the co-ordination of the forces on which the ministry could call and building up an interest under direct Treasury control. How and when the decision was taken to effect this development in organization is uncertain, but there is ample evidence in the

---

[1] When Clive died it was rumoured that he 'had the command of 85 votes' in the East India Company (John Campbell to Philip Francis, 21 December 1774. MS. Eur. E.13, f. 925) but this must include the resources of the 'Nabobs' who threw in their lot with him in self-defence in 1772–3. Already they were beginning to go their own way, and this was probably an over-estimate. Campbell himself thought that his death would not affect the alinement of forces in the Company 'for I conceive that most, if not all, of them will either from hope or fear keep in the same path, and perhaps it will be some ease to a minister to have them dependent upon him, rather than oblige him to depend upon another'.

succeeding years that it had taken place, and well-informed contemporaries realized it. In 1774, shortly after the first election of directors under the new Act, Governor Johnstone attacked Lord North upon it in the House:

Did the Noble Lord pretend to say that the conduct of his Secretary had been without his orders? Did the Secretary on his left hand presume to deny any of the letters which had been given to the public as copies of the originals in his name? That if any subterfuge should arise on this point, he was told to say he had one of those original letters (assuming all management) in his pocket.[1]

The smaller size of the General Courts under the new Act and the four-year tenure of office of the directors, which meant that only six of them were elected each year, eased the problems of 'management' to some extent but their general character remained the same as in the past. The first problem was to obtain the greatest possible number of votes in the General Court in the hands of safe friends and supporters. The Treasury never had the resources to purchase East India Stock for this purpose as Clive and other wealthy Company leaders had done, and though the Pay Offices seem to have invested some of their un-audited funds in East India Stock in the names of their clerks, even this was not done on the scale which Henry Fox's vast balances had made possible in the past. Moreover, the successive changes in the voting qualification imposed by Act of Parliament had made control by the purchase of votes extremely dangerous. The Treasury had to rely therefore on bringing pressure to bear on members of government (already for the most part qualified at the old £500 rate) and on their parliamentary and City supporters and those seeking favours to get them to purchase voting qualifications at India House. The Company's ledgers show that they did this with a good deal of success, and the increasing activity of such government contractors as Richard Atkinson (later to play a prominent part in a crisis in the Company's history),[2] of parliamentary

---

[1] J. Almon, *Debates and Proceedings of the House of Commons*, 1774, xxv. 277.

[2] Richard Atkinson, merchant of Lombard St., partner in the firm of Mure and Atkinson, was one of the biggest Treasury Contractors during the American War and on terms of personal friendship with John Robinson. He had obtained a voting qualification in the Company in October 1771 but disposed of it after the election of directors in 1772. In October 1773, under the new system, he purchased a £1,000 voting qualification and from that time on his name begins to appear at General

supporters such as Sir Herbert Mackworth,[1] and of clerks in public offices and minor office-holders,[2] shows how clearly it became recognized that to assist government in its preoccupations with the Company was a road to its favour. In 1781, when an important General Court was called at short notice, John Robinson sent out personal letters to twelve and circular letters to 150 supporters asking them and their friends to attend.[3] In 1776 for an election of directors North thought they could count on 300 votes quite apart from those of any other interest.[4]

Having obtained the votes it was next necessary to organize the voters. This was done to some extent departmentally. Robinson himself was always early at East India House on the occasion of a General Court or ballot to encourage and control his supporters, but Rigby, the Paymaster-General, also attended 'to vote with his long train of dependents, clerks, and partizans',[5] as an opponent remarked, while after Clive's death Wedderburn, first Solicitor-General and then Attorney-General, took over the organization of this once powerful group, and Lord Sandwich on important occasions personally directed the activities of his own far larger force. On the greatest occasions all prominent members of government would attend the debates in the General Court. At that of 15 May 1776, when North was trying to remove Warren Hastings, 49 'Privy Councillors, Peers and men high in office'[6] were said to have been present to support administration. In general, however, the organization of the debates was left to subordinates, the great leaders turning out when necessary only to register their votes at the ballot.

Courts in support of administration, though he played no prominent part there till 1783-4. For his activities there see below, pp. 380 seq., and H. Furber, 'The East Indian Directors in 1784' (*Journal of Modern History*, 1933, pp. 474 seq.).

[1] M.P. for Cardiff. He made speeches on the Government side in the General Courts and the House of Commons, particularly in 1776 and 1777.

[2] e.g. E. Moore, Receiver and Register for the Office for Hackney Coaches and Chairs and described as Index maker to the House of Commons, W. Chamberlayne, Solicitor to the Treasury, and P. Holford, Master in Chancery.

[3] J. Robinson to C. Jenkinson, 6 June 1781. Add. MS. 38216, f. 192. A personal letter of the kind referred to is preserved in the Francis MSS. (MS. Eur. D.18, f. 67) in which Robinson asks 'the favour of the attendance of yourself, your friends and your connections' at a General Court on 7 December 1773, and particularly asks him to apprize his friends living out of town.

[4] Abergavenny MS. ii. 102, North to Robinson, 6 April 1776.

[5] *The Parliamentary Register*, 1777, vii. 121.

[6] L. Macleane to W. Hastings, 25 June 1776. Add. MS. 29137, f. 253^v.

Even more important than the marshalling of the forces was the decision how to use them. Whatever might be loosely said in Parliament and the Press, the ministry could not hope to achieve a majority in a General Court in which there were still more than a thousand effective voters, or consequently in the Court of Directors, on the basis of its own supporters alone. Alliances with individuals and groups in the Company were necessary; compromises as to persons and policies had to be arrived at; decisions on tactics to be made. Moreover, alliances within the Company were personal and constantly shifting. It was in this that a great part of Robinson's 'management' consisted and it was here that the power of the Treasury was most marked.

Despite the part played by departmental heads in mobilizing the voting forces there is no sign that they stood in any way in the position of heads of private armies, or that they were consulted in the use to which the influence based on their votes was put. There was only one partial exception to this rule, Lord Sandwich. His personal position at India House was now recognized to be unique. So powerful was the interest which this able and indefatigable politician had built up within the Company that with him the Treasury dealt almost on equal terms. Contemporaries were apt to believe, indeed, that he was the senior partner, and, after the Opposition in 1781 had publicly adduced his power in the Company as one of his means of corrupt influence,[1] even comparatively well-informed observers gave highly coloured pictures of his authority there. Nathaniel Wraxall in his memoirs, for instance, wrote:

With consummate ability Lord Sandwich had constructed a species of political citadel within the Ministerial lines which acknowledged hardly any other commander or comptroller than himself. The India House constituted this fortress, of which he was supposed to possess the secret keys. Many of the leading directors, among whom were the two chairmen,[2] looked for orders, as it was

---

[1] Charles James Fox said in the House (quoted N. Wraxall, *Historical and Posthumous Memoirs*, i. 404–5) that in addition to his power as Minister of the Crown and as First Lord of the Admiralty through which 'he could influence a whole profession' he enjoyed a third source of power 'which though not equal to the power of the Crown, forms a material addition to it, and when conjoined with it, is sufficient to crush any individual who shall venture to bring charges against him. The influence to which I allude he derives from the East India Company.'

[2] This was true only in one year, 1778.

commonly believed, not so much to Lord North as to the First Lord of the Admiralty. . . . On all great occasions, when the concealed springs of that complicated machine denominated the East India Company were necessary to be touched, application was made to Lord Sandwich. Even the intimations sent from the Treasury often remained inefficient till confirmed by him.[1]

The papers of Robinson and Jenkinson, however, by showing us the day-to-day workings of East Indian management, correct the exaggerations of this view. They show it is true that questions concerning the support of persons within the Company, including the ministerial candidates for Company elections, were decided by North and Robinson in consultation with Sandwich. In general they aimed at something approaching a balance between them, and Sandwich, always a good patron, was firm in pressing his candidates even when Robinson was doubtful about their suitability.[2] Between 1776 and 1781 his two chief supporters William James and George Wombwell between them held the position of Chairman of the Company for three years and that of Deputy for the same number. Decisions on persons inevitably involved from time to time questions of policy, as in 1780 when the ministry suddenly allied itself with Laurence Sulivan and his group which they had hitherto firmly excluded from favour, and these too were settled only in consultation with Sandwich.[3] But Sandwich's concern in these affairs was strictly limited. Outside the questions which concerned the maintenance of his 'interest'—the patronage he wished to use to strengthen his political situation in general— he seems totally to have dissociated himself from the control of Company affairs. He had no contact with the combatants in the struggle between Hastings and the majority of his council; he took no part in the Madras controversies, or in those centring in the Supreme Court in Bengal, and when questions of the future organization of the Company were raised his name does not appear on the fairly lengthy list of ministers consulted. In short, provided his 'interest' was protected he was prepared to leave all Company affairs to the Treasury and he co-operated

[1] Wraxall, op. cit. i. 403–4.
[2] As in 1778 when Sandwich insisted on their supporting John Pardoe for the Direction, though Robinson (rightly as events showed) was sure he would not be accepted. (Add. MS. 38211, f. 20.) See below, p. 338, n. 1.
[3] See below, p. 348.

loyally to the end in the measures which Robinson devised and North sanctioned for the support of the ministry's policy there.

If there were some misapprehensions about the nature of ministerial influence in the Company there was also mis-understanding about its use. The parliamentary Opposition found it convenient to believe that the ministry fostered their power in the Company to enlarge the patronage by which they could control their majority in the House of Commons. It was claimed for instance that Sandwich's influence there was so great as to give him a 'vast field of exclusive patronage' which made him 'not only independent of his colleagues in the Cabinet but formidable to them'.[1] It was certainly true, and North did not attempt to deny it, that the ministry had a share in the Company's patronage.[2] In a less organized way they had long had some, but now in the normal recruitment of Company servants a fixed proportion of places was by agreement allocated for ministerial nomination.[3] For the rarer but more important openings which occurred in the higher ranges of the service they could also push their nominees, though in deference to Company opinion they very seldom tried to advance the claims of candidates not already in the service.[4] It was also no doubt even more useful than before for 'Nabobs' in fear of investigations into their past or for those with interests to push in the Company to have a vote or votes in the House of Commons which they might find it wise to put at the minister's disposal. But the greater part of the patronage the ministry enjoyed in the Company was in fact needed to consolidate the influence they had to maintain there, and the degree to which Robinson's work in the Company assisted ministers in the

---

[1] Wraxall, op. cit. i. 404.

[2] *Parliamentary Register*, 1779, xiii. 123.

[3] Ibid., 1783, xii. 201-2. Sir Henry Fletcher, late Chairman of the Company, told the House in 1783: 'Much had been said of the patronage of the Company and the influence it might give to his Majesty's Ministers. He had been in the highest situations of the Company in three administrations, and he did declare to that House, that he had never found in any of those administrations any attempts to take the patronage out of its usual course. There was a known and allowed patronage given by the directors to his Majesty's Ministers for their assistance in India affairs, and he never knew them attempt to go beyond it.'

[4] Except in the nominations to the Supreme Council incorporated in the Regulating Act they did so only in the case of Lord Macartney, made Governor of Madras in 1780. The appointment of more independent men from outside as Governors during the period would certainly have been in the public interest.

business of parliamentary management seems to have been comparatively slight. In some ways the management of the Company even added to the burdens borne by the Treasury's patronage. Contracts, as the Opposition forcibly pointed out, were normally awarded to Members of Parliament in return for their support. Now men began also to speak of their awards to East India Company directors to maintain the ministerial majority in their Court.[1] By 1776 at least five of the directors held recently awarded contracts[2] and only two of them were Members of Parliament.

In short there is little reason to doubt that the main object of government intervention and of Robinson's activities was to try to get the Company to administer its Indian possessions in an orderly manner, without the alarms and scandals of recent years. Though there were deviations due to compromise with parties in the Company, and weaknesses due to failure in political leadership and those intrusions of personal interest from which no eighteenth-century government was ever free, Robinson was no doubt speaking sincerely when he said in 1779 that what he had been trying to do for five years was to 'guide imperceptibly' the Company away from the giving of 'personal favours to improper men' and towards 'publick principle and a regular plan'.[3]

The problems which had to be settled by means of 'management' began even before the 1773 settlement in India came into force. Much of the detail of the new machinery had to be omitted from the Acts of Parliament. The Charter of Justice under which the new Supreme Court would function could, it is true, be drawn up without the assistance of the Company,[4] but the instructions on which much of the power of the Governor-

---

[1] *Parliamentary Register*, 1777, vol. vii, pt. ii, 87. Lord Shelburne in the Lords inveighing against Government contractors as tools of the administration: 'To answer the purposes of patronage it has been extended to some of the nabobs of Leadenhall Street, who . . . have now contracts heaped upon them, lest they should be tempted to pay any attention to the interests of the Company, contrary to the opinion of the noble Lord. . . .'

[2] F. Sykes to W. Hastings, 30 May 1776. Add. MS. 29137, f. 204ᵛ. William James, M.P., George Wombwell, M.P., John Roberts, George Tatem, and F. Pigou.

[3] J. Robinson to C. Jenkinson, 9 April 1779. Add. MS. 38211, ff. 20 seq.

[4] It appears to have been drawn up by the new Chief Justice, Sir Elijah Impey, in consultation with the Law Officers.

General and Council depended and even the appointment of General Clavering as Commander-in-Chief of the Company's forces depended on the Company's co-operation. At first this did not seem to present much difficulty. It was known that so long as the Duke of Richmond and Governor Johnstone maintained their grip over the General Court through the support they enjoyed among the £500 proprietors arrangements would be held up; but for the future, the measures taken to obtain votes in the new General Court and the accommodating disposition which the Court of Directors had shown during the passing of the Acts induced an easy optimism. Events soon showed that the task before administration was not so easy as was believed. In the newly constituted General Court hostility to government interference remained strong though largely unexpressed; the reforms, particularly in the Company's shipping, which were going on at the same time[1] displeased influential groups, and the old parties within the Company, disorganized by the cataclysms of the last two years, began to reconstitute themselves. Moreover, even the Court of Directors, lacking in leadership though it was since the debacle of 1772,[2] was well aware that the ministry would be extremely unwilling to reopen controversial issues in Parliament again, and showed a tendency rather to woo the favour of its constituents than to co-operate with the ministry's plans.

In consequence it was ten months before the three new councillors and the judges could leave for India, and the instructions which the councillors took with them were less radical than either they or the ministry had wished. At the same time the hostility of the Company to the new régime had been shown in a series of obstructive motions, ranging from a serious attempt to refuse the Company's commission to General Clavering,[3] to a rejection of all the new councillors' proposals for patronage.[4] When the instructions themselves were under

[1] These were the outcome of the limitation on the Company's shipping as a result of the 1772 Act (see p. 213 above). The directors were concerned with the consequential business throughout 1774, and General Courts were called in this connexion in 1774 and 1775. (Court Books 83 and 84 *passim*.)

[2] Its disorganization increased after the death of the Chairman, Henry Crabb Boulton, an experienced and cunning East India politician, in July 1773.

[3] Court Book 82, pp. 736 seq.

[4] There are a number of angry references to these rebuffs in the correspondence of Philip Francis, e.g. MS. Eur. E.13, ff. 1–2.

discussion the proposals of the directors were thought by the new councillors to be so inadequate that, despite the fact that a Committee of Proprietors led by the Duke of Richmond had put forward even less favourable ones,[1] they had attempted to persuade the ministry to draw up a set of their own and to try to force them on the Company under threat of recourse to Parliament. It took two meetings with North, Robinson, and other prominent supporters of administration to persuade them that there was no hope of the issue being brought to Parliament and that in consequence the best that could be done was to support the directors' proposals 'that the strength of Government being confounded with that of the House, would then appear to the greatest advantage'.[2] Philip Francis noted angrily after a conversation with Robinson on this subject: 'Impossible to come to any conclusion with a man whose own error or over-sight makes it necessary for him to undervalue great difficulties which he ought to have foreseen and prevented';[3] but in reality the full intricacy of the work Robinson had taken on was only gradually appearing. When the councillors finally sailed in April 1774 the framework of the settlement in India was complete. North might welcome this as the end, at least for the time, of a troublesome question; Robinson was fully aware that his troubles were only beginning. He had still to build up in England the essential methods of control.

Though he was already at work on the General Election of that year,[4] the first that either he or North had ever organized from the Treasury, he wasted no time in getting to grips with the Company. Indeed there was no time to spare if the Government were to obtain the powers they needed there, for in April the annual election of directors took place, and this year it was of unique importance. Not only was it the first under the

---

[1] Court Book 82, pp. 544 seq. There is correspondence about Richmond's proposals among the FitzWilliam MSS. (Sheffield). They were drafted by him, assisted by Burke, G. Dempster, and others, and were intended to limit as drastically as they could the powers of the new Governor-General and Council (Richmond to J. Adair, 1 December 1773). See p. 267.

[2] MS. Eur. D.18, f. 128. Quoted in J. Parkes and H. Merivale, *Memoirs of Sir Philip Francis*, 1867, i. 341–2. The ballot between the directors' and proprietors' propositions was finally held on 25 January 1774 (Court Book 82, pp. 714–16) and the directors won by 406 to 308.

[3] MS. Eur. D.18, f. 104. Quoted Parkes and Merivale, op. cit. i. 342.

[4] W. T. Laprade, *Parliamentary Papers of John Robinson, 1774–84*, 1922, pp. 3 seq.

new system, but (to inaugurate the four years' rota) all twenty-four directors were to be elected to hold office for varying periods. Thus both the immediate and more distant balance of forces was in question. As early as 22 February the Treasury took the precaution of circulating to its supporters a warning not to 'engage [their] votes and interest'[1] until a list of the best candidates could be drawn up and distributed. Optimistic supporters of government fully expected that when the date came there would be two lists of candidates, one composed of supporters of administration and the other of supporters of the parliamentary Opposition, that the Government list would prevail and that two-thirds of it would be 'new men'.[2] More cautious observers expected the victory of a House list 'composed . . . generally of former directors',[3] but of men on whom the administration could depend.

In fact the situation was a good deal more complicated. Laurence Sulivan, who knew more of East Indian elections than anyone, had written to Warren Hastings as early as January:

I foresee now that the next election will be hard-fought. The Ministry will be always powerful and Clive has joined them, but to carry their point they must coalise with some strong line, and this will be their difficulty—for Raymond and I are one—the Opposition at present separate but can never join the Court; the Direction more contemptible, if possible, than when Boulton presided, broke to pieces among themselves.[4]

There were, as this extract suggests, three recognizable 'interests' within the Company capable of a variety of permanent or temporary alliances, whose probable actions the ministry in their bid for power had to take into account. The first was that of the majority party in the directors who, weak and disorganized though they might be, could always count to some extent on the support of the 'household troops' which made up

---

[1] A copy is preserved in the Francis Correspondence, MS. Eur. D.18, f. 175.

[2] F. Sykes to W. Hastings, 30 March 1774. Add. MS. 29134, f. 361ᵛ. Quoted by S. Weitzman, op. cit., p. 214, who was misled into believing that the prophecy was fulfilled.

[3] R. Palk to W. Hastings, 22 March 1774. Add. MS. 29134, f. 335ᵛ.

[4] L. Sulivan to W. Hastings, 7 January 1774. Add. MS. 29134, f. 251ᵛ. Sir Charles Raymond was a prominent member of the shipping interest, at that time in disarray and angry with the directors. The year before he had quarrelled with Sulivan; we do not know when they came to terms.

the 'strength of the House'. The second was that of the Company Opposition led by George Johnstone who were still the allies of the Duke of Richmond and the Rockingham section of the parliamentary Opposition, though with the disappearance of the Indian issue from Parliament the alliance was becoming less close. The third was a liquid but formidable middle party composed of those who had been ejected from power in the Company in 1773 and led by the only man of first-class ability in Company politics, Laurence Sulivan. Though they had lost their control over the Company they were by no means broken and they still on occasion could call on ten supporters in the outgoing Direction.

The aim of this group was quite frankly to return to power as soon as possible by any means whatever. Sulivan's friends, as well as his enemies, sometimes spoke mockingly of this determination as idle ambition.[1] In fact there were deeper reasons for it, reasons both creditable and discreditable. In the first place Sulivan was the chief supporter of Warren Hastings and there is no reason to doubt that he, like his protégé, really believed that the Company could achieve great things in India if they had the chance as a combination to carry them out. Even his enemies had to admit that when he was in power there was an initiative in the Company which was lacking when he was not. In the second place he was driven by personal urgencies of a less respectable kind. The financial difficulties into which he and his friends were thrown in 1769 had not been resolved and now the final crash of Sir George Colebrooke's fortunes had left him very near disaster. In 1774 he and his son were writing to their old friend Robert Palk almost in despair[2] and even six years later he had to accept a gift of £10,000 from Warren Hastings to keep himself on his feet.[3] If he could return to the Direction there was the possibility of engineering profitable jobs for his son and his other connexions or even for himself. Moreover, his difficulties, like those of Lord Shelburne and other victims of the 1769 disaster, were bound up with the crash of the adventurer Lauchlin Macleane. In 1773 before he

---

[1] For instance Robert Palk who complained that Sulivan 'cannot be prevailed upon to give up the vain pursuit'. R. Palk to W. Hastings, 22 March 1774. Add. MS. 29134, f. 335ᵛ.

[2] H.M.C., Palk MSS., pp. 240–3.

[3] See p. 192.

fell he had managed to get Macleane out to India with a special recommendation to Warren Hastings to put him in a position to retrieve his fortunes.[1] This Hastings was doing with more loyalty to his friends than consideration for the public interest, and already Macleane had sent a remittance;[2] but the transaction had not escaped notice,[3] and Sulivan was well aware of the fragility of his hopes under the new régime.[4] 'If I can return to the Direction', he frankly stated, 'and keep him upon his legs a very large debt will be secured.'[5]

With one or other of these three groups within the Company Robinson had to come to terms, and it was his weakness that his choice was restricted. With the opposition party, as Sulivan said, no alliance could be made. Nor was he prepared to come

---

[1] Sulivan had hoped to get Macleane a seat on the Bengal Council, but the introduction of the new system checked that, and he went out on the military establishment as Commissary General of Musters in Bengal. Macleane had handed over all his property to his creditors and was still deeply embarrassed. Sulivan implored Hastings to help him, 'so many worthy persons depending upon his prosperity'. Among these persons Sulivan particularly stressed the Vansittarts and himself. L. Sulivan to W. Hastings, 28 April 1773. Add. MS. 29133, ff. 535ᵛ–6. The following year Lord Shelburne also wrote on his behalf to Hastings, alluding to his own claims. (30 March 1774. Add. MS. 29134, f. 366.) In a volume of Laurence Sulivan's correspondence preserved in the Bodleian (Bodl. MS. Eng. Hist. c. 271, f. 2) there is a letter from Macleane to Sulivan of 18 January 1774, reporting Hastings's anxiety '. . . to do everything that can be either pleasing or favourable to you. A disposition which I shall in proper time put in the way of acting.'

[2] H.M.C., Palk MSS., pp. 241 seq. Hastings had enlarged the functions of the Commissary General in such a way as to make them very profitable (directors told Sulivan the extension cost the Company £10,000 a year). Add. MS. 29136, f. 171.

[3] The original appointment was mentioned with a jibe by Strachey to Francis before Francis left England. H. Strachey to P. Francis, 30 August 1773. MS. Eur. E.21, Doc. 4. Quoted Parkes and Merivale, op. cit. i. 335.

[4] Writing to Hastings on 13 October 1773 to tell him of the new arrangements, Sulivan ends by earnestly entreating him 'that [Macleane's] situation to the extent you intend him may be strongly and firmly fixed as soon as possible' in the hope that 'when your Council arrive they will never venture to alter your arrangements' (Add. MS. 29134, f. 70). The hope was ill-founded. On 12 April 1775 the directors sent instructions to reduce Macleane's 'employment and emolument' to 'the limits of his original appointment'; and in Bengal in a Minute of 11 January 1775 the three new councillors made scathing comments on the openings that had been made for him (Home Miscellaneous, vol. 118, f. 152). By this time Macleane had resigned and was returning to England.

[5] L. Sulivan to R. Palk, 23 August 1774. H.M.C., Palk MSS., p. 242. In 1782 Macleane's estate (which was non-existent) still owed Sulivan £15,000 'in which Mr Macleane had . . . most cruelly involved me'. L. Sulivan to W. Hastings, 25 March 1782. Add. MS. 29153, f. 478ᵛ. He hoped Hastings would be able to reclaim it by enrolling it on the consolidated debts of the Nawab of Arcot.

to terms with Sulivan. In the first place the old enmity between Sulivan and Clive would alone have rendered this impossible, and the hostility was shared by the other 'Nabobs' who had joined Clive in 1772 and who bitterly resented the lack of support from the directors, with Sulivan at their head, in the parliamentary assaults upon them of that year. In the second place Sulivan and his supporters represented to the ministry all the vices of Company politics which they hoped to check in the future. Though in the years to come North's amiability some-times misled Sulivan into believing that ministerial favour might be won, it remained a fixed principle of Robinson's manœuvres, which he made no effort to disguise, that Sulivan and his group should not return to power. Robinson was there-fore obliged to rely on the majority party in the directors, and it looked at first as if the situation would be fairly clear.

As early as January Sulivan recognized that for this year at any rate he had nothing to hope for from the ministry or the majority of the directors.[1] He therefore allowed his name and that of some of his most prominent supporters to appear with those of Governor Johnstone and his friends on a 'Proprietors' list' of candidates. This list was supported by all the enemies of administration; the Duke of Richmond for instance wrote to the Marquess of Rockingham urging him and all their friends to support it and going out of his way to explain why he thought they should vote for Sulivan. 'I am sensible of your particular aversion to vote for Sulivan. I have already said I have not a much better opinion of him than you have, but in the present instance he will be of use in supporting our friends and in return I think it but fair to vote for him.'[2] This coalition might have been expected to throw the majority of the directors into the arms of the ministry and to make them accommodating in the choice of candidates. In fact, however, Sulivan was playing a double game and was at the same time negotiating for the inclusion in a House list of the minority among the directors who were favourable to him, through whom he could build up a position for himself in the future. As a result of this 'old Director's trick' the ministry were disgusted to find a House list accepted and published without their consent in which the

---

[1] L. Sulivan to W. Hastings, 7 January 1774. Add. MS. 29134, f. 251ᵛ.
[2] Richmond to Rockingham, 8 April 1774. FitzWilliam MSS. (Sheffield).

fourteen directors they were prepared to support were joined by the ten whom they were not. Robinson called it 'the cursed manœuvre' whereby 'our *fourteen friends* . . . taking in the ten opponents have distressed us beyond expression'.[1]

To accept this rebuff was to admit defeat at the first encounter and to risk serious difficulties in the future. The ministry therefore decided to fight, and a 'House List Amended' was duly published, containing the names of the fourteen directors approved by administration, but offering alternatives to the ten of whom they disapproved. The new ten were drawn from supporters of Clive, from certain elements of the shipping interest (possibly brought in by Lord Sandwich and the Admiralty) and some friends of administration.[2] Robinson said of them:

We are hard at work to secure a tolerable good Direction; we can't make a compleat good one. We have been obliged to comply too much with different classes and parties of men to make it so, for the security of the main points, but we have done the best we could and we fight hard . . . All business is now at an end but the Election and all hands at work I assure you.[3]

The election was hard-fought even by Company standards. It was believed that of some 950 voters in the British Isles no fewer than 890 voted.[4] The result showed that the ministry had not yet achieved its end. To the mortification of those in high places[5] only three of the ministry's ten special candidates were successful and these were not their closest friends. Apart from them, the House list easily triumphed. Nevertheless, the ministry had in reality met with more success than might appear, as may be seen from the views of Sulivan on the election:

I have not time to state the different manœuvres [he wrote to Hastings]; suffice it to say that we played a desperate game. This necessity [*sic*] risqued our own prospects for this year to secure a

---

[1] J. Robinson to P. Francis, 9 April 1774. MS. Eur. D.18, f. 236.

[2] Two were put forward by Clive; three were representative of shipping interests. Of the other five, two were close supporters of Sandwich (John Pardoe and George Wombwell). The other three seem to have had Treasury connexions. Only the three shipping candidates were returned.

[3] J. Robinson to P. Francis, 9 April 1774. MS. Eur. D.18, ff. 235–6.

[4] *London Chronicle*, 1774, p. 358.

[5] *Correspondence of George III*, iii. 92, 93, and 411 (the last wrongly attributed by Fortescue to 1776).

majority of the late directors who were pledged to bring me and others in next year, but the loss of Ducane, Hurlock and Chambers [the three defeated candidates on the House List] puts an end to those views for we have now only eleven . . . and whether we shall keep these firm and have address to gain two more are points to be laboured, but the chances are against us.[1]

His fears were well founded. The weakness and disunity of the directors made them easy game, and Robinson went patiently to work. To increase the ministry's hold on the General Court a new campaign to qualify friendly voters was begun,[2] and to capture the Court of Directors the support of individuals was gradually gained by the measures always open to administration. Two years later five of the directors held contracts,[3] one had been promised preferment at Trinity House[4] and two had hopes of ministerial support for positions within the Company.[5] This quiet consolidation of power was helped by the absence of controversial issues within the Company. No news could yet be received of the workings of the arrangements in Bengal and in England the recent controversies had died down as new and more urgent problems diverted men's attention.

There were only two flurries of excitement during the year which forced the Government to try its strength in the Company. The first arose out of a demand from Clavering on his way to India for the appointment of an Adjutant General, a demand which revived recent dissensions in the Company. On this issue the ministry with some difficulty won a very modified victory in the General Court.[6] The second was the contest between Lord Pigot and Thomas Rumbold for the Governor-

---

[1] L. Sulivan to W. Hastings, 15 April 1774. Add. MS. 29134, f. 407.

[2] J. Caillaud to W. Hastings, 8 February 1775. He speaks of a number of friends of administration who 'purchased stock immediately after the last defeat, in time as they thought to be qualified for the ensuing election'. Add. MS. 29136, f. 44ᵛ. In fact they proved just too late.

[3] See p. 280, n. 2.

[4] William James, see p. 181, n. 2.

[5] Edward Wheler, who hoped to succeed Barwell on the Supreme Council, and Robert Gregory, a very uncertain friend with strong connexions with the opposition (see pp. 241 and 376) who hoped to obtain the Chair.

[6] The matter occupied much time in December 1774 and January 1775 (Court Book 83, passim). The directors refused to appoint Clavering's nominee, and an attempt was made to force another man on him. The ministry were obliged to intervene and prevent any appointment. A special 'Whip' from North to Francis Sykes to support the ministry's line is preserved. Add. MS. 29135, f. 412.

ship of Madras.[1] The contest arose in connexion with what was, though no one recognized it, an important issue. Alexander Wynch, Governor of Madras, had been recalled for his support of the Nawab of Arcot in his attack on the Raja of Tanjore. The question at issue was not merely who should succeed him but what policy should be adopted to these two native princes whose rival claims were in the future to be so actively canvassed in England and to become a party issue. Two 'Nabobs', Lord Pigot and Thomas Rumbold,[1] were rival claimants for the vacant position. A ministry stronger in the Company and with more understanding of the position in the Carnatic might reasonably have set its face against the choice of either. It would certainly, as Robinson did in 1776–7, have tried to check the proposal for a complete reversal of policy in the Carnatic which Pigot was advising and which an ill-led Direction precipitately adopted after his appointment. As it was, since Pigot had identified himself with the parliamentary and Company opposition in 1773–4 while Rumbold had thrown in his lot with Clive and the ministers, they agreed with the directors in supporting Rumbold's appointment. Pigot, however, determined to defy them, mobilized his recent allies in the General Court, and, somewhat to the surprise of the well informed, scored a victory.[2] But as it was only by the narrow margin of four votes, and even this was attributed to over-confidence on the part of Rumbold,[3] it was not taken too seriously. Later experience was to show that neither the events which led to the election nor the instructions which Pigot was allowed to take out to reverse this policy, had been taken seriously enough, but this intrusion of Indian realities into the manœuvres of Company politics was a problem for the future.

In the meantime all went well for the ministry in the campaign for the next election of directors. Sulivan made another determined attempt to get on the House list,[4] apparently

---

[1] For Pigot see p. 135, n. 2, above. In 1773 he had wished to return to Madras and hoped for the appointment of Governor-General with his headquarters there. Disappointed in this aim he had joined the parliamentary and Company Opposition. He had sat in Parliament from 1765 and was said to control three votes. He was understood to have reasons connected with his private fortune for wanting to return. For Thomas Rumbold see p. 213, n. 2, above.

[2] Court Book 83, pp. 422–62.

[3] F. Sykes to W. Hastings, 3 March 1775. Add. MS. 29136, f. 58ᵛ.

[4] L. Sulivan to R. Palk, 12 February 1775, *H.M.C., Palk MSS.*, p. 245.

misled by North's incurable good nature, and only when he failed, reluctantly allowed his name to appear on the Proprietors' list, which was duly and heavily defeated.[1] In the drawing up of the House list the ministry met none of the difficulties which had troubled them the year before. Of the six names put forward (now that the four years' rota was working) four were those of good friends of administration who had been defeated in the last election.[2] Its resounding success in the ballot won an expression of gratification from the king himself,[3] and, among the defeated, Sulivan gloomily noted that henceforth power in the Company must be sought 'through the line of Government, for there's an end of opposition'.[4] Robinson might be pardoned if he believed that the 'management' of the Company was now solidly established.

R. Orme to L. Macleane, 16 February 1775, R. Orme to R. Heron, 28 March 1775. Orme MSS. O.V. 202, ff. 43 and 48.

[1] Some of Sulivan's friends agreed with him in thinking the Ministry well disposed, e.g. R. Palk (Add. MS. 29136, f. 38), though Orme was more correct in thinking them an 'impediment'. R. Orme to L. Macleane, 16 February 1775. Orme MS. O.U. 202, f. 43. Later events showed that they were determined not to make terms with him, but North certainly seems on this occasion to have given him false hopes. He gave his own account of his defeat in a letter to Hastings on 14 April 1775: 'Yesterday the India Election ended with a total defeat of me and those I was joined with. It was perfectly contrary to my judgment . . . that I stood this year but Sir Charles Raymond with some new lines of interest (particularly Boulton's) pressing me to support the Company I suffered my name to go forth . . . I think you will believe I had acted right if I had adhered to my own opinion, when I tell you that in an intercourse with Lord North he expressed his wishes to see me in the Direction—he was pleased to say I was much wanted there. All things were settled, but the ghost of Clive haunts me. His friends took the alarm, and headed by Wedderburn held a language that obliged his Lordship to give me up and he sent me such message in kind terms. As I knew it was not the India but the Parliamentary interest that influenced him (greatly wanted at this American crisis) it seemed plain that I should not wantonly offend but wait quietly for next year. However from the many acquisitions promised me it grew to be the general opinion that I should succeed and said so by Lord North. This dreaded event caused Mr Walsh at the head of 25 Bengal proprietors to form themselves into a canvassing club for opposing me alone—and thus ends this foul history.' Add. MS. 29136, f. 171.

[2] Richard Becher, Benjamin Booth, John Roberts, and George Wombwell.

[3] *Correspondence of George III*, iii. 204.

[4] Add. MS. 29136, f. 171.

XI

LORD NORTH'S REGULATING ACT IN OPERATION: STAGE II

THE establishment of the machinery whereby the ministry hoped to maintain indirect control over the Company proved not, as they hoped, the end of their problems but only the beginning. The machine which they had constructed was to be submitted to a series of strains as a result of events in India (unforeseen though by no means unforeseeable) against which its builders struggled gallantly to strengthen it but which ultimately proved too strong for it to bear. These shocks, together with the weakness of government and the multiplicity of problems which it had to face in other spheres, finally reduced North's East Indian settlement to ruins.

The shocks administered from India swept on in three waves. The first was the conflict which faulty machinery combined with acute personal antagonisms brought about in Bengal. The news of this reached England in the middle of 1775 and absorbed all the attention of the Company, much of that of Robinson, and even a good deal of that of the king and ministers, preoccupied though they were with the American question. The second was the palace revolution in Madras engineered by rebellious Company servants and by the Nawab of Arcot and his dubious court against Lord Pigot in his attempts to implement the Company's ill-judged instructions for the Carnatic. This occupied much attention at home in 1777. The third was a combination of the unsolved problems of both these conflicts complicated by the Mahratta war and the attacks of Hyder Ali in India, and by the troubles of the Franco-American war at home, which spelt the general collapse of plans for India.

The trouble in Bengal began as soon as the new councillors reached Calcutta and the attempt was made to put the plans they brought with them into operation. When General Clavering, Colonel Monson, and Philip Francis were sent out to join Hastings and Barwell and to make up the new body of Governor-General and Council, there is no doubt that ministers hoped that they had the material for a strong and united government. Hastings, who had already been doing remarkably well in Bengal, had at that time a reputation unique among Company servants. Though he had been for some years, through his former association with Vansittart, a protégé and friend of Laurence Sulivan, he had widespread support among the 'Nabobs' from Bengal and Madras with whom he had served and many of whom were his personal friends, and even Clive had overcome his hostility to his connexions sufficiently to give him personal support. The man who was held in the days of his power so difficult to work with had been liked, as well as respected, as a colleague while he held subordinate positions. The high opinion held of him in the Company soon spread to the ranks of government when they began to look for a Governor-General (it is to their credit that they were looking for capacity rather than connexions), and Charles Jenkinson in particular from his key position on the Committee of Secrecy 'contributed greatly', as he later regretfully admitted, 'to spread his reputation'.[1]

But already before the new councillors sailed there was some abatement in the unanimity of Hastings's support within the Company. His continued association with the Sulivan group at home and apparently some pique among Clive's friends in Bengal, had led to a coolness towards him among Clive's entourage which may have been shared by Clive himself.[2] This

---

[1] C. Jenkinson to J. Clavering, 13 December 1776, preserved in the Francis Correspondence. MS. Eur. E.16, f. 33.

[2] The chief source of the difficulty seems to have been dissatisfaction with Hastings felt by the Fowkes father and son; Joseph Fowke, the father, had formerly been a Company's servant but lost his money and returned as a 'free merchant' in 1771. He had married a sister of Clive's lieutenant John Walsh, who was a strong supporter of his relatives' interests, though a somewhat exigent patron. (MS. Eur. E.3, Fowke MSS., the notes from the excellent *Catalogue of Minor Collections* drawn up by Kaye and Johnston, are valuable for the persons concerned.) In a private memorandum Francis (quoted Parkes and Merivale, op. cit ii. 49), speaking of the first actions of the newcomers, says 'Clavering had been shaken by the private representations of Joseph Fowke, who I suspect had laid a plan with Nuncomar to take possession of us, as soon as we arrived.' On Clive's own attitude there is some ambiguity. It seems clear he had no great liking for Hastings, but he wrote him a most friendly letter at this time (Clive to W. Hastings 25 October 1773. Add. MS. 29131, f. 102) and Hastings was still acting as his attorney for the receipt and remittance of his *jagir*. Francis, however, implies in a letter to Wedderburn (3 April 1777, quoted by S. Weitzman, op. cit., p. 217) that Clive had expressed to them both (and to others) a very unfavourable view of Hastings's character, and as this was the only time Francis was in personal contact

was significant since Philip Francis, the most active of the new councillors, identified himself with Clive's group in the months while waiting to sail for India, and he left England expressing, it is true, a determination to co-operate with Hastings but also 'to adopt and unite all Lord Clive's friends [in Bengal] to me'. It seems that it was the pursuit of this determination as much as anything which drove him and his colleagues into almost instantaneous opposition to Hastings on their arrival.[1]

The delay in the introduction of the new system, moreover, served to emphasize serious inconsistencies in its principles. However sincere might be the hope that the old and the new elements would fuse, even North himself, and still more other supporters of administration, continued to stress the reforming and inquisitorial functions of the new councillors. Francis after his first interview with North 'conceived we were to be armed with extraordinary powers to correct enormous abuses'.[2] The official attitude, to which, for instance, Robinson always adhered,[3] was that the Government supported Hastings but disapproved of his chief supporters in the Company at home and in consequence of those of his past measures which might be held to have been dictated by them when they were in power; but the distinction was not an easy one to maintain, particularly in an atmosphere still heated by the revelations and controversies of Burgoyne's Committee. There was only too much point in the criticisms of the Dissenting Peers in June 1773 of

the manifest contradiction and absurdity of this Bill, which, stating abuses as now existing in India for the ground of its Regulations, yet appoints the very persons to preside there who, if the allegations in the Bill be true, must be concerned either by neglect or actual commission in all the abuses complained of.[4]

The result was what might be expected. Though the ministerial nominees went out with the declared intention of

with Clive, he must have done so then. Mervyn Davies, *Clive of Plassey*, pp. 489 seq., has an interesting analysis of Clive's influence on Francis and his policy.

[1] In his 'Hints for my own Conduct' quoted by Parkes and Merivale, ii. 17, he adds, it is true, 'without however offending others', but this, like many others of his good resolutions, he found it impossible to keep.

[2] From Francis's mutilated autobiography, written not later than 1776, reproduced in Parkes and Merivale, op. cit., vol. i, appendix ii, p. 367.

[3] J. Robinson to W. Hastings, 19 February 1781. Add. MS. 29148, ff. 38–40.

[4] *Journals of the House of Lords*, xxxiii. 681.

supporting Hastings in his new administration, they had also a feeling that any close union with the representatives of the old order would be injudicious,[1] while Hastings and Barwell (necessarily very imperfectly informed of intentions at home) awaited their arrival with uncertainty and suspicion. Abuses in Bengal still existed in plenty and, though wiser men might not have launched an attack on the Governor-General within seven days of their arrival or within a few months have reached a position where any reconciliation was impossible, serious friction was probably inevitable. Actions are not capable of such fine distinctions of meaning as words, a fact discovered by many sent out by their country to implement a compromise, and essentially the newcomers were bound, as Francis said, to consider themselves 'the representatives of Government deputed to act generally for the nation; in contradistinction to Mr Hastings and Mr Barwell who may be supposed to act for the Company'.[2] The attitude of the representatives of the old régime may, on the other hand, be summed up in the words of a letter to Hastings from Sulivan:

It will require all your philosophy to bear with temper the Parliamentary system which in a great degree annihilates the Company's powers and privileges, disgraces and degrades the service in India and essentially wounds your own authority. . . . As the Minister and this new Council publicly profess an implicit dependence upon Mr Hastings, I am still willing to hope that those excellent rules you have and mean to establish for the perfect government of Bengal will be confirmed and pursued . . . Yet even with harmony in your Council (so much to be desired) your task is extremely arduous—Scripture says it is impossible to serve two masters.[3]

In these circumstances the only hope of success rested with the qualities of mind and character of those composing the Council, and these, given the paucity of administrative talent and experience and the absence of a tradition of overseas service by men of first-class abilities, could hardly be expected to be high.

[1] Francis, Private Memorandum quoted Parkes and Merivale, op. cit. ii. 48–49. 'Considering the nature of our appointment, and the curiosity and expectation with which our conduct was likely to be observed, a union with Mr. Hastings would have been a very dangerous measure even to men who might not be scrupulous enough to be stopped by any consideration but danger.'

[2] P. Francis to C. D'Oyly, 1 March 1776, printed in S. Weitzman, op. cit., p. 273.

[3] L. Sulivan to W. Hastings, 8 December 1773. Add. MS. 29134, ff. 250–250ᵛ.

Of the Company's representatives Hastings did his masters far more than justice; he stood head and shoulders above his colleagues in the Company's service as he did above the ministerial nominees; but Richard Barwell was in his merits and demerits no more than a typical 'Nabob' of the kind that had grown rich since Clive's conquests.[1] On the other side the ministers encountered serious difficulties in finding the new men to bring into the Council, as also in recruiting the judges for the Supreme Court, despite the enormous salaries that were offered. General Clavering, who possessed, though he hardly deserved, the confidence of the king as a soldier and man of good sense and integrity, was the linch-pin of the new arrangements,[2] but was always causing alarm by his tendency to hand in his resignation. Colonel Monson was no more than a mediocre soldier of good political connexions;[3] while their ill-success in filling the junior post by a 'man of business' led to the last-minute appointment of Philip Francis, who had the support of his former chief, the Secretary-at-War, Lord Barrington, but who, despite real ability and much energy, had entirely failed to carve out a career for himself among the rising 'men of business' of his day.[4] That he was also both desperately am-

[1] See his correspondence in *Bengal Past and Present*, vols. 8–18. Hastings, however, paid tribute to him as an official (W. Hastings to L. Sulivan, 6 January 1780, Bodl. MS. Eng. Hist. C. 271, f. 22). 'At the same time he possesses much experience, a solid judgment, a much greater fertility of official resources than I have, and his manners are easy and pleasant, which I am sometimes inclined to consider as the first accomplishment of a Man of Business.'

[2] Clavering had also valuable political connexions, his brother Sir Thomas Clavering being an important north-country M.P. George III's belief in him and affection for him were, however, real (*Correspondence of George III*, iv. 101). Of his character Philip Francis, who was often on bad terms with him, said: 'General Clavering is unquestionably one of the most resolute men I ever met with; however, in these times, and in this place particularly, some other qualities are necessary to revive a country going fast to ruin . . .' (Quoted, S. Weitzman, op. cit. 232.)

[3] He was son of the first Lord Monson, had married a sister of Lord Darlington, and their income was very moderate.

[4] See Parkes and Merivale, op. cit., and S. Weitzman, op. cit., pp. 18 seq. The surprise often expressed at his appointment is excessive. North had been quite apologetic about offering it to C. W. Cornwall, who had refused it as 'I had rather take my chance at home' (Add. MS. 38207, f. 359), and had tried at least one other candidate of no great distinction. Men doing well in England did not find these positions attractive, and the same applied to the judges of the new Supreme Court. The Chief Justice Elijah Impey was grateful for it because of his heavy losses in speculation in 1772–3. E. Impey to J. Dunning, 23 August 1773 (Add. MS. 16259, ff. 80–80ᵛ), and Sir Richard Chambers, one of the Puisne Judges, some years later said that in 1773 when the Chancellor approached him 'my prospects and situation

bitious and so virulent in tongue and pen as to wreck the success of any team of which he formed part was a misfortune of which they were still unaware.

The conflict of personalities which began as soon as the new-comers arrived in the always quarrelsome atmosphere of an Indian presidency developed rapidly in the heat, isolation, and disease of eighteenth-century Bengal into a warfare so savage and personal hatreds so bitter that they did not end till the final collapse of Warren Hastings's impeachment in 1795. It is unnecessary here to trace its unpleasant details or to take a side in the perennial controversy on the characters and motives of those involved. Some evaluation of the achievements and personality of Warren Hastings is, however, essential for an understanding of the situation which arose in England out of this conflict.

A great deal of time has been unprofitably spent in white-washing or blackening the character of this remarkable man in terms of the standards of official rectitude built up in the nineteenth century. These standards are even more inapplicable to the eighteenth-century servants of the East India Company than they are to their contemporary equivalents in England. Hastings had served through the most corrupt period of the Company's history, had worked with men who had made vast fortunes either as victors in war or as the administrators who seized the chances which the conquerors opened up for them. With these men he remained on intimate terms; he did not feel called on to condemn their actions, and he assisted them, even when he was Governor, in the remittance of their dubious gains and in covering their tracks when inquiry threatened.[1]

were such that it was not ... thought unreasonable in me ... to annex conditions to my acceptance', and he was promised succession to the position of Chief Justice if it fell vacant while he was in India. R. Chambers to C. Jenkinson, 31 December 1785 (Add. MS. 38409, f. 36).

[1] An illustration of this is seen in his correspondence with Francis Sykes, who acted as his attorney in England and from whom he took Cantu Baba as his 'banian' or native agent. Sykes made no attempt at disguise in discussing his affairs with Hastings. In 1773, when threats from Burgoyne's Committee were looming, he expressed great anxiety about the investigations ordered by the directors into the administration of Mahomed Reza Khan; Add. MS. 29133, f. 347: '... the whole will depend on the mode of enquiry and the line of conduct given M. Reza Cawn. I hope you have taken care that I am not involved as I did as much as possible when the examination took place relative to Vansittart. Contoo [Cantu] could inform you particularly how I was situated, and therefore I shall certainly expect

'I am', he once remarked, 'neither a prude nor a hypocrite.'[1] The fortune he himself amassed in the course of his service was not by their standards a great one, but he retired with a fortune nevertheless and he had spent considerable sums while still in office. Moreover, one of the private reasons which he gave for resigning when he learnt the contents of Pitt's Bill was his incapacity to make without perjury the statement as to the sources of his private fortune which was called for by the Act before it was amended.[2] Nevertheless, the fact remains that he had been in a position to tap the two great sources of East Indian wealth in his day, the conquest of Bengal and the system of loans (real and fictitious) of the Nawab of Arcot, and he had made his fortune by neither, and he was widely known among Company servants for his indifference and carelessness about his private fortune.

This moderation seems to arise less, however, from his subscription to a code of financial integrity higher than that of his day, as some of his admirers would suggest, than as a by-product of other virtues. A Company servant to make and maintain a fortune in India had to give a great deal of time, energy, and attention to it. Hastings, an excellent administrator of the Company's affairs, was always too much absorbed in them to give more than a modicum of attention to his own, and his friends and attorneys in England were constantly complaining of the confusion and neglect into which his private finances fell.[3] In the same way his devotion to duty and a constant sense of the historic importance of his position prevented him from accepting from Indian princes favours which would have hampered his

---

to hear that an attention has been paid to my character and interest. Towards the Company I have ever been attentive, nor would one sixpence I enjoy ever come into the Company's Treasury; it was this, whether it would go into a black man's pocket or my own'; and 'I beg you immediately get my stock of cash in bond to run in yours in the name of Messrs Redfearn and Ducarell (sic)'.

[1] W. Hastings to J. Scott, 20 January 1782. Add. MS. 29129, f. 13. Printed Gleig, op. cit. ii. 458.

[2] W. Hastings to J. Scott, 27 December 1784. Add. MS. 29167, ff. 265 seq. The letter was not sent, but was seen by Scott later.

[3] Their complaints became less serious in his later years of office. His attempt to obtain from the Company a grant of the £100,000 he had obtained from the Nawab of Oude in 1781 (an attempt pursued very seriously by his friends and agents) was made by analogy with Clive's gains and seems to have been inspired by a desire for maintaining a standard of living after his retirement to which his wife was accustomed.

freedom of action or reduced his prestige, even though he might condone and even encourage his personal friends and followers in taking advantage of the same opportunities.[1] As a result, though it is hard to claim that his financial principles transcended the conventions of the day, his hands were a good deal cleaner than those of most of his contemporaries, and an age that accepted Clive's great gains and failed to penalize Thomas Rumbold or even Paul Benfield could hardly take very seriously the much less grave irregularities of Hastings. North himself in his good-natured way conveyed the impression to one of Hastings's agents that he thought he would be justified in retiring with a fortune of £200,000.[2]

But those who disapproved his actions in his lifetime were less concerned with the accusations of personal corruption against him than with his growing autocracy and disobedience to orders in his later years; the idea disseminated towards the end of his career that he was a warmonger; and, where financial corruption was in question, the shady nature of his immediate entourage and the very large and profitable contracts he certainly gave to reward friends and keep the support of doubtful allies in his fight to maintain his control of the Bengal Government. In the use of contracts and 'jobs' to maintain political power, Hastings's methods of government differed from those of the Government of England only in degree.[3] In his choice of personal followers and agents to speak for him in England, however, he was certainly unfortunate, and those who came to

[1] For instance, a letter to Shelburne reassuring him of the chances that Macleane would repay him his large debt. W. Hastings to Shelburne, 30 March 1775, Add. MS. 29127, f. 194, makes it clear that he must have known the promises which the latter had obtained from the Nawab of Arcot. In 1779–80 he took great pains to make secret approaches to the same Nawab (whose financial position was then notorious and desperate) to put Laurence Sulivan's son in the way of a profitable connexion with him. W. Hastings to L. Sulivan, 30 January 1780. Add. MS. 29128, f. 227v, and f. 259, 30 August 1780.

[2] J. Scott to W. Hastings, 25 December 1781. Add. MS. 29152, f. 232v.

[3] When General Sir Eyre Coote succeeded Clavering, Hastings gave him perquisites, which the Governor-General's best friends admitted were inordinate, to get the support on Council of that rapacious and difficult soldier and thus maintain his majority there. 'Coote will never change. . . . The motives for granting him those large allowances are well understood.' L. Sulivan to W. Hastings, 23 October 1780. Add. MS. 29146, f. 175v. P. E. Roberts. 'Warren Hastings and his Accusers', *Journal of Indian History*, iii, pt. i, 1924) compares the way in which he charged large disbursements on the revenues of Oude to the use of pensions on the Irish establishment by the English Government.

be associated with him in the public mind had about them an air of dubious intrigue that was marked even in the Company of that day.

This was not altogether his fault. Such Company servants as George Vansittart and John Graham were, whatever Francis might say,[1] neither better nor worse than most of their contemporaries. The Hon. Frederick Stuart, son of Lord Bute, and Alexander Elliot, son of Sir Gilbert Elliot, the king's friend (both pressed on Hastings by North before the passing of the Regulating Act), were conspicuous chiefly as political appointments, and though Stewart was disreputable, of Elliot at least most men spoke very well. But Hastings suffered from being the nominee of a party in the Company which had not only won a dubious reputation in Company politics but which, through the speculative disasters of 1769 and 1772-3, had become associated with many broken men. These they urged him to take under his wing in India so that he could give them the opportunity to restore their shattered fortunes. Lauchlin Macleane was only the most conspicuous of them; of very similar type was John Stewart, Macleane's old friend and associate, and for a time the 'jackal' of Sir George Colebrooke,[2] and there were other lesser victims of speculation who were sent out for his patronage.

While, however, it would have been difficult for him to ignore these recommendations, it would hardly seem necessary for him to enter into such close relations with these men, to employ them on secret missions, and to enrol them among his personal friends. Nor had he the same excuse for employing on confidential business and entering into friendship with John

---

[1] George Vansittart, nephew of the Governor, after holding various positions, was a member of Bengal Council in 1773. John Graham, previously a Madras civilian, was Resident at Burdwan. Francis's views of them were expressed in his private Memorandum, Parkes and Merivale, op. cit. ii. 45-46.

[2] John Stewart, wine merchant of Buckingham Street, who was associated with Macleane in America and in their earlier days in England, carried on much of Colebrooke's East Indian business and was 'jackal' in his speculations. Like his patron he crashed, and in 1771 there was talk of sending him to Madras as Secretary to Council. With Hastings's move to Bengal his appointment was transferred there, too, and he became Secretary of the Council and Judge Advocate General until his dismissal by the Majority in 1775. Hastings, while welcoming him as a person and soon making him one of his intimate friends, expressed concern at his being sent out from England to supersede servants of experience. W. Hastings to L. Sulivan, 10 February 1772. Add. MS. 29126, ff. 111-12.

MacPherson,[1] the more specious adventurer of Madras, with whose intrigues at the Nawab's court he was already familiar and whose letters to him convey a peculiarly unpleasant impression. That he should have first empowered Macleane and then permitted MacPherson to act as his agent and spokesman in England, and this without making any attempt to limit their activities in pursuit of their other interests, was to show an extraordinary unawareness of the degree to which they could be trusted, of the impression that they were likely to create, and of the means which they were likely to employ on his behalf.[2]

Nevertheless, if Hastings for these reasons hardly appeared to observers in England as a monument of personal integrity, even those who disapproved of him were bound, if they were honest and well informed, to respect his ability. Many of the criticisms of conditions in Bengal advanced by his opponents so intemperately were well founded, and some of their alternative proposals were sound; but in a few years he had built up an administration in Bengal from nothing, he knew the strange world of India as few have known it, and everything he wrote has about it an indefinable element of quality. His capacity for decision, his grasp of essentials, and his combination of daring and dogged determination were of incalculable value in the dangerous last years of his reign. Had a strange combination of circumstances not kept him in power long after he would have been recalled under modern conditions of communication, it is difficult to think of any other man then concerned in Indian affairs who would have averted disaster.[3]

[1] MacPherson was introduced to him in a letter from Lord Shelburne. W. Hastings to Shelburne, 16 July 1771. Add. MS. 29126, f. 73. Professor Dodwell, in his Introduction to his edition of *Warren Hastings' Letters to Sir John MacPherson*, 1927, gives a more favourable estimate of John MacPherson's character than I have been able to form.

[2] Hastings seems to have been deeply impressed by these two adventurers, who had much in common, though MacPherson was either the luckier or the more adroit. It seems as if their boasts of backstairs influence and their contacts with those in high places in England caught him at one of his weakest points, his knowledge that he had been so little in England that he was ignorant of English affairs. Indeed, he admitted as much in a revealing letter to MacPherson in 1777 (Dodwell, op. cit., p. 52): 'I am certain of your friendship, your honor, and of the benefit which I would derive from your judgement and especially from that knowledge in which I am most deficient, I mean the knowledge of the British world to which all my designs ought, if they can be, to be squared.'

[3] Perhaps the best summing up of Hastings's character and achievements is that

The first news of the conflicts in Bengal reached England in June 1775, when dispatches arrived from the new Majority attacking Hastings for undertaking the Rohilla War (which the directors had already condemned) and reporting their use of their majority vote to recall the Company's troops (which the directors had refrained from doing). At the same time Hastings and Barwell had written defending themselves and accusing their opponents of intemperance and ill judgement. The two sides had agreed to send to the directors and administration only documents they had shown each other, but everyone concerned wrote voluminously to their friends and relations, who brought their letters to ministers and directors, passed them from hand to hand, and even published them in the Press.

Nothing could have been more unwelcome to a king and ministers struggling with the intractable colonial question. North sent the king copies of the Bengal correspondence agreeing with the majority of the Council that Hastings's conduct was 'not quite free from suspicion', but adding that 'he appears in other matters to have been a very able and useful servant to the Company and in particular to have put their finances in Bengal into a much better situation than they were before his time'. He added rather gloomily: 'The worst part of the business is that the two parties in the Council appear too much irritated against one another to act together with any cordiality for the future.'[1] The king judged Hastings more harshly but suggested no action.[2] It was already not difficult to forecast that the Government's first reaction would be to try to calm down the contesting parties, but that if this were not successful to support the recall of the representatives of the old régime.

This was in fact what happened. There was at first some talk of using the ministerial influence in the Company to secure the recall of Hastings at once, possibly leaving Barwell in office to ensure some continuity with the past,[3] but by November

of P. E. Roberts in the *Cambridge History of British India*, vol. v, and his article in the *Journal of Indian History*, vol. iii, pt. i, 1924, 'Warren Hastings and his Accusers'.

[1] *Correspondence of George III*, iii. 228–9.   [2] *Ibid.* 230–1.

[3] Welbore Ellis to P. Francis, 28 September 1775: 'Before I left Twickenham I had opportunities to converse with those whose opinions must have great weight in the decision on these great points; and I had the satisfaction to perceive good reason to believe that H—— would be recalled and your proceedings highly approved. It did not seem equally clear that B—— would be recalled.' MS. Eur. E.13, f. 267.

Welbore Ellis reported to Francis that 'the state of the Colonies and the constant fatiguing attendance and mass of business in Parliament have driven all consideration of your matters out of doors'.[1] Others noted a tendency in administration, while supporting the Majority in general terms, to say in private that 'they might have acted with less precipitation and more moderation'.[2] Soon the belief became general, as Palk told Hastings reassuringly, that Government had no desire 'to be further embarrassed with disputes in India, nor are they very anxious to vindicate your opponents further than what men will naturally do to justify their own nomination'.[3]

As a result a General Letter was finally dispatched in December, after extensive emendation by Robinson,[4] in which some censure and some praise were administered to both parties and they were adjured to work together in the future. Soothing letters were dispatched privately by the supporters of each, exhorting them not to take offence at the compromise, and though the king said he found the General Letter ambiguous and prophesied that the directors, as they 'manifestly neither choose to hurt Hastings nor his Adversaries . . . therefore will most probably disoblige both',[5] there was some hope that a crisis had been averted.

But only the slowness of communications which at this time made nonsense of so many of the settlements for India had permitted these hopes to flourish. Less than a month after the dispatch of the General Letter the first ships of the new season brought tidings which showed that the newcomers and the old Company servants had quarrelled openly and irreconcilably. It was learnt that the Majority were pressing sinister charges against Hastings, amassed through the disreputable channel of Nuncomar, and against Barwell on more legitimate grounds; that the Judiciary had been swept into the factions that ensued. It also became clear that investigations by Clavering into the affairs of

---

[1] MS. Eur. E.13, f. 269, 17 November 1775.

[2] Ibid., f. 304. S. Fraser to John Bristow, 12 January 1776. Printed by S. Weitzman, op. cit., p. 280.

[3] R. Palk to W. Hastings, 19 November 1775. Add. MS. 29136, f. 341.

[4] A copy with his amendments and queries for further discussion with the Chairman is among North's East India papers in the Public Record Office (T49 8. 52). The General Letter as dispatched on 15 December 1775 is partially printed by S. Weitzman, op. cit., pp. 254–6.

[5] *Correspondence of George III*, iii. 293.

the army and by Francis into those of revenue were producing allegations of past misdeeds which involved not only nearly all the prominent servants still in Bengal but (either directly or through their 'banians') most of the Bengal 'Nabobs' who were now in England.[1] When the news of Nuncomar's execution, so disconcertingly convenient in its timing,[2] was added there seemed to be the material enough for a new Burgoyne's Committee. A crisis in the Company's affairs was in fact unavoidable.

When this became clear certain developments of the preceding year, which might then seem of only secondary importance, began to assume a new significance. They were connected with the return to England which began in that year of Bengal servants whose careers were threatened by the activities of the Majority. By the later months of 1775 four of Hastings's close friends were back in England, and more were to follow.[3] Most important among them was that ubiquitous adventurer Lauchlin Macleane, both in personality and in the powers which he brought with him. Macleane had justified the belief of his creditors that he would show enterprise and vigour in seeking his fortune in India.[4] He was quick to see that his best prospects lay at the disorganized Court of the Nawab of Arcot, and he had not been six months in the country before he was employing a period of convalescence in Madras in the most grandiose intrigues with the Nawab and his fellow-adventurer John MacPherson, out of which he clearly hoped to obtain both financial advantages and an early return to England.[5] When

---

[1] There is, for instance, among North's papers in the Public Record Office (T49 5. 23) a set of interrogations and accounts from Burdwan, showing payments made to certain Company servants and a number of natives. The latter were evidently 'banians' of other servants. The employer's name and office is endorsed on each document in a different hand.

[2] This controversial subject has been extensively discussed by Sir James Stephen, *Nuncomar and Impey*, London, 1885. A balanced summing up is given by P. E. Roberts, *Cambridge History of British India*, v. 235 seq.

[3] George Vansittart, John Graham, the Hon. Frederick Stuart, and Lauchlin Macleane. John Stewart and Alexander Elliot came the following year.

[4] Richard Barwell much admired his 'abilities and address' (*Bengal Past and Present*, xi. 50). He added the caution, however: 'His appointments are handsome, but I fear will not equal his expectations in point of consequence or profit, though in the latter point he told me he should be satisfied. My only reason for doubting he may not be so, is his advanced age and the anxiety with which he wishes to return to England.' (Ibid., p. 298.)

[5] How far Hastings was concerned in them is not clear. He was certainly kept fairly well informed of what was going forward (e.g. J. Macpherson to W. Hastings,

the hostile Majority began their investigations into his position
and activities in Bengal he had quickly adapted himself to the
position, had resigned before they could dismiss him, had done
his best to clinch his agreement with the Nawab, and he now
appeared in the threefold capacity of applicant to the directors
for reinstatement, agent for the Governor-General, and representative from the Nawab of Arcot to the British Government
to complain of his treatment by the Company's servants in
Madras. In the last capacity he had promises of the Nawab's
bounty with which he reassured his numerous creditors and
made it safe for him to enter again the scenes of his past mis-
adventures.

The arrival of this able and highly experienced exponent of
backstairs politics was an indication for the future of the
problems which the ministry had assumed in taking over their
indirect control of India. As an applicant for reinstatement he
stood in an old, bad tradition of Company intrigue which the
ministry hoped to use its influence to check. As representative of
the Nawab of Arcot (for which he boasted he drew a salary
which he variously stated at £6,000 and at £3,400 a year)[1] he
was exploiting a field first opened up by John MacPherson,
with whom, moreover, he had struck up a close alliance on the
basis of their friendship for Hastings when he was in Madras
laying his plans. They were to be followed in the coming years
by a line of other shady adventurers exercising their powers of
intrigue on their own and their patrons' behalf. As agent for the
Governor-General, with a right to spend up to £10,000 on his
behalf,[2] he was opening up new ground.

27 September 1774. Add. MS. 29135, ff. 230 seq.). Macleane's activities caused the
Madras Government much anxiety (Governor Wynch's account to the Chairman
of the Company, 5 February 1775. Home Miscellaneous 118, ff. 235 seq.). Macleane's
own official account to the Company is in Appendix 107 to the *Ninth Report of the
Select Committee, 1783. Reports from the House of Commons*, vi. 356 seq.

[1] Abergavenny MSS. i. 62. J. Robinson to North, 12 August 1775, quotes him
as giving the higher figure. The lower one was included in the account (to be
accepted with great reserve on many points) which he gave to the Court of Directors of his mission. See p. 303, n. 5. Judging by the experience of John Mac-
Pherson he was lucky if he ever drew it. Robinson urged North not to receive him
but 'to act consistently with the plan you have in part adopted, and mean to pursue' and 'acquaint the Indian powers, that if they have anything to offer, either
by way of complaint for redress or as compliment, it is wished that it may come
through the Governor-General and Council of Bengal'.

[2] F. Sykes to W. Hastings, 16 December 1775. Add. MS. 29136, f. 431.

His arrival (which was marked by a picaresque incident of the kind which made his career spectacular)[1] was unwelcome to the ministry, who were not at all inclined to do business with him on behalf of the Nawab, and to the directors. who could not be expected to wish to reinstate him. As agent for the Governor-General he had clearly arrived at a fateful hour and he flung himself energetically into East India politics in his defence. It is doubtful whether the threats and adjurations he addressed to North and Robinson, the publications issued, and manœuvres planned by him and a committee of Hastings's friends, and the considerable voting power in defence of Hastings which he got together in the General Court,[2] affected in more than detail the decision of the ministry to work for a compromise. He had, however, certainly played the leading part in producing an organized interest on behalf of his patron which was a useful nucleus for further development.

It was now to be called into service.[3] The reaction of North and Robinson to the new allegations was immediate. Unless Hastings was dismissed and the judges controlled the 1773 settlement was in danger. Moreover, it might already have been irrevocably damaged by the letters recently sent from England since, on receipt of them, Clavering and his colleagues might throw up their positions. They hastened to assure Clavering of their sympathy and support, and to let him know that, though it might take the Company some time to examine the charges, administration would press for 'a speedy determination', asserting their conviction that there was only 'too great ground for censure' of his opponents.[4] Shortly afterwards they referred the accusations against the judges to the Attorney-General for his opinion[5] and it became known that pressure was being

---

[1] In the letter quoted in n. 1, p. 304 above, Robinson reports that Macleane's colleague on the mission, James Johnson, a bankrupt servant of the Nawab, had tried on their arrival to trick him by stealing the box containing his credentials and presents and offering them himself. He was unsuccessful in the attempt.

[2] L. Sulivan to W. Hastings, 7 December 1775. Add. MS. 29136, ff. 379 seq. Printed S. Weitzman, op. cit., pp. 259–62.

[3] Accounts of this great contest have been given by all biographers of Hastings. The best are those of Mervyn Davies and S. Weitzman (op. cit.). Gleig prints in full a number of letters from Hastings's correspondence, in particular those of Lauchlin Macleane.   [4] S. Weitzman, op. cit., pp. 282–3.

[5] The Government attempt to deal with the question of the Supreme Court is dealt with in a letter from Charles Jenkinson to Clavering of 13 December 1776 (MS. Eur. E.16, ff. 33 seq).

brought to bear on the directors to petition for the recall of Hastings and Barwell.

They were now to see what those with experience of the Company's recent history had seen before, the turmoil which arose there when prominent servants and ex-servants were under attack. All the Company servants endangered by the Majority's investigations had their friends and supporters in the Company. The rally of Hastings's friends the previous year had already shown that they included many who normally supported the Government. In addition, Barwell had a considerable personal interest, headed by John Purling, a former Chairman of the Company, and organized by his redoubtable and indefatigable sister Mary, the only woman who ever organized an 'interest' at India House. The lesser servants also had supporters, some of them important because they threatened the unity of the Government front. Alexander Elliot brought into action his father Sir Gilbert.[1] Frederick Stuart wrote that his father, Lord Bute, was a friend, 'but, alas, he *dare not* produce himself in public', and their not inconsiderable connexions were mobilized in their relative's support.[2] The case of the judges being bound up in the issue, their connexions were also brought in, particularly those of the Chief Justice Elijah Impey who, as a close friend of Dunning, was thought to bring the Opposition interest headed by Lord Shelburne into line. He also had his friends within the ministry, as he enjoyed the patronage of the Chancellor, Lord Bathurst, and of the formidable Attorney-General Thurlow.

In addition to ties of friendship there were still more important ties of interest. Since interest rates in India were high and remittance to England very difficult nearly all the returned Company servants still had financial interests in India. Some of them found these directly threatened by the Majority's

---

[1] L. Macleane to W. Hastings, 25 June 1776: 'Sir Gilbert Elliot and his sons came together to the ballot and gave in their papers open.' Add. MS. 29137, f. 254; Gleig, op. cit. ii. 65.

[2] Frederick Stuart to W. Hastings, 6 January 1776. Add. MS. 29137, f. 5. The Bute influence was still a mystery or, rather, a myth. General Fraser told John Bristow that opinions differed as to whether Lord Bute had intercourse with the king and his ministers, but 'be this as it may, it is certain that he carries great weight in any point; many have been obliged to him when in power: others believe him still to have a secret influence, his brother and his son Lord Mountstewart have a great share of consideration'. (Printed S. Weitzman, op. cit., p. 280.)

accusations—the 'banian' of Richard Becher, for instance, a director normally a supporter of administration, was involved in the Burdwan scandals;[1] Francis Sykes still had a strong interest in the prosperity of Cantu Baba, his former 'banian', who now worked for Hastings and who was specifically attacked.[2] Others not yet directly affected feared that a widespread investigation would revive the inquisitions threatened in 1773. Carefully guided by the leaders of the organized Hastings party these discordant elements were drawn together until they formed, at least temporarily, a united body. By May it could be said that every prominent 'Nabob', with the single exception of John Walsh, was reconciled with Sulivan, whom they had so recently attacked, and was prepared to fight for Hastings against ministers and directors alike.[3]

This coalition was in itself formidable. There was, however, still another source from which it could be strengthened; Governor Johnstone and his opposition group in the Company, with Richmond and the Rockingham opposition in Parliament behind them. This group had, indeed, no great reason for friendship with Hastings or for Sulivan's middle party which was the core of his support. Governor Johnstone had recently condemned Hastings in public for the Rohilla War,[4] and though Sulivan had occasionally worked in harness with their party, he had done so only for his own convenience and had made it abundantly clear that he would have preferred a ministerial alliance if he could have got it. He was, moreover, personally suspect to their parliamentary allies. But the opportunity of harassing the Government was too good to resist, and, though Macleane was too cautious to clinch with them until he was sure that no terms could be obtained from administration, a complete union was finally effected, Johnstone and all his Company supporters declaring vigorously for Hastings and against the 'cruel treatment of the best servants the Company

---

[1] See p. 303, n. 1.

[2] e.g. F. Sykes to W. Hastings, 31 January 1776. Add. MS. 29137, ff. 56 seq. (Printed S. Weitzman, op. cit., p. 264). Richard Barwell had told some scandalous stories of Sykes and Cantu in a letter to his father in 1768 (*Bengal Past and Present*, x. 30).

[3] L. Macleane to W. Hastings, 25 June 1776. Add. MS. 29137, ff. 255 and 256v (crossed out).

[4] *London Chronicle*, 1775, p. 242.

ever had abroad'.[1] When the day of battle finally came not only the Duke of Richmond but the Marquess of Rockingham came in person to register his vote on their behalf.[2]

Against these numerous, if somewhat heterogeneous, forces the ministry had their more united and organized body of voters (somewhat reduced by defections) but little else. They could call on the remnants of Clive's personal connexion, it is true, and Clavering and his colleagues had some friends in the Company who depended on their patronage, but it soon became clear that even in an open vote the ministerial majority was uncertain, while in a vote by secret ballot (a part of the Company's constitution much deplored by ministerial managers who were unaccustomed to the limitations it imposed) it was even more problematical.

The results showed the limitation of their powers of 'management' both in the Court of Directors and in the General Court. A first attempt to get Hastings and Barwell recalled by the directors led to no more than an inconclusive resolution.[3] This check was not taken very seriously as the annual election of directors was imminent and there was some mild friction between directors and ministers about the composition of the next House list.[4] After the election Robinson returned to the charge but difficulties were still encountered there. It was not till 8 May that the ministerial supporters were able to bring the issue to a vote and when they did the results were somewhat disconcerting. Three of the directors normally supporting administration absented themselves;[5] others, either 'Nabobs' or

---

[1] *London Chronicle*, 1776, p. 64.

[2] L. Macleane to W. Hastings, 25 June 1776. Add. MS. 29137, f. 256. Printed Gleig, op. cit. ii. 68. Cf. an undated letter from D. Weir to Rockingham in the Fitzwilliam MSS. (Sheffield).

[3] Court Book 84, pp. 550–1.

[4] This arose from the persistence of North in including among the three candidates they were pushing for the List one Amyatt, recommended by Clavering. Robinson was sure that they could not carry Amyatt, but that he could have got in their other two candidates (J. Robinson to C. Jenkinson, 9 April 1776. Add. MS. 38398, f. 323) but North took the negotiation out of his hands and then bungled it in such a way that finally he gave the impression he had given up all three (Abergavenny MS. II. 102. North to J. Robinson, 6 April 1776). However, it was decided to make the best of a bad job, and the directors were formally congratulated on their unanimity. J. Caillaud to W. Hastings, 5 April 1776. Add. MS. 29137. ff. 150ᵛ–151.

[5] P. Francis to J. Fowke, 19 September 1776. MS. Eur. E.15, f. 222. They were J. Stables, J. Moffat, and J. Woodhouse.

connected with them, abandoned their allegiance,[1] and the motion was passed by one vote only. Macleane, watching the scene, at once whipped up nine proprietors to demand the calling of a General Court, and the battle was transferred to this much more tempestuous and incalculable scene seven days later.

Every preparation was made by both sides in the short time available for one of those spectacular General Courts the debates in which, from time to time, attracted almost as much attention as those in Parliament. The Treasury Whips were out; Macleane and the other leaders of Hastings's friends were tireless in their activity, and the Press was employed on a big scale. When the day came a distinguished gathering including the parliamentary leaders of Government and Opposition thronged India House, where they listened to a debate in which there was much display of oratory and a good deal of heat and which lasted from noon until about midnight.[2] It ended with a vote by show of hands which gave the ministerial supporters an uneasy majority of 17. A ballot was, however, immediately demanded, and ministers had the mortification of finding the directors' decision to recall Hastings and Barwell referred back to them for further consideration by the substantial majority of 377 votes to 271.

The disgust of the ministry was only equalled by the jubilation of Hastings's friends, who adopted the attitude always assumed by Hastings himself, that their victory was one of the unbiased and uncorrupted proprietors over the 'managed' voters of administration, and that in consequence their majority represented the true will of the Company.[3] The ministry's view was very different. North told the king: 'Many of those who profess attachment to the government and who openly support it, have, upon this occasion, either through connexion with the parties concerned or dislike of reformation, acted against us and by that means rendered the majority so considerable.'[4] Robinson said more shortly: 'We have been defeated by Party, joined with friendships, personal connexions, and interested

[1] F. Sykes to W. Hastings, 30 May 1776: e.g. R. Becher, T. Rumbold, and George Cuming. Add. MS. 29137, f. 204ᵛ.
[2] *London Chronicle*, 1776, p. 474.
[3] e.g. John Woodman, Hastings's brother-in-law.
[4] *Correspondence of George III*, iii. 535.

views.'[1] The truth lies between the two, but it is difficult to avoid the conclusion that the explanation given by Robinson is nearer than that of Hastings and his friends. There was certainly some real support for Hastings, both on account of his services (particularly towards the financial revival of the Company which touched the proprietors very nearly) and as a symbol of the Company's independence. These factors were to remain constant and even to increase throughout his career. But in themselves they would not have won a victory in the General Court. This was the result of an organization as complex as, though more ephemeral than, that of the Treasury itself, and Macleane, its chief architect, remarked himself on its miscellaneous and unstable character and the impossibility of keeping it together for any length of time.[2] There was some excuse for the exasperation which made Philip Francis write with his customary savagery:

Mr. Hastings with an air that would become Cato the Censor, declares that for his part he is satisfied with the absolution given him by 377 plain, honest men, obtained without influence or intrigue and extorted by the force of truth in opposition to the whole power of the Ministry. *Risum teneatis!* This is admirable. Macleane, Frederick Stuart and young Elliot were undoubtedly determined by nothing but the opinion of his integrity. . . . Such impudence is a vomit for a dog.[3]

But humiliation and jubilation apart, nothing that had happened had settled the question of what to do to solve the deadlock in Bengal. Here, however boldly Hastings's supporters might talk, they knew that the Government had the whip-hand. North, declaring he would 'have nothing to do with India matters out of Parliament',[4] indicated that he would now have recourse to Parliament for the removal of the two men. Nothing could be done in the present session, which was drawing to its close, but Parliament was summoned to reassemble in October, largely—it was understood—on Indian affairs. In preparation

---

[1] J. Robinson to J. Clavering, 26 April 1777, quoted S. Weitzman, op. cit., p. 322.
[2] L. Macleane to W. Hastings, 10 November 1776. Add. MS. 29137, f. 448ᵛ. Printed Gleig, op. cit. ii. 80.
[3] P. Francis to J. Bourke, 21 August 1776. Printed S. Weitzman, op. cit., p. 288.
[4] L. Macleane to W. Hastings, 25 June 1776. Add. MS. 29137, f. 254. Printed Gleig, op. cit. ii. 65.

for this, moreover, an extensive Press and pamphlet campaign was begun by the Treasury,[1] and Robinson occupied the summer recess in drawing up and getting printed a collection of documents to be used as the basis of the Government's case.[2]

At this point, however, the development of a contest which might well have brought Indian affairs back into the field of controversial politics and brought about in 1776 some of the features of a scene which was not enacted till 1781, were cut across by one of the most debated incidents of the confused relations between Hastings and the administration. This was the opening up of negotiations between the ministry and Macleane as Hastings's agent, which ended in Macleane's handing in his principal's resignation.

When Macleane left Bengal Hastings had resignation much in mind, and though in 1775 his friends were anxious to dissuade him from it, as soon as the ministry declared unequivocably against him they, too, had assumed it was inevitable. Their policy had aimed in the first place at ensuring him an honourable retreat; only when this failed had they ventured to defy the Government.[3] Indeed, even after the directors' decision for his recall and after the summons of the General Court of 15 May, negotiations between Robinson, Macleane, and Sulivan were still in progress.[4] But the terms Hastings's supporters asked were too high. They demanded in return for Hastings's resignation not only reinstatement of those of his supporters in Bengal who had been dismissed or who had resigned to forestall dismissal, but that the Crown should confer on Hastings a peerage or other high honour. These terms the ministry could not accept without giving the impression that they were taking his side against Clavering and his colleagues.

---

1 It was reported to be run by Hugh Kelly, as James MacPherson (of *Ossian* fame), the ministry's chief pamphleteer, had refused to undertake it owing to the connexion of his cousin John MacPherson with Hastings. L. Macleane to W. Hastings, 10 November 1776. Add. MS. 23137, f. 441. Printed Gleig, op. cit. ii. 71.

2 *Correspondence of George III*, iii. 392. This was later seen by John MacPherson, who inaccurately described it to Hastings as his 'impeachment'. John MacPherson to W. Hastings, 16 June 1778. Add. MS. 29141, f. 77.

3 L. Macleane to W. Hastings, 25 June 1776. Add. MS. 29137, ff. 249 seq. Printed Gleig, op. cit., ii. 59–61.

4 J. Robinson to C. Jenkinson [10 May 1776]: 'Lord North told me this afternoon . . . that they are trying again to let down Hastings *easily*, but great care must be taken if it is so, that it is with honour to —— [Clavering].' Add. MS. 38209, f. 13.

In the summer recess, however, feelers were put out again, this time by the ministry through unofficial channels.[1] Macleane, after consultation with Hastings's closest friends, thought it wise to take the suggestions up, and a fear of the consequences of parliamentary action now made him more accommodating. By the middle of September, when Robinson took the negotiations in hand officially, it had been agreed that while the claims on behalf of Hastings's Bengal supporters should be pressed, the demand for an honour for Hastings himself should be dropped, provided that he was promised honourable treatment on his return. Under Robinson's capable direction terms were soon drawn up, the king and North consulted,[2] and on 11 October a letter conveying Hastings's resignation and drafted by Robinson was handed in to the Direction. That part of the terms of the agreement which dealt in detail with the reinstatement of individuals was not, of course, made public. The directors, after considering Macleane's credentials to act for Hastings, accepted the resignation, a successor acceptable both to directors and ministers was appointed,[3] and it seemed as if both the crisis and the Indian career of Hastings had come to an end.

It was not till nearly two years later that it was learnt in England that the result was quite different. Hastings, whom the death of Monson had placed in control of a majority in his Council, was, when the news reached Bengal, disinclined for resignation; he had no clear impression of the situation in England (the last news had been jubilant after the General Court), he felt that Macleane had exceeded his powers, and he was, moreover, so much incensed by the violent behaviour of his opponents in Bengal on the receipt of the news that he

---

[1] There were two approaches, one by William Eden, then Under-Secretary to the Northern Department, through Alexander Elliot, into whose family he was marrying (Macleane was at first puzzled by this as it looked like poaching in Robinson's department, which he knew Robinson kept under close control), and the other from Robinson through one of the directors, John Woodhouse. See Macleane's account. L. Macleane to W. Hastings, 10 November 1776. Add. MS. 29137, ff. 441 seq. Printed Gleig, op. cit. ii. 71–94, and a rather exaggerated account of Woodhouse's activities in a letter from him to Francis, 22 November 1776. MS. Eur. D.18, ff. 395–7.

[2] John Robinson to the King, 24 September 1776, Add. MS. 37833, ff. 36–36ᵛ. The King gave his approval the same day (f.38).

[3] Edward Wheler, one of the directors who supported administration. On his choice see Robinson's letter to the King, 15 October 1776. Add. MS. 37833, ff. 83ᵛ seq.

determined to stand his ground and repudiate the agreement made in his name.

Even before this the compromise had become a subject of controversy in England. The first reactions were enthusiastic. The king considered it 'material intelligence' which 'will prevent much irksome business from coming before the House of Commons'.[1] Laurence Sulivan told Hastings that he was extricated with honour from an untenable position.[2] Only the Opposition in the Company and Parliament, who had been looking forward to the coming contest, were furious at being dropped without even a warning of the agreement which was under discussion. They were so much incensed that Governor Johnstone and the Duke of Richmond called a General Court to censure the directors for accepting Hastings's resignation. But they had been thrown into such disarray that they made a miserable showing and the Duke of Richmond did not even appear.[3]

Soon other voices began to be heard. Only a few of Hastings's supporters had been consulted, and those who had not were hurt and angry and soon began to complain of the terms which had been obtained.[4] The indignation became more general when it was learnt that the red ribband had been awarded to Clavering (as part of an arrangement that had nothing to do with India),[5] and even Macleane counselled Hastings to hold up his resignation until he got some equivalent. By the end of the year dissatisfaction with the terms of the compromise was fairly general and there were some who challenged its necessity altogether.

On the ministry's side there were also some doubts. The indignation which the Majority in Bengal expressed in a blistering letter when the news reached them extended to the terms of

[1] Abergavenny MS. ii. 116. The King to [North or Robinson], 8 October 1776.
[2] L. Sulivan to W. Hastings, 18 October 1776. Add. MS. 29137, f. 408.
[3] 20 November 1776. *The London Chronicle*, 1776, p. 498, gave an account of it. The king expressed his pleasure at the 'poor figure' they cut. *Correspondence of George III*, iii. 404.
[4] e.g. Francis Sykes, 31 October 1776. Add. MS. 29137, ff. 421 seq.
[5] North explained when Hastings's friends remonstrated with him that the occasion of the award was the conferring of a similar honour on General Howe. Sir Thomas Clavering had long had the promise of this honour for his brother and complained that Howe had obtained it first. L. Sulivan to W. Hastings, 23 December 1776. Add. MS. 29138, f. 54.

the agreement (in particular the restoration of Hastings's friends) as well as to the failure in its implementation.[1] Some supporters of administration in England also feared lest the terms had been too liberal to Hastings's supporters,[2] but most of their doubts arose from fear lest Hastings should refuse to consider himself bound by his agent and that in consequence they had failed to achieve their purpose. Robinson wrote as early as November: 'It is said many of Opposition have wrote to Mr Hastings pressing him to remain in his Government and not to avoid it (sic) in compliance with the engagements of his friends here, but I trust he will receive advice counter to this from his friends.'[3] The protests against Clavering's Order of the Bath and the news of Monson's death increased the doubts, North even approaching Macleane at his levée to ask him the direct question.[4] The news of the breakdown of the agreement which reached England and exasperated both king and ministers in April 1778 was by no means altogether unexpected.

As time went on, Hastings began to feel not only that his agent had exceeded his powers but that he and his other Bengal friends had betrayed him. On the first point it is difficult to form an opinion. None of the correspondence in existence specifically gives Macleane this power, but both he and the other supporters of Hastings who had recently come from Bengal obviously believed that he had it. The second is only tenable if it is believed either that the Government would not or could not take the parliamentary action which they threatened, or that they could have been diverted from doing so on less onerous terms. Since Hastings did not wish to consider resignation on any terms, it was on the grounds that resignation was unnecessary that his argument rested. The correspondence of the king, North, Robinson, Jenkinson, and others make this view untenable. North was certainly worried about bringing India again into

[1] MS. Eur. E.15, ff. 795 seq. J. Clavering to J. Robinson, 14 July 1777. The letter was written by Francis.

[2] Jenkinson thought the negotiation justified only if 'improper conditions respecting others besides Mr Hastings are not annexed to it' (which they were). He had not been concerned in it and doubted whether he was 'fully acquainted with the bottom of it'. C. Jenkinson to J. Clavering, 13 December 1776. MS. Eur. E.16, f. 34.

[3] J. Robinson to J. Clavering, 20 November 1776. MS. Eur. E.15, f. 716.

[4] L. Macleane to W. Hastings, 12 May 1777. Add. MS. 29138, f. 404ᵛ. Printed Gleig, op. cit. ii. 102.

Parliament,[1] but the king was determined he should do so and everything was in train for the purpose. It was realized that when India came before the House again the business was likely to be unpleasant both because of the use Opposition would make of this new act of Government interference and because the supporters of administration would be themselves divided, but no one in a responsible position suggested that administration would be unable to carry their point, or that they should give in. Charles Jenkinson, who was somewhat critical of the agreement, summed up the arguments in its favour.

We expected to have had much business in Parliament respecting America and in consequence of that to have had a troublesome and fatiguing session, though the reverse of this has proved to be the case. To have added to this a painful investigation into Indian affairs and the guilt of individuals would not only have augmented our troubles, but we should, I fear, have necessarily broken among ourselves which would have had, perhaps, a bad influence on our American business.[2]

It is perhaps more open to doubt whether or not Hastings's agents held out for the best terms possible, and in this connexion a somewhat disconcerting fact soon became apparent. In the negotiation Macleane appeared to have gained nothing for himself. His name did not even appear among those of the Bengal servants promised restoration. It soon appeared, however, that he had obtained a substantial advantage. From that time on his negotiation with the ministry on behalf of the Nawab of Arcot, which had hitherto made no progress, began to move.[3] Macleane began to see much of Robinson[4] and to present his client's case with, he believed, much success. In March 1777 he abandoned his claims for reinstatement as a Company servant and it became known that he rested his hopes on employment by the Nawab or by the British Government at the Nawab's court.[5] By the middle of the next year one of Francis's friends was reporting (with some exaggeration, it

[1] The King to J. Robinson, 14 September 1776. Add. MS. 37833, f. 28.
[2] C. Jenkinson to J. Clavering, 13 December 1776. MS. Eur. E.16, ff. 34–35.
[3] R. Palk to W. Hastings, 28 December 1776. Add. MS. 29138, f. 70; L. Macleane to W. Hastings, 4 January 1777, ff. 96 seq.
[4] L. Macleane to W. Hastings, 12 May 1777, ibid., f. 402[v]. Printed Gleig, op. cit. ii. 102–3.
[5] 31 March 1777. Court Book 85, p. 675.

must be admitted) that 'This very extraordinary man seems lately to have been the adviser most relied on by our minister.'[1]

When this was observed friends of Hastings began to speculate, as did Samuel Pechell, for instance, whether 'the interest of the Nabob of Arcot may in some instances have occasioned more hurry than there should have been in such a transaction';[2] and though these suspicions may not have been just, Macleane's history and character were not such as to make them ridiculous. But whether or not Macleane intended to sacrifice Hastings's interest to his own, there is no doubt that in the event it was the ministry, not Hastings, who was tricked.

Had an Act of Parliament reached India in 1777 instead of the outcome of an informal agreement it could not have been disobeyed and Hastings would have left India before the most crucial years of his tenure of office. As it was the result was so much in Hastings's favour that Philip Francis would not believe that it was not a deep-laid plot. 'He may say what he pleases now', he wrote in his diary in 1779, 'but I am convinced that the whole was a juggle, in which John Stewart and Vansittart were as much concerned as even Macleane, and all by instructions from Hastings himself to gain so much more time and trust to accidents.'[3]

But if Macleane did Hastings and the country a great unintentional service, he also did him a grave disservice. He had angered the Company Opposition and the Rockingham parliamentary interest by his abrupt desertion of them and he had associated Hastings's cause in his own person both with the support of the ministry and the claims of the Nawab of Arcot, just at a time when circumstances were leading the Opposition to attack both of them. The association was not yet permanent nor its results evident, but the first move in a game that was to have far-reaching consequences had been made. The first signs within the Company were noted by Robinson in the General Court of 20 November 1776: 'Some oblique insinuations tending to show the disposition of the opposing party to criminate Mr Hastings were thrown out, but were not well-received or attended to.'[4]

---

[1] C. D'Oyly to P. Francis, 9 July 1777. MS. Eur. D.18, f. 494. Quoted Parkes and Merivale, op. cit. ii. 105.
[2] S. Pechell to W. Hastings, 7 June 1778. Add. MS. 29141, f. 18.
[3] 22 November 1779. MS. Eur. 23, f. 204.
[4] J. Robinson to J. Clavering, 20 November 1776. MS. Eur. E.15, f. 716.

Whatever its future implications, however, the resignation ended for the time the crisis of East Indian affairs in England. About the judges nothing was done. Though the king still hoped for some action to control the Court of Judicature and Jenkinson and Robinson continued to press for it, legal obstruction was too serious and, for the time, the issue was allowed to lapse. The lull enabled Robinson to restore ministerial prestige within the Company, 'bringing them back' as he said 'from their revolt at home'. His power in the Company had been temporarily dislocated but not permanently shaken. Despite the new friendliness to Hastings and his agent, Sulivan was once again disappointed in his hopes of ministerial support for the election of directors in the following spring. Jenkinson, summing up the results of their experience, wrote: 'As to the General Court of Proprietors, I think that Government grow to have every day more influence in it. But when the whole body of Indians join the opposition against Government (as they did in Mr. Hastings' case) it will always be defeated.'[1]

The end of the crisis in the Company caused by the events in Bengal was, however, almost immediately followed by a new strain on ministerial 'management' caused by startling developments in Madras. The arrival there at the end of 1775 of Lord Pigot as Governor with his revolutionary instructions on the relations to be imposed on the Nawab of Arcot and the Raja of Tanjore had caused the uproar that was to be expected. The indignation arose less from a reasoned disapproval of the sudden reversal of policy vis-à-vis the native powers than from injured personal interest. The Nawab of Arcot and his entourage, already angry with the Company servants,[2] were now overcome with indignant dismay. The dismay spread farther when Pigot sought to limit the access of Company servants to the Nawab and dismissed John MacPherson from the Company's service on the grounds of disloyalty in present and past relations with him.[3] Finally, the restoration of the territory

---

[1] C. Jenkinson to J. Clavering, 13 December 1776. MS. Eur. E.16, f. 37.

[2] There is much material bearing on this question from the correspondents of Robert Palk in H.M.C., Palk MSS.

[3] The reason given for his dismissal was that there came into Pigot's hands a document he had submitted to the Nawab some years earlier describing the services he alleged he had performed for the Nawab in England, obviously with the

which the Nawab had taken from the Raja of Tanjore raised an acute financial problem for the numerous holders of the assignments which the Nawab had granted on the revenues of this territory. Nearly all the most important Company servants were involved either in their own names or in that of the biggest holder of these securities, Paul Benfield,[1] a man soon to become notorious. Before these threats the differences between the Nawab and the Company's servants and those between the various groups of hangers-on at the Nawab's court[2] faded away, and Pigot found himself faced with a powerful opposition which controlled the majority on his Council.

In this position, resembling, superficially at least, that which Warren Hastings had faced in Bengal, Lord Pigot attempted measures which his colleague had wisely avoided. To force his measures through he declared two of the Council suspended. The response was a coup planned by the majority of the Council aided by MacPherson and Benfield and backed, as there seems no reason to doubt, by the Nawab of Arcot and his sons.[3] The Majority seized the Governor's person, declared themselves the Government, and placed Lord Pigot in confinement, where, to

intention of seeking a reward. This remarkable document was printed in Appendix I to the Third Report of the Select Committee, 1782. (*Reports from Committees of the House of Commons*, v. 641 seq.) and in the *Defence of Lord Pigot*, 1777, attributed to John Lind, barrister: Appendix I, pp. 48 seq. A copy of it had already been sent to England by Admiral Harland in 1772 (Home Miscellaneous, vol. 110, ff. 495 seq.) together with a scathing account of MacPherson's activities. The admiral stated that the document had been drawn up in October or November 1771, so that five years had elapsed since it was written. The Minutes of the Council also make it clear that MacPherson was believed still to be intriguing with the Nawab (*Reports from Committees of the House of Commons*, v. 644), and the suspicions are supported by references in *H.M.C., Palk MSS.*, pp. 263-4 and 270.

[1] Paul Benfield had come to Madras in 1764 as civil architect and engineer. In 1769 he became engineer of the ramparts for the Black Town, and in this and other contracting work he made considerable sums which he increased by loans to the Nawab, for whom by 1774 he was acting as banker. He had twice been in trouble with the authorities, in 1770 and 1772, and there seems no doubt that his activities were corrupt and most undesirable.

[2] John MacPherson and Benfield, for instance, had been bitter rivals for the Nawab's favour, and MacPherson in his correspondence with Hastings had made accusations against Benfield no less damaging than those later made by Burke (e.g. 27 September 1774). Add. MS. 29135, ff. 232ᵛ seq. After this date, however, they became and remained fast friends.

[3] *Vide H.M.C., Palk MSS.*, loc. cit., pp. 289-90; also *Defence of Lord Pigot*. Mac-Pherson told Hastings (Add. MS. 29137, f. 375, 13 October 1776) that he himself had dictated the Proclamation against Pigot to a trembling Councillor, since he 'neither was nor would be neuter'.

increase the scandal, he unexpectedly died some months later. Meantime both parties had appealed to the Governor-General and Council and to Admiral Hughes, then in Indian waters, as well as to the directors in England. The sympathy of their colleagues in India was with the Majority, however much their actions might be deplored. For once (and in view of political reactions in England to these events, there is some irony in this fact) Warren Hastings and the majority of his Council were in agreement. They recognized the Majority in Madras as the Government *de facto* pending further instructions from home.

The decision was a reasonable one, but as a court of appeal they had the disadvantage of having a *parti pris*. Clavering and his friends had no reason for friendliness towards Pigot, the representative of Opposition interests in England,[1] and Clavering early expressed his sympathy, in terms of which Pigot justifiably complained, with his military colleague General Fletcher, who was implicated in the revolt.[2] Warren Hastings was even more deeply implicated. His experience in Madras had left him with clear ideas on the correct policy to the native powers of the Carnatic, ideas which ran counter to Pigot's instructions, and with close personal ties with the Nawab.

His main channel of intercourse with the Nawab was none other than John MacPherson, and not only had Macleane's relations with the latter caused a good deal of suspicion in Madras the year before, but now another of Hastings's personal followers, John Stewart, had been in Madras on his way to England and had entered into equally close relations with MacPherson, just at the time when MacPherson was dismissed and the combination was forming against the Governor.[3] When, as if to underline the connexion between the Governor-General and those responsible for the coup, he wrote a private letter to Stratton, leader of the Majority, in which he made clear where his sympathies lay,[4] and when Stratton indiscreetly published

[1] P. Francis to D. Godfrey, 16 September 1776. MS. Eur. E.13, f. 749. 'We have advice from Madras of Lord Pigot's deposition and imprisonment. He was caught like a canary bird and there he may whistle.'

[2] Ibid., ff. 807–13. Copies of correspondence from Lord Pigot to Hastings complaining of Clavering's letter to Sir R. Fletcher (enclosed) and Clavering's minute of 30 October 1776 in reply.

[3] John Stewart to W. Hastings, 13 February 1776. Add. MS. 29137, ff. 66 seq. Cf. *H.M.C.*, *Palk MSS.*, loc. cit., p. 264.

[4] W. Hastings to G. Stratton, 18 September 1776. Add. MS. 29137, ff. 338 seq.

the most damaging part of it, the conclusion that he was an interested party was certain to be drawn and the suspicion (an unjust one) that he had been concerned in the intrigue which led to Pigot's overthrow was not surprising. This was the unpleasantly sensational story, tricked out in all the trappings of melodrama, that began to reach England in the early months of 1777.

The issues which it presented to the Government were similar to those which had assailed them from Bengal in that they represented the incursion of the hard facts of Indian misrule into the manœuvres of Company 'management', but they were different in almost every other respect. In the first place, the Government was not directly concerned in the way which it had been in the Bengal disturbances. In Bengal they were implicated from the beginning, since it was a question of preserving the settlement which they had imposed by Act of Parliament. In Madras they held no brief either for Lord Pigot or for the Majority which opposed him. The king expressed a general view when he remarked: 'I have not the smallest doubt but both parties have been stimulated by motives alone of private interest.'[1] In the second place, even when Robinson had been forced to intervene on behalf of Government in an attempt to clear up the trouble there was not the serious threat to their majority in the Company which there had been in 1776. Lord Pigot's case was, it is true, immediately taken up by the Company and parliamentary Opposition interests which had won him his position. A vigorous Press campaign also gained him some general sympathy among the proprietors; but this time there were not the elements of a solid combination in the Company against ministerial control. The Majority of the Madras Council had their friends just as Lord Pigot had his. Moreover, returned Company servants from Madras, like Robert Palk and General Caillaud, had obligations to, or expectations from, the Nawab of Arcot which also led them to oppose the Pigot Party.[2] Finally, Lauchlin Macleane as the Nawab's agent was this time active in support of the ministerial policy and succeeded in bringing at least some of Warren

[1] The King to J. Robinson, 29 March 1777. Add. MS. 37833, f. 189.
[2] e.g. J. Caillaud to W. Hastings, 24 May 1778. Add. MS. 29140, ff. 440 seq.

Hastings's friends into the Government camp for the occasion, though the wisest of them preferred to remain neutral.[1] The result was that in the General Court of 9 May when Admiral Pigot, Governor Johnstone, and the Duke of Richmond pushed for Pigot's reinstatement against a resolution framed by Robinson which involved the recall of both parties, they were defeated on a ballot by 414 to 317 votes.[2]

In the third place, just because the issue was less serious, ministers in their other preoccupations paid little attention to it. Robinson complained that he could not persuade North to think seriously about it,[3] and though he dutifully consulted both the king and North,[4] the solution which he imposed on the Company—a compromise on relations with the Nawab and Raja 'until the expiration of the Charter, when there may be lights for arranging them on a more solid foundation',[5] and the succession of Thomas Rumbold to the Governorship, the reversion to which had already been promised—was virtually his own.

But if the crisis within the Company in 1777 was both less severe and less directly the concern of administration than that of 1776, it was in some ways even more significant. In the first place, just because the ministry was not directly concerned in the personal issues involved, it emphasized the degree to which they had now taken over the initiative in the Company. The ministry had no doubt been at fault in not checking the reversal of policy contained in Pigot's instructions in 1774, and the more so since the Carnatic was an area in which for reasons of security the State had already a well-established tradition of intervention.[6] Now to the old fear that chaos in the Carnatic would encourage French intrigue among the 'country powers' was added the new danger that faction in the Company at home would endanger the success of Robinson's 'management'.

[1] L. Macleane to W. Hastings, 12 May 1777. Add. MS. 29138, f. 405ᵛ. Printed Gleig, ii. 103. 'It gave me much uneasiness that I could not persuade many of your friends to give their assistance, or to think you were anywise concerned in the issue.'

[2] Court Book 86, pp. 77–80.

[3] J. Robinson to C. Jenkinson, 12 April 1777. 'Lord North will not think of India business while the Civil List is on hand.' Add. MS. 38209, f. 112.

[4] *Correspondence of George III*, iii. 434.

[5] The King to J. Robinson, 22 March 1777. Add. MS. 37833, f. 182.

[6] See above, pp. 193 seq.

Y

Robinson had become alive to the first of these dangers when he began to listen to Macleane's representations on behalf of the Nawab of Arcot, and he had all but pushed some modifications of Pigot's policy through the directors before the news of Pigot's arrest was received.[1] On the receipt of the news it was again he who took the initiative and drew up and forced through the directors a settlement for the future.[2] From within the Court of Directors itself there came neither policy nor leadership. With the control which he had established over the Company there had come, however little it had been recognized by those who had aimed at it, the responsibility for all the major problems of the administration of India which had hitherto fallen on the Court of Directors, but which in their present weak and dependent condition they were in no position to sustain.

The events of 1777 were therefore significant in the development of the administrative responsibilities of the State in India. They were also significant as showing the way in which under the North Administration these responsibilities would be met. The settlement imposed was that which could be achieved with the minimum of disturbance, without the co-operation of ministers or the need of parliamentary decision. It represented, indeed, the best contrivance which Robinson could think of to control the situation there by compromise until the day when the whole Indian question would once more have to come before Parliament and become again a major political issue. Within these limits the instructions sent out with Rumbold, the new Governor, were sensible and moderate; but events were soon to show that stronger measures and different men were necessary to restore the Carnatic to peace and security.

The events of this year gave other indications of the lines of future development. In the Bengal crisis of the previous year, the supporters of Hastings had been reluctant to call to their assistance the parties of the parliamentary Opposition and had

---

[1] Robinson describes in outline these intentions in his letter to the king of 21 March 1777. (*Correspondence of George III*, iii. 432–4). George Vansittart gave a more detailed account of some of its provisions in a letter to Hastings of 18 March 1777. Add. MS. 29138, ff. 249 seq.

[2] See his correspondence with the king. Add. MS. 37833, ff. 180 seq. At the end of March he quoted North's opinion that Government would have to take up the question and act decisively themselves.

been quick to repudiate them when they found the chance to negotiate with the ministry. Pigot's connexions, on the other hand, were with the Rockingham section of the Opposition, and his supporters immediately called on their assistance. As a result party feeling outside the Company was more fully and quickly aroused by the issue than it had been on any Indian matter since 1773. John Bourke wrote to Philip Francis that 'the extraordinary revolution at Madras, brought about with as much ease as that of Mr Bayes in the *Rehearsal* has kindled a spirit of party strife and contest greater than you can imagine'.[1] As a result, when the Company opposition had failed to carry their demand for the restitution of Lord Pigot in the General Court of 9 May, Governor Johnstone and the parliamentary Opposition promptly raised the question in the House of Commons.

The session was drawing to a close and the debate was of little political importance, but was of some interest as indicating the development of the future; it showed the willingness of the Rockingham group to take up Indian questions to harass the Government, and it also laid some of the foundations of the great attacks which, with Fox and Burke at their head, they were later to launch against the Government. This debate saw, for instance, the beginning of one of the myths in which this greatest of eighteenth-century Oppositions became so prolific, the myth of the secret influence wielded over the ministry by the Nawab of Arcot. In the attacks which they were to launch in the last days of the ministry, they singled out for their most violent philippics the wrongs of Bengal and its neighbouring states, groaning under the tyranny of Warren Hastings, as depicted by Francis, and the chaos of the Carnatic brought about, as they maintained, by the corrupt partnership between administration and the Nawab of Arcot. At a time when this impoverished prince could not even pay his agents their salaries,[2] the Opposition believed that he had purchased the direct control of seven or eight seats in the House of Commons and that he enjoyed the means of bending the Government,

[1] Letter of 29 April 1777. MS. Eur. D.18, f. 483.
[2] e.g. John MacPherson to W. Hastings, 17 May 1779. Add. MS. 29143, ff. 272^v–273. In 1781 he got part-payment in India on a large bill he had drawn on the Nawab for expenses in 1779, the rest being still unpaid at the Nawab's death. (Home Miscellaneous 81, ff. 495 seq.; *Case of John MacPherson, bart.* (printed).)

through bribes, to his will.[1] In the debate of 1777 these allegations were heard for the first time. Several Opposition speakers
talked darkly of the intrigues of Lauchlin Macleane, and Burke
called the Nawab 'a most powerful friend in the Court and
ministry of England; so powerful that, for himself, if he wanted
any favour of great magnitude he knew of no canvasser he
should so much wish for as that Nabob'.[2]

If one of the future lines of attack on the ministry became
apparent in 1777 so, too, did the other which was bound up with
the attitude of the Rockingham opposition to Warren Hastings.
For two years Francis, through their common friend John
Bourke, had been trying to rouse Burke's concern at the alleged
misdeeds of Warren Hastings,[3] but the issue was a poor one for
Opposition so long as the ministry itself was cool or hostile to
him. Not only did Burke fail to respond,[4] but in 1776 the
Rockingham group were prepared to aline themselves on
Hastings's side. Now the changed attitude of the ministry towards
him and his friends and the activities of Macleane had com-

---

[1] On 31 April 1781, T. Townshend stated in the House that it was understood
he had seven or eight members 'devoted to his service' (*Parliamentary Register*,
1781, iii. 181). By 7 May 1782 William Pitt had elaborated this to a statement that
he 'had no less than seven or eight members in that House' (ibid. vii. 123).
Precisely the same allegation was made of Paul Benfield in the 1780 Parliament,
and from this the story may have grown, though Benfield's interests were purely
personal and only incidentally tended to coincide at this time with those of the
Nawab's agent. Even in his case the allegation was exaggerated; Benfield returned
in this Parliament only himself and two friends, and had no members in the next
Parliament. In 1780, however, John MacPherson, the Nawab's agent, was one of
his nominees (N. Wraxall, *Posthumous Memoirs*, iv. 91). For MacPherson's connexion with him at that time *vide infra*, p. 336, n. 1.

[2] *Parliamentary Register*, 1777, vii. 231.

[3] Francis to John Bourke, 30 November 1774. MS. Eur. E.13, ff. 37 seq.
Quoted Parkes and Merivale, ii. 18-19.

[4] Edmund Burke wrote his first letter to Francis in India on 9 June 1777, when
he recommended his cousin William to him (ibid., ii. 103-4). Even then he professed to be entirely preoccupied with American affairs. It has been suggested
that Burke was hostile to Hastings as early as 1773, when he made critical remarks
in the debates on the Regulating Act. These seem, however, to be no more than
can be attributed to the party line at the time—Pigot, Hastings's rival, had
joined the Rockinghams in annoyance at being passed over. More interesting
was Burke's friendly reference in 1773 to Francis, which was probably due to
Francis's acquaintance with his relative John Bourke. Strachey at the time advised
Francis to take advantage of this good will by making some reference to Burke in
a letter which Strachey could pass on 'that he may remember you in any opportune
compliment in the House of Commons'. H. Strachey to P. Francis, 3 January 1775.
MS. Eur. D.18, f. 241.

bined to change the situation. In the parliamentary debates of 1777 Hastings's name was freely used by the Opposition and allegations were heard as wild as those which were later to be made against him. 'Tommy' Townshend, for instance, told the House that the Nawab of Arcot

had an ambassador here . . . a gentleman of abilities a Mr Macleane who he heard, as soon as he had effected the Nabob's business by the destruction of Lord Pigot, was to return back as ambassador from the King of Great Britain to the Nabob. It seemed likewise that he had a third master, Mr Hastings . . . that Mr Hastings had recommended Mr Macleane to the Nabob; and it might fairly be concluded from all this, that his Highness and Mr Hastings were the contrivers of the arrest and imprisonment of Lord Pigot.[1]

The hostility of the Rockingham party to Hastings which was to reach such heights in the future was, it is true, not yet irrevocable, for neither was the good will of the ministry. In the following year, when the news of his refusal to resign once again raised the wrath of the king and ministers against him, the Opposition attacks abruptly ceased; but enough had been said to foreshadow the line they would adopt when in 1780 peace was finally made between Hastings's friends and North's Administration.

Changes during this year among the minor personalities of the East Indian scene were also of some importance. Chief of them were the disappearance of Lauchlin Macleane, the return to England of John MacPherson, and the rise to some prominence of William Burke, the relative and life-long friend of the great Edmund and the origin of most of the less creditable aspects of his career.[2] Lauchlin Macleane was nearing the end of his adventurous life. He had staked all on obtaining from the ministry a reversal of policy in favour of the Nawab and, though he had gained some success, he was by no means satisfied with the compromise which Robinson had arrived at or with his own prospects.[3] He still hoped, however, to carve out a position for

---

[1] *Parliamentary Register*, 1777, vii. 227.

[2] For him see Dixon Wecter, *Edmund Burke and his Kinsmen*, op. cit.

[3] L. Sulivan to W. Hastings, 10 March 1777 (Add. MS. 29138, f. 232ᵛ), expresses fears lest he will be disappointed in a matter of such moment to him. J. Caillaud to W. Hastings, 24 May 1778 (Add. MS. 29140, f. 441ᵛ), says that in the Nabob's affair 'I believe he met with some disappointments; at least what appeared as such to one of his sanguine turn of mind'. It was generally thought that he hoped to be accredited by the British Government at the Nawab's court.

himself as intermediary between the Nawab and the ministry.[1] To further this end he decided to make a lightning visit to India, satisfying his creditors by bills drawn on the Nawab before he left. After a rapid overland journey and a crowded three weeks in Madras, he set sail for England, still hopeful and resourceful, but his ship was lost with all hands and the last of his gambles was over. Frederick Stuart remarked shortly that his death was 'a happy event for himself though very distressing to his friends'.[2] Lord Shelburne (whose bill on the Nawab for the remainder of the debt which he had never fully recovered was rescued and returned to him by the tact of some free merchants of Madras) said that his conduct had been 'such as ought to be forgot for the sake of the human species'.[3] But his fellow-adventurer John MacPherson wrote his best epitaph: 'If he involved others he only did to them what he did without mercy to himself'.[4]

His loss made little difference to the political scene, for his place was at once filled by John MacPherson. Though Mac-Pherson had not Macleane's credentials, he took up the work both for Hastings and the Nawab of Arcot where his friend had left it, and added to a capacity for backstairs politics quite as marked as that of his predecessor the further advantage of family connexion with James MacPherson, of 'Ossian' fame, the ablest of North's paid pamphleteers. The links between the cause of Warren Hastings and that of the Nawab and his dubious entourage were thus strengthened, the aura of intrigue surrounding those who supported him was increased, and was soon to increase still farther, as MacPherson pursued his tortuous course, and the possibility of a *rapprochement* with the ministry, if circumstances should make this possible, became stronger.

When Macleane left England on his last voyage to India, another adventurer was leaving on his first visit to the East. Pigot's friends had obtained permission to send a messenger

---

[1] He and MacPherson were apparently playing with an idea which had been thought of before, of getting the Nawab to offer to place his territory directly under the Crown. Hastings knew of this, but not Sulivan or Macleane's other friends in the East India Company, who were indignant when, after his death, they learnt of it.

[2] F. Stuart to W. Hastings, 10 June 1778. Add. MS. 29141, f. 37ᵛ.

[3] Shelburne to W. Hastings, 8 July 1781. Add. MS. 29149, ff. 380–380ᵛ.

[4] John MacPherson to W. Hastings, 13 June 1778. Add. MS. 29141, f. 65.

overland to ensure his immediate release, and the closeness of their ties with the Rockingham Opposition group is shown by their choice of William Burke for the mission.[1] William Burke had risked and lost all in speculation as Macleane had done and, indeed, in 1769 the two men were ruined in the same venture.[2] He had been as anxious as Macleane to obtain a position in India that would help him to restore his shattered fortunes, but he had been less fortunate in his connexions, and this chance, uncertain though it was, was the first that had come to him.[3]

Beginning inauspiciously when Macleane stole a march on him in leaving England,[4] and when, arriving in Madras, he found that Pigot had died in captivity, the enterprise ended in success. In the correspondence of Rockingham, who gave him letters of recommendation, it is made clear that his intention was to take a leaf from Macleane's book and to seek employment, not, it is true, with the Nawab of Arcot, but with his rival the Raja of Tanjore.[5] The year before, when Macleane's ambition led him higher, William Burke had hopes of succeeding him in the position he had held under the Company in Bengal.[6] Now, by 1778, he was back in England as the Raja's agent. The

[1] Court Book 86, pp. 141–2. Alexander Dalrymple permitted to go; p. 145, 6 June 1777, William Burke and Robert Deane allowed to take his place.

[2] See above, pp. 143 seq.

[3] John Bourke to P. Francis, 27 May 1777. MS. Eur. D.18, f. 487.

[4] C. D'Oyly to P. Francis, 9 July 1777. Ibid., f. 493. Reports that as soon as a decision had been reached on Madras Macleane set out [he went by the Suez route] and got a start over W. Burke and his companion by getting to Dover first and engaging the whole of the only packet-boat there.

[5] e.g. E. Monckton to Rockingham, Madras, 15 October 1777. 'I have been so happy as to get Mr. Burke in the line you was pleased to point out.' See also E. Burke to Rockingham, n.d., and Rockingham's reply, 9 June 1777. FitzWilliam MSS. (Sheffield).

[6] W. Burke to Portland (4 and 8 March 1776), Portland MSS., describes his hopes and begs for support in bringing pressure to bear on individuals to vote for 'my immediate succession to Mr. Macleane's office in Bengal. Mr. Macleane has other views and his removal from this office will not impede them.' He reported on 4 March: 'I have today had a whisper that the Treasury will be far from obstructing my Asiatick views.' But on 25 March he wrote to Rockingham (FitzWilliam MSS., Sheffield) '. . . I may possibly be obliged to change my object as Mr. Macleane's further pretensions seem to meet with some check, and consequently the succession to his present situation is at least retarded—but I hope only retarded.'

Other papers in the Portland MSS., a letter of 25 September 1776 to Portland and an annotated list in W. Burke's hand, 'State of East India Directors respecting Mr. William Burke' (endorsed, received 2 December 1776), show he made further attempts to obtain employment in the Company.

importance of this development lies not only in the rivalry in the coming years of the agents of these two Indian princes and the tendency for it to become associated with the contests of parliamentary parties. It also lies in the influence which William's interests exerted directly and indirectly over the development of the thought of Edmund Burke.

XII

THE END OF THE NORTH ADMINISTRATION

BY 1778, had all gone as the 'men of business' had envisaged it, the Government would have been preparing the terms of a final settlement of the relations of the State and the Company. It would have been based on some four years' experience of Indian problems and supported by a control over the machinery of the Company strong enough to withstand the joint attacks of dissident groups within the Company and a parliamentary Opposition certain to make common cause with them when the new measures came before the House.

Much of the information necessary for the task, which as late as 1776 they did not think they possessed, was certainly before them two years later. Not only had the problems of Bengal and Madras been forcibly brought to their attention, but all the main participants had submitted detailed and reasoned proposals for future reorganization.[1] In addition, the agents of the Nawab of Arcot and the Raja of Tanjore were bombarding them with material to support the claims of their patrons; Lauchlin Macleane had in 1776 expounded his views and those of Hastings in long conversations with John Robinson;[2] and Robinson had also had confidential discussions with a number of other men of recent Indian experience, the most important of whom were John MacPherson, on his arrival in 1778,[3] and John Bristow, on a visit from Bengal, who was acting as an agent of Philip Francis.[4] Some points, it is true, gained still further significance from events yet to come; Hastings's plea for increased powers for the Governor-General over the other settlements, for instance, was given greater point by the later stages of the Mahratta War and the invasion of the Carnatic by Hyder Ali. But the 'men of business' already had clear in their minds the

---

[1] S. Weitzman, op. cit., pp. 49 seq. and 302 seq.

[2] L. Macleane to W. Hastings, 12 May 1777. Add. MS. 29138, ff. 402 seq. Printed Gleig, op. cit. ii. 98 seq.

[3] John MacPherson to W. Hastings, 10 February 1779. Add. MS. 29143, ff. 53ᵛ seq.

[4] J. Bristow to P. Francis, 4 February 1779. MS. Eur. E.17, ff. 34ᵛ seq.

main desiderata of a settlement in India, while in the Company's internal administration there was no point of which Robinson had not had long and bitter experience.

By the summer of 1778, therefore, when Robinson employed the parliamentary recess in drawing up for the consideration of ministers a plan for a new settlement in India, he was fairly certain what could and should be done. Indeed, the proposals he drew up formed, when three years later Charles Jenkinson redrafted and elaborated them, the basis of the Bill introduced by Dundas in 1782, and, in consequence, of a considerable part of Pitt's East Indian settlement.[1]

Moreover, public opinion, too, had advanced since 1773. Once again the parliamentary Opposition took up the cause of the Company against the Government, but this time no one advanced the claim that intervention was unnecessary. They now fully accepted, as Burke said, 'the controlling power and guardianship' of Parliament, and attacked only the control of India by 'the executive power of this country'.[2] Still farther, though the claim of both security and national finance still played a great part in men's thoughts about an East India settlement, all sides agreed in giving far more prominence than ever before to the public responsibility for orderly, humane, and equitable government of the peoples of India. Burke and his supporters by their eloquence focused the righteous indignation which had never altogether died down since the revelations of 1772; but the 'men of business' (Robinson and Jenkinson, who had borne the burden of the existing system, and another, Henry Dundas, who was to bear that of the future) shared the attitude that by 1784 made a major reform in Indian affairs a matter of necessity for any administration.

Since this was the case the question arises, why North's Administration failed so signally to introduce a measure of this kind themselves; why, despite all the work that had been done and the more enlightened trend of public opinion, they had recourse first to the wretched expedient of prolonging the exist-

[1] I use this term to include not only the Act of 1784 but the amending legislation introduced by Dundas and passed in 1786 (26 Geo. III, c. 16).

[2] *Parliamentary Register*, xiii. 185. Even in 1772 Burke had stated privately that his party agreed that it was 'the province and duty of Parliament to superintend the affairs of this Company as well as any other matter of public concern' (Burke, *Correspondence*, i. 390), but if so this point became obscured in the heat of debate.

ing Acts for two successive years; and why, in 1781, they succeeded only in passing an Act which was a mere shadow of what
was required and which admittedly needed extensive supplementary legislation before it could be considered a settlement
at all. The answer is twofold: the growing weakness and dislocation of the North Administration as the colonial war
merged into a general conflict and went badly for British arms,
and the breakdown of their existing Indian arrangements followed by the intrusion of the disorders of the Company into
the political sphere.

The first of these causes was the more far reaching in importance. Eighteenth-century experience had shown that unsuccessful war was the only condition in which a ministry could
be brought down by the pressure of public opinion. The fall
of Walpole in 1742 and the capitulation of the Newcastle
Administration to Pitt the elder in 1756–7 had already made
this clear. The fate of North's Administration was to show that
the generalization remained true even when the Crown held
out resolutely against public opinion. The fall of a ministry in
such circumstances came primarily from disintegration from
within. North's Administration, without the coherence of strong
family connexion or the dominance of personality, had always
been weakly articulated, his own position depending partly no
doubt on his parliamentary skill and judgement but chiefly on
the vigorous support he enjoyed from the king. Now, under the
stress of anxiety, overwork, and responsibility, he began to
crack, and even before the Opposition became formidable the
man who still rose so imperturbably to the demands of debate
in the House of Commons became in private subject to what
Robinson called 'his distressing fits'.[1] In these he lost all confidence in himself and almost all power of decision, and during
them he began, with increasing sincerity, to ask for permission
to resign. As early as 1778 he was already weakening, and in
1780 and 1781 his state steadily deteriorated until all associated
with him were aware of his condition and were bound to
speculate on its ultimate result. The king, a man of admirable
nerve and little imagination, tried to bolster him up, at first
through respect and liking for him, ultimately because the
Opposition had grown so strong that there was no acceptable

[1] J. Robinson to C. Jenkinson, 16 August 1779. Add. MS. 38212, f. 62.

alternative. But his position both in the closet and among his colleagues began to weaken, and disunity and ill feeling grew among the members of the ministry as both the strain and the lack of leadership increased.

Lord Sandwich, it is true, remained an unquestioning ally, but he was preoccupied with departmental business, and his administration of the Admiralty became the object of such virulent (though largely unjust) attacks that he was becoming from the purely political point of view a liability rather than an asset. Thurlow, now Lord Chancellor, though a sullen and moody colleague, was perhaps more troublesome than intriguing, and his follower Henry Dundas, the Lord Advocate, was one of North's most effective auxiliaries in debate; but Wedderburn, the Attorney-General, with whom the young William Eden was now associated, gave constant trouble. Moreover, the groups forming round both of them were growing and there was no reason to think that their support extended beyond their immediate interest, or to doubt that it would evaporate at once if through loss of the king's support or wavering on North's part a prospect of a change in ministry appeared. In the closet, Charles Jenkinson, since 1778 Secretary at War, was becoming increasingly important and often critical, and even the invaluable John Robinson was becoming more and more independent as his direct contact with the king grew and his relations with Jenkinson, always intimate, became closer.

For a ministry so situated—divided, burdened with the urgencies of war, and harassed by the rise of an Opposition with the greatest debating power of the century—the problem of an Indian settlement and, even more, of the persons to administer such a settlement both in England and India, was a peculiarly difficult one to tackle. Further, the fact that till 1781 it was believed that India had remained outside the theatre of war made it difficult to obtain serious attention for it.

The breakdown of the day-to-day control over the affairs of India, the second cause of the ministry's failure, was due to a combination of circumstances and came about more gradually. The first step in it was, in occasion at least, accidental. The strains of 1776 and 1777 appeared to leave Robinson's indirect control over the Company unshaken. In the election of directors of April 1778, however, it received a shock. Lord Sandwich had insisted that one of his supporters, John Pardoe, should be put forward as a candidate despite his unpopularity in the Company. Sulivan, tired of waiting for government support and no longer, since 1776, an object of hatred to the 'Nabobs', stood singly against him,[1] and to the surprise and annoyance of Robinson was elected. Once in, this formidable and adroit old Company politican began to make his presence felt both by the weight of his personal ability and knowledge and by building up a party around him in the Direction. Within a year Robinson was complaining that he was 'forming a cabal and party in the Direction and is nearly getting a majority'.[2]

Other problems within the Company which disturbed the ministry and hampered their attempts to plan for the future arose out of their past failures to grapple with problems arising in India. The chief of them was the revival of the problem of the administration of Bengal. In April 1778 they learnt that Warren Hastings had repudiated the resignation proffered on his behalf and that, after a spectacular and public clash with Clavering, he was remaining in power. Though a month before this news reached England word had been received from Cairo of the subsequent death of Clavering, an event which inevitably altered the prospects in Bengal, both the king and the ministry were infuriated at what they considered Hastings's ill faith. The king demanded his immediate dismissal,[3] and there was talk of impeachment or of hostile resolutions in the House. In response, however, there was a rally of Hastings's friends as in 1776. John MacPherson assumed the role formerly adopted by Macleane; Sulivan was now in a position to be even more influential in the Company; the Press was brought to bear and there seemed every reason to fear a revival of the conflict of 1776 in which the ministry had received so severe a set-back.[4] With all their other

---

[1] J. Robinson to C. Jenkinson, 9 April 1779. Robinson was struggling to form the list for the 1779 election, in which North had made a 'most entangling promise' which he thought would have 'ruined us this year as Lord Sandwich did the last by Pardoe, which let in Sulivan'. Add. MS. 38211, f. 20. Sulivan's own account of his triumph was that he got in 'with a very high hand' against the 'united and violent efforts of Governors and Directors'. L. Sulivan to W. Hastings, 20 April 1778. Add. MS. 29140, f. 286ᵛ.   [2] Add. MS. 38211, ff. 20–20ᵛ.
[3] The King to North, 17 May 1778. *Correspondence of George III*, iv. 143.
[4] L. Sulivan to W. Hastings, 10 June 1778 (Add. MS. 29141, f. 35), John MacPherson to Hastings, 23 May 1778 (Add. MS. 29140, ff. 424 seq.), and John

troubles and at a time when they hoped soon to introduce an extensive Indian measure, this was a danger not to be taken lightly. Moreover, when they came to consider the problem more coolly, it was apparent to ministers that the death of Clavering presented them with a new situation. If Hastings were recalled they must either find a suitable public man to succeed him or appoint in his place the only survivor of the three newcomers of 1773, Philip Francis.

The second of these alternatives was not a welcome one. For an intelligent man who was aiming at precisely this opportunity, Francis had played his cards very badly. He had intrigued against Clavering as well as Hastings, had earned the reputation of a trouble-maker, and had pushed his own claims too arrogantly. His agent John Bristow, arriving in England in August 1778, found opinion unfavourable to Francis's claims, and Welbore Ellis, Secretary of State for the Northern Department, told him 'very plainly' that 'a man might over-rate his consequence; it was right for him to carry this point as far as he could, and he showed his judgement in stopping at the limits to which it extended'.[1] It was therefore decided to look out for a well-known man, preferably a soldier, to take Hastings's place, and a number of persons were canvassed, the most prominent and suitable of whom was Lord Cornwallis. But no suitable person seems to have been found ready at that time to take on the position and, indeed, it was hard to expect anyone to do so until future plans for India had been decided on. In consequence ministers finally adopted a policy of temporary non-intervention, leaving the problem to be solved with that of the new Indian settlement when the time came. They contented themselves in the meantime with encouraging their supporters among the directors to send out hostile dispatches to Hastings (possibly, as his friends suggested, in the vague hope of forcing him to resign),[2] and Lord North expressed to visitors from India his surprise that 'the directors should for years following censure Hastings in the severest terms, hardly approve of one of his measures, and still continue him in the Government'.[3]

MacPherson to W. Hastings, 13 June 1778 (Add. MS. 29141, f. 52), give the story at some length, John MacPherson with his customary self-congratulations.

[1] J. Bristow to P. Francis, 4 February 1779. MS. Eur. E.17, f. 40.
[2] F. Sykes to W. Hastings, 15 December 1778. Add. MS. 29142, ff. 168–168ᵛ.
[3] J. Bristow to P. Francis, 4 February 1779. MS. Eur. E.17, ff. 34–35.

In 1779, it is true, another crisis seemed to threaten. The receipt of the news that Hastings had defied the directors' instructions to reinstate Francis Fowke, one of Clavering's supporters, led the king to demand categorically that Robinson should obtain Hastings's recall by the Company.[1] But once again the counter-measures of Hastings's friends taught caution, and once again the issue was avoided. On this occasion Philip Francis most nearly reached the object of his ambitions, the Governor-Generalship of India, and for the last time there was the chance of the Rockingham Opposition taking up Hastings's cause.[2] The failure to take measures to prevent conflict between the Supreme Court and the Council also continued; it, too, was to lead to further serious trouble.

This inertia, with the hint of sweeping measures to come, was not only disorganizing for Bengal but disturbing to the relations of Company and Government in England. The agents of both Hastings and Francis were active with threats[3] and offers and even with short-lived proposals of alliance between their principals against the danger of the appointment of a 'great man' from outside,[4] and an atmosphere of East Indian intrigue began to surround the system of indirect control over

[1] The King to North, 11 May 1779. *Correspondence of George III*, iv. 339.
[2] Robinson tried to carry out instructions. Sulivan told Hastings of the excitement caused by Fowke's dismissal and of moves among the directors to petition the king for Hastings's removal, 'I am afraid pressed on by the Minister'. 15 May 1779. Add. MS. 29143, f. 245. John MacPherson (ibid., ff. 269ᵛ seq.) and S. Pechell (ibid., f. 234) gave accounts of how the attack was countered. It is significant that when the Opposition in April 1779 took up again in Parliament the case against Lord Pigot's opponents they made no attempt to revive the accusations so freely made against Hastings in this connexion in 1777, when the ministry had been temporarily well disposed to him on the mistaken assumption that he was going to resign. John MacPherson threatened Lord North to place Hastings's cause in the hands of Opposition on this occasion. John MacPherson to W. Hastings, 17 May 1779. Add. MS. 24143, ff. 271 seq.
[3] John MacPherson used every means of bringing pressure to bear on Lord North, and John Bristow, describing the tactics he and his friends had employed in pushing Francis's claims to the Governor-Generalship, specifically stated, 'we have endeavoured to follow MacPherson's steps in this particular in bullying the Minister' (MS. Eur. E.17, f. 50).
[4] John Bristow had approached some of Hastings's friends in January 1779 with a hint that arrangements might be made for Francis to support Hastings if the latter agreed to retire in Francis's favour in a short time (S. Pechell to W. Hastings, 3 February 1779. Add. MS. 29143, ff. 10 seq.; J. Bristow to P. Francis, 4 February 1779. MS. Eur. E.17, ff. 43 seq.), but soon took fright and revealed their plans to Robinson, who strongly disapproved, after which they dropped the idea.

the Company. Nor was it in any way dispersed by the developments in the Carnatic. Here the major attacks on and accusations against Rumbold, the Governor sent out to restore order after the Pigot affair, were not yet known, but his instructions had obliged him to open up the perennially controversial issue of the Nawab's creditors. Repercussions of this were already reaching England, while the rival agents of the Nawab of Arcot and the Raja of Tanjore were clamorous, and the case against the assailants of Lord Pigot was proceeding with much publicity. A comparatively minor matter, but one of some significance, was that Paul Benfield, who had been recalled to England for his complicity in the Pigot affair, was laying out his funds and intriguing for permission to return to Madras to supervise the collection of his ill-gotten fortune. In the process he had entered into alliance with John MacPherson, thus identifying his cause not only with that of the Nawab his old patron but with that of Warren Hastings.[1]

The combined result of these strains and cross-currents within the Company was that even before the Government raised the two issues of a new East India Bill and the renewal of the Company's charter, Robinson was beginning to find the maintenance of his control over the Company increasingly difficult. It was in 1779 that he confided to Jenkinson his fear that 'the System I have been for near five years fighting for and had been (sic) attained will be kicked down' and exclaimed in despair that he would 'wish joy to the man who can imperceptibly guide that Company . . . because I despair of its being done'.[2] When it is remembered that the renewal of the Company's charter was always the occasion of the extortion from it of a loan or grant to the State, and that any Indian settlement

[1] John MacPherson was very reticent about this connexion in his correspondence with Hastings. For instance, though he entered the House in Benfield's interest in 1779 he gives no indication of this in the letters in which he refers to his new position, merely stating that he had found it necessary in Hastings's interest and that of the Nawab of Arcot to enter Parliament. (Add. MS. 29143, f. 270ᵛ and f. 357.) Benfield is first referred to by the MacPhersons in their correspondence with Hastings at this time after his reinstatement in the General Court, when James MacPherson recommends him to Hastings as one whom the MacPhersons work with and whom they would like Hastings to have as a political friend. While in England he had, MacPherson said, 'secured such a great political line in a certain Assembly that he cannot fail to acquire the round support of Government in his further views in the East'. 1 February 1781. Add. MS. 29147, f. 263.

[2] See pp. 319 seq., above.

involved not only acute personal questions but the whole
unsolved question of the relations of State and Company, the
difficulties which the Government was facing can be understood.
It was not surprising that the pamphleteer, James MacPherson,
with his shrewd and cynical knowledge of the springs that
moved the administration which he served, should prophesy in
a letter to Hastings:

In my own opinion nothing great or manly will be done. Government will borrow a trifle from the Company and receive a trivial
participation of revenue. The Charter will be continued for ten years
longer, and the present form of Government will be extended to
that period. Some man of family and influence will probably apply
for your seat; and, if the Premier can remove you without much
trouble, you have little favour to expect at his hands.[1]

John Robinson, however, though equally well informed was
less cynical and set himself in the summer of 1778 with energy
and optimism to draft a plan to serve as a basis for future action.
To those concerned with India he stressed the importance of
bringing to an end weakness and uncertainty in its Government.[2]
To the king he also pointed out the opportunity afforded by
the renewal of the charter and the reopening of the question of
territorial rights and revenues for the Government to tap new
resources to meet the heavy claims of war expenditure, now
sharply increased by the outbreak of war with France. The
revival of the Company's prosperity since 1773 is reflected in
words that recall the hopes of Chatham's Administration in
1767, when he wrote in the clumsy third person imposed on
royal correspondents:

Mr. Robinson when he turns his thoughts to the East Indies
cannot but with great satisfaction to his mind feel that with prudence
and attention . . . the moment is at hand which he hopes will not
be lost; a fund of wealth and power will arise to this country and the
public which will surprise almost the warmest imagination.[3]

Copies of the memorandum which he prepared are preserved
among the Liverpool papers.[4] He begins his statement with an

---

[1] James MacPherson to W. Hastings, 25 August 1778. Add. MS. 29141, f. 311ᵛ.
[2] Abergavenny MSS. ii. 186. J. Robinson to T. Rumbold (draft), 14 June 1778.
[3] John Robinson to the King, 7 June 1778. Add. MS. 37833, f. 228.
[4] In Add. MSS. 38398 and 39403-4 among the Liverpool MSS. there are several
copies of two undated memoranda on the future of the Company. One can be
dated from internal evidence 1781 (for it see p. 354, n. 3). The other can be shown

outline of the reasons why the Indian question should be settled forthwith; that the charter would soon expire, that the Act of 1773 was also expiring, that the Company's financial position was re-established, and that the time had come to make it resume its contributions to the State which had been suspended at the time of its financial crisis. While it might be possible to treat these problems independently, it would be better to treat them as one issue. If this were done there were three big decisions to be made: (1) what should be the future Government of the Company and its territorial possessions; (2) if the Company should retain the administration of these possessions, what share of the profits arising from them should be claimed by the State, and (3) what should the Company be asked to pay for the extension of its exclusive trading rights?

He dealt with these questions one by one. In reply to the first he maintained that the Government should permit the Company to retain its control over the administration of its Indian territories subject to new regulations which he would discuss later. His views, based equally on principle and expediency, afford the most reasoned contemporary statement of the relations of State and Company with regard to the Indian possessions.

First, I have never yet seen any plan to my satisfaction by which these acquisitions can be properly transferred from the Company to the Government, or by which they are likely to be managed by the Government in a better manner than they may be by the Company, provided the government of it be amended and made subject to the superintendence and frequent control of the Legislature.

Secondly, the change itself would be very difficult and even dangerous in the present moment when we have a rebellion in our Colonies, a Foreign War and many other difficulties to contend with.

Thirdly, the Government of these acquisitions and the commerce carried on in them are from the nature of the people greatly connected and the manner of remitting any part of the revenue of these acquisitions to which the public may be entitled is still more nearly connected with the general trade of the Company, so that, though

to be John Robinson's composition and to date from the summer of 1778. A letter from Robinson to the King of 3 May 1779 (Add. MS. 37834, ff. 68 seq.) describes enclosures—a paper he had written the previous summer with supporting documents. From the description it is clear that he is describing the memorandum to be found in Add. MS. 38398, ff. 107 seq., and documents in Add. MS. 38403, ff. 2 seq.

I do not absolutely say that these objects cannot be separated, I think it more wise and more politic to keep them in some degree united.

Fourthly, I am violently against pledging the revenues and substance of this country for the security of these acquisitions in return for any advantage by way of revenue that may be derived from them, and yet this must be the case if the Government take the management of them into their own hands.

Fifthly, I think that the errors which must be committed in the management of such acquisitions at so great a distance from the seat of Government, had better fall upon the directors of the Company than fall directly upon the Ministers of the King, who in the midst of the difficulties that at present surround them and of the calumnies to which they are necessarily subject, can hardly now retain a sufficient degree of authority and respect for the Government of this country.[1]

Having reached this conclusion, he required a reply to his second question: what share of the profits from these possessions should be claimed by the State? He favoured an arrangement whereby the Company should be permitted to make an annual dividend of 6 per cent., that further profits go to the State until it, too, had received 6 per cent., and that all other profits, whatever their source, should be divided equally between the State and the Company. This arrangement, like the earlier ones from 1767 onward, had the advantage that it could be made without coming to any clear-cut decision on the right of the Company to its territorial possessions. In the conditions then reigning he calculated (over-optimistically as the future was to show) that this would give an annual income of £400,000 to the public and a dividend of 12 per cent. to the proprietors of East Indian Stock. In addition, he considered that the State should claim from the Company the whole or a part of the expenses of any military or naval force sent East of the Cape to protect the Company's territories. The sums should be paid in Indian money in India, thereby checking 'the payment of enormous bills drawn from the East Indies which it is for the interest of the King's servants to draw and for the interest of the Company's servants to encourage'.[2]

In reply to the third question, what should the Company be asked to pay for the extension of its exclusive trading rights,

---

[1] Add. MS. 38398, ff. 108 seq.   [2] Ibid., f. 110.

he maintained that the Company's charter should be renewed for a short period only, so that Parliament would have further occasion to review the Company's administration. He suggested five or seven years as the term and that the Company in return for this privilege should be required to lend £2,000,000 to the State (being empowered to raise bonds for this purpose), half of which might perhaps be free of interest. He pointed out, however, that any advantage gained by the State in a remission of interest on their loan would be offset by the loss to them as participators in the Company's profits.

Turning next from these major decisions to the no-less-important problems of the control of the Company's administration in India and England, he laid down very briefly the outcome of the experience of the last four years. He considered that the institution of a Governor-General and Council had proved extremely useful and should be perpetuated, and that their powers over the Company's settlements should be increased. He suggested means for maintaining the number of the councillors and (touching on an important question which was to become controversial) added: 'It is doubtful whether some special powers should not be given to the Governor-General singly; Hastings and I believe Clavering recommend this.'[1] The Supreme Court of Judicature also seemed to him a useful innovation despite the opposition which it had raised and the mistakes it had made. He thought that with good membership, and some definition of its jurisdiction and of the law it was to administer, it should be retained. The only other points he stressed on the administration of the overseas possessions was that the clause of the 1773 Act restricting the total of bills of exchange to be drawn on England (which he called 'the salvation of the Company') should be retained, and that a clause, suggested for but dropped from the earlier Act, to prohibit dealings with foreign merchants and Companies, should be introduced.

The Regulation of the Company at home he considered even more important. 'Whoever considers', he wrote, 'the nature of our territorial acquisitions in the East Indies and the constitution of the several Courts of Directors and Proprietors by which they are at present governed, will, if he is a wise man,

[1] Add. MS. 38398, f. 113.

confess that nothing can be more absurd and preposterous than the present system.'[1] He urged that the powers of the General Court should be reduced to the declaration of dividends, the election of directors, the ordering of prosecutions, and the passing of by-laws. These last should, however, only be valid if approved by the directors and the king in Council. He also advocated a drastic reorganization of the Court of Directors, on which he considered the State should be directly represented. Half the directors should be nominated by the Crown. It might be thought desirable for these directors to be chosen from among qualified proprietors of East India Stock and for them to be excluded from the committees responsible for the purely commercial activities of the Company. If this measure be thought too strong, however, the Government should demand that all out-letters be submitted to them and that ministerial sanction be obtained for all major measures of policy or finance. But these he considered 'wretched expedients to supply the place of real authority in the Crown, which it ought to have but which in these times Parliament may not be disposed to give it'.[2] The Governor-General, Commander-in-Chief, and councillors should be chosen either by the Crown or by the directors with the Crown's consent, and should be dismissible by the Crown.

This document, which was to be the basis of all discussions for the next three years, was completed by November 1778[3] and submitted to North, Jenkinson, the Chancellor (Lord Thurlow), the Attorney-General (Wedderburn), Lord Mansfield, Welbore Ellis, and others for their consideration. The king was anxious for it to come before the House early in the next session[4] and if the financial arrangements were to come in time to help North's budget there was little time to lose.

[1] Ibid., f. 114v.

[2] Ibid., ff. 116v–117.

[3] J. Robinson to C. Jenkinson, 9 November 1778, hopes to be ready so that North can discuss East Indian plans with the two of them within a few days. Add. MS. 38567, f. 4.

[4] The King to J. Robinson, 12 September 1778. This was partly to avoid bringing 'undigested and little considered points' before Parliament and partly so that 'gentlemen may be relieved from attendance at Easter, for I have ever found that the moment matters of consequence are not under consideration the Houses generally get into matters that rather bear the semblance of faction than the service of the nation'. Add. MS. 37834, f. 15.

Robinson had hoped that it would be before the king and the Cabinet in November.[1]

The difficulties in the way of such a settlement were, however, various and formidable, and they now began to appear. The first of them was the difficulty of getting ministers to consider the proposals, preoccupied as they were with other matters. No papers were submitted to the king until May 1779[2] and though North, Robinson, and Jenkinson had met to discuss the proposals[3] there is no evidence that anyone else in the ministry had given them consideration. Indeed North complained later that the Chancellor, Thurlow, neglected all East Indian papers sent to him, always returning them 'at a great distance of time without any opinion or assistance at all'.[4] Certain steps it is true had to be taken without delay, but they were all of the nature of stop-gaps. Since the last ships of the season sailed for India at the beginning of 1779, for instance, and the appointments of the Governor-General and Council expired the following September, some instructions had to go out before anything was settled. To the disgust of Francis's supporters and the delight of Hastings's friends, it was decided that the Company would have to renew their appointments for another twelve months.[5]

If ministers had reached no decision Robinson was at work on the Company. In February, after some discussions with its leaders he gave them a list of propositions likely, he indicated, to prove acceptable to the ministry as a basis of discussion.[6] These propositions were based on his Memorandum, but contained some further elaborations, including a new suggestion for strengthening government control over the Company by the establishment of a Secret Committee among the directors nominated by the Crown to consider major problems of policy.

[1] J. Robinson to the King, 25 October 1778, ibid., f. 63v.
[2] J. Robinson to the King, 3 May 1779. Add. MS. 37834, f. 68.
[3] Ibid. 38567, f. 4.
[4] Abergavenny MSS. iii. 285. North to J. Robinson, 13 August 1780. *H.M.C.* x. 6, p. 33 and British Museum Facsimile 340 (i), r. 90v.
[5] Francis's agents tried to get this undone when North, obviously hoping to avoid their importunities, pretended he was unaware of it, but without success. J. Bristow to P. Francis, 4 February 1779. MS. Eur. E.17, ff. 47–48. As late as the previous December the issue had not so much as been raised on the Direction. L. Sulivan to W. Hastings, 26 December 1778, and rumours of all kinds were floating round. Add. MS. 29142, f. 238.
[6] A copy is to be found in Add. MS. 38403, f. 2. See Robinson's description of the document and its purpose in Add. MS. 37834, ff. 68 seq.

It is significant, however, that these propositions lay stress only on the financial aspects of the settlement, while those affecting the reorganization of the Company at home and abroad are still left in a vague and general form.

Now the second difficulty began to emerge, the inevitable resistance from within the Company and with it the rise of interest among the parliamentary Opposition in the question. On this occasion, with strong personal ties between some of the Company extremists and a particularly strong parliamentary Opposition, the fight could be expected to be peculiarly fierce and prolonged. The opposition within the Company fell into the hands of those who had co-operated with the Rockingham Opposition in the past. Governor Johnstone, it is true, no longer led it, for he had changed his allegiance during the American War and, after acting as a Commissioner to treat with the Americans, was now in command of a naval squadron,[1] but another of the opposition leaders of 1773, General Richard Smith, was back in the field and in close touch with his old allies.[2]

The prospect of this alliance was unpleasant to the Government, as was also the delay which the recalcitrance of the Company was likely to impose on their financial plans. The war was placing a heavy burden on the nation's finances and North had already (rather prematurely) announced that he expected to balance his budget with a contribution of £1,400,000 from the East India Company.[3] When the directors' reply to the February propositions was received in March,[4] it was both vague on all questions of Company reorganization and precise but exigent on the financial clauses. As late as May it was still hoped, at any rate by North, that some agreement on the financial side of the settlement could be reached, though only at the expense of postponing all consideration of questions of reorganization until the following session. But the attempt broke down and, after a last interview with the Chairman and Deputy of the Company, North decided that it was better to

---

[1] He broke with the Rockingham group on the American question.

[2] See Holzman, op. cit., p. 54. It was stated that he had run through his fortune while gambling with Charles James Fox and was now making interest to obtain lucrative office again in the Company's service.

[3] *Parliamentary Register*, xii. 16.

[4] A copy is in Add. MS. 38403, f. 5.

give up the struggle for the moment, and in consequence that he must renew the 1773 Act for one year, and defer the consideration both of it and the renewal of the charter till next session.[1] A renewing Act was rapidly passed, North admitted in Committee of Supply that the contribution he had hoped for from the East India Company would not be forthcoming,[2] and the first attempt to make a permanent East India settlement had failed.

The issue could only be postponed, however, for a short time and this at the expense of damaging uncertainty in India and increased opportunities for opposition in England. With less optimism but with undiminished energy Robinson took up again his labour of Sisyphus. In August he complained bitterly to Jenkinson that there was 'nothing done or attempting to be done, no attention to the necessary arrangements at home, none to Ireland, nothing to India and very little to foreign affairs',[3] since North could not be brought to concentrate on them. A few days later North, pressed to consider the Indian question, broke out into laments that he had no time and that everything fell on him.[4] Nevertheless, by 11 September 1779 Robinson had brought him to the point of wishing to see Jenkinson and Welbore Ellis to decide what propositions should be made to the Company[5] and by the end of the month Robinson after working eighteen hours a day on it produced a new draft which he sent to Jenkinson and which he hoped North would submit to the Cabinet.[6] By 18 October a memorandum was ready and would seem to have been given some sanction by ministers, for by November informal discussions with Directors were in train,[7] but even then the issue was not energetically pressed. In December, Robinson was again complaining that he could not focus the attention of Lord North or the Chancellor on it.[8]

---

[1] J. Robinson to the King, 3 May 1779. Add. MS. 37834, ff. 68 seq.
[2] *Parliamentary Register*, xiii. 121.
[3] J. Robinson to C. Jenkinson, 11 August 1779. Add. MS. 38212, ff. 56–57ᵛ.
[4] J. Robinson to C. Jenkinson, 16 August 1779. Ibid., f. 62.
[5] J. Robinson to C. Jenkinson, 11 September 1779. Ibid., f. 92ᵛ.
[6] J. Robinson to C. Jenkinson, 27 September 1779. Ibid., ff. 116 seq. Robinson was working concurrently on the Irish question.
[7] J. Robinson to C. Jenkinson, 9 November 1779. Add. MS. 38567, f. 10.
[8] J. Robinson to C. Jenkinson, 11 December 1779. Add. MS. 38212, f. 281. He enclosed a draft of his own of a reply to the Secret Committee of the East India Company.

Nevertheless, Robinson's negotiations with the directors brought some result for at the end of January 1780 they submitted some propositions, which Robinson thought better than anything hitherto offered though not yet good enough.[1] These proposals the Government was prepared to adopt as a basis for discussion. But at this point they ran into their next difficulty. If the ministry thought the directors' proposals not favourable enough, the Company opposition considered them too favourable and, led by General Smith, a formidable body of opposition was quickly built up in the General Court. On 18 February a vote against a part of the directors' propositions was carried by 311 to 278.[2] Much worse was to follow. Ten days later General Richard Smith and three other proprietors submitted to a General Court eight propositions allegedly designed to serve as a basis for negotiation with the Government but so uncompromising that they were obviously intended rather to torpedo it; the Court jubilantly accepted them by a vote of 466 to 192 and instructed the Chairman and Deputy, accompanied by General Smith and one of his supporters, to present them to Lord North.[3] The Company had got, as so often during such negotiations, completely out of hand. Moreover, as was to be expected, it was not long before the effects of this were seen in Parliament. North, in an attempt to bring the Company to reason, threatened to terminate their charter at the end of the three years' notice incorporated in its terms, and introduced a measure in the House to give weight to the threat.[4] The Rockingham group in opposition promptly rallied to the side of their allies in the Company and, in a rambling debate on East Indian affairs, Burke stigmatized the proposal as 'the most wicked, absurd, abandoned, profligate, mad, and drunken intention that ever was formed'.[5] The Company Opposition, in return, gave its help to its parliamentary friends on one of the issues on which these were baiting the Government, the attempt to exclude Government contractors from Parliament on the grounds that grants of contracts were being made for political

---

[1] The terms are included in an abstract in Add. MS. 38404, ff. 374[v] seq. Robinson refers to them in a letter to Jenkinson of 30 January 1780. Add. MS. 38213, f. 89[v].

[2] Court Book 88, p. 506.   [3] Court Book 88, pp. 512–35.

[4] *Parliamentary Register*, xvii. 388–9.

[5] *Parliamentary Register*, xvii. 392.

reasons. The Company Opposition, echoing their protests, tried to get all directors holding Government contracts (these were of course the most prominent ministerial supporters in the Court) excluded from the Direction.[1]

The combined results of the feelings roused by the negotiations in the Company, of the clamours of parliamentary and Company Opposition, and of the growing discredit of the ministry in the country were very alarming to those managing its affairs for Administration. The anxiety about the Government's hold there, expressed by Robinson as early as 1779, now sharply increased. Even the closest supporters of Administration among the directors were showing an alarming tendency to trim their sails.[2] When the approach of the annual election of directors brought all these tendencies to a head, it became clear to those concerned in Company affairs that, not only was there to be a direct challenge to the ministry's power there, but that there was every chance of it being successful.

All interest in the proposed plans for India was thus submerged while the fight for the ministry's control in the Company went forward. When it ended, the ministry emerged with its authority shaken but intact, but only at the expense of a complete revolution in its alliances within the Company. In April 1780 North and Robinson reluctantly dropped the hostility to Sulivan which had been their consistent policy since 1773 and entered into what has been called that 'curious coalition'[3] with him, the results of which were to be so much more far-reaching than a mere change of personal alliances at India House. The steps by which this change of policy was reached were gradual. Ever since John MacPherson had returned to England he and his cousin had been working (with the interests of Warren Hastings in view) to get North and Robinson to come to terms with Sulivan. In 1778 James

[1] Court Book 88, p. 582, 22 March 1780. A by-law to this effect was proposed, but when the directors sought legal opinion on its validity, the reply was doubtful, and at a further General Court on 30 March, the question was postponed indefinitely (ibid., pp. 601–2).

[2] Even in 1779 Robinson had been complaining of the Government supporters. 'Sir George Wombwell has behaved badly . . . of late in Leadenhall St., affecting to be patriot there and to lay his own ground.' J. Robinson to C. Jenkinson, 9 April 1779. Add. MS. 38211, ff. 20ᵛ–21.

[3] H. Dodwell, *E.H.R.*, 1925, p. 376, 'Warren Hastings and the Assignment of the Carnatic'.

MacPherson told Hastings that they had failed. 'Words are always fair, but no confidence is granted. There are, it would appear, some old sins which cannot be forgiven.'[1] In 1779 they continued their attempts with no more success.[2] At the beginning of 1780, however, when the ministry was meeting with its first serious checks in the General Court on their proposed East India Settlement, Sulivan sent an offer to Robinson through James MacPherson, offering his influence to obtain terms favourable for the Government in return for an alliance. This offer still went unregarded. Sulivan told Hastings that the ministry would like to know what his offer entailed but 'as power and protection did not seem secured to me, I wait for a better hour'.[3]

No further steps were taken till the election was imminent. Early in April it became clear that a joint attack was to be made on the ministerialist supporters by the Company Opposition under General Smith and by Sulivan and his supporters. On 5 April a large meeting of proprietors was held at which a Committee of thirteen, representing a balance of the two opposition interests, was elected to choose a Proprietors' list for the coming election.[4] When the directors drew up their House list, Sulivan and six other directors (representing a variety of interests) refused to sign it.[5]

The House list was drawn up, in the way customary when conflict was not desired, to bring back into the Court all directors out by rotation who wished to stand. It included those prominent supporters of administration, Sir George Wombwell, John Roberts, and Thomas Cheap. The Proprietors' list accepted the other three candidates (one of whom was an old follower of the Rockingham party, Robert Gregory) but in place of the government supporters offered the names of three opponents of the Government, two of them well-known supporters of Sulivan. That the threat to the ministry this time was

[1] 25 August 1778. Add. MS. 29141, f. 312ᵛ.
[2] Add. MS. 29143, ff. 29 and 53ᵛ.
[3] L. Sulivan to W. Hastings, 5 February 1780 Add. MS. 29144, ff. 333–333ᵛ. Cf. Abergavenny MSS. iii. 241. James MacPherson to J. Robinson of the same date.
[4] *London Chronicle*, 1780, p. 336. Cf. Court Book 88, pp. 633–4.
[5] *London Chronicle*, p. 347. Of the six following him, H. Fletcher, W. G. Freeman, J. Manship, J. Moffat, T. Bates Rous, and Nathaniel Smith, only Freeman was his personal supporter.

a real one is suggested by the attitude of the Press and the comments of contemporaries. The actions of the ministry show that they fully endorsed this view. Two days after the public meeting there are signs that Robinson and Sandwich had come to the conclusion that it was necessary to split the opposition by offering terms to Sulivan. On 12 April, the day before the election, the alliance was sealed at a solemn meeting at which the MacPhersons, Robinson, North, and Sandwich were present and to which the Government's main supporters in the Company were later added.[1] Sulivan was promised the position of Deputy Chairman and the support of the ministry for himself in England and Warren Hastings in Bengal, as long as their 'actions may meet public approbation'.[2] In return for this he was to arrange a secret betrayal of his present allies in the Company Opposition by his personal supporters.

The results of this coup were what had been hoped for. At the election the change of forces was just sufficient to swing the tide. In addition to the three double-listed candidates, two Government supporters (Sir George Wombwell and Thomas Cheap) and one supporter of opposition were elected. When it came to the election of the Chairman and Deputy of the new Court, the Government nominees were successful.[3] Though the ministry could not be certain that the directors would be able to control the proprietors, when they resumed negotiations on their settlement, at least they had averted the danger of a hostile Court of Directors as well.

That there was a wider significance to the change both at home and abroad was, however, generally realized by those concerned in the Company's affairs. At home, it caused a good deal of indignation. John Manship, hitherto a supporter, said

[1] Abergavenny MSS. iii. 250 and 251. Sandwich to J. Robinson, 7 April 1780, and reply from Robinson of the same day. Cf. John MacPherson to W. Hastings, 28 April 1780. Add. MS. 29145, f. 61, and J. Woodhouse to W. Hastings, 1 August 1780, ff. 326 seq.

[2] L. Sulivan to W. Hastings, 14 April 1780. Add. MS. 29145, f. 18.

[3] Some care and address was needed to make the alliance work. Abergavenny MSS. iii. 253. James MacPherson to J. Robinson, 13 April 1780: 'S—n has quietly brought forward his party to meet any exertions to support him on your side . . . the greatest address and secrecy has been observed to direct the passions of men to the point requisite. . . . He seems to think that if you will reconcile James, Woodhouse and Stables, everything will go as we wish; but for the sake of absolute security the pulse of others should be felt.'

he would 'rather see the Devil than Sulivan in the Chair unless he came through his friends'.[1] The effects to be expected abroad were shown by the fact that Wedderburn, as Philip Francis's chief patron, sent for John MacPherson and tried through him to get Sulivan to compensate Francis with office outside Bengal, where Hastings's power would now be confirmed.[2] Sulivan refused and in any case it was too late. Already an emissary from Francis was on the way home with the threat that if he was not appointed Governor-General he would return and lay before Parliament his account of the Government of India during the past four years.[3] In August of this year he fought his duel with Hastings and in December embarked for England.

The stir which this revolution caused within the Company was justified by immediate and by long-term results. In the first place by it the Government had abdicated much of the internal control they had recently been exercising over the Company, and the consequences were both good and bad. On the debit side was the immediate revival of some of the practices within the Company which had been at least checked in the last seven years. A lucrative job for Sulivan's son at the Court of the Raja of Tanjore caused, it is true, so much objection from the parliamentary Opposition stirred up by Edmund Burke that Sulivan was forced to withdraw under ministerial pressure. It was put to him that it 'was not a time for Parliament to be broke in upon by matter foreign to the immediate object of its attention, the war and the means of supporting that war', and a compromise was arrived at.[4] On the other

---

[1] J. Woodhouse to W. Hastings, 1 August 1780. Add. MS. 29145, f. 326ᵛ. There were eight votes against Sulivan's election to the position of Deputy Chairman. Some of his opponents later made terms with him.

[2] John MacPherson to W. Hastings, 28 April 1780. Add. MS. 29145, f. 61. Wedderburn apparently took this action even before the new alliance became public.

[3] P. Francis's Instructions to Major Baggs, 1 January 1780. MS. Eur. E.17, ff. 473–5. Baggs was urged to present this intimation, however, in a way that 'must imply defence not menace'.

[4] R. Barwell to W. Hastings, 15 September 1780. Add. MS. 29145, ff. 517–517ᵛ. The Burkes were in touch with Charles Jenkinson at this time both directly and through Lady Waldegrave as an intermediary about alleged injustices to the Raja of Tanjore, including an attempt by Sulivan stated by Edmund, with characteristic extravagance, to be no less than to hand over the whole revenue of Tanjore to his 'son and some other of his creatures'. (Add. MS. 38404, ff. 166 seq. and Add. MS. 38308, ff. 12ᵛ seq.) This would appear to be the same story and if so Jenkinson intervened in it.

hand the rather feeble protests of Lord North against the reinstatement of the Madras servants who had deposed Lord Pigot remained quite unheeded.[1] (He had urged the danger of 'the appearance of a factious desire of assisting their own friends, without attending properly to the peace of these settlements and to the maintenance of the authority of the Company'.) Nor was it surprising, when the other Madras servants had been reinstated, that even government supporters are found actively supporting the claims of Paul Benfield, when he too demanded permission to return. The motion was pushed through the General Court despite the protests of a powerful group of directors and an opposition in the General Court, led for the first time by Edmund Burke himself, on principles of justice and purity of administration. Benfield's cause was not only pressed by a well-known supporter of administration, the contractor, Richard Atkinson (who was personally associated with him), but George Selwyn, who voted with administration, was pressed to give him a vote. 'I took that man to have been a pirate', he wrote, 'till lately that Lord Bathurst asked me to go and give my vote for him at the India House, which I did.'[2]

The breakdown of Robinson's control is shown in this revival of the unabashed party spoils system within the Company which, though certainly not abolished since 1773, had been kept within the bounds of contemporary canons of respectability.

On the other hand, the revolution had certain public advantages. Not only did Sulivan introduce a vitality into the Direction that had been unknown there for seven years, but for the first time both Company and Government were working to assist their able if intransigent Governor-General rather than to thwart him, though the slowness of communications and the autocratic temper which his struggles had encouraged in him did much to neutralize the benefits of this belated change. Sulivan hoped much from the reorganization of the Company

---

[1] North to J. Robinson, 29 May 1780. 'When you see the India gentlemen today you will let them know again that my opinion that it is not for the [good] of the Public or the Company to send back to the Coast of Coromandel or to employ as yet in any station in India, any of their servants who were concerned on either side in the late troubles at Madras.' Abergavenny MSS. iii. 260.

[2] *H.M.C., Carlisle MSS.*, p. 452. For the steps by which the motion was pressed through see Court Book 89, pp. 56 seq. It was first raised on 4 May 1780 and finally passed by ballot on 24 January 1781.

proposed in the new settlement, but even in advance of this did all he could to strengthen the Governor-General's position. It is in this light that certain highly controversial appointments which were made at this time and for which the administration and Sulivan must share the blame or credit, must be considered. One of them, the appointment of Lord Macartney as Governor of Madras, which was pushed through in the teeth of the Company and Parliament Opposition, was certainly a good one and the first serious step taken to clear the Augean stables of the Carnatic. The other, that of John MacPherson to Hastings's Council, was as certainly a bad one, though the Government do not seem to have realized that, and for this the Government, who pushed their protégé on an unwilling Sulivan, must bear most of the blame.[1] Both of them were intended to give Hastings men he could work with. That neither of them did so was due no doubt to faults on both sides.

Whatever the details, the total result of these developments was that the future of Hastings and Sulivan became bound up with the continuance of the administration, and the administration, after all its attempts to remove him, became responsible for Hastings's Indian policy. For both sides this situation contained elements of danger; for Hastings the growing weakness and disrepute of the ministry; for the administration the possibility, which was soon to become an actuality, that things would go badly wrong in India. Already the continuance of the Mahratta War was causing uneasiness and already the financial position of the Company on which Robinson had based his estimates of the contribution which the State could expect for the renewal of the charter was deteriorating. How embarrassing this might become was already being shown by the intensifica-

[1] R. Barwell to W. Hastings, 15 September 1780. Add. MS. 29145, ff. 517 seq. L. Sulivan to W. Hastings, 23 October 1780, 29146, ff. 175 seq. F. Sykes to W. Hastings, 14 January 1781, 29147, ff. 119 seq. L. Sulivan was embarrassed by the rival candidature of George Vansittart, however, and not by any doubts as to MacPherson's suitability. Hastings's confidence in him as a loyal supporter had begun to wane before his arrival in India. Scott to W. Hastings, 18 February 1781, written from Madras on his way to England. Colonel Cummings made this remark of John MacPherson 'that he believed he was much attached to you and would wish to serve you faithfully as far as it did not interfere with his own views of obtaining a seal on the Supreme Council for himself, or as far as the interest of Mahomed Ally [the Nawab of Arcot] was concerned—but that these were his grand points and of course your business only a secondary consideration to him. This is a confirmation of your own opinion.' Add. MS. 29148, ff. 35ᵛ–36.

tion of the interest of the parliamentary opposition in Indian affairs. So long as the Government remained hostile to Hastings, the opposition limited its attacks on Indian affairs to the problems of Madras; but when the object of Francis's unceasing attacks became also the protégé of the Government; when his chief supporter in the Company became the leader of the directors in close touch with administration; and when his friends and his agent were closely associated with the interests of the Nawab of Arcot and of Paul Benfield, the line for the opposition was only too clear. Only a few weeks after the April election, General Smith began to inveigh both in the Company and the House against the continuance of the Mahratta War and to raise issues affecting the Governor-General.

The effects of this development, however, became only gradually apparent. In the meantime the effects of the change on the Government's East India proposals were of more immediate interest. By the time the election was over, it was once again too late to hope to get a settlement through before Parliament went into recess and consequently in May, almost without comment, a further Act was passed renewing existing legislation for still another year.[1] A permanent settlement seemed as far away as ever. But Robinson was soon to find new allies in the struggle in which for three years he had made no progress. Within the Company itself he could now rely on the energies of Sulivan who took the matter up actively[2] and ministers who had hitherto been indifferent also suddenly, if belatedly, began to press for a solution. North was exasperated to learn that in August the Chancellor, hitherto indifferent to the subject, had now taken it up and complained to the king that nothing was being done.[3] It was presumably as a result of this new interest on his part that soon after the vigorous and competent Henry Dundas began to join forces with Robinson and Jenkinson in trying to work out a satisfactory arrangement. With the alarms of the Gordon Riots behind them and with the ministry a good deal strengthened by the public concern at this outbreak, Robinson again urged North to take it up during his

[1] 20 Geo. III, c. 56.
[2] L. Sulivan to W. Hastings, 23 October 1780. Add. MS. 29146, ff. 175 seq.
[3] Abergavenny MSS. iii. 285. North to J. Robinson, 13 August 1780. British Museum Facsimile 340 (i), f. 90ᵛ.

summer vacation, offering him an abstract and sketch of a Bill
to read and assuring him:

That business must now be met in its full extent; the time left
before the expiration of the Charter is barely sufficient to regulate
a constitution to take place. I own I don't see the business, although
of great magnitude, yet so very difficult as to be insurmountable or
to be very discouraging.[1]

He concluded by pointing out that his views had received a
good deal of support and that if North approved the principles
on which he should work he would dedicate the recess to
putting the measure into shape.

Once again, however, he was destined to be disappointed
and this time for a reason which could not be denied. Even as
he wrote, it was decided to seize the opportunity of the reaction
against the Gordon Riots to dissolve Parliament and to hold an
unexpected General Election in the autumn. Robinson, even
more than other members of administration, was submerged
beneath the business of election-management and the excitement of contested seats.[2] Even when it was over and the
Company in November put forward some further proposals,
North's illness led to further delays.[3]

It was not till January 1781 that Indian matters once more
came to the fore. Throughout the month Robinson was again
in correspondence with Jenkinson about a paper for submission
to the Cabinet.[4] On the 12th he even held a meeting with
Edmund Burke ostensibly to consider his views on a settlement
in the Carnatic but in fact covering a much wider range of
subjects.[5] By the beginning of February he was again in despair.

[1] Ibid. 286. J. Robinson to North, 14 August 1780. British Museum Facsimile
340 (i), ff. 102–103ᵛ.
[2] W. T. Laprade, *Parliamentary Papers of John Robinson, 1774–1784*, 1922, pp.
31 seq.   [3] Court Book 89, pp. 364–5.
[4] J. Robinson to C. Jenkinson, 18 January 1781, Add. MS. 38405, ff. 8–9, and
J. Robinson to C. Jenkinson, 20 January 1781, Add. MS. 38215, f. 215.
[5] Minutes of conversation with Edmund Burke on East Indian affairs. Add.
MS. 38405, f. 10. This was the outcome of some contact between Wedderburn
(now Lord Loughborough) and Edmund Burke, of which the first record is
Loughborough's letter of 10 October 1780. FitzWilliam MSS. (Sheffield). Burke
had been trying to ensure the good will of Lord Macartney for his cousin William in
Madras, and the question of policy towards the country powers was raised.
Loughborough in a further letter of 4 January 1781 said he had spoken to North and
Robinson on the question and found their views not dissimilar in principle, and a
private meeting was arranged.

It was Thurlow, the Chancellor, who, as before, came to his assistance. He had, he complained, heard rumours that a settlement had been reached without his knowledge. Assured that they were false he said he was sorry to hear it since he 'was ready to adopt the general conclusion that any decision must be better than none', that things were going from bad to worse and that nothing would be achieved if the matter were dealt with 'by those who can only speculate upon the matter instead of those who can act in it'.[1]

This time his intervention was successful. Soon after there was a 'meeting of the servants of Government when the business was fully discussed' and it was agreed that 'a plan should be prepared on which Parliament might properly proceed to settle by their authority this great concern with the consent of the Company if they could be induced by any honorable means to give it, but without their consent should they still continue to be refractory'.[2] At this meeting, judging from allusions in Jenkinson's correspondence, he was asked to draw up the plan, and a document among his manuscripts, which modifies and brings up to date Robinson's outline of 1778, can be shown from internal evidence to be the result.[3]

The document begins by describing in terms which Robinson must have warmly approved the territorial possessions of the East India Company as the 'most fertile source of wealth . . . at present available to Great Britain both in the commercial gains accruing therefrom, the contributions made in customs duties to the public revenue and in the direct share in the territorial revenues which until the stoppage in 1773 the State had enjoyed'. After a brief account of the events from 1773 onward and of the recent abortive attempts to achieve a permanent

[1] Thurlow to J. Robinson, 13 February 1781. Abergavenny MSS. iv. 347.

[2] Our only record of this meeting seems to be this reference in the memorandum drawn up as a result of it. Add. MS. 38404, f. 72ᵛ.

[3] This document is the second of the undated and unsigned memoranda of which copies are preserved in the Liverpool MSS. See p. 337, n. 4. There are rough drafts in Add. MS. 38398, ff. 70 seq. and Add. MS. 38404, ff. 57 seq. of parts of the finished document. There is a fair copy of the whole in the same MS., ff. 64 seq. It can be dated fairly accurately from internal evidence and there is also internal evidence of Jenkinson's authorship, though the issue is confused by the incorporation in it of large sections of Robinson's memorandum of 1778, which in effect it is bringing up to date. Letters from Robinson to Jenkinson in March and April 1781 referring to 'your paper' and to specific proposals in it provide external evidence to the same effect. Add. MS. 38405, ff. 66 and 70–71ᵛ.

settlement, he concluded that there were three possible means of making such a settlement to the satisfaction of the public interest; either the State must take into its own hands the territories and revenues in the possession of the Company; or it must make a new Company with a new charter to supplant the old one on terms satisfactory to the State; or it must impose on the existing Company by Act of Parliament the terms which it considered necessary. The first of these alternatives he repudiated by quoting verbatim the case against it put forward by Robinson in 1778. The second he rejected on the analogy of the experience of William III, without troubling to go into the details of the intricate problems involved. He therefore came down strongly in favour of the third and argued that Parliament must be prepared to pass legislation both to obtain a share of the Company's revenues for the State and to reorganize and regulate its working. Though such intervention might be opposed as an attack on propertied rights, it was one which could be justified by the argument of necessity. The Company as it stood was quite unfit to control what had become 'a great engine of Government'.

He then proceeded to outline a plan of operations. The House should call for papers and should go into Committee to consider the present position of the East India Company and its future settlement. If the Company under this threat were prepared to accept an amicable agreement no serious problem would arise; but if it did not he could see no way for ministers to avoid making the claim, which they had been successful in avoiding during some twelve years of controversy, that the right to the Company's territorial possessions rested with the Crown. The least controversial way of doing this was, he considered, for the Crown's claims to be stated, but at the same time an assurance be given that for expediency's sake the Company would be permitted to remain in occupation of these territories, and that the charter granting it exclusive trade would be renewed for a period of years to enable it to maintain the administration of these territories. A claim for a share in the Company's profits and for a contribution to the expenses of Crown forces employed in the East should follow. The existing limit of the drawing of bills from the Company's Indian possessions on London should be retained.

Jenkinson then passed to the consideration of the reorganization of the Company's government both overseas and at home, but feeling that the complicated issues here raised required a good deal of further thought he framed his proposals as expressions of opinion rather than as resolutions. The general principles on which he thought decisions should be based were cautious but showed an appreciation of aspects of Indian administration then uncommon.

Parliament should be careful not to meddle too much in this business; they should leave to the Company everything in which they can safely be trusted and the Company will in my opinion act wisely in giving great discretionary power to the Governor-General and Council, being very careful however to chuse proper persons for the execution of so great a trust.[1]

He went more fully into questions of Indian administration than Robinson had done. Like Robinson, however, he considered that the general principles of the 1773 Regulating Act should stand. He stated them as being: the union of the Company's settlements under one authority in India; the separation of the executive power in Bengal (where the problems of territorial control arose) from those of the judicial authority so far as concerned all British subjects resident there; and the exclusion of the Supreme Executive from all participation in trade. To implement these principles he considered that a number of further regulations should be enforced. He suggested the means whereby the Governor-General could on occasion over-ride the Council which Dundas was to adopt in 1783. He endorsed Robinson's proposal for maintaining the size of the Council by co-optation if necessary, and he considered that better measures should be taken to ensure the control of the central administration over the Presidencies and to keep the Governor-General informed of all instructions sent out from home. For the appointment of the Governor-General and Council he approved the temporary arrangements laid down for the replacement of officials in the Regulating Act—appointment by the Company with the consent of the Crown. In this way the Crown would escape the accusation that it was increasing its own patronage yet be able to prevent the appointment

---

[1] Add. MS. 38404, ff. 78ᵛ–79.

of unsuitable men by the Company—an interesting recognition of what was to contemporaries the most politically vulnerable aspect of the growth of State authority over the Company. He then proceeds to review the Bengal constitutional issues most at dispute between Hastings and Francis. He comes down on the whole on Francis's side on the question of land settlement and on Hastings's on that of the judicial system. On the existing Court of Judicature he makes scathing and well-justified comments on the failure of 'four professional men sent from this country with vast emoluments' to show 'wisdom and liberality enough to have put this business on a tolerable footing',[1] and he suggests a variety of judicial reforms as well as some minor miscellaneous measures including those already suggested by Robinson.

On Indian affairs, therefore, he goes farther than Robinson without disagreeing with him. On the home affairs of the Company he is, on the other hand, far more cautious. He begins, it is true, by advocating as the best policy 'if we were able to do all that is right or if it was prudent in the present state of affairs to attempt it' all that Robinson had suggested; but it is significant that what Robinson suggested in 1778 seemed to him in 1781 unattainable ideals, and he fell back on what Robinson thought miserable expedients. In view of the prevailing political temper Jenkinson clearly thought that the Government would be unwise to take any steps which seemed to increase their power over, and patronage within, the Company. The farthest he thought they dared to go was to introduce the provision already suggested by Robinson giving them the scrutiny of all out-letters from as well as in-letters to the Company, and to lay down that the Company's Governors should consider themselves obliged to obey all instructions from the Crown conveyed to them through the directors. In this way he argued the Crown could gradually assume control over all questions of policy in India, leaving all matters of administration, trade, and revenue in the Company's hands, subject to advice and admonition from ministers. To implement these proposals, he suggested that as many as might be approved should be expressed as resolutions and moved in Committee of the House at the same time as the other resolutions. There should then

[1] Add. MS. 38404, f. 85ᵛ.

be an adjournment for a fortnight to enable the Company to consider these terms, during which some modifications might be made if necessary to meet them. If they did not come to terms, which he thought they would, the measure should be imposed upon them without their consent.

There were two important variations in these proposals from those earlier brought forward by Robinson. Both involved a diminution of the State's claims. The first was financial and reflected the deterioration of the Company's financial position caused by the continuance of the Mahratta War in India and the inevitable increase of trading costs which accompanied the maritime war in which Great Britain was involved. There was no longer any suggestion that the Company should pay a large sum down for the renewal of its charter. Attention was concentrated on the annual sums it should pay the State from its profits as a share of its territorial gains and on the contribution it should make towards the Crown's military and naval expenses in the East. The former was indeed made retrospective to cover the years since the Company had extracted itself from its financial difficulties, but the sum involved was small compared with that which Robinson, basing himself on former payments for the renewal of the charter, had been thinking of. Subsequent events proved only too clearly how wise this caution was.

The second difference was in the dropping of all measures for the reorganization of the Company at home and for increasing the Government's control over it. This change was much more serious. For the moment things were still going fairly smoothly for the Government in the Court of Directors; the annual elections were uncontested and Sulivan had succeeded to the Chair, and even in the Court of Proprietors the opposition was less forceful than it had been. Sulivan, however, had been assuming that some of the measures adumbrated for the reorganization of the Company would be incorporated in a new Act and had been relying on them for the future.[1] When he began to realize that nothing was likely to be done he began to show uneasiness. Unless there were some constitutional changes he would be out of the Direction in 1782 by rotation

[1] L. Sulivan to W. Hastings, 23 October 1780. Add. MS. 29146, ff. 175 seq. L. Sulivan to W. Hastings, 3 February 1781. Add. MS. 29147, ff. 296 seq. By 8 June he is less certain. Add. MS. 29149, f. 243.

and a number of the strongest supporters of administration would go out with him. The supporters of opposition within the Direction included some vigorous men, especially Henry Fletcher, whose importance would be enhanced by the disappearance of Sulivan and other leaders, and if the next April election went badly for administration—as might well be the case for reasons both peculiar to the Company and general to the position of the Government—Sulivan foresaw, or maintained that he did, the possibility of a hostile Direction.[1] His warnings and proposals, including a somewhat naïve one to make all directors 'past the chair' (and therefore himself) permanent,[2] were met with vague assurances that something would be done, possibly in later legislation. There was an evasiveness in these replies, however, which showed (as well perhaps as some scepticism of Sulivan's disinterestedness) that others shared Jenkinson's fear of laying themselves open to the charge that their Indian measures would increase the influence of the Crown.

These new proposals made good progress. We do not know on what date they were accepted in principle, but by 23 April Jenkinson and Robinson, now joined in their activities by Dundas, had resolutions and even a Bill drawn up and the matter was brought forward in the Commons.[3] Now Jenkinson's confidence and the work in the Company of Sulivan began to be justified. The following day the Chairman and Deputy brought propositions, though not yet acceptable ones, from the Company,[4] and though the struggle was fierce and at one time it looked as if force would have to be employed, in the end the spirit of compromise triumphed. On 24 June, right at the end of the session, Robinson was able to announce that Sulivan and his Deputy had brought terms on the basis of which ministers were prepared to make a compromise;[5] the Bill incorporating them passed the Commons without controversy on 3 July and

[1] J. Scott to W. Hastings, 20 January 1782, Add. MS. 29152, f. 336, and L. Sulivan to W. Hastings, 20 January 1782, ibid., ff. 433 seq.

[2] L. Sulivan to W. Hastings, 8 June 1781. Add. MS. 29149, f. 243.

[3] J. Robinson to C. Jenkinson, 23 April 1781. Add. MS. 38405, f. 109.

[4] Add. MS. 38405, f. 115. Compare letters from Robinson to Jenkinson about them, ff. 112–14 and 118–118ᵛ.

[5] J. Robinson to C. Jenkinson, 24 June 1781. Add. MS. 38407, ff. 154 seq. This was the result of great efforts on the part of Robinson and his allies, both in the Direction and General Court of the Company, as other correspondence in the volume shows.

the Lords, informed that it was accepted by both Company and Government, accepted it as it stood.[1]

The settlement which emerged from this long and weary struggle was, however, a miserably shrunken thing. The charter was renewed for ten years and the participation of the State in the Company's profits (an illusory advantage as it soon proved) was assured. So too was a contribution by the Company to the military and naval expenses incurred in the East. Some minor regulations for India were included, of which the most important was perhaps the right of the Government to see the Company's out-letters, but all major ones were postponed for incorporation in further legislation which was promised in a vague way. No public reference was made to the reorganization of the Company at home. In short a settlement of a sort rejected in 1779 was accepted with relief in 1781.

The course of this decline in expectations can be traced in letters to India. Both Robinson and James MacPherson warned Hastings not to place much faith in resolutions from home 'for the settling of which', MacPherson said, 'I fear we have not sufficient spirit or unanimity at home'.[2] In May, Richard Barwell, now returned from Bengal, wrote: 'I do not believe my Lord North, although he has thrown it out in private discourse and in public debate, dares to propound those strong measures he has declared necessary for the better regulation of the Government of India.'[3] Sulivan was for some time rather more hopeful. 'Lord N[orth]', he wrote on 2 June, 'wants nerves. All capital resolutions are postponed', but 'your extensive powers he will *hardly* drop, he confesses the necessity of continuing me in the Direction (I am out by rotation in April) and I do not despair of his effecting it';[4] but six days later he is exclaiming:

The timidity of Lord N. is not to be accounted for. He has already agitated and carried the most obnoxious questions against an opposition so feeble as scarcely to deserve the name. Yet he scruples to bring on the essential regulations, though he feels them so necessary; such as, *clearly* extending the authority of the Governor-General and

[1] 21 Geo. III, c. 65. See *Parliamentary Register* (Debrett), iv. 384–7.
[2] James MacPherson to W. Hastings, 10 March 1781. Add. MS. 29148, f. 94. Cf. John Robinson (ibid., f. 40), 19 February 1781.
[3] R. Barwell to W. Hastings, 31 May 1781. Add. MS. 29149, f. 129.
[4] Ibid., f. 173ᵛ.

Council over all India; and making you Dictator; arming the Directors with greater powers; and preventing those who have passed the chairs from being excluded by rotation.[1]

On 15 August, forwarding the Act as it was finally passed, he called it 'a paltry performance'.[2] The only consolation he could offer was the possibility of supplementary legislation next session, but even here 'I, who have experienced so much indecision, have my doubts'. He gave Hastings a list of the most likely regulations both for India (where he thought it likely that the power of the Governor-General and Council over the Presidencies would be increased but doubted whether the former would be given 'Dictatorial authority' though many in the Cabinet thought he should and 'I broach it as my own everywhere') and for England, where he hoped for a clause 'to continue the six gentlemen in the Direction who are else out by rotation next April'. 'Upon these and other points', he concludes, 'I *only* and Mr. Robinson are to meet confidentially in a few days.'[3]

His fears were better justified than his hopes. No further Indian legislation was to be expected from North's Administration. Though it was not till November 1781 that North received the news of the surrender of Cornwallis at Yorktown 'as a man a ball in his heart', and not till March 1782 that he finally forced the king to admit that his government was over, since the preceding summer all initiative had departed from his administration.

In East Indian affairs it had been already undermined, as a result of two developments. The first arose early in 1781 when news had been received from Bengal both of a climax in the friction between the judicature and the executive in Bengal (the solution of which the Government had for so long been shelving) and of a simultaneous crisis in the Court's unpopularity with the English inhabitants there.[4] The issue, though vexatious, was not one on which Government and Opposition

---

[1] 8 June 1781. Ibid., f. 243.
[2] Add. MS. 29150, f. 98ᵛ.   [3] Ibid., f. 99ᵛ.
[4] A petition to the House was received from the European inhabitants of Bengal and, before it had been dealt with, a petition from the Governor-General and Council backed by the Company also to petition for reform of the Judiciary. The breach was the more striking in view of the former alliance between the Governor-General and the Chief Justice, and caused some re-alinement among supporters at home.

either in the Company or in Parliament would necessarily find themselves on opposite sides.[1] When therefore General Smith for the Opposition raised it in the Commons and demanded a Committee of investigation, it did not seem necessary for the Government to oppose it. Carelessness and indifference on North's part, however, permitted (as Robinson pointed out)[2] the election of a Committee in which members of the Opposition preponderated both in numbers and quality, and thus provided a platform for them. Thus came into existence the famous Select Committee, which, continued as it was with increased powers into the next session, was to become the field for Edmund Burke's Indian activities. It became the means by which the Opposition focused its attention on the affairs of Bengal, and on the return of Philip Francis it proved the perfect sounding board for his envenomed attacks on his successful rival. This Committee was, it was true, occupied for the first half of the year with its work on the Bengal judicial system and with the preparation of a Judicature Act which, in an emasculated form, passed the Lords about the same time as the Charter Act. It was only later that it began ranging freely over the problems of Bengal.[3]

In the meantime the second development had taken place. It was the result of happenings alarming in themselves and carrying consequences of great significance for the future; in April news had reached England that Hyder Ali had made a sudden sweep into the Carnatic up to the gates of Madras and that a strong French fleet was operating off the Coromandel coast. India suddenly, at this low ebb of England's fortunes, had to be added to the danger-list and there was little consolation in the knowledge that by the time its plight was known in England the situation might already be lost or saved.

[1] J. Price to W. Hastings, 13 February 1781. 'Many men who always vote on the side of the Majority in the H. of C. would be very glad that the jurisdiction of the Supreme Court was to be very closely limited, but the volunteer forwardness of Smith in forcing the business into the House hath or will give it the air of a party measure.' Add. MS. 29147, f. 423.

[2] J. Robinson to C. Jenkinson, 14 February 1781. Add. MS. 38215, f. 203. He had, he said, warned North what would happen 'which he treated as indifferent and which I wish he may find so but it is entirely in the hands of opposition. What a figure will this make in India?'

[3] 21 Geo. III, c. 70. For a discussion of this dispute and the Act arising from it see *Cambridge History of British India*, v. 240–8.

An emergency meeting of the Cabinet arranged for the dispatch of a strong force to India.[1] It also decided to meet the inevitable parliamentary outcry by setting up another Parliamentary Committee, a Secret Committee to investigate the causes of this war in the Carnatic. In the choice of this Committee no mistakes were to be made—Robinson abandoned his other work to steer it carefully into being;[2] the control must rest in strong hands and in the hands of staunch supporters of administration. It is significant of the strides which Dundas had made in the management of Indian affairs during the past year that he was chosen as its Chairman, with Jenkinson as his right-hand man.[3] This Committee was set up on 27 April and it too, with its able and influential membership and wide terms of reference, was bound to range widely.

These two Committees soon began to exercise a powerful influence in East Indian affairs. The situation had obvious parallels with 1772–3 where, too, there had been a Select Committee largely independent of ministerial control eagerly but discursively examining the abuses of Company rule in India, while a Secret Committee dominated by able ministerial nominees carried out a more limited survey with the intention of discovering what specific action ought to be taken. But the parallel was not an exact one. The Select Committee of 1772–3 was far less well informed and formidable than that of 1781 which became what the other never was, the organ of a formed and powerful Opposition; while the Secret Committee of 1781, though perhaps no abler than that of 1773, was led by far more powerful members of administration and of an administration which was rapidly crumbling to decay. When Philip Francis reached England in the autumn of 1781 he quickly saw that the initiative in Indian matters was passing to those who dominated the two Committees. These 'inquiries', he wrote, 'cannot stop . . . The minister cannot *now* stop them when he pleases. On the contrary if these Committees proceed as they have begun they may hurry both minister and Parliament along with them.'[4]

---

[1] Abergavenny MSS. iv. 362. North to Robinson, 22 April 1781. British Museum Facsimile 340 (ii), f. 238.

[2] J. Robinson to C. Jenkinson, 28 April 1781. Add. MS. 38405, ff. 118–118ᵛ.

[3] A new 'man of business', Thomas Orde, took over the detailed work of the Committee. For him see below, p. 368, n. 2.

[4] P. Francis to E. Wheler, 25 December 1781. MS. Eur. E.19, f. 26.

The danger was not immediate; the Select Committee was only just getting under way and the great impetus which Francis was to give them did not come at once, for even after his arrival Francis hesitated for a time before throwing in his hand against the Government.[1] In the Secret Committee Dundas and Jenkinson were not likely to press matters dangerous to North's Government at so critical a time and so long as the king staked everything on its continuance. But signs began to multiply that they were forming plans and reaching conclusions of their own in which the system of alliances Robinson had so laboriously built up in the service of his chief had no longer a part. Even before North's Administration finally collapsed in the sensational debates in which the Ministry's majority melted away to nothing, the system of relations between the Government and the East India Company which had been built up to implement the Regulating Act had already been gravely compromised.

[1] The ministry were anxious not to antagonize him, and the king and North consulted on the correct degree of favour he should be shown at the *levée* (*Correspondence of George III*, v. 292 and 293). North then thought him 'very well disposed and willing to be directed in a proper course', though he had it 'in his power to do considerable mischief'. Francis himself was playing his own hand, pleased to think 'they are alarmed and uneasy until they know what part I shall take'. P. Francis to E. Wheler, 24 November 1781. MS. Eur. E. 19, f. 12. By January he hints that the ministry is likely to fall (ibid., f. 47). By the end of December it was believed that he was attaching himself to Opposition. J. Scott to W. Hastings, 25 December 1781. Add. MS. 29152, f. 228ᵛ.

XIII

THE EAST INDIAN CRISIS

THE spectacular fall of the North Administration in March 1782, 'the strangest, though not unexpected revolution that has happened in this country for many years',[1] introduced two years of turmoil out of which arose a sharply changed political scene. It was changed not in the wider sense that in 1784 a new relation was established between public opinion and politics, as has sometimes been claimed; nor in the sense that the power of the Crown was overthrown. But it was changed in the narrower sense that none of the major participants in the parliamentary struggle which brought about North's downfall emerged as victor, and that the political groupings of the past twelve years had been thrown into permanent confusion by the tumult through which they had passed. When men in their desperation began to look to the young William Pitt, brilliant son of a brilliant father, as leader, Henry Dundas, himself a man of the future rather than the past, expressed the prevailing demand for a clean sheet and a new start.

His youth appears to me [he wrote to Shelburne] a very material ingredient in the scale of advantages which recommend him. There is scarce any other political character of consideration in the country to whom many people from habits, from connexions, from former professions, from rivalships and from antipathies will not have objections.[2]

In these two years, moreover, the loss of America had been accepted, peace had been negotiated, and the problem of the future of the British in India and the relations of State and Company had reached a point where drastic reorganization was necessary and where the main lines of any such reorganization had become clear.

In the two years between the fall of North and the rise of Pitt the East Indian question had changed its status from one just below the surface of politics to one of the major controversies and problems which claimed the attention of Parliament and

[1] James MacPherson to W. Hastings, 22 March 1782. Add. MS. 29153, f. 468.
[2] H. Dundas to Shelburne, 24 February 1783. Lansdowne MSS.

politicians. The intensity of the conflict arose no doubt chiefly from the circumstances of English politics. That Fox's India Bill should have led to the overthrow of the Fox-North Coalition, for instance, was due, not to any conflicting reactions aroused by Burke's superb rhetoric on the wrongs of the Indian peoples; not to conflicting views for or against Warren Hastings, nor even to alarm at the financial situation to which the Company had been reduced by the claims and difficulties of war.

It was due to the chance which the Bill gave, particularly by the implications of its patronage arrangements, to stage an assault upon a ministry which was hateful to the king. Even the great body of material which was built up and made available to educated opinion on East Indian affairs in the reports of the Secret and Select Committees, material on which all future thoughts on British India were based, was collected and employed primarily for purposes of home politics. It was itself the outcome of what was no more than a political expedient in the first instance, and subserved the political careers of individuals and groups who employed it. Nevertheless, behind the manœuvres of persons and parties there lay the facts of an Indian situation demanding a solution with an urgency which had been absent during the years when North was in power.

The first of these was the growing financial problem which was threatening the Company as a result both of the delays and expenses of shipping imposed on them by the world war in which England was involved, and by the drain of the long-drawn-out Mahratta War in India itself. These were superimposed on the longer-term problems of the finance of British India.[1] Even had no other factor intervened, they would in due course have led to a new East Indian crisis, in which the Government, in the interests of national credit, would have been involved. A second and more immediately alarming factor, moreover, the incursion of Hyder Ali into the Carnatic and the danger of the war with France spreading there, gave a sharper edge to the growing uneasiness with which the Indian scene was regarded. The entry of India into the combat zone at a time when the weariness of the nation with an unsuccessful and expensive war was reaching a climax was the chief reason why

[1] H. Furber, *John Company at Work. A Study of European Expansion in India in the Late Eighteenth Century*, Harvard, 1948, pp. 303 seq.

attention was focused on East India affairs, why individuals and parties took them up, and why the personality, career, and future of Warren Hastings, in whose hands the fate of India lay, became a battle-ground for contending parties.

It is impossible for you to conceive [a friend wrote to Hastings in June 1781] how all the moderate men here pant after a Peace. Give them one in India, Sir, for the love of God and your own good fame. Nothing ever hath done you more honour than a general peace in India will do you, almost on any terms.[1]

To these purely practical considerations others of a different kind must be added. Ever since Burgoyne's Select Committee of 1772 there had been an uncomfortable awareness of the abuses of British rule in India and the growing humanitarian-ism of the age was always well represented in Parliament. The establishment of the Select Committee—at first intended merely to examine the petitions against the Judicature in Bengal, but dominated by the superb imaginative abilities of Burke and quickly extending its sphere[2]—gave a focus to this humani-tarianism. As its long series of Reports came out, mostly in 1782 and 1783, and as the torrent of Burke's oratory poured forth in the House, sentiment became a real force which must drive any government to action. For the first time there were heard in the House expressions of regret (to become common among the humanitarians of the nineteenth century) that Europeans had ever set foot on these distant shores and imposed their wills on these alien societies. Of this humanitarianism Burke was certainly the main inspiration, and it is impossible even now to read his words without being stirred by them. He may have adopted the East Indian question for party and personal reasons; he may have placed his trust in most unworthy wit-nesses, in his contemptible cousin William for Madras and the virulent and disappointed Francis for Bengal; and he showed far more interest in exposing abuses and attacking individuals

[1] J. Price to W. Hastings, 1 June 1781. Add. MS. 29149, f. 167.
[2] The Select Committee was first set up on 12 February 1781 to examine the petitions against the Supreme Court which had been laid before the House (*Jour. H.C.* xxxviii. 202). On 4 December 1781 it was reconstituted to 'take into consideration the State of the Administration of Justice in the Provinces of Bengal, Behar and Orissa' and given the further instruction to 'consider how the British Possessions in the East Indies may be held and governed with the greatest security and advantage to this Country and by what means the happiness of the native inhabitants may be best promoted' (ibid., pp. 599–600).

than in working out a constructive policy of reform. But he was sincere in his savage anger, had mastered a mass of complicated information and at this, in many ways the climax of his career, he was undoubtedly one of the formative influences on the development of a government policy on India.

If Burke and the Select Committee brought the effects of humanitarian anger to bear on the future of India, the influence of the administrators in bringing about reforms was equally great, though quite different. The centre of this group at this time was the Secret Committee, its leader Henry Dundas the Chairman thereof. The Secret Committee, appointed to investigate the invasion of the Carnatic, but with its powers increased to consider the responsibility for the Mahratta War,[1] gave a new chance for those with practical experience of the unsatisfactory nature of the existing East India system to formulate their views. Charles Jenkinson with John Robinson and his own experience to guide him, Thomas Orde, the new 'man of business',[2] and Henry Dundas, when they found themselves the nucleus of a committee to investigate Indian questions, seized the chance to formulate and press their views on the reforms which were necessary both in India and in England.

Henry Dundas, as the only first-class, rising politician among them, became their spokesman and the main driving force in the months ahead. Dundas was even less single-minded than Burke. He used the East India question, as circumstances arose, to further his own political career and to subserve his cautious yet daring personal ambitions. Nevertheless, the persistence and tenacity with which he clung to the proposals which he had formulated for East Indian reform and the terms in which he pressed them show that he, too, was pursuing a principle that lay outside the claims of personal political ex-

---

[1] The motion for setting up the Committee was passed on 30 April 1781, and the members were chosen by ballot on 2 May 1781. It was 'to inquire into the causes of the war that now subsists in the Carnatic; and of the present condition of the British possessions in those parts'. (*Jour. H.C.* xxxviii. 430, 435.) It was renewed on 30 November 1781 (ibid., p. 598) and on 4 December it was instructed to extend its investigations to the 'rise, progress, conduct and present state of the Maratta War, and all other hostilities in which the Presidency of Bengal now are, or have been, engaged . . .' (ibid., p. 600).

[2] 1746–1807; M.P., afterwards first Baron Bolton; Secretary to the Treasury under Lord Shelburne, 1782–3; Chief Secretary to the Lord-Lieutenant of Ireland, 1784–7, when he retired through ill health; 1791, Governor of the Isle of Wight.

pediency. They place him among the small band of men in whose hands the State was slowly to build up once again its administrative machinery and to incur ever-increasing administrative responsibilities. In the two years between the fall of the North Administration and the consolidation of that of William Pitt, two men, Burke and Dundas, dominated the Indian scene. Each had his Parliamentary Committee behind him, each had his own personal and party complications to deal with, which fluctuated with the ebb and flow of party politics in these disturbed years; each had to count on the opposition of vested interests. The contribution of each was different; it was Dundas, building on the experience of Robinson, Jenkinson, and their friends, who laid down the nature of the reforms; it was Burke and his associates who made some sweeping reforms inevitable.

The development of the East Indian question during these years can only be understood against the background of the general party situation; the complex relations of the two Parliamentary Committees and their leaders with each other, with the Government, and with the Opposition; and the situation within the East India Company. This last was complicated by the war waged in pamphlets, newspapers, and on occasion in the House or in the General Court of the Company, between the agents of Warren Hastings and his enemy Philip Francis.

The political situation in the two years following the fall of the North Administration was complex and shifting to a degree. When, despite the king's desperate efforts to retain it, the North Administration fell, there followed the uneasy balance of the second Rockingham Administration. This ministry was pulled between the compact strength of the group which had built itself up in opposition round the Marquess of Rockingham and the supporters of Lord Shelburne, who acted in the knowledge that the king was building him up as a bulwark against the predominance of ministers whom he hated and a group pledged to principles which he abhorred. It fell to pieces with Rockingham's death in July 1782, but was already doomed.

It was followed in its turn by Lord Shelburne's shaky and narrow-based administration, which hardly could have survived the few months it did had Parliament not been in recess for most of its brief life. Its future was known from the beginning to depend on its chance of forming a coalition either with the followers of Rockingham, now led by Charles James Fox, or with those who still accepted the leadership of Lord North, considering it wiser to bide their time than take a part in the formation of weak and transient governments. Both alternatives failed on account of the unwillingness of both Opposition parties to take on the responsibility of the peace settlement, of Shelburne's acute personal unpopularity, and the isolation in which, despite his ability and his political ambitions, he always found himself. When he was overthrown in February 1783 by a coalition between North and a considerable part of his followers and Fox and his supporters, formed in the teeth of the king's known wishes and in indifference to the violent public assaults they had shortly before been making on each other, a political crisis of the first magnitude arose. It was only after six weeks without a ministry at all, and when every alternative had been tried, that the king reluctantly accepted them, and then without pretence of good will or favour. Then followed their brief months of power, the well-planned coup whereby the king and a few resolute men seized the chance of ousting them over their unpopular East India Bill, the prolonged crisis of Pitt's minority Government; then the dissolution and the triumph of the new ministers and the king in the 1784 election. East India affairs were affected by all these changes, at the mercy of conflicting and changing interests, but so far from becoming submerged, they grew in significance until the culmination of Fox's East India Bill and the struggle arising out of it.

In this complex scene the curious situation of the Select and Secret Committees made them, in the hands of their skilful leaders, of high importance in the development of East Indian policy. There was nothing in the terms of reference of either of them to suggest that they were intended to formulate general policies of East Indian reform, or to do more than issue their reports and pass out of existence. But even before the fall of North's Administration they began to take the initiative in bringing forward measures for East Indian reform and in forming a corporate policy. The first sign of this was the Bill, introduced by General Smith as Chairman of the Select Committee (though in fact the work of Burke) for the reform of the Judicature of Bengal.[1] It was introduced as the Committee's

[1] 21 Geo. III, c. 70.

own measure, the outcome of their first report. Though the Committee was notoriously dominated by the enemies of the North Administration and though the ministry might have been expected to wish to frame their own measure and certainly disapproved of some parts of the Committee's proposals, the Bill was actually allowed to pass through the House of Commons and was not drastically amended until it reached the Lords.[1] The long life of the Committee (which did not produce its eleventh and last report until November 1783) and the disturbed political scenes through which it passed after the fall of North's Administration, led to the development of a corporate feeling among the small body of enthusiasts who made up its nucleus. This was strengthened by its rivalry with the Secret Committee.

The growth of an independent policy in the Secret Committee, even during North's Administration, was still more remarkable, for they were essentially a ministerial body containing only two members who did not habitually vote with the Government,[2] and with influential office-holders at their head. It soon became suspected, however (and evidently with reason), that its leaders, while pushing ahead with their reports on the Carnatic, were also occupied in the formulation of general conclusions on East Indian policy, and that these were diverging considerably from that so far pursued by the Government. This was not altogether surprising. As James MacPherson pointed out, the Indian policy of the North Administration had been essentially that of the Treasury, and Indian affairs had little chance 'to come to a Cabinet vote'.[3] With so controversial a question, with the ministry showing serious signs of disintegration, with Dundas always apt to play his own hand and Jenkinson having recently taken umbrage against North on a patronage issue,[4] it was not difficult to understand how differences could arise. As early as June 1781 the rival interests at

[1] *The Parliamentary Register; or History of the Proceedings and Debates of the House of Lords*, iv. 387 seq. and 396 seq.

[2] Robert Gregory, M.P. for Rochester, East India Director, and Philip Yorke, M.P. for Cambridgeshire.

[3] James MacPherson to W. Hastings, 20 January 1782. 'In India politics', MacPherson remarked, obviously uneasy at some of the friends Hastings's agent was depending on, '. . . safety neither comes from the East nor the West but from the *North*.' Add. MS. 29152, f. 425ᵛ.

[4] About a protégé named Rickets. Add. MS. 38307 *passim* and 38309, f. 52.

India House thought it worth while to press their views upon the Committee. North's abortive approach to Dundas in July with an offer of the position of a Lord of the Treasury, 'meaning', as Dundas explained, 'that in that situation with the assistance of a secretary or two under me, I might take the management of India into my hands' and be 'constantly near himself',[1] may well have been an attempt to check the development of a dangerous dichotomy.

After Dundas went to Scotland for the recess, Jenkinson was believed to be the member of the Committee most active in developing an independent policy. James MacPherson, deeply interested in the preservation of the Treasury control, spoke of the need of checking 'the influence and views of interlopers from the Secret Committee'.[2] About the same time Robinson was agitated by opposition on the part of several ministers to the appointment of his protégé John Stables to the Council of Bengal and both he and North attributed it to the intervention of Jenkinson.[3] The idea that the Secret Committee was formulating a new East Indian policy continued to grow throughout the summer. Sulivan, whose warnings always deserved attention, told Hastings that though the Secret Committee had so far confined itself to factual reports on the Carnatic from which Sir Thomas Rumbold, the late Governor, seemed likely alone to suffer, he feared that they were preparing to go farther. By 'pervading every department' of the Company they were collecting material on which to base a proposition for 'a total revolution in the management of India'.[4]

The sketch of this plan on which Sulivan ventured is of some interest. It involved the adoption of the proposals which Robinson and Jenkinson had earlier brought forward; it also involved the abandonment of support of Warren Hastings as Governor-General, and his replacement by a successor believed to be Lord Cornwallis.[5] In view of these rumours, to the correct-

---

[1] C. Matheson, *Life of Henry Dundas, First Viscount Melville, 1742–1811*, 1933, pp. 69–70.

[2] James MacPherson to W. Hastings, 25 August 1781. Add. MS. 29150, f. 171.

[3] North to John Robinson, 1 September 1781, Abergavenny MSS. iv. 382, and J. Robinson to C. Jenkinson, 1 August 1781. Add. MS. 38407, ff. 159 seq.

[4] L. Sulivan to W. Hastings, 15 August 1781. Add. MS. 29150, f. 99ᵛ.

[5] L. Sulivan to W. Hastings, 21 August 1781. Ibid., ff. 143 seq. The knowledge of this attitude among the members of the Secret Committee was no doubt what

ness of which the history of the Committee after North's fall gives a high degree of probability, it was reasonable of Philip Francis when he returned from India in October to be uncertain whether the Select or the Secret Committee was more likely to assist him in his vendetta. As late as January 1782 he still hoped that the forthcoming reports of the Secret Committee would 'be decisive against him [Hastings] in spite of the Minister and all his works'.[1]

But the full development of the Secret Committee's views was checked by political considerations of more immediate significance to its members than their proposals for Indian reform. After the news had been received of the surrender of Cornwallis at Yorktown the ministry was fighting for its existence, and whatever they might think of its prospects, Dundas and his friends could hardly be expected to incur the enmity of the king by introducing an attack on India policy that might well bring it down. Even while Philip Francis was hoping that the Secret Committee's forthcoming reports would ruin Hastings, his friends were conveying to him information, derived from Jenkinson, that he had no cause for alarm.[2] The last four reports of the Committee which came out at the beginning of February and of March contained in fact nothing that could be construed as an attack on him.[3] When in February Dundas announced his intention of bringing before the House propositions based on his Committee's reports,[4] there is no reason to believe that they were intended to do more than launch an attack on Sir Thomas Rumbold and his colleagues for their administration of Madras, a plan he had already discussed with Lord North. It was at this point, however, that the resignation of Lord North led to the fall of the administration and left a completely changed political field against which the East Indian problem had to be considered.

inspired Burke and his friends to renew their pressure when Parliament reassembled for the Secret Committee to take up the question of the Mahratta War. When they did Dundas repeated the Government case against the extension but Jenkinson professed himself converted and the motion went through (*Parliamentary Register*, 1781, v. 84).

[1] P. Francis to G. Ducarel, 23 January 1782. MS. Eur. E.19, f. 37.

[2] J. Scott to W. Hastings, 3 January 1782. Add. MS. 29152, f. 291ᵛ; confirmed by L. Sulivan, f. 430ᵛ, 20 January 1782.

[3] *Reports from Committees of the House of Commons*, vols. vii and viii.

[4] 5 February 1782.

In these changed conditions and under the weak and fluid administrations which followed, the two Committees became increasingly important, but also changed their political status several times. Under the Rockingham Administration it was the Select Committee which enjoyed the power but also suffered the responsibilities and limitations of a ministerial body, while the Secret Committee, whose leaders remained out of office, were able to develop their views without taking into account the expediencies of government. On the fall of this administration, when Dundas took office under Shelburne, the situation was again reversed. It was not till Fox disclosed the daring plans which the Fox-North Coalition adopted and till Pitt, their successor, put forward his alternative proposals that the initiative was once again taken by governments as such instead of by the leaders of one or other Committee.

If the political circumstances of the time and the curious status of the Committees affected the course of East Indian issues, so, too, did certain aspects of affairs within the East India Company itself. The first of these was the growth of its financial difficulties. Already under the North Administration the Treasury had to give their permission for the acceptance (under certain conditions) of bills in excess of the statutory maximum from India.[1] When the Rockingham Administration came into power the Treasury was faced with an urgent petition for legislation to enable the Company to maintain its dividend (its bond debt had now crept above the statutory maximum of £1,500,000) and for concessions about the annual payments to the State reintroduced in the 1781 Act.[2] A Bill for affording it temporary relief was through both Houses by the end of June 1782.[3]

By next January it was clear that the temporary assistance would not be enough and that a further appeal must be made to the Shelburne Administration now in office. The Treasury, after studying the Company's memorial, replied that what they asked was too much to be given without the consent of Parliament and invited them to prepare a petition to lay before the

---

[1] Court Book 90, p. 314. 28 August 1781. These bills were 'for the sole purpose of purchasing an investment'.

[2] Court Book 91, pp. 18 seq. 17 April 1782. The petition had already been under consideration before North's Administration fell.

[3] 22 Geo. III, c. 51.

House.[1] The fall of Shelburne's ministry and the interregnum that followed were acutely inconvenient, for all business was held up and the temporary legislation of the previous year expired in April. On the advent of the Fox-North Coalition, therefore, a hasty Bill for extending the relief had to be rushed through the House, though this time the Act was to operate only until October of the same year.[2] Nothing occurred in the next few months to ease the Company's position; on the contrary large numbers of the bills drawn on them from India and China began to fall due. In September the directors had to approach the Treasury for permission to accept them,[3] but by this time Fox's Bill was on the stocks, and in any case the time for palliatives was by now past. The Treasury indicated, as Treasuries had before, that they could do nothing outside Parliament, and Fox was able to claim when presenting his Bill that it was intended to reorganize the affairs of a Company which if not (as he at first appeared to claim) entirely bankrupt was at least for the time unable to meet its liabilities.[3] As an undercurrent to the controversies over Fox's and Pitt's East India Bills there ran a heated debate on the true financial situation of the Company, out of which it emerged that only by a relaxation of all State claims, a revision of its expenditure, and the right to raise a considerable loan, could it be put on its feet again after the crippling effects of war.

The course of its financial problems at this time is of significance for two reasons, first, that it illustrated how important still in its relations to government was its position as a 'monied company'. In the interests of the support of public credit each government in turn felt obliged not only to save it from stopping payment but even to maintain the level of its dividend. Its financial position was also of importance because, though its plight did not cause the public alarm and anger which it did in the credit crisis of 1772 (partly, no doubt, because it was recognized that Government must give it some support), it continued to keep Indian affairs in the public eye and gave weight to the growing conviction that reform by Parliament was inevitable.

[1] Court Book 91, p. 754. On 15 January 1783 the Company found it necessary to make the appeal. On 19 February (p. 868) the directors received the Treasury reply.   [2] 23 Geo. III, c. 36.
[3] See Fox's speeches on 18 and 25 November 1783 (*Parliamentary Register*, 1783, xii. 29 seq. and 101).

Another important factor was the state of politics within the Company. In the last months of North's Administration Sulivan, who since 1780 had led the Government troops in the Company, had been prophesying the loss of the Government's majority in the Court of Directors,[1] an event that had never happened since Robinson's system got into its stride. This prophecy reflected the decline of the Government's reputation as well as exasperation with the war in India; it also reflected the anti-Government feeling always aroused in the Company by a negotiation with the Government upon their charter or territorial possessions. In this case the antagonism had been skilfully fanned in the Company's General Courts by General Smith and his friends acting in close collaboration with the Rockingham Opposition.[2] The rising ill feeling was, moreover, likely to be more than adequately represented at the coming election of directors. Ever since the 1773 Act it had become customary in order to minimize expensive contests to re-elect each year those of the former directors who had been for a year 'out by rotation' and who wished to stand for election. In 1782 Sulivan himself was due to go out carrying five other strong Government supporters with him. Those coming in were likely to comprise three strong supporters of the Rockingham Opposition, including Henry Fletcher who, with Robert Gregory, was their leading man, and only three who might be expected to support administration. It was, of course, possible to break through this convention, and, indeed, by arrangement new directors thought likely to be useful were sometimes brought in by so doing, and Sulivan himself had returned to power by defying it; but this was clearly not the occasion for the Government to risk a show of strength.

What would have happened had the North Administration remained in office it is hard to say, but its fall only a few weeks before the annual election of directors meant a victory for what had been the Company Opposition and the new ministry formed itself with a ready-made majority (though not a large one) in the Court of Directors and General Court.

This change of fortune caused the greatest alarm among the

---

[1] L. Sulivan to W. Hastings, 20 January 1782. Add. MS. 29152, ff. 433 seq. He had been trying to make provision against it since the middle of the preceding year.　　　　　　　　　　　　　　　　　　　　　　　[2] Court Book 90, *passim*.

the attacks on him, and the organized defence of him. Though Sulivan doubted whether he could have triumphed in the General Court in May 1782 without the support of the followers of other servants more indirectly threatened,[1] he alone had a following among independent proprietors and among the public apart from that which was organized and subsidized by his supporters. And the violent altercations between his agent Major Scott and Philip Francis in the Press and in the House added a personal element to the controversy which was a source of strength as well as weakness. John Robinson said that Hastings had made a mistake in sending over an agent to speak for him, for had he not done so the accusations and the responses to them would have had to travel to and fro to India so slowly as to take the edge off political controversy.[2] It seems doubtful if Robinson were right, now that the controversy had become so much intensified, but he was right in seeing how much this duel itself was responsible for heating the atmosphere of debate. When from time to time in the next few years friends in high places told the credulous Scott that Warren Hastings had overthrown or created ministries, their polite words meant, if anything, that in his personality many of the issues of the East Indian conflict might be said to find at least a symbolic centre.

It is in the light of these complexities of national and Company politics, and the growing urgency of a settlement which would bring political and financial stability to the Company, that the contributions of each of the short-lived ministries of 1782–4 to a solution must be considered.

The Rockingham Administration, March–July 1782

The fall of the North Administration caused a great deal of confusion. 'There never was such a smash as the present', it was said, possibly with some exaggeration. 'The change even goes to under clerks in the public offices.'[3] The situation was moreover, unprecedented in the eighteenth century, since the Rockingham party had come into power pledged to a legislative policy which threatened to change in several respects the face of English politics. Among other important measures expected

---

[1] L. Sulivan to W. Hastings, 12 November 1782. Add. MS. 29156, ff. 449 seq.
[2] L. Sulivan to W. Hastings, 20 January 1782. Add. MS. 29152, ff. 435 seq.
[3] J. Scott to W. Hastings, 28 March 1782. Add. MS. 29153, f. 496.

as a war-monger—'an Alexander or an Aurungzebe'—which he later reinforced by a series of resolutions criticizing his policy over a number of years. The news of the Chait Singh incident came at a time materially to strengthen his case. Burke, Fox, and the Select Committee could not do otherwise than welcome this support, though they were suspicious of it, and Fox made the traditional Rockingham point that the welcome would not extend to any proposal to increase the powers of the Crown at the expense of the Company.[1]

But however pleased the Select Committee and the Government might be at the support they had obtained, they could not feel satisfied that the Secret Committee should monopolize the field in East India affairs. The Select Committee therefore hastily followed Dundas's example and also laid a series of resolutions before the House.[2] Partly, however, because they had as yet made much less progress than the Secret Committee in the collection of their material and the issuing of their reports, and partly, no doubt, because nothing they brought forward must embarrass the Government, the propositions they advanced—an attack on Sir Elijah Impey and a rather minor one on Laurence Sulivan—were much less impressive and important than those of their rivals.[3]

Dundas therefore retained the initiative and continued to drive on, always with the support of the Rockingham group of the Government though not always with that of a united ministry, until on 28 May he got through the House with the support of Burke, Fox, and a number of ministerialists a resolution that the Company should recall Warren Hastings and Hornby, President of Bombay, as having 'acted in a manner repugnant to the honour and policy of this nation and thereby brought great calamities on India'.[4]

The effects of this resolution were as dramatic as those arising from the more indirect attacks on Hastings in 1776. The attacks on Rumbold already in progress had not much disturbed the Company since he had never sought allies there but sought to

---

[1] *Parliamentary Register*, vii. 36.   [2] *Jour. H.C.* xxxviii. 973 seq.
[3] They demanded the recall of Impey and censured Laurence Sulivan for inaccuracies in statements in the Company Minutes, delay in the transmission of an Act of Parliament (the recent Judicature Act) to Bengal, and for restricting the freedom of statement of the Secretary of the Company in giving evidence before the Select Committee.   [4] *Jour. H.C.* xxxviii. 1032.

defend himself by his own exertions and influence in Parliament. The attacks on Impey as Chief Justice were not the Company's direct concern. With the attack on Hastings and the implied threat against other servants the real struggle with the Company began. A General Court was promptly demanded by proprietors representing a wide variety of interests within the 'Old' party,[1] a 'very full and respectable court'[2] was produced by their joint efforts; the party's plan of campaign was decided on at a meeting at the Crown and Anchor the night before; Richard Atkinson 'opened his house for the entertainment of friends', and by an overwhelming majority the Court resolved that to remove Hastings on the mere wish of the House of Commons would be to 'destroy that independency which the Proprietors of East India Stock ought to enjoy in the management of their own affairs', and that the directors should not carry out any resolution for the removal of officers without the approval of the General Court.[3]

The correspondence of Hastings's friends showed that they ventured on this open defiance of the House of Commons in the belief not only that the Government was too weak and divided to harm them but that it must soon fall.[4] In both of these assumptions they were right. The action of the General Court left the Rockingham Administration in precisely the same position as North was left in 1776. They had the choice of capitulation or of taking action at once in Parliament. Fox, Burke, and some of their supporters were anxious to take the strong line, but Lord Shelburne and his supporters stubbornly opposed it.[5]

The concessions which Shelburne had been obliged to make on East Indian questions cannot have been other than humiliating to him. His connexion with Impey, who had been recalled, was well known. Now Hastings, whom he had recently promised to support, was also attacked. When he decided to make his stand he did so, moreover, with an obstinacy born of his other and politically more serious disagreements with his colleagues, and he was successful at least so far as to prevent any action

[1] Court Book 91, pp. 201 seq.
[2] J. Woodman to W. Hastings, 24 June 1782. Add. MS. 29154, f. 480.
[3] Court Book 91, p. 203, 19 June 1782.
[4] S. Toone to W. Hastings, 1 July 1782. Add. MS. 29155, ff. 1 seq.
[5] J. Scott to W. Hastings, 11 July 1782. Ibid., f. 69. Scott is quoting Lord Mansfield, who got the information from the Chancellor.

before Parliament rose in July. The delay served its purpose, for in July Rockingham died, Fox resigned, and the short Rockingham Administration came to an end. In the speech announcing his resignation Fox mentioned as one of the causes of dissension with Shelburne the fact that 'the noble person was inclined to screen from justice and punishment those delinquents who had destroyed our possessions in the East and involved us in all the calamities which that House had so honourably endeavoured to remove'.[1] While the ministry still stood Shelburne had sent Dunning, now Lord Ashburton, to Hastings's friends to assure them of his support and to tell them to await with confidence the next session when 'a new System in all probability will be adopted and that he trusts you will have no reason to complain of the Measure that may then take place'.[2]

The record of the Rockingham Administration in East Indian affairs was thus somewhat ignominious; they had formulated no policy of reform; they had left it to Dundas to make the running even in those measures on which they felt most strongly and which were themselves no more than the preludes to reform; and when they supported these measures they had failed to carry them through. But the debates inaugurated by Dundas and the further reports of the Select Committee, which came out near the end of their term of office,[3] together with the press and pamphlet campaign which accompanied the attack on Warren Hastings, had brought and kept East Indian affairs firmly in the public eye.

The Shelburne Administration, July 1782–February 1783

When it was known that Lord Shelburne was to be head of a new administration it was widely believed in the 'Old' party in the Company that the worst clouds threatening them would disperse. Shelburne himself had confirmed them in their belief that he had fallen in with his late allies unwillingly. Now Laurence Sulivan hoped that his former friend would use him as the link between the Government and the Company, and Major Scott, Hastings's agent, waited confidently to be sent for to discuss his patron's claims and future.[4] Disillusion, however,

---

[1] *Parliamentary Register*, vii. 304.
[2] R. Palk to W. Hastings, 1 July 1782. Add. MS. 29155, f. 6.
[3] Reports 2–6 were published between 6 June and 11 July 1782.
[4] J. Scott to W. Hastings, 11 July 1782. Add. MS. 29155, ff. 67 seq.

soon followed. Shelburne, when he met Sulivan at a public
dinner, gushingly called him his 'old and dear friend',[1] but he
made no approaches to him and Ashburton though amiable
was evasive.[2] Major Scott, after waiting for some time, asked
for an interview, and when he got it found Shelburne friendly
but his words disquieting. James MacPherson was quicker than
he was to provide the explanation. The trouble was, he told
Hastings, that Shelburne 'has found it expedient to connect
himself with men who in some late instances committed themselves on the subject of your being removed'.[3] Lord Shelburne's
most urgent need in fact was to build up a ministry, and
second in importance only to the young William Pitt among
his recruits was Henry Dundas. It soon became clear that,
whatever Shelburne's pledges, the Indian policy of the new
administration was to be that of Dundas, and that Dundas was
determined to take it up just where he had left it off.

This did not mean that the new ministry were averse from
using Shelburne's Indian connexions to rid themselves of
Hastings with the minimum of trouble as a preliminary to the
introduction of reforms. Shelburne spoke Major Scott very
fair. Scott knew, he said, 'the cause of the reserve he had
hitherto been obliged to practise'.[4] He indicated that Hastings
could expect to be received home with honour and need fear
neither Philip Francis nor General Smith as his successor. But
he made it clear that he wished him to return home—he could
not, he said, expect to remain Governor-General for ever. The
room for negotiation was not, however, large. Obviously
Hastings could not be consulted himself unless the East Indian
reform was to be postponed for over a year. He had been careful
not to give Scott authority to resign on his behalf. It was now
suggested that it might be possible to get round this difficulty
if the conditions of his recall were so satisfactory that his friends
could refrain from opposing a motion by the directors to recall
him.[5] A good deal of energy was expended in making this point.

---

[1] J. Scott to W. Hastings, postscript of 16 November to letter of 14 November
1782. Add. MS. 29156, f. 474.
[2] L. Sulivan to W. Hastings, 12 November 1782. Ibid., f. 449.
[3] James MacPherson to W. Hastings, 5 August 1782. Add. MS. 29155,
f. 342ᵛ.
[4] J. Scott to W. Hastings, 31 July 1782. Ibid., f. 258.
[5] J. Scott to W. Hastings, 26 September 1782. Add. MS. 29156, ff. 121 seq.

Dundas went so far as to maintain that he deplored the Resolution which he had himself proposed in the House for the recall of Hastings and to suggest that he had done so solely to forestall a more hostile resolution from the Select Committee, a claim which taxed even the credulity of Major Scott.[1]

In fact the negotiations never went very far. It was well known with what terms Hastings's supporters would rest content; a peerage for him, the rescinding of the resolution for his recall, the right to choose his own time to resign after his successor had been appointed, and (a new issue recently introduced) an understanding that the ministry would not oppose the grant to him by the Company of the 10 lacs of rupees (£100,000) he had received from the Nawab of Oude to serve as a sort of pension for him.[2] These terms meant, in effect, that the Government must espouse Hastings's cause in Parliament; but it was a price which they were not prepared to pay. It was probably indeed impossible for any government at that time, in view of the reports of the Select Committee and the attitude taken by Dundas as Chairman of the Secret Committee, to adopt such a line. William Pitt some twelve months later boggled at just the same demands.[3]

Though the possibilities of negotiation were not neglected, the Government therefore proceeded also with the preparations for more drastic methods. By the end of August Scott was warned that the Government were pressing the directors to take into consideration the Resolution of the House and to prepare a motion in accordance with it to recall Hastings.[4] The rumours that began to fly around at the same time were that Hastings and all his Council were to be recalled, though the recall was to be on public grounds 'without stain on his character'; that Lord Cornwallis would be sent out to replace him in the following spring, and that he was to return home the season after. It is certain that Cornwallis was approached at this time and that

---

[1] J. Scott to W. Hastings, 27 July 1782. Add. MS. 29155, f. 245.

[2] For this attempt to get something which would serve him, as Clive's *jagir* did on a larger scale, to retire on see *Cambridge History of British India*, v. 302–3. There is much on the subject in his correspondence and a number of directors and some ministers were alleged to support the proposal, but the circumstances of the time and the knowledge of the uproar which would follow prevented any progress in the negotiation.

[3] J. Scott to W. Hastings, 4 September 1784. Add. MS. 29164, f. 462v.

[4] J. Scott to W. Hastings, 29 August 1782. Add. MS. 29155, ff. 497 seq.

he was believed to be prepared to go out if the terms were satisfactory.

The terms were under discussion by the Committee of Correspondence and the Court of Directors for more than a month, and their course was eagerly followed by all interested bodies.[1] Eventually it was thought wise to exclude all servants but Hastings from the motions (though this did not split the hostile *bloc* against them, as must have been hoped) and to base the recall on the need for a peaceful policy in India and the belief that this could not be expected from those accustomed to a policy of 'offensive alliances'.

The first problem was to ensure that these motions were accepted by the directors. For this the Government had to rely in the Court of Directors chiefly on the support of the followers of the Rockingham group, but they also had to persuade Shelburne's own supporters to follow their leader in his change of front. It was evidently none too easy. Thomas Orde, the new Secretary to the Treasury, who was trying to assume the duties which Robinson had so expertly carried on before, was said to have 'sent for each Director, closeted him separately and endeavoured to enforce a compliance with the wishes of Government'[2] before they came to the vote. But the result was fairly satisfactory. Despite heated opposition thirteen directors voted in favour of the recall of Warren Hastings and only ten opposed it.

This was, however, only the first step. In the second the Government can have had little hope of success. As soon as the vote was taken the statutory nine proprietors demanded a General Court. James MacPherson, Governor Johnstone, and several of Hastings's friends were among the number.[3] It was clear that all sections of the 'Old' party were massed in opposition, and they had in existence the considerable voting power they had kept in readiness for this purpose since the contest of the previous May. Moreover there were signs that a good deal of independent interest had been aroused by the unremitting publicity which the attacks on Hastings were getting, and that this opinion among proprietors was overwhelmingly against

[1] Court Book 91, pp. 492 seq.
[2] J. Scott to W. Hastings, 28 October 1782. Add. MS. 29156, f. 286.
[3] Court Book 91, p. 503, 16 October 1782. Cf. ibid., p. 544.

the Government. A large Court sat patiently from midday to 9 p.m. listening to speeches on both sides which were considered to reach a high level of eloquence. On a vote then taken by show of hands there was an overwhelming majority in Hastings's favour. A ballot was, however, demanded and Treasury whips went out.[1]

A curious incident illustrates the relationship of Lord North both to the 'Old' party in the Company and to the Government at this time. Though the men best known in the Company as Robinson's henchmen were already actively engaged, Lord North and his political followers had stood aside from this dispute as they were standing aside from all partisanship in politics for the moment. Governor Johnstone, however, when the ballot was coming on, demanded his open support for Hastings. North was greatly agitated at this demand; he had no desire to take sides; he thought the recall of Hastings at this juncture unwise, he said, and certainly did not want to support it, but on the other hand had he not for long opposed Hastings and only ceased to do so 'in despair of success and in the absence of an alternative'? Moreover the Secret Committee whose leaders were demanding the recall had been his creation, and might they not be angry with him? All he felt able to decide was to leave it to Robinson's discretion whether or not to summon his friends to the ballot.[2]

Whatever the decision, the ballot was an overwhelming defeat for the Government by 428 votes to 75. James MacPherson said it had 'thrown disgrace upon a Government too weak before',[3] but Dundas took it calmly and must indeed have expected it. When he met Major Scott at the king's drawing room he said without ill-nature that the House of Commons had been beaten by India House, but Scott added gloomily that he was 'one of those dark, designing and worthless characters'.[4] It was certain that the Government would press on. For the moment they contented themselves with using their powers under the 1781 Act to prevent any official report of the recent

[1] L. Sulivan to W. Hastings, 28 November 1782. Add. MS. 29156, f. 451ᵛ.

[2] North to J. Robinson, 27 October 1782. Abergavenny MSS. v. 483. Quoted Weitzman, op. cit., pp. 370-1.

[3] James MacPherson to W. Hastings, 12 November 1782. Add. MS. 29156, f. 445ᵛ.

[4] J. Scott to W. Hastings, 5 November 1782. Ibid., f. 350.

proceedings being sent to India. Despite their preoccupation with strengthening their own parliamentary position and the problems of the peace settlement, the Indian question figured largely in the king's speech when Parliament reopened on 5 December:

The regulation of a vast territory in Asia opens a large field for your wisdom, prudence and foresight. I trust that you will be able to frame some fundamental laws which may make their connection with Great Britain a blessing to India; and that you will take therein proper measures to give all foreign nations in matters of foreign commerce an entire and perfect confidence in the probity, punctuality and good order of our government.[1]

In the debate which followed East India business was spoken of as 'a very important part of the business of the session',[2] and it soon became known that Dundas was preparing a Bill which would supersede Lord North's regulations now in force. It was assumed that arrangements would be made at the same time for the recall of Hastings and his Council and the succession of Cornwallis.[3]

The Bill which was now under preparation by Dundas, with the assistance, as he later said, of 'some gentlemen of the Secret Committee',[4] is a landmark in the history of Indian legislation. It enjoys this position not for what it did, for it never came on to the Statute Book, but for the fact that it brought together all the major propositions of the 'men of business' of the past, added to them some points which had impressed themselves on Dundas's mind from his experience on the Secret Committee, and, most important of all, that it was the blue-print of Pitt's East India Act of the next year. It was an eminently moderate, sensible, and workmanlike Bill, reflecting strongly the administrative good sense of those who had framed it. It was also in no sense a popular Bill from the contemporary point of view. Indeed the only serious divergencies from it in the Act which Pitt later passed were the result of attempts to remove certain clauses which, in the interest of efficiency, ignored too cavalierly the dislike of the executive characteristic of eighteenth-century political opinion. This fact should be borne in mind to the

---

[1] *Parliamentary Register*, xi. 7.　　　　　　　　　[2] Ibid. ix. 4.
[3] J. Scott to W. Hastings, 22 January 1783. Add. MS. 29157, ff. 489 seq.
[4] He mentioned later that Thomas Orde in particular had helped him.

credit of Dundas. He may have taken the initiative in East Indian affairs to increase his political reputation, but the Bill he introduced was not a vote-catching one.

The main principles of the Bill were fourfold. The first was an increase in the power of the Governor-General and Council over India, and of the Governor-General within his own Council. This was taken straight from the propositions of Robinson and Jenkinson. The second was some increase (though a less marked one) of the power of the Governors of the Presidencies over their Councils, a measure which derived from the same source. The third was a settlement of the claims of the Raja of Tanjore and the Nawab of Arcot, and an investigation of the notorious debts of both. The Burkes and the Select Committee were the chief inspiration here. The fourth was the reorganization of the structure of the Company at home to prevent the General Court from over-riding the decisions of the Court of Directors on political matters, and to strengthen the power of the Government to deal with the Company. Here the influence of both Robinson and Jenkinson was shown, but Dundas added his own special contribution, the belief that there should be a third Secretary of State entirely to handle the Government's East India affairs.

By the third week of January 1783 the terms of the Bill began leaking out.[1] It was expected to come before the House by the middle of February; the date was postponed until 3 March. But once again East Indian affairs were sharply interrupted by a political crisis. Before that date the Shelburne Administration had fallen before a coalition of Fox and North who joined forces in disapproval of the Peace terms, and in the disordered weeks that followed there was no possibility of considering even the urgent financial claims of the Company, still less the problem of its reform.

The Fox–North Coalition, April–December 1783

It was not until the dust had died down and the Fox–North Coalition was established in power that attention could once more be given to the East Indian question. It is significant of its growing importance that it arose immediately from three different angles. In the first place some legislation was im-

---

[1] J. Scott to W. Hastings, 22 January 1783. Add. MS. 29157, ff. 490 seq.

mediately necessary at least to carry on the temporary financial arrangements of the previous year. The new Government were not ready to do more than prolong these temporary arrangements; they did so for an even shorter period than before.[1] In the second place Dundas, undeterred by his fall from power, announced his intention of proceeding with the introduction of his Bill; and in the third place Burke and the Select Committee had been hard at work during their period out of office and a number of powerful reports were coming out in the first months of the new ministry.[2] When on 14 April Dundas introduced his Bill, coupled with a strong plea for Lord Cornwallis as Governor-General, the new Government made it clear that they were no longer prepared to permit him to make the running.[3] His proposals indeed met with little support; the East India Company petitioned against the Bill,[4] the Government attacked its principles, and even those with knowledge of India who, like Major Scott, were obliged in private to express approval of many of its clauses, opposed it hotly for the sake of the vested interests they represented.[5] Dundas saw that it was useless to press the Bill, and the measure seemed at the moment still-born.

There are, however, no signs that the new Government, or even that part of them which followed Fox, had as yet formed a policy of their own on Indian reform. Though Burke was writing the famous Ninth Report of the Select Committee with its masterly analysis of the workings of the Indian system, his references to East Indian reform remained vague and only his attacks on Hastings explicit.[6] All the evidence suggests that from the time the new ministry took office in April until the House rose in July they had not got beyond the problem of the dismissal of Hastings and his replacement (rumour said by a board of supervisors with Francis at their head and William Burke among them, but this was probably unjust).[7] As late as 17 July Fox, when speaking of the India business which must be raised

---

[1] 23 Geo. III, c. 36. Later extended by 23 Geo. III, c. 83.
[2] Reports 7–10.
[3] *Parliamentary Register*, ix. 608 seq.
[4] Court Book 92, pp. 53 seq.
[5] J. Scott to W. Hastings, 24 April 1783. Add. MS. 29158, ff. 480ᵛ–481.
[6] John Scott, reporting his speech on Dundas's Bill, says he still stated that what was needed was a 'change of men and not of constitution'. (Add. MS. 29159, f. 45.)
[7] J. Scott to W. Hastings, 7 June 1783. Ibid., f. 332. Cf. Thurlow to Gower [1782]. *H.M.C., Sutherland MSS.*, 5th Report, p. 210.

next session, spoke of it as delicate, but solely since opposition
would be strengthened by those who would vote 'upon grounds
of personal attachment to this or that Director, or to this or that
Governor'.[1] There was no suggestion yet of what he called the
'vigorous and hazardous'[2] plan which was certain to raise
hostility on a far wider plane. It was not till the beginning of
September that Hastings's correspondents began to tell him of
a plan that was believed to be hatching to transfer the whole
patronage of the Company 'to the west end of the town'.[3]

If the intentions of Fox and Burke and their followers remained
obscure, that of the other section of the Government, the
followers of Lord North, was even more uncertain; this was
only of secondary importance for there were few illusions as to
which section would prevail in this matter. There was, however,
a general feeling both at the beginning and during the course
of the administration that North and his followers might at
least act as a brake on their allies.[4] The confusion into which
North's own relations with the Company were thrown by the
Coalition was shown by an incident which occurred during the
preparation for the annual election of directors in April, while
the Coalition was in the last stages of its negotiation. In the
normal way Laurence Sulivan would return to the Direction
after his year out by rotation. The supporters of the 'Old' party,
however, believed that an attempt was being made to exclude
him. The fact that a report of the Select Committee censuring
him had been produced shortly before the election, was inter-
preted, perhaps justly, as an attempt to influence the proprietors against him.[5]

In these circumstances Sulivan and some of his supporters,
old followers of North and Lord Sandwich in the days of the
North Administration, called on their former leader and asked
him to instruct Robinson 'to take the usual steps' on Sulivan's
behalf. North, with his customary good-nature, gave them a
verbal promise of support and sent them off to Robinson; but
Robinson, uneasy though he was at his master's new alliance,

[1] Lord John Russell, *Memorials and Correspondence of Charles James Fox*, ii. 119.
[2] Ibid. ii. 171.
[3] J. Price to W. Hastings, 3 September 1783. Add. MS. 29160, f. 266.
[4] James MacPherson to W. Hastings, 28 February 1783. Add. MS. 29158,
f. 322.
[5] *The Seventh Report*. Cf. *Parliamentary Register*, ix. 583 seq.

felt obliged to refuse to act until he had the instructions from
North direct. The result of Robinson's caution was that North
began to show a tendency to hedge and to suggest that before
intervening in the election he must discuss the matter with the
Duke of Portland and his other new friends. But he was dealing
on this occasion with men who knew him well. When a deputa-
tion including the impetuous Governor Johnstone, calling to
remonstrate with him, found the Duke of Portland, Fox, and
Burke in his ante-room, they forced their way through into his
bedroom and—telling him that he would be dishonoured and
would alienate his best friends if he withdrew from his pledge—
extracted a letter from him in support of Sulivan before they
left the room.[1] Sulivan was duly elected, to play his part in the
resounding scenes of the next winter, but this was the last sign
of personal contact between North and the 'Old' party in the
Company which Robinson had built up for him. There could
be no hope that they would follow North into the camp of
his new allies. When Robinson began to abandon him, first
privately and finally openly, it was this defection alone that
enabled him to keep the influence within the Company which
was so useful in the crisis to come.

It was during the summer recess that the measure which was
to be known as Fox's India Bill began to take form and that
Fox, Burke, and their friends really began to face the problem
of determining the future relations between the State and the
Company and of laying down the future lines of the British
administration of India. There is evidence that the Bill only
took its final form some time after the end of September. On 20
September the Duke of Portland wrote to the Duke of Manchester offering him the position of Governor-General. In this
letter he indicated that he had in mind an Act of Parliament to
nominate both a government in India and a Court of Directors
in England (on which there should be included some members
of both Houses of Parliament) as a temporary measure for a
period of not less than three and probably not more than five
years. When Manchester replied saying that he would prefer
a temporary dictatorship in the hands of the Government in

---

[1] J. Scott to W. Hastings, 23 March 1783. Add. MS. 29158, ff. 437 seq. Printed,
Gleig, op. cit., ii. 517–18. Lord Sandwich was in the party that called on
North.

India, Charles James Fox replied guardedly on 4 October that their plans were not yet digested, but would be sent to him as soon as anything was settled.[1]

The first indication of the change in their preoccupations was the rumours which began to spread in September. Not only was it said that all the Company's patronage was to be seized, but also that Fox and North had come to an agreement about the sharing out of it.[2] It was about this time that there also took place another significant change. As the ministry began to realize the difficulties they would encounter in introducing a radical alteration in Indian policy, a marked change in their attitude towards Warren Hastings began to be apparent. Though discipline was weak and Burke never allowed his crusade to be deflected by considerations of expediency, a number of members of both sections of the ministry began about this time to approach Hastings's friends in an obviously concerted attempt to discover whether any compromise on his claims was possible so that at least one major issue could be settled before the Bill was introduced.[3]

They were encouraged to make this attempt by the fact that news had been received that the Mahratta War had at last come to an end. This removed one of the major grounds of attack on Hastings, and led to the belief that he would soon be returning home, a circumstance which might make his friends readier to come to an agreement. The supporters of administration continued their attempts to placate Hastings's friends up to the last moment. The very day Fox moved to introduce his Bill he sent Sheridan to one of Hastings's friends in an endeavour, as one of them said, to 'bespeak our neutrality'.[4] While in the first months of the ministry every India debate had re-echoed with ministerial abuse of Warren Hastings, now that the India Bill was coming forward Fox and the more moderate of his followers in the Commons and all the ministerial speakers in the Lords went out of their way to insist that the Bill was no attack on Hastings or on any man. They maintained with emphasis that it was a question of reorganization which Hastings himself had

[1] *H.M.C.*, 8th Report, pt. ii, pp. 132–6. On 23 October 1783 Manchester turned down the offer (ibid., p. 136).
[2] J. Scott to W. Hastings, 10 September 1783. Add. MS. 29160, f. 293[v].
[3] Ditto, 13 September 1783. Ibid., ff. 306 seq.
[4] Ditto, 20 December 1783. Add. MS. 29161, f. 201[v].

declared necessary. Even had Burke and the extremists not counteracted these smooth words by their violence, it is unbelievable that Hastings's friends would have been misled by them, but the beginning of this new attitude in administration is significant as indicating both the time when Fox and his followers began to formulate the terms of their daring Bill, and their recognition of the gravity of the occasion.

There is peculiarly little evidence as to when and by whom the Bill was drawn up. Some have claimed it as Fox's creation and have denied that there is any proof that Burke drew it up or was specially concerned in it.[1] But not only was Burke the acknowledged East Indian expert of his party; there is also evidence which seems clearly to indicate that he was responsible for both its inspiration and much of its form. Among his correspondence there is an undated letter endorsed in Burke's hand 'from Mr. Pigot who finished the India Bill from my drafts'. It runs: 'I shall be particularly obliged to you to send me, as soon as ever you come in, so much of the bill, or instructions for the bill, as you have in the state in which it is; as it will very much forward my work.'[2] So too there is some evidence of the prominent part Burke played in pushing the proposals on the ministry as a whole. Robinson, by this time a hidden enemy of the administration, wrote to Jenkinson on 7 November suggesting that the Coalition might disintegrate: 'India is a rock. Remember what I said to you from Lord N's [North's] conversation with me. Burke drives madly, perhaps to their breach.'[3] Whoever had the greatest part in formulating the Bill it was adopted whole-heartedly by Fox and his followers and accepted, if not with the same enthusiasm, by all members of the administration before it was introduced into the House of Commons. The leaders were well aware how controversial it would be. 'Our India measure will come on soon after the meeting', wrote Fox on 7 November 1783. 'It will be a vigorous and a hazardous one and if we get that well over, I have very little apprehension about anything else here.'[4]

The Bill, which was ultimately carried triumphantly and

[1] *Memorials and Correspondence of Charles James Fox*, ii. 98.
[2] *Burke Correspondence*, iii. 22.
[3] J. Robinson to C. Jenkinson, 7 November 1783. Add. MS. 38567, f. 163.
[4] *Memorials and Correspondence of Charles James Fox*, ii. 171.

rapidly through the House of Commons only to be defeated in the Lords, was intended to be one of several. It was to be the main Regulating Act; another to deal with special problems of misrule in India, based on the findings of the Select Committee and the views of Philip Francis, was to have followed, and there was also a promise to deal with the Company's financial problems, which would no doubt have entailed a third. The subjects with which a Regulating Bill had to deal were those already taken up in Dundas's Bill. But they were handled very differently. Dundas had sought to deal with the problem of the relations between the State and the Company at home by increasing the power of the State over the political activities of the Company, and with the problems of misrule in India primarily by increasing the power and the responsibility of the Governor-General. The Rockingham party in opposition, on the other hand, had for years strongly and consistently opposed both these solutions, and done so on principles which could be relied on to make an instantaneous appeal to an eighteenth-century House of Commons. They had opposed the increased authority of ministers over the Company as opening up a dangerous opportunity of increased patronage for the Crown, and they had opposed the increase of the powers granted to the Governor-General or to any servants in India as leading to tyranny and absolutism. They had also ever since 1766 opposed the distinction between the Company's political and commercial activities as impracticable and unreal. Now that they found themselves in power with the problem of controlling and reforming the Company, they had to find a way of doing so without running counter to their frequently declared principles. It was probably to this need for consistency, more than to any of the deep-laid calculations of party gain attributed to them by their opponents, that the most striking features of the Bill were due.

Fox's Bill had three main features. In the first place it was a more sweeping attack on the independence of the Company than anyone had ever suggested since Beckford had blustered in the House of Commons in 1767. In the second place it gave the powers the Company would lose not to the Crown but to a body of seven Commissioners, nominated in the Act (their successors were to be chosen by the Crown), who were to hold office for at least four years, and to nine Assistant Commissioners[1] who were, under their direction, to manage the Company's commerce, and who were to be nominated in the first instance in the Act though later by an open vote in the Court of Proprietors. In the third place misrule in India was to be checked, not by increasing the power of either Governor-General or Council, but by careful provision for their more complete subordination to the Commissioners sitting in England. The seven Commissioners whom it was proposed to nominate for the first four years were chosen on a ratio among the supporters of the two branches of the Government, care being taken to include only respectable men who had not been concerned with the East Indian feuds; the nine Assistant Commissioners were to consist of practically all the Rockingham supporters in the Court of Directors. For Governor-General it was thought that either Macartney or the rising young politician William Eden was to be the choice.[2]

The measure was the most radical to be given concrete form in the course of the century. To contemporaries its most striking feature was the method of appointment of the Commissioners. The enemies of the administration saw in this nothing but an attempt to seize the extensive patronage of the Company and to preserve it even should they be no longer in power. In fact it seems likely that the origin of this provision lay in no such calculation, but that it arose primarily, if not wholly, from the need felt by the framers of the Bill to preserve consistency with their earlier statements of policy. As late as April 1782 Fox had publicly reaffirmed his party's disapprobation of any settlement which would increase the patronage of the Crown. It was hard to think of any reform that was not open to this objection; an arrangement whereby the Commissioners were to hold office for a fixed term of years might be held to reduce this danger to a minimum. That this thought was foremost in their minds (even though the advantages of patronage in their own hands could obviously not be ignored) is suggested by the reactions of Lord FitzWilliam, who was persuaded (with some unwillingness)

---

[1] The number was at first fixed at eight but afterwards increased to nine. The proposed title of the Commissioners was changed to 'Directors' when the Bill was under discussion.

[2] J. Scott to W. Hastings, quoting Elliot. Add. MS. 29161, f. 221, 11 January 1784.

to undertake the Chairmanship of the Commission. On considering their proposals he urged the importance of consistency with the protest which he and other Peers of the Rockingham party had made against the Regulating Act of 1773. He wrote to Portland on 16 November 1783:

> The particular point of a *Parliamentary appointment* is there argued upon such general principles that I do not see the possibility of getting over it—no circumstances, no situations, can make any change in so general a principle—. It will be ten times better to meet the thing boldly and give the King the appointment for the purpose of creating *responsibility in those who advise him to* appoint.[1]

There is no evidence whether he was converted from this very sensible opinion, or whether he was over-ruled, but the line of argument pursued is significant.

Even were there no external evidence which pointed to Burke as the chief originator of the Bill, the internal evidence would mark it as a product of Burke's intelligence. It has the ingenuity which marks his legislative productions, but also the absence of administrative sense.[2] There can be little doubt that it was a measure far less likely to be practicable and beneficial than either Dundas's abortive Bill or the Act which Pitt later passed. The provision which left the control of India in the hands of a Commission chosen on party lines but holding office for a fixed period would have been open to serious objections when the Commissioners and the Government of the day differed in their party allegiance. Just as questions of war and peace in India had become too important to entrust to a trading Company, so they could hardly have been satisfactorily left in the hands of Commissioners who might at any time be in open hostility to the Government on whom in the last resort the responsibility for these questions fell. Lord Cornwallis, who was not altogether hostile to the Bill, wrote to a friend at the time that he cared little about chartered rights but that

> I think Jenkinson hit one principal blot which can hardly be got over. He supposed the Commissioners to be appointed for three or five years, as proposed by Fox, and that a change of Administration ensued, what would then be the consequence? The directors of East

---

[1] FitzWilliam to Portland, 16 November 1783. Portland MSS.
[2] Compare D. Keir, 'Economical Reform 1779–1787', *Law Quarterly*, l. 368 seq.

India Affairs would probably be acting in direct opposition to the Government at home.[1]

Nor were the provisions for the Government of India more satisfactory. The whole evolution of British rule in India during the nineteenth and early twentieth centuries has shown that the Governor-General must be left with discretion and be given powers commensurate with his great responsibilities, as Warren Hastings had so clearly seen. Lord Cornwallis put this clearly when he had gained some experience in India: 'In regard to the general state of our affairs in India, the power given to the Governor General, however it may now be misplaced, is the only chance of saving this country. Mr. Fox's plan would have ruined all.'[2] Burke's attempt to increase the Governor-General's subordination to a body sitting in England shows how little he understood of the problems of administration—the checking of abuses, not the government of a sub-continent, was what he still had chiefly in mind. There can be no more emphatic illustration of the advantage to a politician of experience in power over experience in opposition than the fact that a man of Burke's eminence entirely missed a point which was perfectly apparent to others so much his inferiors in vision and insight as John Robinson, Charles Jenkinson, and Henry Dundas.

Fox's Bill was thus a poor one; but the opposition to it at the time was not based on its weaknesses, for these were not of a kind which an eighteenth-century House of Commons was prepared to appreciate. It was attacked chiefly on the ground that it destroyed chartered rights; that it was introduced without prior consultation with the Company or any attempt to come to terms with them; and, far and away the most damaging attack, that it gave enormous power of patronage to Fox and his party whether or not they were in power, thereby threatening the royal prerogative (as Jenkinson and the king's friends protested) and making an *imperium in imperio* within Parliament itself.

That it would destroy vested rights was certain, and the Company succeeded in stirring up a number of protests from other corporate bodies on this issue. But its supporters were right in pointing out that breaches in the chartered rights of the Company had already been made and were inevitable if it was

---

[1] *The Correspondence of Charles, First Marquis Cornwallis*, ed. C. Ross, 1859, i. 150.   [2] Ibid. i. 226.

to be reformed. It was also true that the terms of the Bill were an unusually well-kept secret. When Parliament opened on 11 November Fox announced that he would introduce his Bill on the 18th, but as late as the 15th Hastings's agents did not know what was in it.[1] Nor was there any concession to the custom whereby ministers normally tried to get Company support for their measures before introducing them in the House. The Chairman of the Company and their own good friend, Sir Henry Fletcher, told the infuriated proprietors that he had not known its terms in advance, though he later admitted that he had a general idea how ministers' views were shaping.[2] But in view of the sweeping nature of the Bill, and Government's determination to give office only to its own friends, no purpose could have been served by prior consultation, the aim of which, ever since 1773, had been to ensure the co-operation of the Company in working a system of combined Company and State control.

Even before the Company knew the terms of the Bill they had made it clear that they were going to do all they could to embarrass the ministry. The news that the Mahratta War had ended reached England shortly before Parliament reassembled. Five days before it met, the friends of Hastings and the other Company officials, backed by all the forces of the 'Old' party, called a General Court to congratulate Hastings and his Council and to adjure them not to resign precipitately.[3] The correspondence of those concerned, as well as an abortive attempt by the Government to persuade them to give up their intentions, shows that there were wide political implications behind the move.[4] John Robinson, in the process of abandoning his old leader, was active in fomenting the meeting, and told Jenkinson: 'You will see the Proprietors are at work. Hastings should, I think, now be supported for many reasons—it will perhaps break them the sooner—and I know *we can get* Hastings home when it is wanted *for good purposes*.'[5] Thus even before the terms of the Bill were known the possibility of using it as a focus for opposition was being considered.

The centre of the opposition, however, was found not in the

[1] J. Scott to W. Hastings, 15 November 1783. Add. MS. 29161, f. 134.
[2] *Parliamentary Register*, xii. 80.
[3] Court Book 92, pp. 544 seq., 7 November 1783.
[4] J. Scott to W. Hastings, 21 October 1783. Add. MS. 29161, ff. 32v-33.
[5] J. Robinson to C. Jenkinson, 7 November 1783. Add. MS. 38567, f. 163.

Company but among the politicians. It concerned the provision of patronage and the access of strength which this would give to the party in power at the moment. When the Bill came before the House it was received with violent and real as well as fictitious indignation. Reflecting years later on the downfall of the administration, Lord John Townshend said that the Bill was 'really unpopular' and was made more so in debate by 'Burke's ungovernable temper and Jack Lee's extreme indiscretion'.[1] That men had confidence, nevertheless, in the strength of the Coalition to survive both this outcry and the king's antagonism, is shown by the way in which the ministerial majorities were sustained in the House of Commons during the passing of the Bill. In the Lords the ministry had always felt more nervous of success, Fox stressing the point that every vote recorded in the Commons would 'tell on account of the House of Lords afterwards'.[2] But here too there is little doubt they would have been successful had it not been for the actions of the king and certain determined men who now decided to seize the opportunity to exploit the widespread and diversified opposition to the principles of the Bill.

The political turmoil which had raged ever since the preceding February gave every enterprising man in political life his chance of prominence. A number of these men now came into collaboration: Dundas and the still unformed William Pitt, Charles Jenkinson, emerging from his silence to play on behalf of the king a discreet part as an intermediary and perhaps something more, and the formidable Thurlow now for the first time in the wilderness. To these there tended to gravitate those elements among North's followers who had always deplored the Coalition with Fox and would have preferred an alliance with Shelburne on which the Crown would have smiled. The most important of these from the practical point of view was North's Secretary, John Robinson, whose defection was effected with the minimum of ostentation but with consequences which North never forgot and did not, until his death-bed, forgive.[3]

---

[1] *Memorials and Correspondence of Charles James Fox*, ii. 27. Lee, who was Attorney-General, caused an uproar by describing a charter as no more than 'a skin of parchment with a waxed seal at the corner'.   [2] Ibid. ii. 215.
[3] Namier, *Structure of Politics*, i. 48.

Robinson's importance at this crisis lay firstly in his extensive inside knowledge of the springs of political allegiance within both Houses, but secondly in his connexions with the East India Company and the influence he was able to wield there. Though he himself did no more than abstain from voting on the East India Bill and as late as 19 November North wrote to him asking him to whip up his friends to vote for the second reading,[1] Robinson was already encouraging his friends at East India House to oppose it. Moreover reactions in the Company to the threat of the Bill had made events there easy for them to control, for on 21 November the General Court had entrusted the whole defence of the Company to a Committee of nine proprietors of whom Governor Johnstone was Chairman, Laurence Sulivan a member, and of which Richard Atkinson soon became the leader.[2] It is difficult to know when the possibility began to be considered, not only of a combined assault by the opposition elements and the Company against the Bill, but of an attempt to overthrow the Government upon it. It would seem, however, to be after Dundas came down from Scotland for the second reading. He then joined Jenkinson and Robinson in their close contact with the leaders of the Committee of Nine Proprietors, and on the very day of the second reading Francis Baring told Shelburne that forces were beginning to move against the Government and spoke of negotiations which were in progress, he imagined with Pitt and his friends.[3]

By 3 December Richard Atkinson, who was acting as intermediary for Robinson (who thought it wise to keep out of town), wrote telling him that 'everything stands prepared for the blow if a *certain* person has courage to strike it'.[4] It would seem that the plan for overthrowing the ministry by defeating it in the Lords had taken shape. Neither the king nor those who would take the lead in Parliament had, however, pledged themselves. On 5 December Dundas asked Robinson to prepare urgently an analysis of the House of Commons in the event of a change

---

[1] North to J. Robinson, 19 November 1783. Abergavenny MSS. vi. 519.

[2] The Committee of Nine was first set up on 22 November 1782. Court Book 91, pp. 634–5. Atkinson was not a member at first, but by the end of 1783 was its Acting Chairman in Johnstone's absence (Court Book 92, p. 699).

[3] F. Baring to Shelburne, 27 November 1783. Lansdowne MSS.

[4] Abergavenny MSS. vi. 520. Quoted W. T. Laprade, *Parliamentary Papers of John Robinson 1774–84*, xiii.

of government. The next day, while the document was still unfinished, Dundas, Thurlow, and Pitt considered it,[1] and by the 9th, the day after the Bill passed its final reading in the Commons and on which it was given its first formal reading in the Lords, it was complete.[2] Though Robinson warned them of its unreliability in such abnormal conditions, it was thought sufficiently encouraging to justify a bid for power. 'Things are', said Jenkinson, 'in the hands of men of resolution.'[3]

At the same time the Company pressed forward with its opposition, preparing a case to be put by Counsel before the Lords, and organizing with what speed it could petitions from other corporate bodies throughout the kingdom. Full support of Warren Hastings by the leaders of the new movement was evidently felt to be necessary whatever mental reservations they may have made. Thurlow and Temple interviewed his agent Major Scott at some length.[4] Then on 10 December a letter was sent to the king declaring their willingness to 'receive the burthen';[5] the next day the king saw Lord Temple and gave him the famous permission to state that any peer voting for the Bill would be considered his enemy. On the night before the Bill was again before the Lords, Pitt, Dundas, Robinson, and Richard Atkinson met in the deepest secrecy,[6] but the secret was already out and Fox's friends knew the Bill was lost and even that the ministry was doomed.[7] At the second reading of the Bill in the Lords the tide turned against the ministry and on the 17th it was decisively beaten. The next day the king dismissed them and what was to be the Pitt Administration came in.

Thus ended the first attempt at a sweeping reform of the East India Company. Though its defeat was due largely to the political situation and the determination of a few resolute men

[1] J. Robinson to C. Jenkinson, 7 December 1783. Add. MS. 38567, f. 167. The document is printed in Laprade, op. cit., pp. 66 seq.
[2] Ditto, 9 December 1783. Add. MS. 38567, f. 169.
[3] C. Jenkinson to J. Robinson, 13 December 1783. Abergavenny MSS. vi. 528. H.M.C. x. 6, p. 62.
[4] J. Scott to W. Hastings, 20 December 1783. Add. MS. 29161, f. 194. Printed Gleig, op. cit. iii. 99 seq.
[5] R. Atkinson to J. Robinson, 12 December 1783. Abergavenny MSS. vi. 526.
[6] Ditto, 15 December 1783. Ibid. vi. 530. H.M.C. x. 6, p. 62.
[7] Memorials and Correspondence of Charles James Fox, ii. 220-1. R. FitzPatrick to Ossory, 15 December 1783.

to take advantage of it, they were able to do so the more easily because it aroused widespread hostility and dislike, not only among the threatened Indian interests but among a wide body of opinion throughout the country. The petitions and other representations which came in against it and in support of the new Government were no doubt carefully organized and much of what appeared in the Press was subsidized, but the contrast between the difficulty which Burke and the Company found in getting up protests against Lord North's Regulating Act in 1773 and the ease with which they were now obtained, was highly significant. Nevertheless the success of the opponents of the Bill did not mean that the subject was closed. It still remained axiomatic that East Indian reform was necessary. Indeed Pitt came into office pledged to undertake it.

The Pitt Administration

It is outside the scope of this work to trace the stages by which, even before the dissolution of Parliament, the new administration gradually gained credit. The growth of the belief that it would endure began to reflect itself in the steadily shrinking majorities which their opponents could command in the House. The 1784 election, as is notorious, completed their triumph. Throughout this process, the East Indian question remained well in the foreground. It was indeed inevitable that it should, since Fox's Bill had gained such notoriety and since (thanks to his failure) no measure had been taken even to alleviate, still less to remove, the Company's immediate financial embarrassments. Here at least the new minority Government could do something; the Treasury, to tide over the next few months, gave them permission under the 1781 Act to accept an increased number of Bills from India, despite a resolution from the hostile majority of the House of Commons forbidding them to do so.[1] Nevertheless everything remained at a standstill until the Company's future was settled.

The urgency of the problem on the one hand and on the other the new Government's own anxiety not to give time for the support they might expect from a grateful Company to evaporate, led them to drive on at once with the introduction of the East India Bill they had promised without waiting for a

[1] *Jour. H.C.* xxxix. 924, 16 February 1784.

majority in the House of Commons. The importance of pushing on quickly arose largely from the need to take advantage of a situation within the Company highly satisfactory to government and not likely to last long.

The crisis over Fox's Bill had left the Court of Directors hopelessly disorganized. In the face of the fury of the General Court, the Chairman, Sir Henry Fletcher, and his chief supporter, Stephen Lushington (both to be beneficiaries under the defeated Bill), had felt obliged to resign, and even before they had done so they were opposed by a clear majority of directors. During the debates on the Bill all initiative had been taken out of the Court's hands by the Committee of Nine Proprietors, and now, though the purpose for which it had been appointed was achieved, it determined to complete its work before it went out of existence. The two ends its members were aiming at were the re-establishment of the ascendancy of the 'Old' interest in the Company and (so far as Robinson and his agent Richard Atkinson were concerned) the cementing of the alliance between the Company and the new Administration and the pledge of Company support to the India legislation the Administration were determined to introduce. As Richard Atkinson wrote to Robinson, 'We must lay our ground work.'[1] It was with these two ends in view that a General Court was called for 19 December to receive a report on the fate of Fox's Bill and the Committee and its friends met in advance to concert the measures to be adopted at it.[1] At this preliminary meeting it was agreed to propose Governor Johnstone and Richard Atkinson as Directors in the place of Sir Henry Fletcher and Lushington and to propose another supporter, John Woodhouse, to fill a third vacancy. When the Court met these proposals were adopted, and thanks were given to the Counsel who had presented the Company's case before the Lords and Commons, to the fourteen directors who had opposed the 'late violent attempt', and to Governor Johnstone and Atkinson for their work on the Committee of Nine Proprietors.[2] The next day the Committee submitted to the directors a recommendation that 'in the present state of affairs the Company should state its willingness to treat in an

---

[1] R. Atkinson to J. Robinson, 18 December 1783. Abergavenny MSS. vi. 541. H.M.C. x. 6, pp. 63–64.

[2] Court Book 92, pp. 697–702, 19 December 1783.

amicable manner with Ministers on the Company's affairs'; and the measure passed rapidly through the directors and General Court summoned for the same day.[1]

Meantime what they were to be asked to agree to was being equally rapidly drawn up by the new ministry. On the same day Baring wrote to Lord Shelburne: 'Some friends of W. P. are at work about a new plan for India, the groundwork I apprehend to be a separation of the patronage and power (including civil and military) from the commercial.'[2] This seemed to him not disadvantageous but he added: 'One circumstance however is alarming, and that is the direction will be solely in the hands of Mr. Dundas.'

It was inevitable that Dundas, with his clear-cut ideas on Indian reform and indeed his Bill in his pocket, should take the lead in formulating the new Government's Indian policy and that its basis should be the Bill he had so recently introduced.[3] Nevertheless some at least of the criticisms which had been advanced against it in Parliament and the Company had to be met. By the beginning of January Pitt was fairly clear what modifications in Dundas's Bill were necessary to obtain the support of the Company and to make success in the House even remotely possible.[4] In the first place some of the personal powers proposed for the Governor-General must go, to answer the cry that a personal tyranny would be created. His suspensive veto, which Robinson and Jenkinson had at first advocated and Dundas had adopted (echoing Warren Hastings's representations), was dropped, though the strengthening of his power over the subordinate Presidencies was retained. In the second place pains were taken to limit the extent of the Government's declared patronage; Dundas at first clung to and Pitt adopted his favourite plan to create a third Secretary of State to control

---

[1] Court Book 92, pp. 705 seq., 20 December 1783.

[2] F. Baring to Shelburne, 18 December 1783. Lansdowne MSS.

[3] Atkinson on 31 December speaks of the proposed Bill as Dundas's. R. Atkinson to J. Robinson, 31 December 1783. Dundas was steering it through the Cabinet. Abergavenny MSS. vi. 551. *H.M.C.* x. 6, p. 64.

[4] He saw the chief interested members of the Company on 9 January and had his scheme more or less complete then, though at least one modification was made later; see for this R. Atkinson to J. Robinson, 5 January 1784. Abergavenny MSS. vi. 557. Atkinson and Robinson approved the main lines of the Bill but thought it rather too general and depending heavily on further legislation. Ibid. vi. 551.

the political and military affairs of the Company, but when he was opposed by Atkinson and Robinson and was made aware of the unpopularity of the measure, he agreed that this control should be placed in the hands of a Board, the Board of Control of the future.[1] Measures intended to check oppression in India and to bring to light financial abuses by Company's servants were also incorporated to satisfy the demands of opinion in the House of Commons. The Bill in fact differed in principle very little from that finally passed later in the year.

No pains were spared to ensure that the Company gave its support to this measure so closely resembling that which it had strongly opposed only eight months before. Pitt himself discussed it with the Chairman and Deputy, with Laurence Sulivan, and also with representatives of the Committee of Proprietors.[1] On 6 January the Chairman reported that the Government's proposals were complete and a Court of Directors and a General Court were called two days later to consider them. The Committee of Proprietors in the meantime framed a number of resolutions strongly supporting the Government's scheme. When the Courts met, these resolutions were pushed through them (and later confirmed by ballot) at a speed condemned as indecent by the minority group in the Court of Directors who still represented the interests of the former Government.[2] When Pitt introduced his Bill in the House of Commons four days later, he could, therefore, claim that he (unlike his predecessors) enjoyed the full support of the Company for his proposals. Gratitude, fear of the future, good organization by the friends of the Government in the Company, and quick action on the part of the Government itself had combined to win unprecedented support from the Company for a measure which under more normal conditions would have created an uproar there.

This was more important for the future than for the present, however, for Pitt's first Bill was doomed. Despite the majority against him in the Commons he seems to have hoped that the urgency of the matter and the modifications he had introduced into Dundas's former measure might lead his enemies to let it

[1] R. Atkinson to J. Robinson, 5 January 1784. Abergavenny MSS. vi. 557.
[2] Court Book 92, pp. 744–56, 8 January 1784. Protest of six directors, pp. 770 seq., 13 January 1784.

through. But the political situation was far too tense for compromise, and the Bill met the fate of his other measures. The
only response to his plea of urgency was an offer by Fox to
introduce a modification of his own Bill if he were assured that
there would be no dissolution of Parliament until it was passed.
To this debating point no reply was made.[1]

The deadlock therefore remained unbroken. The Company
occupied itself in the meantime in an attempt to disprove Fox's
allegations about its financial stability. Richard Atkinson,
maintaining the prominence he had recently gained there,
'laboured for weeks' on a statement of their position for which
Laurence Sulivan gave him the lion's share of the credit.[2] In
Parliament the Government used their majority in the Lords to
censure the Commons for irresponsibility and indifference to
public credit in trying to prevent the Treasury from giving
what help it could to the Company. The move was a shrewd
one so far as it went, for the majority in the debate which followed was driven onto the defensive.[3]

Events were, however, now reaching a crisis. In the negotiations which followed, inaugurated by certain country gentlemen
at the St. Alban's Tavern to try to bring the new and the old
ministries together, the possibility of an agreed East India Bill
was considered, but the two parties were still far apart when the
negotiations broke down.[4] The failure of these negotiations
marked the beginning of the Government's triumph. By
27 February the majority against them in the Commons was
down to seven; by 8 March it had sunk to one and on the
following day Fox dared not divide the House on the Mutiny
Bill. Even before the dissolution on 23 March and before the
election which confirmed the triumph of the king and his new
ministers, the game had manifestly been won.

In the famous election which followed, the part which East
Indian interests played has attracted some attention. The
election has been considered by historians at different times in
a completely different light; it has been held out on the one
hand as a hitherto unparalleled expression of public opinion

---

[1] *Parliamentary Register*, xii. 603, 16 January 1784.
[2] L. Sulivan to W. Hastings, 1 March 1784. Add. MS. 29162, f. 293.
[3] *Parliamentary Register*, xiii. 73 seq. and 101 seq., 5 and 16 February 1784.
[4] Ibid., pp. 175–6, 20 February 1784.

and on the other as the outstanding illustration of the success of eighteenth-century parliamentary 'management'. The truth seems to be that it was 'managed', and managed expensively,[1] but that the 'management' was assisted in a number of places by a real public opinion whipped up by pamphlets, newspapers, and cartoons.[2]

It has been suggested by those stressing the importance of 'management' in this election, that its importance was intensified by the entrance into the political field of a new factor, the 'commercial magnates' of the East India Company using

their wealth in large amounts in an organized and systematic way, not merely to purchase seats regularly in the market, to provide funds for the satisfaction of electors habitually venal, and to establish interests in the accustomed way, but also frankly in an effort to destroy, by the use of large sums, interests long-established and to corrupt constituencies not hitherto regarded as venal.[3]

Put into more sweeping terms, the suggestion runs that

this new power of organized wealth, aroused to give battle in defence of its privileges, now proposed to depart from the accepted rules of the game and to adopt a policy of winning at any cost.

It may be stated at once that the evidence does not appear to support this suggestion. Whether one uses as the basis of examination the wide definition of the Indian interest in Parliament adopted by Dr. Philips in his careful and comprehensive study[4] —a definition which may be said to include the passive as well as the active members of the interest—or whether an attempt is made to perform the more difficult task of deciding what was the active interest which might indulge in this organized activity, the same thing is clear. Those responsible for managing the election were, as usual, looking for men of wealth friendly to government who would take up expensive seats; the only distinction which can be drawn between this and other elections is that on this occasion they found a larger number of such men than usual among the ranks of those interested in the Company, and that men such as Atkinson helped them to do so.

---

[1] W. T. Laprade, op. cit., pp. 65 seq.
[2] Mrs. E. George, 'Fox's Martyrs; the General Election of 1784', *Royal Historical Society Transactions*, xxi. 133 seq.
[3] Laprade, op. cit. xvii.
[4] C. H. Philips, op. cit., pp. 307 seq.

Among the men most prominent in the Company it is true the movement had already gone so far that it was difficult for it to go farther. Indeed, there were rather fewer members of the 1784 Court of Directors sitting in the new House than there had been members of the 1783 Directors sitting in the old. To the ranks of prominent 'Nabobs' or their representatives sitting in the House the 1784 election also brought few recruits, and even these were men who would probably have sought seats there in any event; Philip Francis (in opposition), Hastings's agent, Major Scott (it had been suggested by the Government representatives that he might purchase two seats on his patron's behalf, one for himself and one for Hastings on his return, but he thought the expense of one sufficient),[1] and George Vansittart. All the other prominent Company servants who had returned recently enough to fear investigation or who were hoping for further preferment had already provided themselves with seats. It was among less prominent men, in particular City men with some East Indian concerns, that the Government found recruits for parliamentary seats at the election.

In the stirring up of public opinion, on the other hand, both the Company and some of its members played an active, though not an outstanding, part. The Company itself, through the Committee which it set up to manage its defence against Fox's Bill, published the case that Counsel put forward for them in Parliament and invited other corporate bodies to come forward in defence of chartered rights. Among the individuals at work those putting the case for Warren Hastings had been far and away the most enterprising in their use of the Press. Since 1781 Major Scott had been actively engaged in writing and sponsoring pamphlets, providing the Press with good copies of speeches in Parliament, and paying for the insertion in newspapers of letters by himself and others answering attacks on Hastings and announcing his merits. In 1783 his campaign reached its height and towards the end of the year the defence of Hastings merged into a defence of the Company. During the election itself, however, it seems rather to have died down and though propaganda against Fox as the would-be tyrant of the East appears to have been the most effective electoral weapon against him in the

[1] J. Scott to W. Hastings, 11 March 1784. He paid £4,000 for his seat at West Looe. Add. MS. 29162, ff. 362 seq.

'popular' constituencies during the election, the pamphleteers who were most successful in exploiting this theme[1] seem to have been employed not by any Indian interest, but by the parliamentary leaders.

Nor can it be said that a great deal of money was expended by the Company interests in their campaigns. Scott, for instance, calculated that his Press campaign in favour of his patron cost him between his arrival at the end of 1781 and the middle of 1784 no more than some £1,700.[2] Of this at least £569 was spent before the end of 1782.[3] Scott himself and other friends of Hastings did much of the writing without pay, and in any case the remuneration of pamphleteers was not high. In so far as the Company or individuals connected with it assisted in this aspect of the election, it was more by the provision of information and the services of experienced writers than by the expenditure of large sums of money. In short, though the East Indian interests were peculiarly concerned in the results of this election, it cannot be claimed that they introduced a new element into it or in any way modified the eighteenth-century pattern of electioneering.

But if the election saw no revolutionary change in method or in the House which resulted from it, and though the new Government stressed with ostentation what was continuous and unchanged in their Indian policy, what was interesting in the relation between State and Company in the future was not what was the same but what was different. Pitt's India Act, based on the Bill of the previous January, has been called a dishonest Act,[4] but no one connected with the Company had

---

[1] e.g. Daniel Pulteney, *The Effect to be expected from the East India Bill upon the Constitution of Great Britain* (1783) (George, op. cit., p. 145). He was a protégé of the Duke of Rutland. (*H.M.C., MSS. of the Duke of Rutland*, iii. 238, &c.)

[2] J. Scott to W. Hastings, 12 July 1784. Add. MS. 29164, f. 491.

[3] Ditto, 5 November 1782. He entered on his accounts

Paid Mr. Debrett	Printers	£110. 5.
To Mr. Wilkinson		£38.
Paid E. Baber and J. Price's Printers		£240.
[i.e. for printing pamphlets by them]		
To the Editors of different Papers for inserting letters etc.		£96.
To Writers		£85.

Add. MS. 29156, f. 409.

[4] Philips, op. cit., p. 34.

any real illusions about its contents. What Pitt and Dundas had set out to do was to give themselves both the sanctions and the machinery for carrying out the methods of government supervision and infiltration which North and Robinson had been seeking to employ ever since the Regulating Act of 1773. When Dundas's supplementary legislation of 1786 had been passed strengthening the hands of the Governor-General, as Dundas had always wished to do, they could also carry out the other intention of the Regulating Act of 1773—the establishment of a central power in India which could ensure the peaceful and stable government of the British possessions there. They were far better informed than their predecessors and they were able, after the return of Warren Hastings and the death of Laurence Sulivan, to build up their new power in the Company without the challenge which Robinson always had to face. In short, though Dundas never found the management of the Company easy, and there remained much to criticize in the methods of government control, in the conduct of the Company, and in the wisdom and foresight shown in the rule of their vast territories, the confusion of the past twenty-five years had come to an end and a new era had begun in the Government of India and in the relations of State and Company.

INDEX

Adair, James, 282 n.
Aix-la-Chapelle, Peace of, 48, 49.
Albemarle, 3rd Earl of, *see* Keppel, George.
American Colonies, 19, 227, 248, 315, 324 n., 338, 365.
American Revolution, War of, 237 n., 275 n., 290 n., 291, 331, 343 and n.
Amherst, Field-Marshal Jeffrey, Baron Amherst, 235 n.
Amsterdam, 10, 11, 41, 111, 139, 141, 142, 146 and n., 207, 208, 219, 228.
Amyand M.P., Sir George, 130 n.
Amyatt, Peter, 88 n., 116 n., 308 n.
Anatomy of Exchange Alley (D. Defoe), 11 n.
Angria, Tulaji, 181.
Anne, Queen, 16, 18
Anson, George, Baron Anson, 79.
Arcot, Nawab of, *see* Mohammed Ali.
Asaf Jah, 45.
Ashburton, 1st Baron, *see* Dunning, John.
Atkinson M.P., Richard, 65 n., 275 and n., 350, 380, 385, 404 and n., 405 and n., 407 and n., 408 n., 409 and n., 410, 411.
Auckland, 1st Baron, *see* Eden, William.
Auditor, The, 95 n.
Augusta, Princess of Wales, 197 n.
Aungier, Gerald, 2.
Austrian Succession, War of, 30, 46.

Baggs, Major Philip, 349 n.
Baker M.P., Sir William, 19 n., 31.
Bank of England, 14, 17, 19 n., 22 and n., 23, 24, 26, 34 n., 111, 223, 224 and n., 233, 259 n.
Bantam, factory at, 13.
Baring M.P., Sir Francis, 377, 378 n., 404 and n., 408 and n.
Barnard M.P., Sir John, 29, 31.
Barne M.P., Miles, 39, 40.
Barré M.P., Colonel Isaac, 102 n., 121 and n., 130, 132, 134, 151, 154, 172 n., 191 n., 192 n., 193 n., 194 n., 195 n., 196 n., 197 n., 202 n., 209 and n., 210 n., 211 and n., 212 n., 235 n., 242 n., 257, 377.
Barrington, William Wildman, 2nd Viscount Barrington, 295.
Barwell family, 244, 246.
Barwell, Mary, 245, 306.
Barwell M.P., Richard, 213, 214 n., 260, 288 n., 291, 294, 295, 301 and n., 302, 303 n., 306, 307 n., 308, 309, 349 n., 351 n., 360 and n.

Batavia, 262.
Bath, 88, 156, 157, 158, 160.
Bath, Earl of, *see* Pulteney, Sir William.
Bath, 1st Marquess of and 3rd Viscount Weymouth, *see* Thynne, Thomas.
Bathurst, Henry, 2nd Earl Bathurst, 306, 350.
Beauclerk, Vere, 1st Baron Vere, 104.
Becher, Richard, 290 n., 307, 309 n.
Beckford M.P., William, Alderman, 22 n., 30, 31, 147, 148 and n., 149, 151, 152, 158, 160, 161, 168, 169, 187, 242, 398.
Bedford, 4th Duke of, *see* Russell, John.
Behar, 367 n.
Belcher M.P., William, 73 n.
Bencoolen, 221 n.
Benfield M.P., Paul, 56, 298, 318 and n., 336 and n., 350, 352, 380.
Bengal, 3; *diwani* of, 32, 56, 136, 137, 138, 140, 149, 218, 225; 39; Nawab of, 45, 75, 82, 83, 87, 115, 116, 136, 137; 47, 53 and n., 55, 63, 64; Laurence Sulivan's interest in Bengal affairs, 65; effect on Bengal of his election as Chairman of Court of Directors (1758), 73, 74; appointment of Clive to Bengal Council, 67; general letter to Bengal forbidding payment of Clive's *jagir*, 111 and n., 112; Clive's plans for Bengal (1765), 130, 131, 136, 137; Clive's measures as Governor of Bengal, 138, 139, 140, 141, 142 and n., 147; 67 n.; J. Z. Holwell as Zemindar of Bengal, 67, 68 and n.; 69, 75 and n., 76 and n.; conflict between Bengal servants and direction, 77 and n., 84, 87 and n., 89, 90; 78 and n., 79, 81, 82, 86; presence of French in Bengal, 93, 95, 97, 98; 100, 105, 109, 115; crisis arising from private trade carried on by Company's servants in Bengal, 116 and n., 117; 119, 125, 126, 127; supersession of Bengal servants by those from other Presidencies, 118, 128; 149, 152, 179, 180 and n., 191, 200; appointment of Warren Hastings as Governor of Bengal, 205; his operations in Bengal, 297, 298, 300, 301; steps to improve Bengal administration (1772), 217, 218; 219, 220, 221 n., 222, 224, 225; financial difficulties of 1770, 226; measures concerning Bengal in Judicature Bill (1772), 230, 231, 232; 237 and n.,

5433   E e

Sackville, Lord George, see Germain, George Sackville, 1st Viscount Sackville.
St. Alban's Tavern, 174, 410.
St. Helena, 76.
Saint-John, Henry, 1st Viscount Bolingbroke, 20.
Salabat-Jang, Subah of the Deccan, 93, 97.
Salvador, Joseph, 105 n., 106 n., 111 n., 118, 119, 129, 130.
Sandwich, 4th Earl of, see Montagu, John.
Saunders, Thomas, 66 n., 109.
Savage, Henry, 62, 66 n., 234 n.
Savile M.P., Sir George, 8th Baronet, 240 n.
Scott M.P., Major John, 297 n., 298 n., 351 n., 359 n., 364 n., 373 n., 378 n.; co-leader of Hastings's supporters and ally of Sulivan, 380, 381 and n.; 385 n., 386 and n., 387 and n., 388 and n., 389 n., 390 and n., 391 n., 392 n.; attitude to Dundas's Bill, 393 and n.; 395 n., 396 n., 399 n., 402 n., 405 and n., 412 and n., 413 and n.
Scrafton, Luke, 102, 117, 133 n., 135 n., 140 and n., 144 n., 145 n., 148 n., 154 n., 156 and n., 183 n., 188, 195, 197 n., 199.
Secret Committee (or Committee of Secrecy) of Court of Directors, 33, 88, 95–99, 128, 234 n., 342.
Secret Committees (or Committee of Secrecy) of the House of Commons, see Commons, House of.
Select Committees of the House of Commons, see Commons, House of.
Selwyn M.P., George Augustus, 350.
Seven Years War, 30, 49, 63, 75, 91, 92, 141.
Shelburne, 2nd Earl of, see Petty, William.
Shelburne, Lady, see Petty, Sophia.
Shepherd M.P., Samuel, 14 and n.
Sheridan M.P., Richard Brinsley, 396.
Shipping, Committee of, 60 n.
Shipping interest, 9, 36, 39, 122, 213, 283 n., 287 and n.
Ships' Husbands, 38, 39, 122.
Shrewsbury, 85.
Shropshire, 236.
Siraj-ud-Daula, 45, 63, 68, 81, 257.
Smith, Adam, 26 and n.
Smith, John, 378 n.
Smith M.P., Captain Nathaniel, 347 n., 378 and n.
Smith M.P., Brig.-Gen. Richard, 78 n., 130, 213, 246, 343 and n., 345, 347, 352, 362 and n., 370, 376, 379, 387.

Smith M.P., Samuel, junior, 378 n.
South Sea Bubble, 22, 24, 41, 191–2.
South Sea Company, 14, 16, 17, 22, 23, 24, 26, 28, 29, 32, 52.
Spain, 92.
Spanheim, Mary Ann, Marquise de Montandre, 104 and n.
Spanish Succession, War of, 46.
Sparkes, Joseph, 378 n.
Spencer, John, 116, 118, 125, 130, 131.
Spice Islands, 2.
'Splitting' (collusive transfer), 16, 34 and n., 72; in campaign of 1763, 101–8; in campaign of 1764, 118–22; 124, 126, 128, 129, 130; Company's petition for prevention of, 132; 133, 134, 139, 140, 176; Government measures against, 135, 173, 176; campaign of 1766, 145; 146, 156, 157, 164 and n., 170, 182 and n., 183 and n., 188 and n., 189 n., 191, 192; effect of Macleane's 'splitting' campaign on Lord Shelburne, 209; campaign of 1772–3, 244, 245.
Stables, John, 308 n., 348 n., 372, 380.
State of the East India Co. (A. Dalrymple), 24 n.
Statutes; Parliamentary:
8 & 9 Will. III, c. 32, to restrain the number and ill-practices of brokers, 11 n.; 9 & 10 Will III, c. 44, to regulate the issue of East India bonds; 11 and n., 12 and n.; 10 Anne, c. 28, continuing the trade and corporation of the East India Company, 16 n., 29; 1 Geo. I, St. 2, c. 38, Septennial Act, 20; 6 Geo. I, c. 18, the 'Bubble Act', 26; 7 Geo. I, St. I, c. 5, its limitations on issue of East India bonds, 12 and n.; 7 Geo. II, c. 8, to prevent the infamous practice of stockjobbing, 11 n., 41; 17 Geo. II, c. 17, permits East India Company to increase bond issue, 12 and n.; 27 Geo. II, c. 9, for punishing Mutiny, &c., in the East Indies, 47 and n.; 7 Geo. III, c. 48, to prevent collusive transfer of East India Stock, 150, 173 and n., 181, 182; 7 Geo. III, c. 49, to limit the Company's dividends, 172 and n., 173 and n., 174, 175 and n.; 8 Geo. III, c. 11, to prolong 7 Geo. III, c. 49, 183 and n.; 9 Geo. III, c. 24, 1769 Settlement between State and Company, 183 and n., 227 and n.; 12 Geo. III, c. 54, to limit East Indian shipping, 281 n.; 13 Geo. III, c. 9, to restrain the dispatch of Super-

PRINTED IN
GREAT BRITAIN
AT THE
UNIVERSITY PRESS
OXFORD
BY
CHARLES BATEY
PRINTER
TO THE
UNIVERSITY